CONTENTS

iv

ACKNOWLEDGEMENTS

I am grateful to many individuals and several institutions for help (financial and spiritual), encouragement and support. I was granted Study Leave from the University of British Columbia for six months in 1979 and a full year in 1984; part of the former was spent at the Institut de Grec at the Université de Strasbourg, where my wife and I enjoyed the hospitality of Pros. Ed. Lévy and J. Jouanna (the latter now at the Sorbonne). In 1984 I was awarded as well a Social Sciences and Humanities Research Council of Canada Leave Fellowship and was able to work at University College, London, and the Institute of Classical Studies, under the courteous auspices of Prof. E. Handley (now at Cambridge). In that year I also held a stipendium from the Deutsche Akademische Austauschdienst and worked for two months at Bonn and Konstanz. I thank Drs. H. Neitzel and A. Köhnken of the former and Dr. Wofgang Rösler and Prof. H.-J. Newiger of the latter for their generous assistance. While I was a visiting professor at Colby College in Maine during 1987/8 that institution provided me with secretarial and other help for which I am deeply grateful.

My more personal debts are numerous. At an early stage Prof. E.R. Dodds (†) encouraged me to undertake serious study of the play. Prof. Wm. M. Calder III kindly sent me detailed references to Eduard Fraenkel's notations on *Eum*. A first draft of the entire MS was read and commented upon by Prof. W.C. Scott (Dartmouth), Prof. D.J. Conacher (Trinity College, Toronto), Prof. David Sansone (University of Illinois at Champaign/Urbana), Prof. M.L. West (Royal Holloway and Bedford New Colleges), Prof. D.M. MacDowell and Dr. Alex Garvie of the University of Glasgow, Dr. S. Ireland (Hull), and Dr. A. S. Brown. To them all and especially to the Press's Editorial Adviser, Prof. M.M. Willcock of University College, London, I am deeply appreciative. Vancouver friends, Dieter Stenschke, Olga Betts, Ron Hatch and Bettye Bongie rendered material assistance for which I am extremely grateful. My wife's support has been (as always) unflagging; ordinarily the book would be dedicated to her but with her approval I have inscribed it to an old, and great, friend of us both, Msgr. Charles Murphy of Portland, Maine.

Vancouver,
Canada,
December, 1988

AESCHYLUS

EUMENIDES

Edited with an Introduction, Translation and Commentary by

A. J. PODLECKI

ARIS & PHILLIPS LTD

WARMINSTER – ENGLAND

British Library Cataloguing in Publication Data

```
Aeschylus
   The Eumenides.——(Classical texts).
   I. Title   II. Podlecki, A.J.   III. Series
   882'.01       PA3825.E7
```

ISBNS   (cloth) 0 85668 381 7
           (limp) 0 85668 382 5

CAROLO AMICO MAGNO

Printed and published in England by Aris & Phillips Ltd, Teddington House, Warminster, Wiltshire.

INTRODUCTION

I. The Myth before Aeschylus: cult of the Semnai: early conceptions of the Erinyes

References[1]

MYTH
Garvie, A.F. *Aeschylus. Choephoroe* ix–xxvi.
Mazon, P. "La legende d¹Oreste avant Eschyle", *Eschyle* II, ii–x.

PRIMITIVE CONCEPTIONS OF THE ERINYES
Neumann, Günter "Wortbildung und Etymologie von *Erinus*", *Die Sprache* 32 (1986) 43–51.
Heubeck, Alfred "*erinus* in der archaischen Epik", *Glotta* 64 (1986) 143–165[2].
Wüst, E. "Erinys" cols. 91 ff.

ART
Davies, M.I. "Thoughts on the *Oresteia* before Aischylos".
Prag, *The Oresteia*.
Vermeule, "The Boston Oresteia Krater".
Dyer, Robert R. "The Iconography of the *Oresteia* after Aeschylus", *American Journal of Archaeology* 71 (1967) 175–6.

THE CULT AND ITS ORIGINS
Brown, A.L. "Eumenides in Greek Tragedy", *Classical Quarterly* n.s. 34 (1984) 260–281.
Dietrich, B.C. *Death, Fate and the Gods* (London: Athlone Press, 1967) ch. iv, "The Erinyes", pp. 91–156.
Farnell, L.R. *The Cults of the Greek States* (Chicago: Aegaean Press, 1971; repr. of the ed. Oxford, 1909) V. 437–442.
Harrison, J.E. "The *Ker* as Erinys etc.", in *Prolegomena to the Study of Greek Religion* 3rd ed. (Cambridge: Cambridge University Press, 1922) 213–256.
————, "Delphika".
Marinatos, Sp. "Demeter Erinys in Mycenae", *Athens Annals of Archaeology* 6 (1973) 189–192.
Rohde, E. *Psyche; the cult of souls and belief in immortality among the*

Greeks (Engl. trans., London: Routledge & Kegan Paul, 1925) pp. 174–182.
Sansone, D.   "The Survival of the Bronze-Age Demon".

When, in about 459 B.C., Aeschylus set to work to compose a trilogy on the Orestes legend, what mythic material did he have at hand and what aspects of the story would have been familiar to his audience? Orestes' vengeance on his mother and her lover for their murder of Agamemnon was firmly embedded in the tradition known to the Epic.   In the *Odyssey* (3. 306–310) Nestor tells Telemachus how Aegisthus had reigned in Mycenae for seven years after killing Agamemnon, but "in the eighth evil came in the form of Orestes who returned from Athens and killed his father's slayer ... and made a funeral feast for the Argives over his hateful mother and cowardly Aegisthus" (this turn of events is also mentioned as a possibility by Proteus in his prophecy to Menelaus, 4. 546–7).   The passage is noteworthy for Orestes' provenience, Athens (which the Alexandrian scholar, Zenodotus, wished to change to "Phocis"), for the precise timetable of Aegisthus' reign, and for the fact that Clytemnestra is implicated both as sharing responsibility for Agamemnon's murder[3] and – more to the point – as fellow-victim with Aegisthus of the retribution wrought by Orestes.   Zeus tells the assembly of gods at the beginning of the poem that he had sent Hermes to warn Aegisthus that, should the latter persist in his plan to slay Agamemnon and marry Clytemnestra, Orestes would bring retribution, *tisis*, "when he grew to manhood and longed for his land" (1. 40–41).   Already in the Epic, then, Orestes is in some sense a pre-ordained agent of vengeance, and there is also a hint that he acted from motives at least in part personal: a "longing for his land".

The story of Orestes and Clytemnestra was told in full in the lost Cyclic epic *Nostoi* ("Returns"), ascribed to Hagias of Trozen, and in a papyrus fragment of the archaic *Catalogue of Women*, transmitted under Hesiod's name but probably to be dated to the sixth century B.C., we read that Clytemnestra's and Agamemnon's third child, after Electra ("who rivalled the immortals in beauty") and Iphimede (Iphigeneia), was Orestes "who when he grew to manhood paid back his father's slayer and slew his overbearing mother with pitiless bronze" (fr. 23 a, Merkelbach-West, vv. 29–30).   Towards the middle of the sixth century an *Oresteia* in at least two books was composed by a lyric poet of Sicily, Stesichorus.[4]   Stesichorus' version left its imprint on Aeschylus' *Libation Bearers* in three specific details: Electra's recognition of her brother through the lock of hair; Orestes' nurse, whom Stesichorus named

"Laodameia"; and an ominous dream in which Clytemnestra saw "a snake with a man's head at the end, and from it the King, son of Pleisthenes, appeared" (fr. 219 Page; "Pleisthenes" is a name in the royal family, but it is uncertain to whom it refers here). In the tradition we possess, it is in Stesichorus' version that Apollo and the Erinyes first make their appearance: the god gave Orestes a bow and arrows with the instructions that he was to use them to fend off the attacks of the Erinyes. It is possible (but of course by no means certain) that Apollo's command to Orestes to slay his mother, and perhaps also his purification of the slayer after the deed, found a place in Stesichorus' *Oresteia*.

The story was handled again about 500 B.C. by Simonides of Ceos, who worked extensively at Athens and developed close ties of patronage there. It is reported by a late source that Simonides followed Stesichorus in placing the scene of the action at Sparta and a papyrus commentary on his works mentions a sacrifice of a human being in honour of a divinity, and great lamentation arising therefrom − could this have been anyone but Iphigeneia ? − but no reference survives to Orestes or the Erinyes in Simonides' version. In Pindar's retelling in the *Eleventh Pythian* Ode, probably to be dated 474 B.C. (for this date, rather than 454, which is another possibility, see Garvie, Intro. xxiv–xxv), where the action is set at Amyklai near Sparta and the nurse's name given as "Arsinoë", the lyric narrative stops with Orestes' return from Phocis and his vengeance on Clytemnestra and Aegisthus.

Scholars have sought to supplement the literary remains with evidence from the visual arts (see Garvie, Intro. xvi–xvii). Two important classes of sculptural relief survive, both of which have been taken as depicting the Orestes legend. The first, more imposing and certainly more significant if the identification of their subject be accepted, is a set of stone sculptured reliefs discovered at Foce del Sele southeast of Naples; they appear to have been metopes from a small temple of Hera on the Silaris River. They are to be dated about 540 B.C. and allude to a variety of mythological subjects; three seem to be closely connected with events in an *Oresteia*. Number 24 shows a woman advancing with a double axe in her hand, while another female character stands behind her and attempts to hold her back; in Number 25 one male character is driving a sword through another; Number 26 depicts a huge snake, its coils wrapped around a man's legs and its head curving down over him threateningly as he attempts to fend it off with a sword. The scenes have been identified as follows: the first is Clytemnestra, who has just called for her "man-killing axe" (*Choephoroi* 889), trying to defend herself against her son, with the nurse ("Laodameia" in Stesichorus,

"Cilissa" in Aeschylus) holding her back; the second is Orestes stabbing Aegisthus; and the third is the snake-Erinys pursuing Orestes[5] (note that this is a divergence from Stesichorus' version, where Apollo's bow figured prominently). Artistic evidence for the early development of the story survives also in several small bronze reliefs found at Olympia; the first two are decorations for shield straps, which the excavators date about 580 B.C., that is, about a generation earlier than the Foce del Sele sculptures. On one Aegisthus is shown holding Agamemon's head down while Clytemnestra stabs him from behind and on the other Orestes drives his spear through a seated Aegisthus. A third, slightly later than the other two, embellished the foot of a tripod; according to Karl Schefold it is of the Ionian style of Magna Graecia (and thus has a Stesichorean ambience). It is a more elaborate grouping with a central scene of Orestes stabbing Clytemnestra while Aegisthus, panic-stricken, rushes off to the right and an Electra-type female figure, holding a veil over her head, looks on at the left.[6] If this figure is indeed Electra, this is the first depiction to bring her into the revenge-plot.

Sometime around 470 B.C. a vase-painter of the first order chose the murders of Agamemnon and Aegisthus for a striking diptychal arrangement on an Athenian red-figure kalyx krater now in Boston.[7] Pictorially this is the culmination of a series of late-sixth and early-fifth century Athenian vase-paintings, which are characterized by Garvie as "evidently deriving, but with variations, from a single model, which show the murder of Aegisthus on his throne .... Clytemnestra intervenes, but, in several of the vases, her arm is seized by Talthybius" (the Greek herald prominent in the Trojan cycle).[8]

Aeschylus, then, found in the tradition about Orestes details regarding his pursuit by the Erinyes (in one version, at least, in the form of snakes) and Apollo's protective custody of him. One very important element in the plot of *Eumenides* cannot be traced to an earlier version, either literary or graphic: Orestes' trial and acquittal before the Court of the Areopagus. To be sure, Athenian mythology explained the name in terms of an early trial on the site, but as the etymology indicates ("Ares' Rock"), the defendant was Ares himself who, in the standard version of the myth, was prosecuted there by Poseidon for having slain the latter's son, Halirrhothios, who had raped Ares' daughter, Alkippe. Felix Jacoby argued vigorously that in Aeschylus' remodelling of the myth Orestes' crime replaced Ares' as the "first ever" for which the Areopagus was asked to adjudicate; to lend credibility to his version, Aeschylus invented a new etymology for "Areopagus" at *Eum.* 683 ff. (see commentary on those lines below).[9] Of course the importance of Athens in the Orestes story may have suggested itself to Aeschylus, as was remarked above, by the detail preserved at *Odyssey* 3. 307 that Orestes had come "from Athens" to exact vengeance on his father's murderers. The sources assign him a variety of prosecutors: the Spartans (Hellanicus, *FGH* 323 a F 22) or, more specifically, kinsmen of the victims: Aegisthus' daughter Erigone (Parian Marble A 25), or Tyndareus (Euripides' *Orestes*), or Clytemnestra's cousin Perilaos (Pausanias 8. 34. 4). Various places are named as the site of the trial: Argos (Euripides' *Orestes* 612 ff.), Mycenae (Hyginus, *Fabula* 119), Trozen (Pausanias). There was a variant that had Orestes tried before the Twelve Gods sitting at the Athenian Areopagus (Euripides, *Orestes* 1648; Demosthenes 23. 66 and 74; Scholiast to Aristides, III p. 67, 108.7 and p. 68, 108.10 Dindorf). In a sequel, or perhaps alternative, to the Athenian episode, Orestes removed to Lesbos (Hellanicus in his *Aeolika*) or to Arcadia, where he founded a settlement named after him Oresteion (Pausanias 8. 44. 2, Euripides, *Orestes* 1646–7, cf. *Electra* 1273–75), or Oresthasion. Some of these variants are hinted at already in Euripides but it is unclear whether they go back to a period earlier than Aeschylus. Jacoby, for example, maintained that the version which made Orestes' court consist of the twelve Gods was a post-Aeschylean invention, perhaps by Euripides for his *Orestes* (vv. 1648 ff.).[10]

What may have suggested to Aeschylus a trial before the Areopagus with the Erinyes as prosecutors was the fact that there was an association of some antiquity between the Areopagus and the cult of the Semnai Theai, or "August Goddesses". Both Thucydides (1. 126.11) and Plutarch (*Solon* 12.1) mention an altar of these goddesses in the vicinity of the Acropolis "by the cleft in the NE side of the Areopagus" (Marchant's note on the Thucydides passage). In the fifth century their shrine became a place of refuge (Aristophanes, *Knights* 1312, *Thesmophoriazusae* 224), "the most inviolable asylum for all who sought it" (B.B. Rogers on *Knights* 1312). A scholiast on Aeschines (*Against Timarchus*, 1.188) reports that three days each month were allotted to them, and that the Areopagus held its sittings only on those sacred days; according to Lucian (*Hermotimos* 64, *de domo* 18), the sessions took place at night. At the beginning of trials before the Areopagus, both parties took oaths by "the Semnai Theai and other gods", (Dinarchus 1. 47[11]) and those acquitted in a trial before the Areopagus were expected to make a sacrifice in their honour (Pausanias 1. 28. 6). According to several sources, the Areopagus selected the *hieropoioi* (cult-supervisors) of the Semnai Theai.[12] Offerings to them consisted in certain sacred cakes and milk in clay pitchers; compare the allusion at *Eum.* 107 to the teetotal nature of the Erinyes and similarly the Eumenides at Sophocles, *Oedipus at Colonus* 100 and 481. Pausanias describes the cult of the Eumenides at Sicyon: "each year [the Sicyonians] hold a one-day festival for them, slaughtering pregnant ewes, and making ritual use of a mixture of milk and honey and of flowers instead of garlands of leaves" (2. 11. 4, trans. P. Levi). Their cult at Athens may have been similar.

The question of whether, and to what extent, Aeschylus on the one hand conflated pre-existing but previously distinct cults and on the other simply gave free rein to his inventive imagination is notoriously difficult to answer. A.L. Brown, who attempts to dissociate both the notion and the very title of "Eumenides" from Aeschylus' play entirely[13] – in his view, there is no real evidence for the identification Erinyes-Eumenides until Euripides' *Orestes* of 408 – argued that "the goddesses worshipped beneath the Acropolis were essentially nameless, but Aeschylus wished to suggest that these nameless beings were originally reformed Erinyes".[14] Others believe that the curse-goddesses (Erinyes) and fructifying vegetation divinities (Semnai and/or Eumenides) were totally separate until Aeschylus united the two aspects in *Eum.*[15] However that may be – and with the evidence mainly late and sparse, any investigator's selection and use of it risks appearing tendentious – by the late-fifth century, Semnai, Erinyes and Eumenides were virtually indistinguishable, as Sophocles' description of the Eumenides in the *Oedipus at Colonus* shows: they are "Dread (*emphoboi*) goddesses" (39–40), "furious maidens whom [as the Chorus say] we tremble to mention" (127–8), Eumenides (42; cf. 486) and Semnai (89–90).[16] By the fourth century Eumenides occur in company with Erinyes in the Derveni papyrus.[17] If Aeschylus did take over the Semnai Theai for his own dramatic purposes, he probably went out of his way to exaggerate their more horrific aspects; as Pausanias succinctly puts it in the passage already cited, Aeschylus was "the first to introduce snakes among the hair of their heads, but their statues, and those of all the underworld gods, have nothing fearful about them".[18] Conversely, it is possible that the Erinyes for their part were originally if not more benign, at least more constructive than Aeschylus portrays them as being early in the drama, and that consequently their conversion under Athena's soothing persuasion is not so radical or miraculous as it appears to be at first sight. It is therefore appropriate to consider here the few known facts about the "primitive" Erinyes.

The parentage of Erinys or the Erinyes is not given by Homer, but in Hesiod they are daughters of Earth fertilized by the genital fluid of Ouranos after Cronos castrated him (*Theogony* 184–5). A little further on Hesiod lists, among the children of Night, the "Moirai and avenging

Kēres [Death-spirits], who pursue transgressions of gods and men" (*Theogony* 217–20). Since the functions and to some extent the identities of these Vengeance-demons are not kept scrupulously separate but rather superimposed in later Greek popular belief, Aeschylus' genealogy, according to which the Erinyes are made daughters of Night (*Eum.* 321–2, 416, 745, 792 = 822, 844 = 878, 1033), was innovative, but not radically so; for Sophocles, the Eumenides (who are not, I believe, to be distinguished from Erinyes) are children of Earth and Skotos, Darkness (*Oedipus at Colonus* 40, 106). In the Orhpic *Theogony* the Erinyes are daughters of Chthonian Zeus and Persephone.

The name *E - ri - nu* occurs on several Linear B tablets from Knossos, apparently as a divinity to whom a gift of oil is being offered.[19] In several passages in the Epic we hear of "Erinyes of a mother" or those "invoked by a mother" and some of the time they function as protective spirits called on to redress a wrong (*Odyssey* 11. 279–80, 2. 135). We are not so very far from the relationship between Clytemnestra and Erinyes at the opening of *Eum.* The usual method of invoking these agents of vengeance is a curse (cf. *Iliad* IX. 571–2); they are taking on a more independent, substantive status. They are not restricted to female victims: Phoenix's father "invoked the dread Erinyes" that the boy should never have a son (*Iliad* IX. 454–6). Nor is their agency limited to members of a family circle, for in cursing the suitors the disguised Odysseus calls on the "gods and Erinyes of beggars" (*Odyssey* 17. 475). It therefore looks as though the Epic conceived of the Erinyes as supernatural agents whose efficacy could be invoked to come to the assistance of an oppressed party; it seems to be a secondary development that this "oppression" sometimes took a violent form, and that the Erinyes were summoned to avenge a murder. The regular if not invariable means of activating their power was a curse by the victim against his oppressor. Noteworthy in this light is the remark by the Chorus-leader in *Eum.* (416–7), "we … are named 'Curses' in our homes beneath the earth". Alcaeus (c. 600 B.C.) fr. 129. 13 f. Lobel-Page shows that their agency as redressers of wrong could be invoked also in political contexts.

Recourse to etymology has not proved very enlightening. Pausanias (8. 25. 6) connected it to a putative Arcadian verb *erinnuein*, "to be angry", but the noun may be the primary, and the verb a derived, formation. Recently Neumann has revived a suggestion, made fleetingly also in antiquity, of a connection with the Greek word *eris*, "strife".[20] On the other hand, functions are assigned to the Erinyes in our sources that have nothing to do with anger, strife or curses. In a famous scene towards the end of the *Iliad* in which Agamemnon is apologizing to

Achilles and the rest of the Greek army for his earlier, inexplicably offensive, behaviour, he avers: "I am not responsible, but Zeus and Moira (Fate) and Erinys who walks in darkness – they cast Atē (blind folly) on my mind" (*Iliad* XIX. 86 ff.), and very similar is Theoclymenus' description of his father Melampus as afflicted with "the heavy Atē which the frightening (*dasplētis*) goddess Erinys put in his mind" (*Odyssey* 15. 234). The Erinys has apparently become liberated from any connection with a curse pronounced by an injured party and is moving towards a more abstract, quasi-independent agency of her own. In a strange (indeed, in the Epic, unique) passage, the Erinyes stop the voice of Achilles' talking horse, Xanthus, just after he foretells his master's death at Troy (*Iliad* XIX. 418). In the course of an enlightening discussion E.R. Dodds cites the comment by the scholiast that the Erinyes are "overseers of things contrary to nature", and Dodds' own explanation is that "the Erinys is the personal agent who ensures fulfillment of a *moira* [allotted portion or 'destiny']".[21] It is not so far a step from this to the cosmic and almost mystical function of the Erinyes in Heraclitus: as "helpers of Justice" they keep the sun from leaving its course and following any other than its own predetermined, *i.e.*, "natural", route.[22] This cosmic aspect reappears in Prometheus' answer to the chorus' question, "Who then is the steersman of Necessity?", "The tri-form Fates and remembering Erinyes" (*Prometheus Bound* 515–16).

There is nothing in the early literary evidence to justify Rohde's celebrated dictum that the Erinys is "nothing else but the soul itself of the murdered man, indignant at its fate and seizing its revenge for itself".[23] Other writers have emphasized their more benign aspects, which they seem to share with other early "fertility" spirits.[24] In my opinion it was precisely this aspect of them as chthonic powers, concerned to ensure fertility in crops, animals and – especially if such fertility should be threatened by children's murderous attacks against parents – the human family, that was the important strand taken over by Aeschylus from the tradition and adapted by him to his own dramatic purposes. Heubeck notes the variety of activities performed by the Erinyes in the early tradition and concludes,

It was obviously the co-existence and fusion (*Miteinander u. Ineinander*) of diverse functions and spheres of activity that gave Aeschylus the possibility and the intrinsic preconditions for drawing his monumental picture, in which a sequence develops from this co-existence. The change of the demonic figures from inexorable Spirits of Revenge to benevolent Divinities of Assistance, from the 'Erinyes' to the

'Eumenides,' is predetermined in the complexity of their portrayal before Aeschylus.[25]

II. Staging

A. The design of the early theatre

References

Arnott, Peter *Greek Scenic Conventions in the Fifth Century B.C.* (Oxford: Clarendon Press, 1962).

Bieber, Margarete *A History of the Greek and Roman Theater* (Princeton: Princeton University Press, 1961).

Dinsmoor, W.B. *The Architecture of Ancient Greece* 3 ed. (London: Batsford, 1950) pp. 119–20, 207–211, 244–50, 297–319.

Gould, John "Tragedy in Performance", in P.E. Easterling and B.M.W. Knox, edd. *Cambridge History of Classical Literature, I. Greek Literature* (Cambridge: Cambridge University Press, 1985) ch. 10. 2 pp. 263–281.

Hammond, "Conditions" pp. 438–41.

Hill, I.T. *The Ancient City of Athens* (London: Methuen, 1953) 107–8, 114–24.

Pickard-Cambridge, A.W. *The Theatre of Dionysus at Athens* 2 ed. (Oxford: Clarendon Press, 1946).

Simon, Erika *The Ancient Theatre* Engl. trans. by C.E. Vafopoulou-Richardson (London & New York: Methuen, 1982).

Taplin, *Stagecraft* Appendices B and C, pp. 434–459.

Travlos, John *Pictorial Dictionary of Ancient Athens* (New York: Praeger, 1971) 537–552.

Webster, T.B. L. *Greek Theatre Production* 2 ed. (London: Methuen, 1970).

Winter, F.E. "The Stage of New Comedy", *Phoenix* 37 (1983) 38–47.

Wycherley, R.E. *The Stones of Athens* (Princeton: Princeton University Press, 1978) 204 ff.

Almost nothing can be asserted with complete confidence about the physical arrangements of the early theatre at Athens. There is evidence that choral performances *of some type* (not necessarily dramatic) were held in the Agora.[26] These performances probably took place on a round packed-earth dancing floor, the spectators seated or standing on *ikria*, wooden benches or "stands". If there was a "skene", the word later used to designate the scene-building but which ordinarily meant "tent" or "hut", its function in this early period is not known. Possibly even this early it served as the actors' changing-room and was available to be included in the action of the play, as need or opportunity arose. At some early date (perhaps soon after 500 B.C.; the date is inextricably connected with a dubious anecdote about the collapse of the *ikria* during a competition in which Aeschylus, Pratinas and Choerilus participated) the site of the performances was moved to a specially prepared area on the south slope of the Acropolis. There is little agreement among scholars about the physical arrangements of this fifth-century theatre. Although the usual view is that the dancing-floor or orchestra was circular, a case has also been made for a rectangular shape.[27] Hammond argued that a rocky outcrop or *pagos*, shown by archaeological excavation to have been levelled in a later reconstruction, was in fact a conspicuous feature incorporated into the action of Aeschylus' earliest suriving plays. The position of the skene in Aeschylus' early plays, according to Hammond, could shift vis-à-vis the dancing floor as the action of the play required. At some time after *Persians*, *Seven against Thebes* and *Suppliants*, but before *Oresteia*, its position became fixed: "In the *Oresteia* a palace background appears for the first time in the extant plays of Aeschylus".[28] Hammond believes (and I concur) that "the forecourt or rectangular area immediately in front of the facade was probably raised above the orchestra by some two or three continuous shallow steps" ("Conditions" p. 449), but other scholars would argue just as strenuously that no truly raised stage existed until the ten-foot-high structure for which there is evidence in the Hellenistic period.

Hammond uses the hypothetical rocky outcrop in his visualisation of how *Eum.* was staged; thus he locates the council-chamber mentioned in v. 570, in which the Areopagites deliberate, "on the eastern side of the *orchestra* against the *pagos*, or on the *pagos* itself" (p. 441). Taplin believes that the *pagos* was removed prior to *Oresteia*, when the position of the skene was fixed. But it may have been removed even earlier in the century – perhaps when the performances were moved from the agora – as has been posited by some archaeologists. Furthermore, it seems to me quite possible that a scene-building, however modest its dimensions, had a fixed symmetrical position vis-à-vis the spectators right from the beginning and perhaps also a temple-like appearance, which could be incorporated (or not) into the action. At *Persians* 140–1, the Chorus of

Persian elders refer to *tod(e)* ... *stegos archaion*, "this ancient structure", which is obviously not to be taken as the royal palace, which, as Hammond rightly points out ("Conditions" p. 429), the Queen at v. 159 says that she has "left".

The traditional view has been that in the latter part of the fifth century (say, around 420 B.C.), the theatre was refashioned in stone and thus given more permanent form, although this was challenged by Travlos, who argued that this did not occur until well into the fourth century.[29] We shall have to wait until the archaeologists come to an agreement about the date of this permanent structure, but in any case, there was another rebuilding of the theatre under the politician Lycurgus in about 330 B.C., and it is this construction, with its later modifications by the Romans, that is to be seen (albeit in somewhat ruinous condition) by visitors to Athens today.

B. The Staging of *Eumenides*

References

Hammond, "Conditions", pp. 438–441.
-------, "More on Conditions", pp. 22–33 ("The Production of *Eumenides*").
Melchinger, Siegfried *Die Welt als Tragödie, 1. Aischylos – Sophokles* (Munich: C.H. Beck, 1979) 109–158.
Taplin, *Stagecraft* ch. VIII, pp. 362–415.

The setting is Delphi, as the audience is soon made aware both by the appearance of Apollo's priestess and her reference at v. 11. She enters either directly from the temple of Apollo or walking in by one of the entrance ways called in the sources *eisodos* or *parodos*, which ran as a kind of ramp that divided the seating area from the skene and acting place at (roughly) the ten- and two-o'clock positions. She goes in for the consultation which, as she says at vv. 30–31, she hopes will be "the best ever", but she quickly re-appears, this time probably on all fours, to report that she has seen Orestes within the temple and the sleeping Furies in front of him (v. 46). When she finishes her speech, she departs and Apollo, his suppliant Orestes, and the mute Hermes appear, almost certainly through the temple-doors and onto the playing area. After a brief scene they in turn exit, Apollo probably back into his temple and Orestes to Athens.

It is unclear at what point and how the Chorus of Erinyes entered the orchestra,[30] but the direction from which they appear, that is, from inside the temple where the Pythia said she had seen them, is itself an element of surprise, for the normal way for a chorus to enter the orchestra was by the parodos already mentioned (or possibly by both, if they entered in two symmetrical halves). Scholion *Eum.* 64b says that an apparatus known as the *ekkyklēma* was "turned" to reveal the interior of the shrine. Although some scholars deny that the device was available as early as 458 B.C. – its first indisputable use is for Aristophanes' *Peace* of 421 B.C. – I find it difficult to see how the gory tableau of Clytemnestra standing over her victims at *Agamemnon* 1372 ff. could have been staged without it. If scholion *Eum.* 64b is correct and the ekkyklema was employed here to reveal the scene inside the temple, this may explain why Aeschylus has the Pythia at v. 47 describe the horrible creatures she has seen inside as both asleep and "sitting on chairs". As A.L. Brown has remarked, such an arrangement has the effect of "saving space on the ekkyklema, since a body on a chair takes up less room than one lying on the ground" ("Some Problems", 28 n. 15). We need not suppose that the scene at v. 64, however it was managed, showed more than several Erinyes, but Apollo's reference at v. 67 to "these women", presumably accompanied by a gesture, would be (so it seems to me) incomprehensible if none were visible to the audience. Clytemnestra's ghost appears before v. 94, either emerging through a trap door (again, as with the ekkyklema, it is unclear whether it was in use this early), or – more probably – walking in along a parodos. She addresses the sleeping Erinyes, trying to rouse them from sleep but with only limited success. It is unclear at what point the full chorus entered the orchestra. Taplin argues that "the chorus is not seen at all until 140 ff. .... This would mean that, although Clytemnestra's words are all directed at the Erinyes, they are none the less out of sight, and their responses (117 ff.) are therefore heard from within" (*Stagecraft* p. 366). Taplin's theory receives some support from the stage directions at vv. 119, 120, 123, 126 and 129 for which (unlike Taplin) I believe Aeschylus himself to have been responsible; the need for indicating them in the text would have been even greater if the Erinyes were at this point only to be heard and not seen. But the theory that the chorus remained inside the temple until line 140 must meet Hammond's objection that "it would not have been possible for spectators sitting at a distance of 300 to 700 feet and at varying heights to see through a doorway into a shaded interior and discern there fifteen people in various attitudes" ("More on Conditions", 26). Since, following Hammond against Taplin, I believe the demonstrative at v. 67 to entail the visibility of some Erinyes at least, I think these same ones were available for Clytemnestra to address. However many or few were there to receive the ghost's rebukes are now roused to full wakefulness by the chorus-leader at vv. 140 ff. The easiest assumption for those like myself who posit use of the ekkyklema in the opening scene is that it is rolled in (or away) after the chorus-leader's spoken trimeter at v. 142 and before the Entrance Song or "Parodos", vv. 143 ff. There are indications in the text of this song that it was not all sung by the entire chorus (see n. on vv. 143–178 below). A comment in the ancient *Life of Aeschylus* (section 9) implies that the chorus entered "sporadically"; if so, the Entrance Song may have been begun by a few choristers (those including the leader who had been present, on my hypothesis, from v. 67), who were joined by others as the Parodos progressed. I take it that by the end of the song all the chorus-members were in the orchestra and that v. 179 means not that Apollo is ordering stragglers out of his temple but that he is exasperatedly expelling them all from his sanctuary and the vicinity of Delphi. At the scene's end both Chorus and Apollo depart, he probably back into his temple and they in the direction that Orestes had taken to continue their pursuit of him.

References to Athena's statue at vv. 242, 259, 409, 439 and 446 (cf. 1024) make it clear that a stage-property statue of the goddess was prominently visible to the audience. The easiest assumption is that it was carried in by stagehands in the pause after v. 234. This modification of the scene will also have served to indicate that the locale of the action had changed, from Delphi to Athens. It is unclear where this statue was placed. There are suggestions in the text not only that Orestes clings to or stays seated near it throughout much of the action from vv. 235 to 489 (cf. 259, 409, 439 [440 in the trans.] 446), but also that the chorus' Binding Song (vv. 307 ff.) was sung by them while they danced around their would-be victim. This interpretation was disputed by Pickard-Cambridge (p.44): "The ancient *bretas* [statue] was of course inside the temple, as every Athenian would naturally assume: to this Orestes clings, and the fancy that in the *humnos desmios* [binding-song] the Furies dance around him is therefore untenable". Pickard-Cambridge, in referring to the "actual" state of affairs in the fifth century, signals a discrepancy with matters in the theatre in 458 B.C.: the statue to which the text clearly refers cannot have been inside any structure at all, but somewhere in front of the building which the audience is now to take as representing Athena's temple. If this was immediately in front of the temple-doors rather than somewhere in the orchestra, it is, indeed, difficult to see how the chorus could have danced around their victim, although this would have been theatrically a very effective – and frightening – grouping. In my opinion, the question of the statue's placement must remain open.

Although the point is controversial, I personally accept the tradition reported by several ancient sources that the provenience of arriving Chorus and actors was conventionally differentiated according as they entered from (stage-) right or left. Such a conventional marker to audiences who did not have programme notes in their hands, and some of whom may not have been very clear on details of the stories they were about to see performed, would have been very helpful in following the action. The distinction, however, cannot have been exactly as stated by Pollux (4. 126) who makes an entry from the west (i.e. spectators' right, stage-left) signify an arrival "from the countryside or the harbour or the city". Plutarch reports (*Life of Themistocles* 19.5) that the so-called Thirty Tyrants turned the bema, or speaker's platform, in the Pnyx *away* from the sea and *towards* the countryside. Therefore, it is clear that most Athenians made a fundamental distinction between these two regions. Vitruvius (*On Architecture* 5.68) and an anonymous ancient *Life of Aristophanes*[31] are nearer the mark in distinguishing the two directions, so that an entry or exit through the west parodos indicated, because of the special situation of the Theatre of Dionysus, an arrival from or departure to the city or harbour, whereas one on the other, eastern, side signified the countryside or, by an extension of this, a distant journey overland.[32] If Aeschylus observed this convention for his production of 458 B.C., Orestes will have re-entered at v. 235, followed closely by the pursuing Erinyes at v. 244, by the stage-right, or eastern, parodos, and Athena later enters from this same direction "from the Scamander" at v. 397. After the preliminary hearing, Athena departs with the intention of "selecting the best of (her) citizens" (v. 487); this ought to indicate her exit in the conventional direction of the city (proximate), that is, by the western, stage-left, parodos. After the Second Choral Ode Athena re-enters, again from the left, probably with ten mute extras representing charter members of the court of the Areopagus.

Was there, as some commentators have maintained, a further change of scene, with the audience expected to visualize (or having its imagination helped along by a different set of props) that from here to the end of the play the action was occurring on the Hill of the Areopagus? My own fairly strong inclination is to reject this suggestion. Athena leaves to assemble her jury and returns with them, apparently to the same place (Orestes probably exited with Athena; see n. on v. 489

below). Verrall argued vigorously that vv. 685 ff. were inescapably specific, but the pronouns may have a vaguer designation than Verrall and others have thought; Athena may be referring to her new court as an institution rather than to the particular place where its sittings were held in historical times.

How the trial-scene was staged we can only surmise. I take it that seats or benches of some kind were provided for the jurors towards the rear of the acting area. The defendant and his patron, Apollo, take up their positions upstage and to the (stage-) right; the Chorus-leader representing the prosecution moves forward from the orchestra, ascends the steps and takes a corresponding position at stage-left. Athena, in charge, stands in a commanding position at the centre facing the audience. After both sides have been heard, Athena issues her proclamation founding the Areopagus as a court "for all time" and after she has finished her speech the voting begins (v. 710); the ensuing couplets by the Chorus-leader and Apollo cover the actual casting of the ballots by the jurymen, who file past two urns,[33] probably centrally located, and return to their places. At v. 734–5 Athena says that she will cast her vote in Orestes' favour and this, as she says at 741 (although the line is not free from ambiguity; see my note there), will constitute acquittal if the jurors' votes should be tied. Two of the jurors turn out the urns and count the votes, a procedure which takes place during the four lines of stichomythic exchange between Orestes and the Chorus-leader (vv. 744–47), and the following four lines, whose ascription is uncertain (see note on vv. 746–751). Athena inspects the results and, at v. 752, pronounces a verdict of acquittal. Orestes gives his speech of thanks and departs after v. 777, presumably accompanied by Apollo, although this is not made clear in the text. (As I indicate in my n. on v. 777 below, the possibility should at least be entertained that Apollo remains onstage though mute through the whole last part of the play, and departs with the others in the procession at the end).

The remainder of the play is a remarkable depiction of "white" magic. As Athena, still standing magisterially at stage-centre, uses all her powers of cool reason and persuasion to dispel the Erinyes' venomous rage against herself and her citizens, the Chorus dance and sing their refrains of hate (778–793 = 808–823; 837–847 = 870–880) until, gradually assuaged by her calm, authoritative persistence, they are ready both to listen to and ultimately to accept her proposal. The Chorus-leader again speaks for them all in a brief stichomythia with Athena framed by two short speeches by the goddess, vv. 881–915. The play ends lyrically, with the Chorus singing three pairs of stanzas given to prayers of blessing on their new colleagues, the citizens of Athens, and Athena interposing chanted anapaests (the exchange between the Chorus and Clytemnestra after the murder of Agamemnon is structurally similar, *Agamemnon* 1407–1576). At v. 948 Athena addresses the jurors, at v. 997 the Chorus call on the "people of the city". Athena then refers to "escorts" (v. 1005) and, at 1010–11, she calls upon those "who are in charge of the city, Kranaos' sons" to lead the Erinyes, now turned Eumenides, to their new chambers below the soil of Attica. How this was managed is not quite clear, but the most satisfactory assumption is that a group of individuals representing both sexes and all ages of Athenian citizens had begun to make its way into the orchestra along the (audience's) right-hand parodos at about v. 1003; possibly they were then joined by the Areopagite jurors from the stage. The text at vv. 1022–23 makes it clear that the procession was equipped with torches and was led by Athena herself, and vv. 1024–5 suggests that her image, which figured significantly earlier in the action, was taken up and carried in the procession. V. 1028 has been taken as showing that the Erinyes donned crimson cloaks over their previous costumes, but it is not by any means a necessary inference. The final exit-song (vv. 1032 to the end) is sung by ⁺he procession of Athenians, who escort the Eumenides to their new home in tones of joyfulness and praise.

How lavish or spare the actual production was in terms of properties, costumes, number of extras and so on depended largely on the munificence or otherwise of the "choregos", whose duties extended beyond the mere "chorus sponsorship" that the term suggests. What in later times became a debilitating financial drain was, we must assume, in the palmy days of the tragic and other choral performances a sought-after privilege, a means whereby established or aspiring leaders brought themselves before the public eye; it can hardly be accidental that Themistocles was choregos for (probably) Phrynichus' *Phoenician Women* in 476 B.C. and the young Pericles for Aeschylus' *Persians* in 472. From an inscription[34] we know the name and ancestral residence of Aeschylus' choregos in 458, Xenocles of Aphidna, but he is not encountered again in the historical or epigraphical records. It may be significant that Aphidna was "one of the most radically minded demes of Attika".[35] Xenocles would have been responsible for putting up enough money for the director – at this period, the playwright himself – to feed, house and train the chorus (numbering probably 12 in Aeschylus' later dramas), as well as such extras, mute actors or subsidiary choruses as the script might call for (in *Eum.*, for example, the Areopagite jurors and the singing "escorts" at the close). The only major expense which he was not expected to defray was that of providing the three actors; their masks and costumes, however, were probably his concern, as those of the chorus certainly were. Xenocles seems to have ensured that the mask-maker spared no expense in creating suitably horrific Erinyes (see *Eum*. 46 ff., 192 ff., 410 ff., 990 below). That the city paid for all actors for all the competitors is probably at core the reason for the restriction to three actors who, however, might fill any number of roles. In *Eum*. there was no need for particularly quick changes of costume or breathless re-entries. The "protagonist" (first actor) will have played Orestes, the second actor Apollo and the third actor the Pythian priestess, Clytemnestra's Ghost and Athena, with Hermes' part, if he appeared (see note on v. 89), being taken by a "mute".[36]

III. Philosophy – and Politics

References

Beer, D.G.   "Tyranny, *anarkhia*, and the problems of the *Boule* in the *Oresteia*", *Florilegium* 3 (1981) 47–71.

Dodds, E.R.   "Morals and Politics in the 'Oresteia'", *Proceedings of the Cambridge Philological Society* 186 (n.s. 6) (1960) 19–31 = *The Ancient Concept of Progress* (Oxford: Clarendon Press, 1973) ch. III, pp. 45–63.

Dover, K.J.   "The Political Aspect of Aeschylus' *Eumenides*", *Journal of Hellenic Studies* 77 (1957) 230–237 = *Greek and the Greeks' Collected Papers* I (Oxford: Basil Blackwell, 1987) ch. 17, pp. 161–175.

Jones, Lesley Ann   "The Role of Ephialtes in the Rise of Athenian Democracy", *Classical Antiquity* 6 (1987) 55–76.

Macleod, C. "Politics and the *Oresteia*", *Journal of Hellenic Studies* 102 (1982) 124–144 = *Collected Essays* (Oxford: Clarendon Press, 1983) ch. 3, pp. 20–43.

Podlecki *Political Background* ch. v. "Oresteia", pp. 63–100.

Quincey, J.H.   "Orestes and the Argive Alliance", *Classical Quarterly* n.s. 14 (1964) 190–206.

The *Eumenides*, like the trilogy which it completes, was not composed in some timeless, "mythical" vacuum, but was (for the original audience) anchored to the Athenian present. As L.A. Jones has recently written, "The 'mythical' Athens may be functioning on one level as a timeless ideal state, but, on another, Aeschylus was very anxious to anchor it in the shared experience of his countrymen" (Jones p. 71). The lifeline between heroic past and the Athens of 458 B.C. is, of course, that venerable but also contemporary institution, the Court of the Areopagus, which had been "reformed" (as he maintained) by a certain Ephialtes, perhaps with the collaboration of Pericles, some years previously in 462/1 B.C. It is not clear what precisely the reform consisted in. The account given by the *Constitution of Athens* ascribed to Aristotle is not free from ambiguities and problems (for example, at ch. 25. 3–4 it associates Themistocles' name with Ephialtes', but this seems impossible), but we ought probably to accept the bare assertion that Ephialtes "took away from the council all the accretions [*epitheta*] which gave it its guardianship of the constitution, giving some to the council of five hundred and some to the people and jury-courts" (ch. 25.2, trans. P.J. Rhodes).[37] It would be difficult to deny that a play written within five years of the event and one in which the foundation of the Areopagus featured so prominently has something to say about Ephialtes' reforms. The question is, exactly what?

I am personally convinced by Jacoby's demonstration that Aeschylus modified the transmitted myth in (a) creating the connection between Orestes' acquittal and the Areopagus-court, and (b) making this the "first ever" trial for homicide. Jacoby further maintained that the poet "wrote his trilogy because of the Areopagus" and that he "defends the democratic restriction of the old Council to jurisdiction in cases of homicide because that was the function Athena had assigned to it, all additional functions falling under the concept *epitheta*".[38]

But account must also be taken of several passages in the play whose tone appears to be "conservative" and which have therefore been called in to support a contrary view to Jacoby's: that Aeschylus opposed the Ephialtic reforms of the Areopagus. In the Second Choral Ode the Erinyes descant upon the virtues of *to Deinon*, a salutary fear, which, they say, "ought to abide seated majestically, overseeing men's thoughts. There is an advantage in learning prudence under duress .... Give approval to a life that is neither anarchic nor ruled by a despot. God grants mastery always to the middle way ...." (vv. 517–21, 526–30). These sentiments are echoed by Athena in the course of the great speech in which she outlines the rights and responsibilities of her newly founded court: "I counsel my citizens to cherish and revere neither anarchy nor despotism, and not to expel fear entirely from the city, for what man who fears nothing can be just?" (vv. 696–98). Athena and the Erinyes are at one not only in their advice to the Athenians to avoid the extremes of tyranny and anarchy, they express themselves in strikingly similar language. But are these eulogies of "the mean" to be taken in general, "philosophical" terms, or do they have some special political point? In other words, is Aeschylus recommending some particular, perhaps narrowly partisan, course of action to his fellow Athenians?

What seems to me to weigh heavily on the side of a general interpretation here is the fact that the Areopagus' main role, to be Athens' premier court for homicide at which cases of premeditated murder were tried – the very function, in fact, with which Athena endows her newly established court – was left untouched by Ephialtes' reforms. The Areopagus continued to exercise this jurisdiction in homicide cases, along with certain other responsibilities, down into the fourth century.[39] I believe that it is in this light that Athena's words at *Eum*. 760 ff. are to be understood: it is precisely because such matters as Orestes' killing of his mother are henceforward to be dealt with by legal, civically sanctioned means rather than by Clytemnestra's (and Atreus' and also Orestes') vendetta, that the new court will constitute an "ever-watchful guard-post of the land". So in this respect, at least, Aeschylus seems not to be criticizing the changes made by Ephialtes (whatever they may have been) in the Areopagus' judicial functions.

Another theme in the play must be considered before we can assess fully the stance that Aeschylus took to the reforms of 462 B.C., that is, the prominence that it gives to Argos and the perpetuity and firmness of the bond struck by Orestes between his people and Athena's. As we saw above in Section I, earlier poets had located the house of Atreus in different places around the Peloponnese: Homer at Mycenae, Stesichorus and Simonides at Sparta. Aeschylus – and he appears to have been an innovator in this respect – sets the action at Argos. At three places in *Eum*. Orestes' Argive nationality is not only alluded to, but given special emphasis (vv. 289–91, 670–3 and 762–74). Why this repeated emphasis on the perpetuity of the alliance with Argos and the dependability of the Argives as allies? I believe it is because the alliance with Argos was part and parcel of the reformers' program in 462. When Athens repudiated her alliance with Sparta and entered into a thirty-year alliance with the Spartans' long-term and bitter rival in the Peloponnese, Argos, it was, as Thucydides makes clear (1.102.4), not only a repudiation of Sparta but also a bitter blow to Cimon, the conservative politician and friend of Sparta who was in fact subsequently "removed" through the constitutional tool of ostracism. The Argive alliance can thus be seen as signalling a turn towards a more liberal stance in internal Athenian politics as well. Dover writes: "... the alliance was an achievement – or perhaps it would be more accurate to call it a gesture – of the democrats, inseparable from their renunciation of the Spartan alliance to which the conservative elements in Athens gave their loyalty .... If [Aeschylus] was positively conservative in sentiment, it is difficult to believe that he would have written the *Oresteia* in anything like the form which it actually has" (Dover pp. 235–6). This conclusion seems to me to be inescapable.[40]

Topical allusions have been detected in several other passages in the play. When Orestes is praying to the still absent Athena for assistance, he begs her to come, whether she is "in Libyan regions of the land ... or whether she is overseeing the Phlegraean plain" (vv. 292, 295–96). No very specific point has been suggested for the reference to the Phlegraean plain (near Potidaea) beyond the fact that, since it was, as Dover points out, "the scene of the victory of the gods over the giants ... in which Athena took a prominent part", it was "naturally associated with her" (Dover p. 237). Orestes' mention of Libya, however, may have struck a more immediate and topical chord in the audience's attention. Thucydides reports (1.104) that two or three years before *Eumenides* was produced the Athenians had sent a large expedition to support the attempt of a certain Inaros, self-styled King of the Libyans, to revolt from his vassalage to the King of Persia. This ambitious, and as it turned out misplaced, venture was in mid-course precisely at the date of the play. Would, then, the reference to Libya have had a special point for Aeschylus' audience? Dodds argued that it would: "when ... [Orestes] speculates on the possible presence of Athena in Libya, 'helping her friends' (295), I imagine they asked themselves, 'What friends?' and quickly guessed the answer, 'Of course, our other ally [*i.e.*, besides Argos], those Libyans whose king we are just now helping to break the yoke of Persia'" (Dodds p. 20). Dodds also mentions, although he does not endorse, the suggestion that Athena's own reference to the Trojan plain in v. 398 may somehow be connected with an Atheno-Persian confrontation over Sigeum for which there is evidence dating from 451 B.C.[41]

In her foundation speech Athena warns her new court (and, ipso facto, the Athenians at large) not to "make innovations in the laws – if [she warns] by evil in-pourings and mud you pollute bright water, you'll never find a drink" (vv. 693–95; there follows the injunction to avoid extremes of anarchy and despotism, already discussed). Some scholars have interpreted these lines as an allusion to a constitutional change which, they argue, must have been the topic of debate at the time of the play, since it is known actually to have been passed and made into law in the next archon-year. The Aristotelian *Constitution of Athens* (26.2) reports that in 457 B.C. the elegibility requirements for the archonship

were lowered, and the office, hitherto restricted to the top two –
relatively wealthy – of Solon's four property classes, was in that year
opened to the third, "zeugite", class. Was the change being mooted in
the preceding year, when *Eum.* was produced, and if so, is Athena
warning against the lowering of property requirements for eligibility for
the archonship as a "pollution" of the Areopagus, which was composed of
ex-archons? Dodds argued[42] that this is in fact the case and that such an
interpretation makes sense of what appears to be the special point of
Athena's rather strong language in vv. 694–95. Jones has recently
restated and somewhat modified Dodds' case. In her view, relaxation of
the property-standards for the archonship had been an additional proposal
by Ephialtes, who proposed to go further in weakening the Areopagus
than the judicial reforms already discussed: "... the conservatives would
have viewed Ephialtes as a continuing risk to the constitution, as he was
still held in high regard and there was a danger he would win more
people over to his side. It was for this reason that he was murdered
[mentioned by *Const. of Athens* 26.4, although the date is left vague:
"not long after" the reforms] – for what he was about to do, rather than
for what he had achieved. .... The murder of Ephialtes may well have
been the incident that Aeschylus feared might signal an outbreak of
factional violence" (Jones p. 75). Many commentators have felt that
there is more to the passages of warning or admonition than meets the
modern reader's eye, and Jones may well be correct in her suggestion of
the message that Aeschylus wished to communicate to his audience
"between the lines".

IV. Influence

A. Ancient Literature

References

Xanthakis-Karamanos, G. *Studies in Fourth-century Greek Tragedy*
(Athens: Academy of Athens, 1980).
Ribbeck, O. *Scaenicae Romanorum Poesis Fragmenta*, vol. I *Tragicorum
Romanorum Fragmenta* 3rd ed. (Leipzig: Teubner, 1897).
Warmington, B.H. *Remains of Old Latin* (London: Wm. Heinemann,
and Cambridge, Mass.: Harvard University Press, 1961 [Loeb
Classical Library]) vols. I and II.
Tarrant, R.J. *Seneca's 'Agamemnon'* (Cambridge: Cambridge Univ.

Press, 1976).

Jocelyn, H.D. *The Tragedies of Ennius* (Cambridge: Cambridge Univ. Press, 1967).

The ancient Hypothesis to *Eumenides* reports, "in neither [sc. Sophocles or Euripides] is the story to be found". If this is technically correct (Sophocles wrote a *Clytemnestra*, but this dealt with the sacrifice of Iphigeneia), episodes in certain plays of Euripides show that his predecessor's work made a strong impression upon him. Castor, *deus ex machina* at the end of *Electra* (c. 420), prophesies Orestes' frenzied wanderings pursued by the "dread dog-faced death goddesses" (1252), who are described as "aflutter with dreadful snakes" (1255–56), "black-skinned with snaky hands" (1345). He will go to Athens, where he is to find protection with his arms wrapped around Athena's statue; he will be tried on Ares' Hill and, the jury's votes being equal, acquitted (1265, 1269). The defeated Erinyes will "sink down into a chasm by the rock, an august oracle for pious men" (1271–72[43]). Euripides took up the story again in *Orestes* of 408 B.C., this time developing the psychological effects of the matricide; we are shown a chillingly realistic portrayal of a killer in the grip of a madness brought on by guilt and remorse for his deed. As the action progresses, the Argives conduct an offstage trial at which, in spite of a spirited defence of his action and a plea for his acquittal on grounds that his condemnation would constitute an inducement to faithless wives to murder their husbands (reminiscences here of Apollo's argument at *Eum.* 213 ff.), Orestes is condemned to death by public stoning. After a series of bizarre twists the action ends with Apollo's appearance *ex machina*, to prophesy, much as Castor had done in *Electra*, Orestes' wanderings, first to Arcadia, thence to Athens,[44] where he will "be brought to trial by the three Eumenides" – the first surviving occurrence of any reference to their number and official title – "and the gods will judge your case at Ares' Hill" (1649–51[45]). In *Iphigeneia among the Taurians* (c. 414 B.C.) Orestes recounts some of these events for his sister's benefit, and adds one or two details: the Athenians' treatment of him as an outcast, and the subsequent commemoration of their reception of him by the "Festival of Pitchers" (Choes), the second day of the Athenian Anthesteria (vv. 959–60). Probably earlier than these Euripidean forays into the myth was an *Agamemnon* by Ion of Chios; the few surviving fragments (Snell *TrGF* 19, F 1–5) yield no knowledge whatever about the plot.

The title *Orestes* is ascribed to several other dramatists: a younger Euripides, a namesake of but apparently unrelated to the fifth-century tragedian;[46] Theodectes, pupil of Plato and Aristotle, whose works enjoyed a large vogue and from whose *Orestes* Aristotle quotes a line in the *Rhetoric* (1401 a 35 = *TrGF* 72 F 5); Carcinus, whose version may have dramatized Orestes brought to trial by Clytemnestra's cousin, Perilaos (*TrGF* 70 F 1g; cf. Pausanias 8.34.4); and Aphareus, whose *Orestes* came third at the Dionysia in 341 B.C.[47] In the first century B.C. a *Clytemnestra* is attributed to a certain Polemaios of Ephesus, and the Suda-lexicon lists an *Orestes and Pylades* to the credit of a tragedian named Timesitheus, of unknown date.

Improbable as it may seem, Aeschylus' play appears to have exerted some influence on later comic writers. A *Eumenides* by Cratinus is fairly well attested, and another by Telecleides rather less so.[48] In the late-fourth century the popular comic writer Philemon, in a work whose title is not recorded, had one of his characters maintain that the Semnai or "August Goddesses" were not the same as the Eumenides (fr. 217 Kock). Two writers of farces, Rhinthon and Sopatros, who were active about 300 B.C., wrote dramas with the title *Orestes*, but virtually nothing is known about their plots.

The early Roman dramatists turned to the main cycles of Greek myth for their inspiration, and the Orestes story provided material for numerous dramas.[49] Of most of them not enough survives, unfortunately, for us to be sure to what extent their authors were influenced directly by Aeschylus' *Oresteia*. A description of Agamemnon's storm-tossed return from Troy featured in the *Aegisthus* of Livius Andronicus, as in Accius' *Clytemnestra* (compare Seneca, *Agamemnon* 470 ff.). The action of Livius' *Aegisthus* involved the murder of Agamemnon as he sat at table with Clytemnestra and their daughters Electra and Chrysothemis, and in another scene Aegisthus ordered his servants to drag Electra from her place of refuge in a temple. Accius' *Clytemnestra* depicted the murder of Cassandra, and Clytemnestra told Electra (probably), "You blame your mother for a just deed; you approve your father for an unjust". In Accius' *Aegisthus* a reference was made to Orestes' hand "filthy with the sprinkled blood of his mother". Pacuvius wrote a drama entitled *Dulorestes*, probably a reference to Orestes' return to his ancestral home disguised as a slave, in fulfilment of an oracle. In this play, which certainly was unaeschylean in some of its plot developments (for example, it told how Clytemnestra had betrothed Electra, against the latter's will, to Oeax, son of Palamedes), someone, probably Aegisthus, threatened Electra with imprisonment and torture. Orestes complained, in regard to the power exercised by Aegisthus, of the "rashness of tyrants" and Aegisthus, warned of the danger to his rule, made enquiries about the sources of Orestes' support. In a memorable line, Orestes steeled himself for the deed he was about to perform by praying that he might "become like his mother" (*matrescam*) in order to deal with her as she had dealt with Agamemnon. According to the Virgilian commentator Servius, Pacuvius portrayed Orestes "entering a temple on Pylades' advice in order to avoid the Furies". It is this play to which, according to Jocelyn, Cicero is alluding when he several times mentions the friendship of Orestes and Pylades.[50] Of an *Electra* by Atilius nothing is known beyond Cicero's dismissal of it as a mere copy of Sophocles' play (*de Finibus* 1.2).

The only Roman play which drew directly upon Aeschylus' *Eumenides* was Ennius' tragedy of the same name; even though it is represented by only four citations in Jocelyn's edition of Ennius' tragic fragments, it is nevertheless quite clear that it closely followed its Aeschylean model. In fr. 63 (Jocelyn) Orestes says, "Unless I avenged my father by pouring a libation of maternal blood ..." (the reference presumably is to the threats of punishment for disobedience of Apollo's oracle; cf. *Eum.* 463–67, *Choephoroi* 271 ff.) and another citation preserves the conclusion of Orestes' trial, with Athena pronouncing the verdict: "I say that Orestes has won, depart ye from him!" (fr. 64). Possibly, as Jocelyn notes, Cicero had this trial scene in mind when he referred to Orestes "acquitted by the vote of one who was not merely a goddess, but a goddess pre-eminent for wisdom" (*pro Milone* 8). Although the following lines are quoted by Nonius as coming from Ennius' *Eumenides*, it is not clear whether they were spoken by Athena (compare *Eum.* 571–73) or Orestes (cf. *Eum.* 276–79): "I think it is best to be silent and wise according to one's strength, *tacere opino esse optimum et pro viribus sapere...*"[51]

Ennius' Orestes so far departed from his Aeschylean exemplar that, as Jocelyn remarks, he "pretends confidence about not only the justice but the equity [*aecum*] of his act".[52] In the first century B.C. Varro, who is himself credited with a Menippean satire entitled *Eumenides*,[53] cites a line of Ennius in which the "Areopagitae" were mentioned,[54] but since the Varronian passage has suffered some corruption, it is unclear whether the allusion was made in *Eum.* or somewhere else in Ennius' writings. Finally, it must remain an open question whether Cicero was thinking specifically of Ennius' drama when he mentioned stage Furiae pursuing polluted criminals with blazing torches.[55]

The last of the Roman dramatists to treat the story was Seneca. His *Thyestes* dealt with events recapitulated briefly in Aeschylus' *Agamemnon*, while the action of the Senecan *Agamemnon* coincides roughly with that of Aeschylus' play although, as R.J. Tarrant has written, "nothing in Seneca's play requires direct knowledge of Aeschylus".[56]   A passage from Cassandra's vision is worthy of consideration, however: "The filthy sisters press on, flail their snaky whips, half-burnt torches held in their left hands, their cheeks bloated and pale, black mourning robes around their wizened flanks.   Fearful shrieks shudder through the night, and a huge corpse's bones lie rotting in a dark and distant swamp" (vv. 759–68). This goes far beyond Aeschylus' Cassandra who alludes fleetingly to the "band insatiable for the family" which she tells to "raise a cry over the sacrifice of stoning" (Aeschylus, *Agamemnon* 1117–18), a dark but unmistakable reference to the Erinyes, as the Chorus are quick to remark. Seneca's more rococo portrayal has as its spiritual ancestor the fierce and rabid creatures of *Eum*.

A curious late Latin poem survives, an *Orestis tragoedia* in 974 dactylic hexameters, which has plausibly been ascribed to one Blossius Aemilius Dracontius, active at Carthage in the latter part of the fifth century A.D., who wrote verse on Christian as well as secular topics.[57] The poem is a pastiche of various elements from the tradition about Orestes and earlier poetic treatments, including Aeschylus', although some details seem to be Dracontius' own invention. On his way from Troy Agamemnon is blown off course to the Chersonese where, to his amazement, he encounters Iphigeneia in Diana's temple; she tells her father that a hind had been substituted for her as the victim of his sacrifice at Aulis. Back in Mycenae, Clytemnestra incites Aegisthus to regicide: it is he who lays Agamemnon low with an axe, while Clytemnestra entangles him in a tunic. Electra spirits Orestes away to Athens on the same ship which had brought Agamemnon home and there, in the company of Pylades, he engages in "scientific studies" and physical exercise. A dream-apparition of Agamemnon urges the young men to seek vengeance; their secret return, to which Orestes is incited by his friend, is prepared by a freedman of the royal house, Dorylas, who had originally accompanied Agamemnon's children into exile but returned with a lying tale that they had been killed in a shipwreck (shades of Sinon in *Aeneid* 2). Pylades runs Aegisthus through with his sword; Clytemnestra is left to her son, who is unmoved by her rhetorical pleas and bared breast. After the murders, a messenger arrives to report that Achilles' son Pyrrhus has snatched away Hermione, daughter of Helen and Menelaus, although the girl had been betrothed (and in some versions, actually married) to Orestes. Leaving Pylades in charge, Orestes rushes away and slays his rival as he is entering a temple ("at his father's altar" according to *Aeneid* 3. 330 ff.; a commoner version had

Pyrrhus killed at Delphi, either by Orestes or through his agency). Orestes returns home and, as at *Aeneid* 4. 471–2, is haunted by his mother's ghost; she, armed with snakes and with faggots from her own funeral pyre, pursues him through the palace and, Harpy-like, prevents him from eating or drinking anything. Molossus, the son of Pyrrhus and Andromache, arrives to avenge his father's murder. Pylades sends Orestes off to foreign parts, including the Chersonese, where he encounters his sister Iphigeneia and is purified by her. Molossus hales Orestes to Athens and prosecutes him before the Areopagus for the two murders he has committed; when the jurors' votes are split, Athena casts her ballot for Orestes' acquittal.

B. Ancient Art

References

GENERAL

Junge, M. *Untersuchungen zur Ikonographie der Erinys in der griechischen Kunst* (diss Kiel, 1983).

McPhee, Ian "Elektra", *Lexicon Iconographicum Mythologiae Classicae* [LIMC] III.1 (Zurich: Artemis, 1986) 709–719, esp. 715 catalogue B.2, Electra and Orestes at Delphi.

Prag, A.J.N.W. *The Oresteia*. (P in the catalogue of vases below)

Sarian, H. "Erinys" (S below).

Vermeule, E.T. "The Boston Oresteia Krater".

VASE-PAINTING

Dyer, Robert Rutherford "The Evidence of Apolline Purification Rituals" (Dyer).

Goldman, Hetty "The *Oresteia* of Aeschylus as illustrated by Greek Vase Painting", *Harvard Studies in Classical Philology* 21 (1910) 11–159 (G).

Kossatz-Deissman, Anneliese *Dramen des Aischylos auf westgriechischen Vasen* (Mainz: von Zabern, 1978) (K).

Séchan, Louis *Etudes sur la tragédie grecque dans ses rapports avec la ceramique* (Paris: Honoré Champion, 1967; repr. of the 1926 ed.) pp. 93–101 (Sé).

Trendall, A.D. and Webster, T.B.L. *Illustrations of Greek Drama* (London: Phaidon, 1971) pp. 41–49 (T/W).

Webster, T.B.L. *Monuments illustrating Tragedy and Satyr Play (2nd edition with Appendix)* (University of London: Institute of Classical

Studies [Bulletin Supplement No. 20] 1967) pp. 140–141.

ETRUSCAN ART

Bates, Wm. N. "The Purification of Orestes", *American Journal of Archaeology* 15 (1911) 459–464.

Brunn, E. *I Rilievi delle Urne Etrusche* vol. I (Rome: "L' Erma" di Bretschneider, 1965; repr. of the ed. Rome 1870) plates LXXVIII–LXXXIII.

de Ruyt, Franz *Charun, démon étrusque de la mort* (Rome: Institut historique belge, 1934).

SARCOPHAGI

Ruth M. Gais, "Aigisthos", LIMC I (1981) p. 376 no. 34.

Robert, C. *Die antiken Sarkophagreliefs, II. Mythologische Cyklen* (Rome: "L' Erma" di Bretschneider, 1968, repr. of the ed. Berlin 1890).

Koch, G. and Sichtermann, H. *Romische Sarkophage* (Munich: Beck, 1982).

Sichtermann, H. and Koch, G. *Griechische Mythen auf romischen Sarkophagen* (Tübingen: Wasmuth, 1975).

McCann, A.M. *Roman Sarcophagi in the Metropolitan Museum of Art* (New York: Metropolitan Museum of Art, 1978) pp. 53 ff.

THE "COPPA CORSINI"

Hafner, G. *Iudicium Orestis. Klassisches und Klassizistisches* ([Berliner Winckelmannsprogramm No. 113] Berlin: de Gruyter, 1958).

de Luca, G. *I Monumenti antichi di Palazzo Corsini in Roma* (Rome: Accademia Nazionale dei Lincei, 1970) pp. 127–132.

The action of *Eum.* seems to have been more popular with South Italian vase-painters than with Athenian artists; Webster, *Monuments* 140 lists only 6 Attic vases, and Prag E9 adds a red-figure column-krater in Bologna (Mus. civ. 2212, C 660). How is this to be explained? Companies of travelling actors, or local dramatic troupes, probably account for some of this interest in Athenian drama. In Dyer's view (p. 53), "The evidence of the vases is that the legend of Orestes enjoyed great popularity in Magna Graecia throughout the first half of the fourth century, and it may not be overbold to suggest that this is related to revivals of the *Oresteia* and the *Iphigeneia in Tauris*". The figure of Orestes in particular appears to have captured the religious imagination of various civic groups in southern Italy, for he was the object of a heroic cult at Tarentum and Rhegium and, eventually, Rome.[58] There is also the possibility that some of the vase-pictures were inspired not by actual productions but by outstanding visual models, striking wall-paintings or plaques which lent themselves to copying in the more restricted medium.

I set out selectively and schematically those depictions on which it seems to me that Aeschylus' version may have exerted an influence, with references to plates or illustrations in the works cited at the beginning of this section.

(1) Louvre K 343: Athenian red-figure column-krater by the Duomo Painter (450–425 B.C.) [P pl. 31a; S 42 with pl.; Lacroix in *L'Antiquité classique* 15 (1946) 211–212 pl. 7] Orestes kneels, his right leg bent and his left leg outstretched, on a rock-pile which some have taken to be an altar, between Athena (l.) and Apollo with laurel branch (r.), all looking right to a snaky-locked, winged Erinys, who menacingly holds out an uncoiling snake in her right hand. Orestes has just drawn his sword; cf. *Eum.* 42 below.

(2) East Berlin, Staatl. mus. inv. 4565: Apulian (S. Italian) bell-krater by the Hearst Painter (415–390 B.C.) [K 33, pl. 23.2; Dyer pl. V.8; S 74 (ill. as "Athena" no. 166)] Orestes seated on a base which may be a temple plinth with his left arm grasps a statue of an armed Athena as at *Eum.* 259; with his right hand he fends off winged, snake-bedecked Erinyes who stand in a framing pattern to left and right.

(3) Vatican W1, Inv. 17.137: red-figure Lucanian amphora (350–325 B.C.) [Sé p. 100, fig. 33; S 56 not illustrated] Orestes at an altar and again with his sword drawn, but in a pose opposite to (1) above with his left leg bent, his right outstretched; to upper left a towering, fully armed Athena stretching out her left hand which has the aegis draped over it in a gesture both protective of Orestes and to warn off the running Erinys at upper right, who is snaky-locked but wingless and seems about to thrust a spear at Orestes with both hands. Apollo stands rather casually at lower left, his feet crossed, a laurel branch held in his right hand and his left elbow resting on a pillar. In the centre of the upper register between Athena and the Erinys is a seated Nike: merely a space-filler, or an assurance that Orestes' cause will prevail?

(4) Boston, Museum of Fine Arts 1976.144: Apulian bell-krater by a follower of the Judgement Painter (c. 360 B.C.) [S 49, not illustrated] (Cf. A.D. Trendall and A. Cambitoglou, *The Red-figure Vases of Apulia* [Oxford: Clarendon Press, 1978] vol. I, p. 264 no. 33, pl. 87. 5–6; E.T. Vermeule, "More Sleeping Furies", *Studies in Classical Art & Archaeology... H. von Blanckenhagen* [Locust Valley, N.Y.: J.J.

Augustin, 1979] 185–8, pl. 51.2) Orestes at altar, his left knee bent as in (3) above; similarly, an armed Athena to Orestes' left, balanced by a standing Apollo on right holding a laurel branch in his left hand and his right arm bent upwards. Orestes holds a sword in his right hand and with his other arm appears to be clutching the omphalos shown above and behind the altar. His flapping cloak betokens a speedy journey (Vermeule 186 n. 10 calls this "the whirling pivot pose"). At bottom of scene, 2 sleeping Erinyes, wingless.

(5) London BM 1917.12–10, 1 (Hope Collection): Paestan krater by Python (350–340 B.C.) [K cat 36, pl. 21.2; T/W III.1, 11; P pl. 33a; Sé pl. II facing p. 101; S 52, not illustrated but cf. LIMC II.2 (1984) "Athena" p. 765 pl. 626; M. Bieber, *History of the Greek & Roman Theater*, p. 27, fig. 97] The scene is again Delphi. A majestic, armed, gorgeously attired Athena stands to the left, looking down benevolently at Orestes who kneels with both knees bent, his back propped against the omphalos and two spears clutched in his left hand. Above Orestes, a large tripod, surmounted by a bust of an Erinys who holds a snake in her outstretched right hand with additional snakes streaming from her hair. To Orestes' right stands Apollo who looks behind him at an Erinys standing at the right of the picture, gloriously winged, a snake held in her left hand and coiling up over her head. In the upper left and right corners busts of, respectively, a female in a conical headdress who may be either Clytemnestra or Leto, and Pylades.

(6) Berlin (West), Staatl. Mus. V.1, 3164: Campanian hydria by the Ixion Painter (330–300 B.C.) [S cat. 58, pl. p. 600] Orestes, seated against a net-covered omphalos, holds his sword in his right hand and with his left clutches a tripod which rises behind and above him. He turns a worried gaze to the left of the scene, where an Erinys with large wings and snakes coiled around her body lowers her torch as if daunted by the sight, at the right of the picture, of Athena in full armour, standing behind Apollo, seated, who holds his bow in his left hand and raises his right in warning to the Erinys.

(7) Leningrad, Hermitage B 1743 (St. 349): Apulian calyx-krater by the Konnakis Painter (c. 360–350 B.C.) [K cat. 35, pl. 21.1; Sé p. 95 fig. 30; Dyer pl. V.7; T/W III.1, 10; S cat. 46, pl. p. 599] Orestes is seated in a small Ionic shrine ("the painter is thinking of the stage-building at Taras rather than of the marble temple at Delphi", T/W p. 46); his left arm is around the omphalos and he holds a drawn sword. On the steps below Orestes are five little white-haired, black-skinned (cf. *Eum.* 52) Erinyes. Fright has gripped the Pythia who runs off to the right, clutching the temple-key in her left hand; she looks back and thrusts her

right hand before her, as if to avert the evil of the scene. Dyer (p. 53) remarks that, although there are significant differences between the painting and the Pythia's description at *Eum.* 46–59, "the resemblances are so striking that we can be certain that the painter was working very close to a text or production of Aeschylus".

(8) Louvre K 710: Apulian bell-krater, the name-vase of the Eumenides Painter (c. 390–380 B.C.) [K 41, pl. 20.2; Dyer pl. II.1; G XXII; Sé pl. I, bottom, facing p. 92; Bates 459 fig. 2] Orestes sits on a low pedestal, his back resting against the omphalos and a sword held upright in his right hand; he has rather a pensive look ("madness seems to have given way to melancholy", Goldman p. 145). A special problem is presented by the fact that Apollo, who stands to Orestes' right, not only clutches the laurel with his left hand but at the same time in his right hand holds out a piglet, which he has grasped by its left hind leg, over Orestes' head, thus apparently illustrating *Eum.* 282–3 below (see my note). This purification is also shown on an Apulian bell-krater of the same period "formerly Milan market" (Dyer), illustrated at Dyer II.2, and on a Paestan squat lekythos in Paestum, Mus. naz. 4794, c. 340 B.C. by Asteas [Dyer IV.6; T/W III.1, 12; S 64].

Late depictions of the myth apart from vase-painting include a silver stater from Cyzicus, dating from the later fourth century B.C.[59] Orestes at a rocky outcrop, which may be the omphalos, kneels on his left knee with his right leg bent. The scene has been thought to go back to a late-fifth century original, perhaps by the artist Timanthes, who is reported to have made a pathetic and moving rendition of the "Sacrifice of Iphigeneia".[60]

ETRUSCAN ART

The scene of Apollo purifying Orestes with the blood of a young pig is depicted on an Etruscan mirror of the 4th century B.C. now in the Museum of the University of Pennsylvania in Philadelphia [Bates 462 fig. 2], where the purification is witnessed by two female figures named, on left and right respectively, Vanth and Metua, Etruscan underworld demons who may have been intended to represent Erinyes. Sarian reports two other Etruscan mirrors, one in West Berlin and the other in Tübingen, showing Orestes about to murder his mother (respectively S 28, illustrated, and 29, not illustrated).

Orestes' slaying of Aegisthus and Clytemnestra, generally in the presence of one Erinys or several, is depicted on many Etruscan cinerary urns. The Erinyes are usually (not always) winged; they wear short tunics and are more Etruscan than Greek of mien, and they generally make threatening gestures at Orestes with their torches. Occasionally the artist, following a route which we can no longer trace, will come close to his Greek exemplar and portray his Erinys holding a snake (see Brunn, pl. 80. 11; LIMC I.2 [1981] "Aigisthos" p. 291 pl. 30). In Brunn pl. 80. 10 (LIMC I.2 p. 291 pl. 33) the demon is seen emerging from the depths at lower left with a snake extending upward sinuously and menacingly from her head, while in Brunn pl. 81. 12 Orestes is shown with his right leg bent, crouching at a rocky projection that was perhaps meant to be the omphalos; he is beset by torch-wielding Erinyes.

ROMAN SARCOPHAGI

A fairly large number of late Roman sarcophagi (2nd–3rd cent. A.D.) depict, in a confused and turbulent scene, the murder by Orestes of his mother and her lover, who lie in undulating, if somewhat disheveled poses at the young man's feet. The story is often told sequentially. The two ends of the scene show early stages of Orestes' quest. On the right Orestes proceeds to his terrible task with drawn sword from Delphi (signalled by a tripod; on a version in the Museo del Opera in Florence a snake coils up underneath). He steps over a sleeping Erinys who always holds a torch and generally also around whose arm a snake uncoils; she is usually rendered reposing on the ground and facing right, but in an atypical rendering in the Vatican, Museo Chiaramonti (inv. 1226), the Erinys sleeps in a sitting position to the right of the tripod, with her back propped against some rocks. An interesting added touch: an axe – probably Clytemnestra's murder weapon – leans against her knee. The detail of the sleeping Erinys is picked up on the left side of almost all these reliefs, where the space is filled by three gracefully curving Erinyes in various attitudes of repose; the one lower left has her head on her arm which is propped up on, once again, an axe. The head of the topmost figure rests on her bent left arm from which, in most of the copies, a snake can be seen uncoiling. In a unique variant of this composition in the Vatican, Museo Gregoriano Profano (inv. 10450) [S 36, not illustrated = "Aigisthos" 34 in LIMC I.2; Koch and Sichtermann (above) pl. 192; Sichtermann and Koch (above) pls. 133.2, 135–140], the lower Erinys with axe remains but the other two have been replaced by a hooded ghost of Agamemnon, whom Orestes and Pylades have come to consult.

It is only when we move to the centre of the scene that violent action breaks out (hence E. Vermeule's designation of this as the "usual mass-mêlée type"). Not all details can be seen clearly on the half-dozen or so examples, but it is likely that the original, whether painting, sculpture or pattern-book, showed Orestes (whose figure is duplicated) at various stages of slaying Aegisthus, who has fallen head-and-shoulders downwards from an overturned throne and whose robe of office is being dragged out from under him. The horror of the act is marked by the dramatic rendering of an elderly female (the nurse Cilissa?), who turns away with outstretched hands and averted gaze. Orestes is invariably shown in the centre of the composition about to slay his mother, who lies on the ground with bare neck and breasts thrust up to him; the depiction is perhaps inspired, if only indirectly, by *Choephoroi* 896 ff., where Clytemnestra appeals to her son by the breasts which gave him suck. He turns from his mother as he is about to offer the coup de grâce, as if she were the Gorgon to which the Chorus in *Choephoroi* (834 ff. with Kirchhoff's emendation) had compared her.

Perhaps the most remarkable part of the whole composition is the group formed by two snaky-locked Erinyes immediately to Orestes' right Usually they are shown behind a vast, drooping winding-sheet, the right part of which is, in some versions, held up by a herm. In the Vatican Gregoriano Profano rendition however, which, as we have already seen, contained a bold variation in the ghost of Agamemnon, the Erinys on the left stands in front of the sheet, a huge snake coiled around her hefty left arm which she stretches threateningly towards Orestes; in the background can be seen a lighted torch, probably held by the Erinys to the right, also pointed menacingly at him. In most versions careful inspection reveals traces at least of this snake, quite close to Orestes' raised right hand holding his poised sword; many, such as the copies in the Vatican, Galleria dei Candelabri (inv. 2513) and those in Madrid and Cleveland, which is illustrated at S 35, also have the torch. All the copies add an effective genre touch: a male attendant, sometimes young, sometimes old, is shown crouching down, his right knee bent, beneath the folds of the sheet and partially hidden by them. He holds an inverted footstool in front of his face, seeking what feeble protection it can offer.

Not only is the rendering of the whole design theatrical, and several details of the scene, as remarked above, perhaps inspired by Aeschylus' story; on two of the copies (Vatican Gregoriano Profano, and Cleveland) there are actors' masks as decorations at the corners of the carved lid, and the left mask in Cleveland suggests, even if it does not actually depict, snaky locks.

ROMAN EMBOSSED SILVER

The actual trial of Orestes is illustrated on a Roman silver kantharos of the Augustan period, the so-called "Coppa Corsini" (De Luca, above;

S 75, partially illustrated [cf. also LIMC I.1 "Aletes" 3; ill. I.2 p. 368]). In the central scene a helmeted Athena lets fall a pebble into an urn; flanking her are one Erinys in a standing position on her left and another, just awakening, on her right. The other side of the cup shows three figures who have been variously identified as Orestes, Clytemnestra and the ghost of Aegisthus; or as Pylades, Electra and a male accuser. It has been suggested that this scene, the decisive moment of Orestes' acquittal, goes back to a lost original by the silver worker Zopyrus, who is mentioned by Pliny the Elder (*Natural History* 33. 156). In any case, it has left traces in other art-forms, for example, – the best-preserved version – on the end panel of the Madrid Oresteia sarcophagus mentioned above (Madrid, Museo Arquelógico inv. 2839); on a panel in the Vatican, Belvedere (Robert no. 164), which shows an almost fully preserved Erinys with whip who casts her vote into a tripod; a similar one in the Villa Doria Pamfili in Rome (Robert no. 179), on which the Erinys' arm-with-ballot is missing, but the voting urn is clearly visible; and one in the Doges' Palace in Venice, where the Erinys is shown as a young, semi-nude figure seated on a rock, holding the vote in her left hand and before her are shown a small tree and a tripod, between whose legs a snake unwinds (compare the extreme right of the scene on the sarcophagus in Florence, Museo dell' Opera, mentioned above).

Variations of this scene of voting occur also on terracotta lamps and gems; for example, a terracotta lamp from the first century A.D. in Vienna, which Sarian illustrates (S 77), shows Athena casting her vote, watched by a standing Erinys (see in general Hafner, above).

C. The Myth in later literature and music

The story of Orestes' pursuit by the Furies is treated only sporadically in post-classical literature and music. Voltaire wrote an *Oreste* (1761), but Aeschylus' works did not begin to exert a significant influence on French writers until the nineteenth century. There is a translation of the trilogy, *L'Orestie*, by Alexandre Dumas père (1856), and an extended poem in Alexandrines by Alfred de Vigny, *Destinées* (written in 1849, but only published posthumously in 1864), in which the Fates are described as "D'un mouvement pareil levant leurs mains fatales / Puis chantant d'une voix leur hymne de douleur / Et baissant à la fois leurs fronts calmes et pâles". In 1873 Leconte de Lisle produced *Les Erinnyes*, with incidental music by Jules Massenet, who scored the work for 36 strings, tympani, and three trombones representing the Furies; the piece was revived, with expanded musical accompaniment, in May 1876

at the Théâtre Lyrique de la Gaîté.   French critics have pronounced
rather harshly upon Leconte's stately verses.   Although the third play of
Aeschylus' trilogy has been eliminated, the Erinyes are introduced as
mute figures in the opening piece, *Klytaimnestra*, where the author
describes them as coming and going, "grandes, blêmes, décharnées, vêtues
de longues robes blanches, les cheveux épars sur la face et sur le dos".
The hint in Aeschylus (*Agamemnon* 1117 ff., 1186 ff.) is expanded to a
full-scale vision by Cassandra of "Les Chiennes, l'odeur de ceux qui vont
mourir, / Les monstres à qui plaît le cri des agonies, / Les Vieilles aux
yeux creux, les blêmes Erinyes ...", etc. (pp. 278–9 of the 1884 ed.).   In
Part II, *Orestes*, Clytemnestra, as she is about to be slain by her son,
warns him that he will be pursued by "le troupeau haletant / Des spectres
d'Hadès".   After the murder, which occurs onstage, Orestes holds out his
arms to his father's tomb and asks for help, but in response there appear,
first, two Erinyes from either side of the tomb, then three more
encircling Clytemnestra's corpse ("Ah! Monstres, vous grincez des dents
affreusement!").   Finally, they attack him from all sides.   "Ce sont Elles,
ce sont les Chiennes furieuses de ma mère!", he cries, and, his last
words, "Ah! ah! vous vous taisez, Monstres!" (Les Erinnyes se jettent
toutes sur lui).   "Horreur!" (Il s'enfuit. D'autres Erinnyes lui barrent le
chemin).   "Horreur!"

Musical renditions include an operatic trilogy by the Russian
composer S.I. Taneyev (1895 – a recording of this work is currently
available), an opera in five acts by the Austro-American Ernst Krenek
(1929) and a "musical dramatic trilogy" by another Austrian composer, F.
Weingartner (1902).

The diplomat-poet Paul Claudel produced a translation of
Agamemnon in 1896, which he followed with *Choéphores* and *Euménides*
in 1920.[61]   Incidental music for all three works was composed by
Claudel's friend Darius Milhaud.   In his autobiography Milhaud reports
that *Les Euménides*, alone among his musical works for the theatre, was
never produced in its entirety.[62]   During this same period the American
poet and cult-figure Robinson Jeffers published a long poetic rendering of
the first two plays of the trilogy to which he gave the title *Tower Bevond
Tragedy*.[63]

In 1931 the American playwright Eugene O'Neill presented his
trilogy, *Mourning Becomes Electra*, a powerful adaptation to a New
England, post-Civil War setting.   In the last play, *The Haunted*, while
not introducing the Furies in any literal way on stage – much less
assigning to them any choral component – O'Neill translates their effects
upon Orin, the Orestes-figure, into post-Freudian psychological terms:

they are in a sense internalized as the fierce and passionate ravings of the boy's demented spirit. The audience is told that at his mother's funeral Orin "acted like someone in a trance", and when he returns from a trip to China with his sister Lavinia (Electra), O'Neill's explicit stage-directions report that he "walks like an automaton"; "his face wears a dazed expression and his eyes have a wild, stricken look". At the same time the Erinyes' role as "haunters" is divided between these internal guilt-feelings of Orin's and an externalization of the evil ("the evil destiny out of the past") which pervades the house, here symbolized by the intimidating Mannon family portraits which stare down on Orin from the sitting-room wall. "They're everywhere", he says at one point, and he refers to them as "the souls". As his moral and mental powers begin to crumble he challenges the portraits: "You'll find Lavinia Mannon harder to break than me! You'll have to haunt and hound her for a lifetime!" (p. 239 of the ed. New York 1931). After Orin's suicide, to which he has been goaded by his sister, she addresses the portraits: "Why do you look at me like that? Wasn't it the only way to keep your secret, too? But I'm through with you forever, now, do you hear? I'm Mother's daughter – not one of you! I'll live in spite of you!" (p. 242). (One of O'Neill's main themes is the corruption of the family, a corruption particularly transmitted through the male, Mannon, line. Christine / Clytemnestra represents a more earthy and fruitful feminine strain which, under less tragic circumstances, might have prevailed.) Towards the end of the play, Lavinia expresses the futile hope that she may be able to close up the house and seek happiness elsewhere: "The portraits of the Mannons will rot on the walls and the ghosts will fade back into death" (p. 247).

Within a decade of O'Neill's fairly close imitation, T.S. Eliot produced *The Family Reunion* (1939), a play in which the major elements of the story have been transformed, or very freely adapted, out of all recognition. Paradoxically, Eliot kept the Furies as onstage, but mute, characters. (Later, Eliot wrote that he wished he had left them invisible: "I should either have stuck closer to Aeschylus or else taken a great deal more liberty with his myth. One evidence of this is the appearance of those ill-fated figures, the Furies .... We tried every possible manner of presenting them .... They never succeed in being either Greek goddesses or modern spooks ...."[64]) Harry, the Orestes figure, who has come home from pilgrimage-like wanderings abroad to the grim "family reunion" at the ancestral mansion in the north of England, catches sight of them standing in a window-embrasure and tells his uncle (to whom they remain invisible): "You don't see them, but I see them, / And they see me. This is the first time that I have seen them / .... I knew they were coming / .... They were always there. But I did not see them. / Why should they wait until I came back to Wishwood?"[65] Later in this same scene he remarks, "... *they* are always near. Here, nearer than ever. / They are very close here. I had not expected that" (p. 236). He has another vision of them in the next scene: "When I remember them / They leave me alone: when I forget them / Only for an instant of inattention / They are roused again, the sleepless hunters / That will not let me sleep ...." (I. ii, pp. 252–53) and, when they become momentarily visible only to disappear again, he shouts, "I must face them. / I must fight them" (p. 253).

In Part II Eliot produces his "revelation", intended to clear up Harry's – and the audience's – by now considerable perplexity: the "Eumenides" (as Eliot terms them in the stage-directions) are indeed "Well-Wishers", redeeming not revenging spirits. There is, in fact, no sin on Harry's part which they could avenge, for although his wife had fallen overboard during a transatlantic voyage and he, in a somewhat morbid excess of guilt, entertains the idea that he may have pushed her over, the text makes it far likelier that she committed suicide. When the Eumenides appear again Harry tells them, "... you were already here before I arrived. / Now I see at least that I am following you" (II.ii, p. 278). And later, "... now I know / That my business is not to run away, but to pursue, / Not to avoid being found, but to seek .... Now they will lead me. I shall be safe with them .... I must follow the bright angels" (pp. 280–1). Harry's aunt, Agatha, increasingly acts and speaks as an agent of the Eumenides (somewhat confusingly, since she does not repudiate the charge made by Amy, her sister and Harry's mother, of having seduced Amy's husband thirty-five years before); "... Harry has been led across the frontier: he must follow .... *They* have made this clear" (p. 285). Downing, Harry's valet and something of a Pylades-figure, has also seen them, as has Mary, a younger, distant cousin. The play ends with Agatha and Mary reciting a kind of binding-song which is obviously modelled on Aeschylus: "... in the night time / And in the nether world / Where the meshes we have woven / Bind us to each other / Follow follow" (p. 292).

If the American and English dramatists have renamed their characters and put them in situations which appear at times to have little connection with the original plot, two masters of the modern French theatre adhere rather more closely (at first glance, at least) to the ancient characters and plot-line. Jean Giraudoux's *Electre* and Jean-Paul Sartre's *Les Mouches* appeared within five years of each other, in 1938 and 1942 respectively, but the spirit and intent of the two works are quite dissimilar. Giraudoux's play begins with the return of Orestes and ends with his murder of Aegisthus and Clytemnestra, as reported by a beggar-messenger. The main "action" involves various revelations about how members of this family feel about and respond to one another: Electra and Orestes as infants vying for their mother's attention; Electra formerly trying to play surrogate-wife to her father and now overwhelming (Giraudoux uses the word "smother", *étouffer*) her brother with a pent-up and neurotic affection; Clytemnestra despising her arrogant and somewhat oafish husband and doting on her son. Giraudoux's plot encompasses the action of the original trilogy's middle play but he has the Eumenides intervene at regular intervals through the action, though at each appearance they are somewhat older. At the beginning, when Orestes returns, they are three little girls who greet him with a certain grim playfulness and who, incidentally, supply the audience with information about the family's guilty past: Atreus' slaughter of Thyestes' children and the murder of Cassandra. Later, in a parody of a dialogue between Orestes, Clytemnestra and Electra, they appear as adolescents wearing the actors' masks and one of them makes an accusation to the mock-"Orestes": "you are weak and you are a man of principle".[66] In Act II they return, now aged fifteen, to try to warn Orestes that if he succumbs to Electra's prodding, he can no longer entertain the illusion that he might live to become a glorious and respected ruler of Argos; instead, he must do his duty as Electra has presented it to him and incur the guilt of matricide. "She's going to poison everything with her venom", warns the first of the Eumenides, and the second chimes in with, "the venom of truth, the only one for which there is no antidote" (II.3, p. 208). It is psychologically revealing, as well as symbolic, that at the play's end they emerge as girls of Electra's own age and appearance and go off to hound Orestes for the matricide: "We shall never leave him", one of them says, "until he begins to rave and then kills himself, cursing his sister" (II.10, p. 247).

Sartre presented his reworking of the story in the German-occupied Paris of 1942; the title he gave it, *Les Mouches* (*The Flies*), probably derives from Giraudoux's earlier treatment, where one of the characters says of the Eumenides, "You buzz like flies". In the first two acts the Furies are as it were embodied in this plague of flies infesting Argos. Orestes at one point says, "I am plagued with all those pangs of conscience, innumerable as the flies of Argos",[67] and later Aegisthus, just after he has been stabbed by Orestes, warns him, "Beware of the flies, Orestes, beware of the flies" (II.ii, p. 106). After the murder of

Clytemnestra Electra suddenly senses an attack of the flies, "hanging from the ceiling like clusters of black grapes; the walls are alive with them". "... They'll follow us everywhere in a dense cloud", she warns Orestes; "they're the Furies, Orestes, the goddesses of remorse" (pp. 108–9). In Act III the Furies take on a more substantial shape and become speaking participants in the action. They dance around the sleeping killers with a macabre gleefulness, much like the weird sisters in *Macbeth*, threatening to suck the blood and pus from the guilty pair's "rotten hearts, juicy, luscious hearts" (III.i, p. 111). Far from his previous affectionate admiration for his sister Orestes now feels revulsion at her clawed and ravaged face and – much as in O'Neill – claims that she now resembles Clytemnestra. Electra, deranged, offers herself to them and they fall on her to rend her to pieces when Zeus appears (one Fury addresses him as "the Master") and orders them off. Zeus then offers brother and sister the opportunity to show repentance for their crime (in Sartre's existentialist philosophy, to disavow the act by which they defined themselves as free human agents). Orestes refuses, staunchly adhering to his new, more authentic existence as a man; Electra on the other hand, shocked by what she sees as her brother's "blasphemy" to Zeus and overcome by a new attack of the Furies-Flies, repudiates her share in the deed and thus deflects their assaults onto her brother: "That man is ours", gloats the First Fury, "and ours, I think, for many a day. His little soul is stubborn. He will suffer for two" (p. 124). To the silent amazement of the people of Argos Orestes reveals himself to them as at once their legitimate king and as the scapegoat for their collective sins. The play ends as he "strikes out into the light. Shrieking, the Furies fling themselves after him" (p. 127).

V. The *Eumenides* and its place in the work of Aeschylus: *Dikē* (Justice) in the *Oresteia:* the moral of the trilogy

References

Podlecki, *Political Background* pp. 1–7.

Ireland, *Aeschylus* ch. II, pp. 4–7.

S. Radt, *Tragicorum ... Fragmenta v. 5 Aeschylus*, with a useful collection of testimonies arranged by subject-heading. A selection of fragments is translated by H. Weir Smyth (see General Bibliography, "Translations") pp. 373–518, with an *Appendix* of papyrus fragments by H. Lloyd-Jones, pp. 525–603.

------, "Der unbekannte Aischylos", *Prometheus* 12 (1986) 1–13.

T. Gantz, "Aischylos' Lost Plays: the Fifth Column", *Rheinisches Museum* n.f. 123 (1980) 210–222.

——, "The Aischylean Tetralogy: Prolegomena", *Classical Journal* 74 (1979) 289–304.

——, "The Aischylean Tetralogy: Attested and Conjectured Groups", *American Journal of Philology* 101 (1980) 133–164.

When Aeschylus died at Gela in Sicily in 456 B.C., at not quite seventy years of age, he was the most acclaimed Athenian dramatist of his day. He began competing at the public dramatic festivals shortly after 500 B.C., and won his first victory in 484; the sources, who assign to him a total of about 90 plays in all, tell us that he won first place with 52 plays. According to Aristotle he was "the first to introduce a second actor; he also made the chorus less important and gave first place to the spoken parts" (*Poetics* ch. 4, trans. G.M.A. Grube). Antiquity remembered him particularly as a successful writer of satyr plays, but since so little of his work in this genre survives, we cannot know the degree to which this reputation was justified. Twelve of the preserved titles have definitely been identified as satyric and about six more are possible. The longest excerpts come from his *Net-fishers*, discovered on papyri and published in 1933 and 1941; these and other scattered fragments total barely a hundred lines, some exceedingly fragmentary.

After his death, his memory was honoured in a quite unparalleled way: anyone who wished might be "assigned a chorus" to revive his works, that is, the normal procedure was circumvented by which the chief archon chose the competitors for the next year's festival. The anonymous *Life of Aeschylus* included in some manuscripts, which is our source for much of this information, adds that "he won not a few victories after his death". We have no way of knowing when the title "Father of Tragedy" was bestowed on him (our earliest source is Philostratus, c. A.D. 200 [*Life of Apollonius of Tyana* 6.11 = T 106 Radt]), but it seems fully deserved.

Of his work there survives *The Oresteia*, produced in 458 B.C. and comprising *Agamemnon, Libation Bearers* (abbreviated *Cho.*, from its Greek title, *Choephoroi*) and *Eumenides*; the satyr play, *Proteus*, has not been preserved, but its plot is known from Homer's treatment in *Odyssey* 4, where Menelaus, on his way from Troy, is driven off course to Egypt and enquires from Proteus, an ancient, multiform sea-god, about the fates of the Greek heroes, especially his brother. In addition there is *The Persians* (472 B.C.), which seems not to have formed part of a connected trilogy, *Seven against Thebes* (abbreviated *Sept.*) of 467 B.C., which stood third to the lost *Laius* and *Oedipus*, with *Sphinx* as its satyr play, and *The Suppliant Women* (*Suppl.*), produced (probably) a few years later and standing first in a *Danaid* tetralogy. The date of *Prometheus Bound* is unknown and its authenticity has been questioned; it is admittedly an unusual play, but for all its peculiarities, it seems (to me, at least) quite Aeschylean in language and dramatic conception.

The range of myth represented by the lost titles is astonishingly wide. There was an *Achilleis*, which covered the action of the *Iliad*, a further tetralogy on Memnon and Achilles, a *Lycurgeia*, and an additional tetralogy involving another human opponent of Dionysus, Pentheus. There were tetralogies which dramatised the stories of Jason and the Argonauts, the award of Achilles' armour and Ajax's subsequent suicide, the attack on Thebes by the "Epigonoi" (Descendants) of the *Seven*, and Odysseus' return and recognition by Penelope. There were also works whose exact place in tetralogies is uncertain: *Ixion, Philoctetes, Telephus, Europa, Palamedes,* Alcmaeon's transformation into a stag and grisly death, Athamas' slaying of his son Melicertes, and, of relevance to the present study, a separate *Iphigeneia*, which presumably told the same story as Euripides' *Iphigeneia at Aulis*.

In his final masterpiece Aeschylus grappled with – we might almost say, was consumed by – the notion of "justice": what it is, how it is to be realized in the sphere of human activity, and (most difficult of all), what part the gods play in helping men to achieve it. Of course, the notion of "justice" figures in his other plays to some extent, but the characters' quest for justice could fairly be said to constitute the action of *The Oresteia*. Whatever else it may be in addition, Agamemnon's attack on Troy is an attempt to vindicate his rights as a host and a husband. "Wealth provides no defense against greed for the man who kicks and obliterates the great altar of Justice" sing the Chorus in the First Choral Ode (*Ag.* 381–4). The Messenger from the Greek army reports that Troy was razed "by the pick-axe of justice-bearing Zeus" (*Ag.* 525–6); Paris was "found guilty in this case of rape and thieving" he continues at v. 535, using language which carries a hint of legalism (a point to which we shall return). The Chorus in *Libation Bearers* revert to the theme: "to the sons of Priam there came eventually Justice, requital that brought heavy justice" (*Cho.* 935–6). Agamemnon's cousin and hereditary enemy, Aegisthus, claims almost obsessively to have had justice on his side in helping Clytemnestra plot her husband's murder (see *Ag.* 1604, 1607). It is with some irony that he insists, rather bombastically, that he is ready to face even death now that he beholds his victim "in justice's snares" (*Ag.* 1611), for in the sequel Orestes will not only slay him but refute his claims to having acted justly; on the contrary, Aegisthus himself has "received just punishment" (*Cho*. 990; compare *Ag*. 1615–6, where the chorus warn him that he will eventually have his just deserts, public execution by stoning).

The Chorus of elders, well-intentioned, loyal, but overawed by Clytemnestra's forcefulness or just inept, or perhaps truly ignorant of the full enormity of the crime she intends, try to warn their long-absent lord that "many mortals even as they transgress justice pay ostentatious honour to its semblance" (*Ag*. 778–9); Clytemnestra picks up the thread in a chilling, barely veiled vaunt that "justice guided him home against expectations" (*Ag*. 911). If it was Aegisthus who "justly stitched" the murder plot (*Ag*. 1604), Clytemnestra insists that its execution was "the deed of this [that is, her own] right hand, a just craftsman" (*Ag*. 1405–6). Sacrilegiously she asserts that if she could fittingly pour a libation of the dead man's own blood (or possibly, of her curses; the meaning is rather obscure), "this would be done justly, nay, more than justly" (*Ag*. 1396). She caps her exultation over the corpse with an oath by "the accomplishing Justice of my daughter [Iphigeneia, whom Agamemnon had slain as an offering to Artemis before the fleet sailed for Troy], by Atē (the personified Spirit of Madness or Destruction), and the Erinys", to all of whom she says she offered her husband's death as a sacrifice (*Ag*. 1432–3). The chorus, horrified, ask how she can wail a dirge for the man she killed; they call it a "graceless grace" (or "unkindly kindness", Fraenkel) which she "fulfills unjustly" (*Ag*. 1545–6).

In the sequel, when Orestes returns from Phocis where, according to Clytemnestra at least, the boy had been sent for his own safety (*Ag*. 880 ff.), Agamemnon's children plot death for their mother and her lover, Aegisthus. Electra assures her brother that he must now absorb all the love she would have given to their dead sister, Iphigeneia, and to their mother whom, she says, she now hates "with total justice" (*Cho*. 241). She then prays that they may be assisted by a trinity of gods that balances Clytemnestra's (*Ag*. 1432–3, above): "Power, Justice and the third, Zeus greatest of all" (*Cho*. 244–5). "After injustice, I demand justice", she says later (*Cho*. 398). As he stands over his victims' bodies, Orestes holds up the fatal robe that had ensnared his father and calls on the Sun to be his witness "in justice" (the phrase also suggests "in a court of law") that he pursued his mother's death "justly" (*Cho*. 988) and that Aegisthus, too, has had just punishment meted out to him (*Cho*. 990, quoted above). At the play's close, even as he begins to feel himself haunted by his mother's avenging Erinyes, he says he wishes to "proclaim to dear ones and assert that I slew my mother not without justice" (*Cho*. 126–7).

In *Eum.* words derived from the root that designates "justice", *dik-*, occur with striking frequency. As is only to be expected given the plot, the meaning that connects the terms to a "legal proceeding" is predominant, but even here there is sometimes a hint of a wider signification (see, for example, vv. 243, 573, 719 and 795). All the characters express concern for justice or profess to be acting to achieve it: Athena (vv. 414, 430, 432, 439, 675, 691, 699, 700, 804, 805, 888 and 891); Apollo (vv. 218, 221, 615, 619 and 725); Orestes (vv. 85, 291, 468, 610 and 612); and the Erinyes, whose references to justice are clustered in the Second Choral Ode (vv. 511, 516, 525, 554 and 564; but cf. also 154, 163, 433, 749 [the attribution of this line is doubtful], 785 repeated as 815 and 966). Even Clytemnestra's ghost in her brief appearance calls her reproaches against the Erinyes "just" (v. 135).

What, then, is this "justice" that has become such an easy catchword, a driving compulsion, to those who participate in these violent actions? Etymology is of only limited help. Kirk, Raven and Schofield in their survey of Presocratic thought interpret *dikē* as "the 'indicated way' (from the same root as *deiknumi* [to show]), or the normal rule of behaviour".[68] This definition occurs in a discussion of Heraclitus' dictum that "... justice is strife, and everything comes into being according to strife and necessity" (fr. 80 Diels-Kranz). (We should recall that it was Heraclitus who, in fr. 94 cited in section I above, called the Erinyes "helpers of Justice" in the realm of celestial or cosmic phenomena.) It seems clear that built into the notion of an "indicated way" or "normal rule of behaviour", whether by cosmic bodies or humans, is not merely a description of *how* things happen but a prescription for what *ought* to happen. If a way is being pointed out, it is to a direction that events should take, although perhaps they do not always do so in real life (the situation of the sun's leaving its course in Heraclitus fr. 94 is a hypothetical, and rather extreme, case). In actual fact the term *dikē* is used across a wide spectrum of meanings, from the frequent occurrences (especially in *Oresteia*) of it as a prepositional equivalent, "in the manner of ..." (*dikēn* with noun in the genitive, usually preceding), or the invariable *dikē esti(n)*, which generally means no more than "it is right that ..." something or other should happen (cf. *Eum.* 277), to a personified *Dikē* as Zeus' maiden daughter, a conception at least as old as Hesiod (*Works and Days* 256, *Theogony* 902; compare *Sept.* 662, *Cho.* 949). She has an altar (*Eum.* 539 below, where I cite *Ag.* 383–4 in the n.) and is equipped with a scale (*Cho.* 61) and an anvil (or some slab-like object, *puthmēn*, *Cho.* 946–7). Human agents refer to her as a potential ally (*Sept.* 662, *Suppl.* 343, 395, *Cho.* 947); Orestes says that she "guided his hand in battle" (*Cho*. 949). She stands guard over the marriage-bed (*Eum*. 218). She exacts debts and cries aloud as she does so (*Cho*. 310 ff.). She enters into potent triads as the object of prayers: with Atē (Spirit of Madness or Ruin) and the Erinys (*Ag*. 1432–3); with unnamed gods and Earth (*Cho*. 148); with Power (Kratos) and Zeus (*Cho*. 244–5).

Somewhere in the middle of the spectrum *dikē* is frequently used in a quite concrete sense to refer to the state of affairs which parties who believe they are aggrieved wish to have restored. Thus the phrases "to go after *dikē* (or *dikas* in the plural)" and "to give *dikē*" are the equivalent of, respectively, "to prosecute or seek redress from" the allegedly guilty party, and "to pay the penalty", "be punished". It is a short step from this to the use of *dikē* (or, again, the plural) and its cognates with a specific, concrete legal or judicial connotation: "prosecute at law", "institute (or undergo) legal proceedings". It is precisely this field of meaning which enables Aeschylus to bring Justice as an abstract concept or personification into the everyday reality of an Athenian lawcourt. In fact, there are numerous occurrences of the *dik*-root in the first two plays of the trilogy; it is as though Aeschylus were preparing the ground for the major development of *Eum.*, the establishment of a court of law to adjudicate the conflicting claims of the dead Clytemnestra and her son.[69] Here are some instances of the way the legal dénouement is foreshadowed. Menelaus is described by the chorus of Elders in their opening lines as "Priam's great *antidikos*, adversary-at-law" (*Ag*. 41). In the First Choral Ode they refer to Agamemnon and Menelaus as *prodikoi*, "principals in the lawsuit" (*Ag*. 451). The army's messenger, who has come in advance of Agamemnon to confirm the beacon's report of Troy's capture, reports that, "found guilty in this case of rape and thieving, Paris both lost the property he took and mowed his country down" (*Ag*. 534–5, trans. Douglas Young). After Agamemnon's murder Clytemnestra tells the chorus, "you adjudicate exile from the city against me" (*Ag*. 1411–1), and a few lines further (*Ag*. 1420–1), "you are a harsh judge (*dikastēs*)". At the beginning of *Libation Bearers* the chorus-leader urges Electra to pray that "some spirit or mortal come –", and the latter interrupts, "Do you mean some *dikastēs* [judge] or bringer-of-*dikē*?" (*Cho*. 119–20). As was already noted, Orestes calls on the Sun to be a "witness in *dikē*" that he was just in his pursuit of his mother's death (*Cho*. 987–9). With these advance clues, it should have come as no surprise to the audience (or to us) when, early in the action of *Eum.*, Apollo told his suppliant to go to Athens where "we shall get us judges (*dikastas*) of these matters" (*Eum*.

81).

  As emerges in the course of the play the Erinyes see themselves as the primeval upholders of Dikē. Aeschylus seems to have invented this part of Orestes' story (see Section I above), but attentive members of his audience might have been able to follow another series of clues about this development in the action from the numerous references to the "Erinys" and "Erinyes" in the first two plays. At the beginning of the Entrance Song in *Ag.* the chorus prefigure the punitive expedition against Troy as a "late-requiting Erinys" (*Ag.* 58–9), where the second member of the compound adjective suggests the association between Requital, *Poina*, and the Erinyes, a relationship to be explored more fully in what follows. In the sequence of mythic events this is not the first time that an Erinys has been sent against Troy. In the Second Choral Ode we hear Helen herself called an "Erinys who brings tears to brides [that is, both herself and the brides, or widows, of other Trojan warriors]", sent against Priam's sons through the agency of Zeus, god of hospitality (*Ag.* 747–9). In the First Choral Ode the Argive elders hint in a rather obscure way that Agamemnon is to become their victim: "the black Erinyes rub out the life of one who prospers without justice ..." (*Ag.* 462 ff.). Even this early in the trilogy the Erinyes are conceived of as in some way agents of justice. Cassandra's disquieting visions include an "insatiable band", whom the Chorus immediately identify as connected with the Erinyes (*Ag.* 1117–20). They are the "chorus singing in unison but not euphoniously" which she says will never leave the house (*Ag.* 1186–7, cited in my note on *Eum.* 307 below; compare the Chorus' earlier reference to the "lyreless dirge of the Erinys" which their spirit forebodes, *Ag.* 990–2), "a revel band which the house cannot get rid of, kindred Erinyes who have quaffed human blood" (*Ag.* 1188–90). As we have already seen, Clytemnestra after the murder takes an oath by an unholy trinity which includes the Erinys (*Ag.* 1432–3) and Aegisthus describes the victim lying at his feet "in a robe woven by the Erinys" (*Ag.* 1580). In *Libation Bearers* Orestes tells how Apollo's oracle had threatened "assaults of the Erinyes from his father's blood" if he were to ignore the command to hunt down the killers (*Cho.* 283–4). In the Choral Incantation the chorus-leader remarks that "the Erinys cries 'havoc'" as disaster piles on disaster (*Cho.* 402 with Schütz's emendation). Orestes sums up his plot to gain admission to the house disguised as a Phocian stranger bringing news of "Orestes'" death: "the Erinys, not stinted of gore, will drink the third, unmixed draught – of blood!" (*Cho.* 577–8; compare *Ag.* 1188 ff. just cited). At the very end of the First Choral Ode the women slaves who have, at Clytemnestra's command, brought a libation to

Agamemnon's tomb and thus give the play its title, sing of the action to come in a stanza which gains in importance because of the divinities that are juxtaposed: "Dikē's foundation (or anvil) is fixed firmly. Fate [Aisa, a synonym for Moira] the sword-maker stokes up the forge. The famous, deep-pondering Erinys introduces to the house a child of old blood-deeds to pay in time the debt owed, a new defilement" (*Cho.* 646–51). As Garvie in his note on this complex passage remarks, the image recalls an earlier one at *Ag.* 1535–6, "Moira is sharpening Dikē at other whetstones for another deed of harm". In the final play we shall hear the Erinyes refer repeatedly to their half-sisters, the Moirai (see my n. on *Eum.* 173 below), for it is in their immediate interests to show how irreversible, pre-ordained, is their championing of a mother's claims, even over those of a husband. We may compare *Cho.* 306, where the Chorus-leader, at the beginning of the great Choral Incantation, calls on the Moirai and then goes on to report (or perhaps pray) that Dikē will exact a debt which has been owed. Both here and in the passage just discussed, *Cho.* 646 ff., the language of "exacting payment for a debt" foreshadows how in the final play the Erinyes will be closely associated, perhaps even identified, with another abstraction, *Poina*, Requital or Retribution; see *Eum.* 322–3 with my notes on 322 and 543. This association, too, has been anticipated in the preceding play. After Orestes has led his mother into the palace to her death the chorus in the Third Choral Ode attempt to see his deed as the working out of a larger pattern (the passage was cited above): "There came eventually to the sons of Priam Justice, Requital (*Poina*) that brought heavy justice" (*Cho.* 935–6), and again, in the "stealthy battle" by Orestes against his adversaries, "Poina of devious intent came ... and Zeus' daughter, whom we mortals correctly call 'Dikē', truly guided his hand ..." (*Cho.* 946–51). Garvie in his note on this passage cites the phrase used at *Ag.* 58–9, *husterpoinon* [late-requiting] ... *Erinun*, and remarks "*Poina* is to be thought of as the Erinys".

I shall close by taking up several more general questions raised by the trilogy: How free are Aeschylus' characters in their actions? What role do the gods play? Finally, what moral lesson are we to draw from the work?

At one level, it is clear that Agamemnon's expedition to Troy was sanctioned by Zeus Xenios, protector of the sanctity of hospitality (*Ag.* 61–2, 362, 367, 704, 748), although the chorus express some – perhaps not very serious – doubts at *Ag.* 55 ff., a passage cited in part above, where the sending of the late-avenging Erinys is attributed to "some Apollo or Pan or Zeus". There is a note of uneasiness, even of doubt, in the "Zeus Hymn", sung by the Chorus as part of their Entrance Song: "Zeus, whoever he is .... I am not able to compare him, as I weigh up everything, to anything else except Zeus, if I must truly rid myself of this foolish burden of worry" (*Ag.* 160–6); and later, "Zeus cause of all, worker of all: for what is achieved among mortals without Zeus?" (*Ag.* 1485–7). Is this an act of faith, or a barely veiled groan of despair? And what of the interposition of Artemis who, in anger at the "sacrifice" and "feast" made of the pregnant hare by her father's eagles (*Ag.* 136), "is eager for [just as the Erinyes are "eager", *Eum.* 360 ff., although the text there seems gravely disturbed] another sacrifice, an unlawful one, unsuited for a feast, an inborn craftsman of quarrels ..." (*Ag.* 151 ff.). Artemis seems, in other words, to be allowed by Father Zeus to require the sacrifice of Iphigeneia before the Greek fleet can set sail (I say "seems" because the much-discussed v. 144 can hardly be cited as conclusive evidence). What choice, then, did Agamemnon have? The dramatist portrays him as vexed, even tormented, but ultimately he decides that his responsibilities as a commander outweigh his love for his daughter; "How can I abandon the fleet?" (*Ag.* 212). In killing their daughter Iphigeneia he stirs his wife's lust for revenge, unforgetting and unforgiving. As the prophet Calchas foresees (*Ag.* 154–5 in Weir Smyth's translation), "... there abideth wrath – terrible, not to be suppressed, a treacherous warder of the home, ever mindful, a wrath that exacteth vengeance for a child". The chorus of elders at the end of *Ag.* and her son at a crucial moment in *Cho.* (917) charge that Clytemnestra was motivated by sexual desire for Aegisthus (who himself insists that he was merely seeking revenge for the wrong done his father, Thyestes, by Agamemnon's father, Atreus). But after the murder, Clytemnestra's tone of confident self-assurance seems to weaken. She repeatedly invokes the Spirit of Vengeance, the Alastōr (see n. on *Eum.* 236 below, where, however, it has a different meaning), or Daimōn, that stalks this violence-prone family. She instructs the chorus to think of her not so much as Agamemnon's wife as the "ancient, bitter Alastōr" roused by Atreus' grim feast (that is, his serving up to Thyestes the latter's own children, *Ag.* 1497 ff.). If only, she says, she could make a sworn pact with the Daimōn of the Pleisthenidai (another way of referring to the family of Agamemnon) to settle for the intolerable crimes already committed and leave the house to work his evil elsewhere (*Ag.* 1568 ff.). There are other references as well to the Daimōn as a quasi-personal force at *Ag.* 1468, 1482, 1660 and 1667, where the chorus-leader suggests that the Daimōn may "direct Orestes' path" to return for vengeance; compare the chorus-leader's instructions to Electra at the opening of the next play to pray that "some Daimōn [which above I have translated "Spirit"] or mortal come" to aid her against her enemies (*Cho*. 119). When Clytemnestra hears of her son's purported "death", she cries aloud to the "Curse of this house, hard-to-wrestle-with", to which she attributes some responsibility, at least, for her troubles (*Cho*. 692; this is in the same vein as Eteocles' outburst, "O Curse and my father's Erinys of mighty power", *Sept*. 70). In the Choral Incantation Orestes despairingly calls upon the "widely powerful Curses of those who have died" (presumably, curses uttered by the family's various victims, Thyestes and his children as well as Agamemnon) to bear witness to the dishonour inflicted on him and his sister (*Cho*. 406 ff.). Clytemnestra will soon have curses to utter, with which the Erinyes identify themselves (*Eum*. 417 with n.). Seeing her son intent on murder Clytemnestra tries to buy time: "Moira", she insists, "shares responsibility" for Agamemnon's death, to which Orestes retorts, "then Moira is inflicting your death as well" (*Cho*. 911); it is his "father's Aisa" that is hastening on the deed (*Cho*. 927).

Why do Aeschylus' characters invoke these various supernatural beings whose agency they claim to detect operating within the family? Can they seriously hope to absolve themselves of responsibility for what is occurring? If so, they are mistaken. At *Pers*. 724 the Queen Mother of Persia is trying to explain her son's misguided and ultimately self-destructive attempt to conquer Greece: "Some Daimōn joined in his intent". But the ghost of her husband, Darius, offers a significant modification: "When anyone is eager, the god, too, joins in" (*Pers*. 742). The characters in *The Oresteia* are, in their own ways, "eager" for results which, however desirable they may appear at the time, can only be achieved through crime. In Orestes' words, "Ares clashes with Ares, Dikē with Dikē" (*Cho*. 461). Besides their sexual involvement with each other, Clytemnestra to some extent and Aegisthus more markedly seek political rule in Argos (see, for example, *Ag*. 1638-9). Electra and Orestes see themselves as children of a war hero (*Cho*. 363 ff.) who deserved better than the mutilation that their mother allegedly inflicted (*Cho*. 430 ff., 439 ff.; cf. *Eum*. 458 ff. below). Their insistence on Aegisthus' unworthiness to succeed to their father's throne and bed (*Cho*. 572, 975 ff.) has in it a large admixture of pride. Orestes may be able to plead diminished responsibility because of the punishments which Apollo's oracle had threatened for disobedience (cf. *Eum*. 466-7 below, where reference is made to *Cho*. 271 ff., 1032-3), but the children are also driven, and fairly strongly, by the prospect of the material advantages which they stand to gain from restoration to their patrimony

(*Cho.* 237; cf. *Eum.* 757 below). As Orestes himself admits, "many desires converge to one end – the god's command, great sorrow for my father, and in addition being destitute of money presses me, to the result that citizens who are the most glorious of mortals, men who razed Troy with confident spirit, should no longer be subservient to two women" (*Cho.* 299–304). If the maxim "learning through suffering" which we hear repeated in various forms throughout the trilogy means anything, part of what the various victims learn is that their own motives have not been entirely untinged by thoughts of self-interest. In addition, they all in their turns learn the truth of another adage, "the doer must pay" (*Ag.* 1564, 1658; *Cho.* 313).

Modern criticism has made the point with perhaps excessive emphasis that the Aeschylean world is "overdetermined", with causality and motivation at the human level reinforced at the divine. But all this really means is that Aeschylus gives due weight to the complexity of motives from which humans often (perhaps always) act. When we look back upon our actions, especially ones that may have had some serious consequences (for good or ill), can we invariably and confidently explain why we acted? "Something made me do it ...." And in really critical situations do we not sometimes pray to supernatural powers named or unnamed that our actions may be part of some larger scheme of things where (we hope) "the good prevails"?

There has been a good deal of discussion in recent years about the trilogy's possible significance in sociological terms, both for its day and for ours. It is possible to read the work as an anti-feminist tract. Clytemnestra slays her husband in a deed which is assimilated to some of the worst women-against-men crimes in all of Greek mythology (*Cho.* 585 ff.). Orestes kills his mother and not only gets off with impunity (except for some preliminary hounding and affrighting from vengeance-demons) but is judged innocent by a wise divinity who says she "approves the male principle in all things and with all her heart" (*Eum.* 737). Furthermore, the killer is rewarded by being permitted to conclude an alliance between his people and one of the most powerful states in Greece "for all time to come". Apollo, never subdued in his championship of male values, "tramples down" aged female divinities who are in the end made to settle for what is, after all, a decidedly minor place in Athenian cult. All this might have been, as Vellacott contends, elaborately ironic: Aeschylus was "really" telling his predominantly if not solely male audience that they were misguided to acquiesce in a state of affairs that was so patently unfair.

A number of things can be said in response. First, it is difficult to take seriously a theory of "covert meanings", ironical or otherwise, in ancient drama (at least in Aeschylus). This was a public performance, intended for a mass audience, and its meaning ought, therefore, to be fairly accessible. Now there can be no doubt that the Athenian social and political system was unfairly weighted against women. In that light, it is a wonder that the females in *Eum.* receive as much recognition as they do. Clytemnestra's ghost makes a valid point when she complains that, "even though I was treated so terribly by loved ones .... though I was slaughtered by a mother-killer's hands" (vv. 100–103), no one (at least among the Olympians) is looking after her interests. Some of the play's best lines – noble sentiments about justice and a salutary fear and upholding the rights of a mother and a wife almost at all costs – go to the Erinyes. They show passion and determination in arguing their, and incidentally Clytemnestra's and woman's, point of view against a spokesman, Apollo, who for sheer pettiness and preening must have made even those who accepted his arguments feel uneasy. And Athena had no easy task in winning them round, as the entire final portion of the play attests. When the Erinyes don their crimson cloaks to become "Well-wishers" to their new adoptive homeland and join the solemn procession in Athena's honour they do so with enthusiasm and not at all half-heartedly, but they do not weaken in their fierce determination that justice, a healthy balance, must be preserved in all human undertakings, both civic and private. "From these frightening visages", Athena says (and we must believe her), "I see great profit accruing to these citizens" (990–1). The fearful power they embody is now to be turned to the social benefit of Athens and her citizens, but it is not completely eradicated. In future as in the past, "anyone who encounters them as oppressive adversaries does not know what has knocked his life to pieces" (*Eum.* 932–3); and we sense that Athena, who herself is not above threatening use of Zeus' thunderbolts (vv. 826–8), quite seriously means what she says. The fact that half the human jurors voted against Orestes is a victory, if only a moral one, for the women's side. "It was not a defeat for you, but a true outcome of a trial in which the votes were equal ..." (vv. 795–6). Athena casts her vote as she does not only because the myth must work itself out as it does, but – as she herself admits at 736 ff. – for the most personal and subjective of reasons: "there is no mother who gave birth to me and I approve the male principle ...." Aeschylus carefully does not have her argue, as Apollo had done at vv. 658 ff., that the mother is *never* entitled to be considered a child's true parent, but merely that Athena's own individual, and on any account somewhat peculiar, mode of birth gives her an instinctive (and, could

Aeschylus perhaps be hinting?, somewhat irrational) predisposition to the masculine. We may draw a corollary. The message of the play does not seem to be (as some critics maintain): The ancient but now outmoded principle of matriarchy must give way to the enlightened masculinity of the *polis*, but rather: Life must go on. An accommodation must sometimes be made between evenly balanced but conflicting points of view. A choice for either alternative risks stirring the aggrieved party to reprisals (see vv. 470 ff., and especially 480–1, below). But the *polis* has a right and obligation to ensure the safety of its citizens against private acts of violence, no matter how much one can comprehend and may perhaps even sympathize with the motives behind these acts. In the end, justice, and even "Justice", in an imperfect world is only partial and relative. What matters is that the community be able to adjudicate opposing claims in an orderly way and that all sides agree to accept the verdict. "Ultimately", as J. Michael Walton has recently written, "the *Oresteia* is a paean to affirmation".[70]

VI. The text of *Eumenides* and its transmission

References

TEXTUAL CRITICISM
Maas, Paul   *Textual Criticism* Engl. trans. by B. Flower (Oxford: Clarendon Press, 1958).
West, M.L.   *Textual Criticism and Editorial Technique applicable to Greek and Latin Texts* (Stuttgart: Teubner, 1973).

HISTORY OF SCHOLARSHIP
Pfeiffer, Rudolf   *A History of Classical Scholarship from the Beginnings to the End of the Hellenistic Age* (Oxford: Clarendon Press, 1968).
------, *History of Classical Scholarship from 1300 to 1850* (Oxford: Clarendon Press, 1976).
Reynolds, R.D. and Wilson, N.G.   *Scribes and Scholars* 2nd ed. (Oxford: Clarendon Press, 1974).
Wilson, N.G.   *Scholars of Byzantium* (London: Duckworth, 1983).

MSS OF AESCHYLUS AND THEIR TRANSMISSION
Smyth, Herbert Weir   "Catalogue of the Manuscripts of Aeschylus", *Harvard Studies in Classical Philology* 44 (1933) 1–62.
Turyn, Aleksander   *The Manuscript Tradition of the Tragedies of*

Aeschylus (New York: Polish Institute of Arts & Sciences in America, 1943; reprinted Hildesheim, 1967).

Wartelle, A. *Histoire du texte d'Eschyle dans l'antiquité* (Paris: Les belles lettres, 1971).

Helm, James J. *Demetrius Triclinius and the Textual Tradition of the 'Oresteia'* (Ph.D. dissatation Univ. of Michigan, 1968).

——————, "The Lost manuscript *tau* of Aeschylus' *Agamemnon* and *Eumenides*", *Transactions of the American Philological Association* 103 (1972) 575–598.

Dawe, R.D. *The Collation and Investigation of Manuscripts of Aeschylus* (Cambridge: Cambridge University Press, 1964).

Gruys, J.A. *The Early Printed Editions (1518 – 1664) of Aeschylus. A Chapter in the History of Classical Scholarship* (Nieuwkoop, The Netherlands: D. de Graaf, 1981).

The science of textual criticism assumes that, given adequate evidence, it will be possible to establish with a fair degree of certitude what Aeschylus actually wrote, undoubtedly in multiple copies for use by chorus-members (who, so far as we can tell, were not professionals) and the actors, in 458 B.C.

Our oldest and best manuscript (abbreviated below as MS, plural MSS) of *Eum.* is M, the so-called "Medicean", Laurentianus Mediceus 32.9, which is now in the Laurentian library in Florence; it was written between A.D. 950 and 1000. How was the intervening space of some 1,400 years bridged? There was probably a fairly extensive market for privately produced copies of successful plays among literate Athenians and other Greeks. Euripides is reported to have had a large personal library, and the frequent and sometimes recondite allusions to other dramas in Euripides' works and to tragedies in Aristophanes' comedies presuppose a close familiarity by some members at any rate of their audience; the most natural assumption is that this was the result of reading (there is also the somewhat problematic reference by Socrates in the *Apology* [27 D–E] to the availability of Anaxagoras' books "at the orchestra", perhaps that in the Agora which was mentioned above in Section II). With Aeschylus' works the need to have accurate acting versions was critical because of the official encouragement to posthumous productions, as noted above in Section V. Reproductions of "old" tragedies formed part of the programme of the City Dionysia from at least 386 B.C. and inscriptional evidence survives for several of Euripides' works being so presented, although we hear nothing of Aeschylus'. In addition, productions of tragedies were part of the celebration of the Rural Dionysia held in the country districts of Attica. The orator and politician Lycurgus had legislation enacted c. 330 B.C. that official versions be made of the works of the three main tragedians which should be deposited in the state archives housed in the Old Bouleuterion. Actors were now obliged to keep to this official text, and it was this which Ptolemy III of Egypt (246–221 B.C.) borrowed, allegedly returning a copy instead, to have copied for the library founded at Alexandria by his grandfather Ptolemy I. Although there is evidence for widespread activity of a philological nature by the early librarians, "tragedy seems to have been neglected by scholars of the third century", according to Rudolf Pfeiffer (*History* I [1968], 192). Alexander of Aetolia is reported to have made critical editions of the tragedians. Since there is evidence of scholarly work on Sophocles and Euripides by Aristophanes of Byzantium (c. 200 B.C.) and Didymus (c. 25 B.C.), it has been assumed that they also studied Aeschylus. A fleeting reference survives to a treatise on Aeschylus' *Lycurgus*, a satyr drama, by Aristarchus (c. 175 B.C.).

Educated Romans were familiar with Greek tragedy, as can be seen, for example, from imitations by their own dramatists like Ennius (see above), and the numerous citations and translated excerpts in Cicero.[71] When in the second or third century of our era interest in and the teaching of Greek literature began to decline, and the papyrus roll had been replaced by the "codex", ancestor of the modern book, a selection was made of 7 works by each of the three tragedians (that we have more by Euripides is due to a lucky accident), although to judge from papyrus fragments and quotations by later authors, other plays still were occasionally read. The plays of the "Selection" were copied, more or less faithfully we must assume, in medieval monastic *scriptoria* (copying rooms) in the script known as "uncial" or "majuscule", a form of writing in capital letters that derived ultimately from the lettering-style of inscriptions. About A.D. 900 the "minuscule" (small letter) style was introduced and copying became easier and faster. The text of *Eum.* produced by the scribe of **M** is descended from one of these minuscule codices.

The first printed edition was the "Aldina" or Aldine, edited by Franciscus Asulanus and published in Venice in 1518 by Aldus Manutius (see Gruys 17 ff.). It was based not on **M** itself, but on a copy, probably that designated by Turyn "**Mc**", the latter part of Guelferbytanus Gudianus Graecus 88, in Wolfenbüttel, written in the fifteenth century (Garvie, Intro. to *Cho.* lix, n. 143; Turyn 20–21). For his celebrated edition of 1552 Robortello used, according to Gruys (p. 64), "a fairly bad copy of **M"** made c. 1145. **M** itself did not enter the editorial stream until it was used as the basis of the edition made by Victorius and published, after some additional editing, by Stephanus (Henri Etienne) in 1557 (Gruys 77 ff.) All subsequent editors have acknowledged **M's** superiority to the other surviving MSS.

Errors in **M** were corrected, sometimes by the original scribe, sometimes by a supervisor or "corrector", who referred to the exemplar from which **M** had been copied and occasionally to MSS from a different family as well. These stages of editorial change and correction are distinguished in the "apparatus", that is, the variants that follow the printed pages of text. The notations M^{ac} and M^{pc}, for example, designate readings in **M** "before" and "after correction". M^s designates that the variant is due to the scribe who also wrote the scholia; M^Σ or simply Σ refers to these scholia, explanatory notes written between the lines or, more frequently, in the margins or at the bottom of the page that are generally thought to reflect Alexandrian scholarship on the text (Didymus, mentioned above, has been suggested, but there is no substantiating evidence).

Besides **M**, there are four other manuscripts which are known to be related because they all omit vv. 323–4 (from *poinan* ... to ... *tithēsin*), 582–644 and 778–807. These, as Prof. M.L. West informs me by letter, "are copied from a lost (13th cent.?) model known as **tau**, which Triclinius worked over but which was in itself just an ordinary copy of the time". These MSS respectively are (with dates suggested by West): **G**, in Venice, Venetus graecus 616 (663), ca. 1320; **T**, in Naples, Neapolitanus II F 31, which was Demetrius Triclinius' "final edition of Aeschylus" (Helm [1972] 581), ca. 1325; **F**, in Florence, Florentinus Laurentianus 31.8, ca. 1340; and **E**, in Salamanca, Salamancensis Bibl. univ. 233, ca. 1460. By analyzing the readings which these MSS have in common and in which they differ from **M**, and by taking account of variants that may have occurred by "contamination" (that is, a change introduced only occasionally when the scribe or corrector had recourse to another MS outside the family), it has been possible to reconstruct the lost MS **tau**, which seems to have descended in an independent tradition, separate from and inferior to that of **M**.

The text I print is based on Page's Oxford text of 1972, which I have compared closely with Murray's second edition of 1955 and other printed editions.

I have listed in the General Bibliography at the end those editions and commentaries which are (in principle, at least) still available and may prove useful to those intending to study the play further; an edition with commentary by A. Sommerstein has also been announced by the Cambridge University Press. Two commentaries which are cited in my notes, which I consulted with profit but which are unfortunately no longer in print, are those by F.A. Paley (4th ed., London: Whittaker, 1987) and A.W. Verrall (London: Macmillan, 1908). Other annotated editions which I have used for individual passages are those by Stanley 1663/4 (see Gruys 153 ff.), Schütz 1810, Drake 1853, Hermann 1859, Weil 1861, Davies 1885, Wecklein 1888, Barnett 1901, Mills 1901, Sidgwick 1902, Blass 1907, Wilamowitz-Moellendorf 1914, P. Ubaldi 1931, P. Groeneboom 1952, G. Ammendola 1961, and G. Pompella 1972.

1. Full refs. to works given **in short title** are to be found in the General Bibliography at the end; citations **by author only** are to works listed at the beginning of each section of the Introduction and the Appendices.

2. I owe this and the preceding ref. to Prof. Sansone.

3. The *Odyssey* reflects both versions, Aegisthus as solitary agent (1.299–300, 3.194 ff., 4.524 ff.), and that he acted with Clytemnestra's help (3.235, 11.410, 24.97).

4. Fragments can be found in D.L. Page, *Poetae Melici Graeci* (Oxford: Clarendon Press, 1962) nos. 38–42 (215–219 in the consecutive numbering). Athenaeus' cryptic comment (12.513 A) that Stesichorus "took over" (*parapepoiēken*) his *Oresteia* from an earlier writer, Xanthos, cannot be verified.

5. Prag pls. 7a, 7b, 28b.

6. Prag pls. 2a, 6a, 23a (for the last, see also Karl Schefold, *Myth and Legend in Early Greek Art* [London: Thames and Hudson, 1966] pl. 80).

7. Boston 63. 1246 (= Prag pls. 15, 16a); cf. Vermeule, "The Boston Oresteia Krater".

8. Garvie xxii.

9. F. Jacoby, *Die Fragmente der griechischen Historiker* (Leiden: Brill, 1954) III b (Supplement) i, p. 24 (note on Hellanicus 323a F 1).

10. Ibid., vol. ii, pp. 23, 24.

11. For this oath see further Appendix I below.

12. Dinarchus VIII.2, pp. 86–7 Conomis; scholion on Demosthenes 21. 115 (*Scholia Demosthenica* II, p. 213 Dilts).

13. His article "Eumenides in Greek Tragedy", as cited in the refs. to this section; at p. 276 he suggests that the play's original title may have been *Erinyes*. In my n. on v. 992 below I take up the point of the play's title and the report in the Hypothesis that "Athena mollified the Erinyes and called them 'Eumenides'".

14. Brown p. 276.

15. Conacher, *Aeschylus' 'Oresteia'* pp. 176–7, citing Reinhardt.

16. I find it difficult to accept Brown's arguments (276 ff.) that Eumenides are kept distinct from Erinyes in Sophocles' *Oedipus at Colonus*. The Eumenides' descent from Earth and Darkness (vv. 40, 106), which even Brown admits (p. 278) "may have been suggested by that of the Erinyes", seems to me, if not decisive, strongly confirmatory.

17. *Zeitschrift für Papyrologie und Epigraphik* 47 (1982) following p. 300; M.L. West, *The Orphic Poems* (Oxford: Clarendon Press, 1983) 78 (cf. Brown 266 n. 45).

18. 1.28.6, trans. P. Levi (later statues by Scopas and Calamis). I note here the unterrifying depiction of the Eumenides as "three stately goddesses, each with a snake in one hand and a flower in the other", on votive tablets found near Tiryns which date from the fourth to the first centuries (the description is by Brown 261 with refs. at n. 7; cf. Harrison "Delphika" 217 f.). They are discussed and illustrated by Sarian, "Erinys" nos. 112–119.

19. The tablets are Fh 1.8, Fh 390 and V 52, on the last of which the scribe has struck out the name, which occurred originally in the company of (apparently) Athena, Enyalius, Paian and Poseidon. See Neumann (p. 43) and Heubeck (pp. 144–5). Cf. M. Gérard–Rousseau, *Les Mentions religieuses dans les tablettes mycenéennes* (Incunabula Graeca no. 29; Rome: Dell' Ateneo, 1968) 103–4.

20. Neumann, pp. 48–9.

21. *The Greeks and the Irrational* (Berkeley: University of California Press, 1954) p. 21 n. 35 and p. 7, respectively.

22. H. Diels and W. Kranz *Die Fragmente der Vorsokratiker* 11th ed. (Zurich: Weidmann, 1964) No. 22, fr. 94. Compare the cryptic statement attributed to Anaximander (D–K 12, fr. 9) that elements in the natural world "pay penalty and retribution to each other for their injustice according to the assessment of time".

23. Rohde 179.

24. Dietrich 117; Harrison, "Delphika".

25. Heubeck 165.

26. Wycherley 204–5 with 204 n. 3.

27. E. Pöhlmann, "Die Prohedrie des Dionysostheaters im 5 Jhrdt. und das Bühnenspiel der Klassik", *Museum Helveticum* 38 (1981) 129–146 (drawn to my attention by A.L. Brown); cf. Wycherley 213 n. 18.

28. "Conditions", 434; so also Taplin, *Stagecraft* 453–459. West accepts the existence of the *pagos* down to and through *Oresteia* ("The Prometheus Trilogy", *Journal of Hellenic Studies* 99 [1979] 130–148 at 135).

29. Travlos 537; cf. Wycherley 210–11.

30. In the view of some they are there from the beginning (see Rosenmeyer, *The Art of Aeschylus* 68–9, W.C. Scott, *Musical Design in Aeschylean Theater* 113 and 115), but this seems to me unlikely.

31. Dindorf, *Proleg. de Com.* p. 36, cited by Pickard-Cambridge 236 n. 3.

32. See on this point A.E. Haigh, *The Attic Theatre* 3rd ed. rev. by A. Pickard-Cambridge (Oxford: Clarendon Press, 1907) 194–5; Pickard-Cambridge 236–7; M. Bieber, "Entrances and Exits of Actors and

Choruses in Greek Plays", *American Journal of Archaeology* 58 (1954) 278 ff.

33. See Appendix I below.

34. I.G. ii² 2318 col. i, line 4.

35. J.K. Davies, *Athenian Propertied Families* (Oxford: Clarendon Press, 1971) 383. Aphidna was the deme also of Themistocles' critic, Timodemus (Herodotus 8.125) as well as of descendants of the "tyrannicides", Harmodius and Aristogeiton (Davies 472 ff.).

36. For this distribution, see Pickard-Cambridge, *Dramatic Festivals of Athens*, 2nd ed. rev. by J. Gould and D.M. Lewis (Oxford: Clarendon Press, 1968) 140.

37. See in general John V.A. Fine, *The Ancient Greeks* (Cambridge, Mass. and London: Harvard University Press, 1983) pp. 386–91. According to Fine, "... one has to admit that it is futile to try to spell out in detail the exact measures which Ephialtes carried through the Assembly" (p. 389). For some theories, R. Sealey, "Ephialtes", *Classical Philology* 59 (1964) 11–22; R.W. Wallace, "Ephialtes and the Areopagus", *Greek, Roman and Byzantine Studies* 15 (1974) 259–69.

38. *FGH* III B Suppl. (cited in n. 9 above) i, p. 25 (commentary on Hellanicus F 1). Jacoby left open whether the terms "epitheta", accretions or additions, was a slogan used by Ephialtes himself or was introduced by the author of the *Constitution of Athens* in his discussion of Ephialtes' reforms.

39. *Constitution of Athens* 57.3 (cf. 60.2).

40. See in general my *Political Background* pp. 80 ff.

41. See my n. on v. 398 below.

42. "Morals and Politics", pp. 21–2, and "Notes on the *Oresteia*", *Classical Quarterly* n.s. 3 (1953) 11–21 at 19–20; so, too, Beer p.65.

43. There is no other evidence for such an oracle at the Areopagus, and *kritērion* has been suggested for *chrēstērion* at *El.* 1272, but, as Denniston remarks ad loc., "we cannot be sure that Euripides has not made one of his innovations in mythology".

44. This reverses the order of *Electra*, where his founding of the Arcadian Oresteion comes after his acquittal at Athens.

45. A jury composed not of Athenian citizens but of the 12 gods may be a mere transference from the trial of Halirrhothios (see Euripides, *Electra* 1258–60); it occurs at Demosthenes 23. 66 and 74 (see above, p. 5).

46. *TrGF* 17; Dana F. Sutton, "The Theatrical Families of Athens", *American Journal of Philology* 108 (1987) 9–26 at 16.

47. *TrGF* DID A2a, 11; cf. Xanthakis-Karamanos p. 16. She also

notes a play by Timocles, *Orestautocleides*, dating from the 320s, in which a notorious pederast, Autocleides, was shown surrounded by sleeping hetairai (this, as Xanthakis-Karamanos suggests, was perhaps a satire on Theodectes' *Orestes*).

48. Brown (cited in *References* to Section I, above) 276 with nn. 102 and 103.

49. The standard collection of the fragments is by Ribbeck, but much more accessible is Warmington's text and translation in the Loeb *Remains of Old Latin*. For a brief discussion of the Roman antecedents see Tarrant 13–4, and Jocelyn 284.

50. Jocelyn 284. The Ciceronian passages are *de Finibus* 1.65, 2.79, 5.63; *de Amicitia* 24.

51. Fr. 65 Jocelyn. Another possibility is that the lines formed part of Apollo's admonition to Orestes at the opening (cf. *Eum.* 81–2); see on this Robert A. Brooks, *Ennius and Roman Tragedy* (New York: Arno, 1981) 242–3.

52. Jocelyn 289 (commentary on Ennius fr. 66).

53. Brown 266 n. 46 citing J.-P. Cèbe, *Varron, Satires menippées* IV [Rome: L'école française de Rome, 1977] 545.

54. *Lingua Latina* 7.19 = fr. 192 Jocelyn, 349 Ribbeck.

55. *Pro Sext. Roscio Amerino* 24.67, *in Pisonem* 20.46 (Orestes is mentioned in sect. 47), *de Legibus* 1.40 (cf. Jocelyn 284). In a poem sprinkled with mythological conceits, Propertius tells his mistress that, if he should ever forget her favours to him, "you, tragic Erinys, may then afflict me" (II.20.29). Cf. also Virgil, *Aeneid* 4. 471–3.

56. Tarrant 10; he suggests as a possible intermediary the *Agam.* of Ion of Chios, about which virtually nothing is known.

57. See the article by A. Hudson-Williams and F.J.E. Raby in the *Oxford Classical Dictionary* 2 ed. (Oxford: Clarendon Press, 1970) 364. The most accessible edition of the *Orestis Tragoedia* is by E. Rapisarda (Catania: G. Reina, 1951 [2 ed. 1964, which I have not seen]). So far as I know, no English translation exists.

58. Dyer p. 53; cf. G. Giannelli, *Culti e miti della Magna Graecia* (Florence: Sansoni, 1967) 42.

59. British Museum Cat. *Mysia* pl. VII.1, where the date is wrongly given as "450–400 B.C."; cf. L. Lacroix, "A propos des monnaies de Cyzique et de la legende d'Oreste", *L'Antiquitè classique* 15 (1946) 209–225.

60. J. Overbeck, *Die antiken Schriftquellen zur Geschichte der bildenden Künste bei den Griechen* (Hildesheim: Olms, 1959; repr. of the ed. Leipzig 1868) nos. 1734–7.

61. Cf. Wm. H. Matheson, *Claudel and Aeschylus* (Ann Arbor: Univ. of Michigan Press, 1965) 142–5.

62. *Notes without Music* (Engl. trans., London: D. Dobson, c. 1952) p. 183. The finale of *Les Euménides* along with *Les Choéphores* was presented with great success at Antwerp in 1927 and afterward in Paris.

63. In *Roan Stallion, Tamar and other Poems* (New York: Boni & Liveright, 1925).

64. *Poetry and Drama* (London: Faber & Faber, 1951) 30, repr. in Toby Cole, *Playwrights on Playwriting* (New York: Hill & Wang, 1960) 256.

65. Part I, sc. 1, p. 232 in T.S. Eliot, *The Complete Poems and Plays* (New York: Harcourt, Brace, 1952). Later, Harry will say, "I thought foolishly that when I got back to Wishwood, as I had left it, everything would fall into place. But *they* prevent it. I still have to find out what their meaning is" (II.ii, p. 272).

66. Act I, sc. 12, p. 198 in the translation by P. LaFarge and P.H. Hudd, *Jean Giraudoux, Three Plays* (paperback ed., New York: Hill and Wang, 1964).

67. Act II, sc. i, p. 94 in the trans. by Stuart Gilbert, *No Exit and Three other Plays by Jean Paul Sartre* (paperback ed., New York: Vintage Books, 1955).

68. *The Presocratic Philosophers* 2nd ed. (Cambridge: Cambridge University Press, 1983) p. 194.

69. See my *Political Background*, 63 ff.; Fraenkel's n. on *Ag.* 41 and 451; Taplin, *Stagecraft* 328.

70. *Living Greek Theatre* (New York: Greenwood Press, 1987) 64.

71. On Cicero's citations see H.D. Jocelyn, "Greek Poetry in Cicero's Prose Writing", *Yale Classical Studies* 23 (1973) 61–111.

Madrid, Museo Arquéologico inv. 2839; side-panel of a Roman sarcophagus from Husillos, 2nd cent. A.D.: a helmeted Athena casts her vote for Orestes in the "urn of mercy" (the "urn of death" lies overturned beneath the table) while a pensive Erinys, a torch barely visible in her left hand, looks on. *See p. 33.* *(photo German Archaeological Insitute, Rome)*

EUMENIDES

ΕΥΜΕΝΙΔΕΣ

Αἰσχύλου Εὐμενίδες

ὑπόθεσις Ἀριστοφάνους γραμματικοῦ

ἡ ὑπόθεσις· Ὀρέστης ἐν Δελφοῖς περισχόμενος ὑπὸ τῶν Ἐρινύων βουλῇ Ἀπόλλωνος
παρεγένετο εἰς Ἀθήνας εἰς τὸ ἱερὸν τῆς Ἀθηνᾶς· ἧς βουλῇ νικήσας κατῆλθεν εἰς Ἄργος·
τὰς δὲ Ἐρινύας πραΰνας προσηγόρευσεν Εὐμενίδας. παρ' οὐδετέρῳ κεῖται ἡ μυθοποιία.
τὰ τοῦ δράματος πρόσωπα· Πυθιὰς προφῆτις, Ἀπόλλων, Ὀρέστης, Κλυταιμήστρας εἴδωλον,
χορὸς Εὐμενίδων, Ἀθηνᾶ, προπομποί.

ΠΡΟΦΗΤΙΣ

πρῶτον μὲν εὐχῇ τῇδε πρεσβεύω θεῶν
τὴν πρωτόμαντιν Γαῖαν· ἐκ δὲ τῆς Θέμιν,
ἣ δὴ τὸ μητρὸς δευτέρα τόδ' ἕζετο
μαντεῖον, ὡς λόγος τις· ἐν δὲ τῷ τρίτῳ
λάχει - θελούσης οὐδὲ πρὸς βίαν τινός -   5
Τιτανὶς ἄλλη παῖς Χθονὸς καθέζετο
Φοίβη, δίδωσιν δ' ἣ γενέθλιον δόσιν
Φοίβῳ· τὸ Φοίβης δ' ὄνομ' ἔχει παρώνυμον.
λιπὼν δὲ λίμνην Δηλίαν τε χοιράδα,
κέλσας ἐπ' ἀκτὰς ναυπόρους τὰς Παλλάδος,   10
ἐς τήνδε γαῖαν ἦλθε Παρνησοῦ θ' ἕδρας.
πέμπουσι δ' αὐτὸν καὶ σεβίζουσιν μέγα
κελευθοποιοὶ παῖδες Ἡφαίστου, χθόνα
ἀνήμερον τιθέντες ἡμερωμένην.
μολόντα δ' αὐτὸν κάρτα τιμαλφεῖ λεώς   15
Δελφός τε χώρας τῆσδε πρυμνήτης ἄναξ.
τέχνης δέ νιν Ζεὺς ἔνθεον κτίσας φρένα
ἵζει τέταρτον τόνδε μάντιν ἐν θρόνοις·
Διὸς προφήτης δ' ἐστὶ Λοξίας πατρός.
τούτους ἐν εὐχαῖς φροιμιάζομαι θεούς.   20
[Παλλὰς προναία δ' ἐν λόγοις πρεσβεύεται]
σέβω δὲ Νύμφας, ἔνθα Κωρυκὶς πέτρα
κοίλη, φίλορνις, δαιμόνων ἀναστροφαί.
Βρόμιος δ' ἔχει τὸν χῶρον, οὐδ' ἀμνημονῶ,

EUMENIDES

Aeschylus' "Eumenides"
Hypothesis [of Aristophanes the Grammarian]

The Hypothesis: Orestes was hard pressed by the Erinyes at Delphi but through Apollo's will he came to Athens to the santuary of Athena. It was through her will that he won and was restored to Argos. After she mollified the Erinyes she called them "Eumenides" [Well Wishers.] The story is not handled by either of the other two dramatists. Characters in the drama are: the Pythian priestess, Apollo, Orestes, Clytemnestra's Ghost, Chorus of Eumenides, Athena, Escorts.

The setting is Apollo's shrine at Delphi. Enter the priestess.

THE PYTHIAN PROPHETESS

1   I give pride of place in this prayer first of all the gods
     to Earth, primeval prophetess, and after her to Themis,
     for she was second to sit in this, her mother's
     shrine of prophecy (so the story goes). In third
5   assignment – the change was voluntary; no one exerted pressure –
     another Titaness, daughter of Earth, took up the seat,
     Phoebe by name, who then gave it as a birthday-gift
     to Phoebus, who thus has Phoebe's name besides his own.
     Leaving Delos' lake and ridge of rock
10   he put in at Pallas Athena's shores, haunt of ships,
     then came to this land and a place to settle on Parnassus.
     He was given escort and shown great reverence
     by Hephaestus' sons, builders of roads,
     who made tame the savage land.
15   Upon his coming the people greatly honoured him
     as did Delphos, lord and steersman of this land.
     Zeus inspired Apollo with the seer's art
     and made him fourth and present prophet on the throne:
     the spokesman, then, of Father Zeus is Loxias.
20   These are the gods I pray to by way of prelude,
     [Pallas of the Fore-shrine is given pride of place in the account]
     but I also reverence the Nymphs, who dwell at the Corycian
        hollow
     rock, delight of birds and haunt of powers divine.
     Bromios, too, inhabits the place (as I am fully aware)

ἐξ οὗτε Βάκχαις ἐστρατήγησεν θεός   25
λαγὼ δίκην Πενθεῖ καταρράψας μόρον.
Πλειστοῦ δὲ πηγὰς καὶ Ποσειδῶνος κράτος
καλοῦσα καὶ τέλειον ὕψιστον Δία,
ἔπειτα μάντις εἰς θρόνους καθιζάνω.
καὶ νῦν τυχεῖν με τῶν πρὶν εἰσόδων μακρῷ   30
ἄριστα δοῖεν· κεἰ πάρ' Ἑλλήνων τινές,
ἴτων πάλῳ λαχόντες, ὡς νομίζεται·
μαντεύομαι γὰρ ὡς ἂν ἡγῆται θεός.

ἦ δεινὰ λέξαι, δεινὰ δ' ὀφθαλμοῖς δρακεῖν,
πάλιν μ' ἔπεμψεν ἐκ δόμων τῶν Λοξίου,   35
ὡς μήτε σωκεῖν μήτε μ' ἀκταίνειν στάσιν·
τρέχω δὲ χερσίν, οὐ ποδωκείᾳ σκελῶν·
δείσασα γὰρ γραῦς οὐδέν, ἀντίπαις μὲν οὖν.
ἐγὼ μὲν ἕρπω πρὸς πολυστεφῆ μυχόν,
ὁρῶ δ' ἐπ' ὀμφαλῷ μὲν ἄνδρα θεομυσῆ   40
ἕδραν ἔχοντα προστρόπαιον, αἵματι
στάζοντα χεῖρας, καὶ νεοσπαδὲς ξίφος
ἔχοντ', ἐλαίας θ' ὑψιγέννητον κλάδον
ἀργῆτι μαλλῷ σωφρόνως ἐστεμμένον.
[◡ – ◡ – ◡ τῇδε γὰρ τρανῶς ἐρῶ]   45
πρόσθεν δὲ τἀνδρὸς τοῦδε θαυμαστὸς λόχος
εὕδει γυναικῶν ἐν θρόνοισιν ἥμενος.
οὗτοι γυναῖκας ἀλλὰ Γοργόνας λέγω,
οὐδ' αὖτε Γοργείοισιν εἰκάσω τύποις.
εἶδόν ποτ' ἤδη Φινέως γεγραμμένας   50
δεῖπνον φερούσας· ἄπτεροί γε μὴν ἰδεῖν
αὗται μέλαιναί τ', ἐς τὸ πᾶν βδελύκτροποι,
ῥέγκουσι δ' οὐ πλατοῖσι φυσιάμασιν,
ἐκ δ' ὀμμάτων λείβουσι δυσφιλῆ λίβα·
καὶ κόσμος οὔτε πρὸς θεῶν ἀγάλματα   55
φέρειν δίκαιος οὔτ' ἐς ἀνθρώπων στέγας.
τὸ φῦλον οὐκ ὄπωπα τῆσδ' ὁμιλίας
οὐδ' ἥτις αἶα τοῦτ' ἐπεύχεται γένος

25 from the time when the god commanded an army of Bacchants
and wove a net of death for Pentheus, as for a hare.
I call, too, upon the springs of Pleistos and Poseidon's might
and Zeus Fulfiller and Most High;
Then I, as prophetess, take my seat upon the throne;
30 may the gods grant me now a consultation far better
than any before, and if any enquirers from the Greeks are
    present,
let them enter in allotted order, as is customary,
for my task is to prophesy in whatever way the god may lead.

(The Pythia goes into the building here taken to represent Apollo's temple and, after a short time, returns. She stumbles – or even crawls -- out of the shrine in a state of obvious fright.)

A sight terrible to tell, yes, terrible for eyes to see
35 sent me out again from Loxias' shrine,
so that I have no strength and cannot raise myself upright;
I run on all fours; my legs have no speed left in them,
for an old woman when afraid is nothing, no better than a child.
I proceeded to the interior of the shrine with its many garlands
40 and saw at the navel a god-polluted man.
His posture was that of a suppliant: blood dripped
from his hands and he was holding a fresh-drawn sword
and a tall branch of an olive-tree
modestly garlanded with bright fleece.
45 [so much I can say with certainty]
But in front of this man an astonishing troop
of women sleeps, sitting on chairs –
no, I don't mean women, Gorgons rather –
but I won't liken them to Gorgon-shapes either;
50 I once saw a picture of women taking away
Phineus' supper – but *these* females have no wings
and are black, thoroughly loathesome.
They snore with unapproachable exhalations
and drip from their eyes a hateful stream;
55 their attire, too, is such as cannot fitly be brought
either before images of gods or into homes of men.
I never saw the tribe to which this company belongs,
nor a land which might boast that it could rear this race

τρέφουσ' ἀνατεὶ μὴ μεταστένειν πόνον.

τἀντεῦθεν ἤδη τῶνδε δεσπότῃ δόμων   60
αὐτῷ μελέσθω Λοξίᾳ μεγασθενεῖ.
ἰατρόμαντις δ' ἐστὶ καὶ τερασκόπος
καὶ τοῖσιν ἄλλοις δωμάτων καθάρσιος.

ΑΠΟΛΛΩΝ

οὔτοι προδώσω· διὰ τέλους δέ σοι φύλαξ
ἐγγὺς παρεστὼς καὶ πρόσω δ' ἀποστατῶν   65
ἐχθροῖσι τοῖς σοῖς οὐ γενήσομαι πέπων.
καὶ νῦν ἁλούσας τάσδε τὰς μάργους ὁρᾷς
ὕπνῳ, πεσοῦσαι δ' αἱ κατάπτυστοι κόραι,
γραῖαι παλαιαὶ παῖδες, αἷς οὐ μείγνυται   70
θεῶν τις οὐδ' ἄνθρωπος οὐδὲ θὴρ ποτε·
κακῶν δ' ἕκατι κἀγένοντ', ἐπεὶ κακὸν
σκότον νέμονται Τάρταρόν θ' ὑπὸ χθονός,
μισήματ' ἀνδρῶν καὶ θεῶν Ὀλυμπίων.

ὅμως δὲ φεῦγε, μηδὲ μαλθακὸς γένῃ·
ἑλῶσι γάρ σε καὶ δι' ἠπείρου μακρᾶς   75
βιβῶντ' ἀν' αἰεὶ τὴν πλανοστιβῆ χθόνα
ὑπέρ τε πόντον καὶ περιρρύτας πόλεις.
καὶ μὴ πρόκαμνε τόνδε βουκολούμενος
πόνον· μολὼν δὲ Παλλάδος ποτὶ πτόλιν
ἷζου παλαιὸν ἄγκαθεν λαβὼν βρέτας·   80
κἀκεῖ δικαστὰς τῶνδε καὶ θελκτηρίους
μύθους ἔχοντες μηχανὰς εὑρήσομεν
ὥστ' ἐς τὸ πᾶν σε τῶνδ' ἀπαλλάξαι πόνων.
καὶ γὰρ κτανεῖν σ' ἔπεισα μητρῷον δέμας.

ΟΡΕΣΤΗΣ

ἄναξ Ἄπολλον, οἶσθα μὲν τὸ μὴ ἀδικεῖν·   85
ἐπεὶ δ' ἐπίστᾳ, καὶ τὸ μὴ ἀμελεῖν μάθε.
σθένος δὲ ποιεῖν εὖ φερέγγυον τὸ σόν.

Απ.   μέμνησο, μὴ φόβος σε νικάτω φρένας.
σὺ δ', αὐτάδελφον αἷμα καὶ κοινοῦ πατρός

without harm, and not regret the labour.
60 What happens from now on is up to this temple's master;
mighty Loxias himself must make it his concern.
He after all is a healer-priest and diviner,
and purifier of others' houses.

(*Exit the priestess. The temple doors open. Apollo emerges, accompanied by Orestes, and probably also Hermes, a non-speaking part. Some sleeping Erinyes may also be present (see v. 67)*).

APOLLO

I shall not betray you, but to the end will be your guardian,
65 both when I stand by your side and even from afar;
I shall not be gentle to your enemies.
Why even now, you see these savage women overcome
by sleep; the abominable maidens have fallen,
aged antique children, with whom no one consorts,
70 not any of the gods, nor man, nor beast;
no, even their coming to birth was for evil's sake, since evil
darkness and Tartarus-under-earth is their abode,
objects of hatred as they are to men and Olympian gods.
Nevertheless, persist in fleeing, show no softness,
75 for they will stalk you even over vast continents
as you progress over broad tracts of trodden earth
and over sea and to sea-girt island cities.
Do not grow weary in your tendance of this
task, but go to Pallas Athena's city;
80 sit as a suppliant, holding her ancient statue in your arms,
and there we shall get us judges of these matters and words
that cast a spell, and thus shall find expedients
to rid you of these toils once for all.
For I in fact persuaded you to kill your mother.

ORESTES

85 Lord Apollo, you know how not to do wrong;
and since you know it, learn as well your duty not to neglect me.
But your strength is a pledge of your benefaction.

Ap.   Remember, let fear not gain a victory over your judgement.
(*He turns to his brother, Hermes.*)
As for you, my own brother in blood and of a common father,

Ἑρμῆ, φύλασσε, κάρτα δ' ὢν ἐπώνυμος 90
πομπαῖος ἴσθι, τόνδε ποιμαίνων ἐμὸν
ἱκέτην. σέβει τοι Ζεὺς τόδ' ἐκνόμων σέβας
ὁρμωμένων βροτοῖσιν εὐπόμπῳ τύχῃ.

ΚΛΥΤΑΙΜΗΣΤΡΑΣ ΕΙΔΩΛΟΝ

εὕδοιτ' ἄν, ὠή· καὶ καθευδουσῶν τί δεῖ;
ἐγὼ δ' ἐφ' ὑμῶν ὧδ' ἀπητιμασμένη 95
ἄλλοισιν ἐν νεκροῖσιν, ὡς μὲν ἔκτανον,
ἔχω μεγίστην αἰτίαν κείνων ὕπο· 99
αἰσχρῶς δ' ἀλῶμαι. προυννέπω δ' ὑμῖν ὅτι 98
ὄνειδος ἐν φθιτοῖσιν οὐκ ἐκλείπεται· 97
παθοῦσα δ' οὕτω δεινὰ πρὸς τῶν φιλτάτων, 100
οὐδεὶς ὑπέρ μου δαιμόνων μηνίεται
κατασφαγείσης πρὸς χερῶν μητροκτόνων.
ὁρᾶτε πληγὰς τάσδε καρδίᾳ σέθεν;
εὕδουσα γὰρ φρὴν ὄμμασιν λαμπρύνεται,
ἐν ἡμέρᾳ δὲ μοῖρ' ἀπρόσκοπος βροτῶν. 105
ἦ πολλὰ μὲν δὴ τῶν ἐμῶν ἐλείξατε,
χοάς τ' ἀοίνους, νηφάλια μειλίγματα,
καὶ νυκτίσεμνα δεῖπν' ἐπ' ἐσχάρᾳ πυρὸς
ἔθυον, ὥραν οὐδενὸς κοινὴν θεῶν·
καὶ ταῦτα πάντα λὰξ ὁρῶ πατούμενα, 110
ὁ δ' ἐξαλύξας οἴχεται νεβροῦ δίκην,
καὶ ταῦτα κούφως ἐκ μέσων ἀρκυστάτων
ὤρουσεν, ὑμῖν ἐγκατιλλώψας μέγα.
ἀκούσαθ' ὡς ἔλεξα τῆς ἐμῆς περὶ
ψυχῆς· φρονήσατ', ὦ κατὰ χθονὸς θεαί· 115
ὄναρ γὰρ ὑμᾶς νῦν Κλυταιμήστρα καλῶ.

ΧΟΡΟΣ

μυγμός
Κλ. μύζοιτ' ἄν· ἀνὴρ δ' οἴχεται φεύγων πρόσω·
† φίλοις γάρ εἰσιν οὐκ ἐμοῖς προσίκτορες †
Χο. μυγμός 120

90 Hermes, guard over him; live up to your title
and be truly "the Escorter", shepherding this suppliant
of mine. Be sure that Zeus reveres this sanctity of outcasts
who are sent to men with an auspicious escort.

(Orestes and Hermes exit; Apollo returns into his temple. After a pause, Clytemnestra's ghost appears.)

CLYTEMNESTRA'S GHOST

Sleep on, then! You, there! What need of sleeping women?
95 I, who have been thus cast away from honour by you
among the other corpses, because I committed murder,
99 endure the greatest possible blame from them,
98 and so I wander in disgrace. But I tell you publicly that
97 reproaches do not cease among the dead;
100 even though I was treated so terribly by loved ones,
none of the divinities is angered on my account,
though I was slaughtered by a mother-killer's hands.
Do you see these wounds in your heart?
For the sleeping mind is brightened with its own eyes,
105 while by day man's lot is to have no foresight.
Sure enough, you lapped up many offerings of mine,
wineless libations, appeasements for the sober,
and I offered at a hearth-fire sacrificial meals
sanctified by night, a time not shared by any of the gods.
110 And I see all these offerings now being trampled on,
while *he* has escaped and is off, like a fawn,
and this with no effort at all; he leapt out lightly from
inside the nets, having thumbed his nose at you as he went.
Listen to me, for I spoke about my very
115 being! Awake and be conscious, goddesses of the nether world!
I, a dream, Clytemnestra, am summoning you now.

CHORUS

(snorting)

Cly.   Snort on, then! The man has gone off, escaped!
*For he has friends, friends who – are not at all like mine![1]

Cho.   (snorting)

---

1. Phrases preceded by an asterisk are dubious or conjectural.

ΚΛ. ἄγαν ὑπνώσσεις, κοὐ κατοικτίζεις πάθος·
     φονεὺς δ' Ὀρέστης τῆσδε μητρὸς οἴχεται.

Χο. ὠγμός

ΚΛ. ἄζεις; ὑπνώσσεις; οὐκ ἀναστήσῃ τάχος;
     τί σοι τέτακται πρᾶγμα πλὴν τεύχειν κακά;   125

Χο. ὠγμός

ΚΛ. ὕπνος πόνος τε κύριοι συνωμόται
     δεινῆς δρακαίνης ἐξέκηραναν μένος.

Χο. μιγμὸς διπλοῦς ὀξύς
     λαβὲ λαβὲ λαβὲ λαβέ· φάρξον.   130

ΚΛ. ὄναρ διώκεις θῆρα, κλαγγαίνεις δ' ἅπερ
     κύων μέριμναν οὔποτ' ἐκλείπων πόνου.
     τί δρᾷς; ἀνίστω· μή σε νικάτω πόνος,
     μηδ' ἀγνοήσῃς πῆμα μαλθαχθεῖσ' ὕπνῳ.
     ἄλγησον ἧπαρ ἐνδίκοις ὀνείδεσιν·   135
     τοῖς σώφροσιν γὰρ ἀντίκεντρα γίγνεται.
     σὺ δ' αἱματηρὸν πνεῦμ' ἐπουρίσασά τῳ,
     ἀτμῷ κατισχναίνουσα, νηδύος πυρί,
     ἕπου, μάραινε δευτέροις διώγμασιν.

Χο. ἔγειρ', ἔγειρε καὶ σὺ τήνδ', ἐγὼ δὲ σέ.   140
     εὕδεις; ἀνίστω, κἀπολακτίσασ' ὕπνον,
     ἰδώμεθ' εἴ τι τοῦδε φροιμίου ματᾷ.

         ἰοὺ ἰοὺ πόπαξ· ἐπάθομεν, φίλαι·   [στρ. α
     ἦ πολλὰ δὴ πέπονθα καὶ μάτην ἐγώ·
         ἐπάθομεν πάθος δυσαχές, ὦ πόποι,   145
         ἄφερτον κακόν.
     ἐξ ἀρκύων πέπτωκεν, οἴχεται δ' ὁ θήρ·
         ὕπνῳ κρατηθεῖσ' ἄγραν ὤλεσα.

         ἰὼ παῖ Διός· ἐπίκλοπος πέλῃ,   [ἀντ. α
     νέος δὲ γραίας δαίμονας καθιππάσω   150
         τὸν ἱκέταν σέβων, ἄθεον ἄνδρα καὶ
         τοκεῦσιν πικρόν,

Cly.   You are too deep in sleep, and have no pity for my suffering.
            Orestes, who murdered me, his mother, has gone!
Cho.   (whimpering)
Cly.   Do you whimper? Do you sleep? Get up at once!
125   What business have you been assigned except to work harm?
Cho.   (whimpering)
Cly.   Sleep and Toil, the arch-plotters,
            ruined and drained away the dread dragoness' force.
Cho.   (snortings redoubled and louder) [*perhaps uttered by individual*
                                          choristers]
130   Catch, catch, catch, catch! Bar him!
Cly.   You're chasing your prey in a dream. You're baying like
            a hound that never abandons its troublesome task.
            What are you doing? Stand up! Don't let toil gain a victory over·
               you,
            nor sleep make you soft and neglectful of my misery.
135   Let your insides ache because of my just reproaches,
            which, for those with feelings, are as sharp as goads.
            Send someone on his journey with a gale of blood,
            shrivelling him up with your breath, the belly's fire!
            Follow, wither him by renewing your pursuit! (*Exit*)

CHORUS-LEADER
140   Rouse, rouse her I tell you, just as I'm rousing you.
            What? You want to go on sleeping? Up, I tell you, kick off
               sleep!
            Let us see if our dream-prelude is empty imagining.

Entrance Song
                                         Stanza 1

            Aoo! Aee! We have suffered, my sisters!
            Indeed I have suffered much, and all in vain.
145   A dreadful, aching hurt we suffered – aah! –
            a wrong beyond all bearing.
            He has escaped the net; the beast has gone.
            Sleep overcame me and I lost my prey.
                                      Stanza 1'

            O son of Zeus, you're a thief!
150   Young, male, you rode roughshod over aged female divinities
            by reverencing the suppliant, a godless man,
            cruel to his mother.

τὸν μητραλοίαν δ' ἐξέκλεψας ὢν θεός.
  τί τῶνδ' ἐρεῖ τις δικαίως ἔχειν;

ἐμοὶ δ' ὄνειδος ἐξ ὀνειράτων μολὸν   [στρ. β
  ἔτυψεν δίκαν διφρηλάτου   156
  μεσολαβεῖ κέντρῳ
  ὑπὸ φρένας,
  ὑπὸ λοβόν.
  πάρεστι μαστίκτορος δαΐου δαμίου   160
  βαρύ τι περίβαρυ κρύος ἔχειν.

τοιαῦτα δρῶσιν οἱ νεώτεροι θεοί,   [ἀντ. β
  κρατοῦντες τὸ πᾶν δίκας πέρα.
  φονολιβῆ θρόνον
  περὶ πόδα,   165
  περὶ κάρα,
  πάρεστι γᾶς <τ' > ὀμφαλὸν προσδρακεῖν αἱμάτων
  βλοσυρὸν ἀρόμενον ἄγος ἔχειν.

ἐφεστίῳ δὲ μάντις ὢν μιάσματι   [στρ. γ
  μυχὸν ἐχράνατ' αὐ   170
  τόσσυτος, αὐτόκλητος,
  παρὰ νόμον θεῶν βρότεα μὲν τίων,
  παλαιγενεῖς δὲ Μοίρας φθίσας.

κἀμοί γε λυπρός, καὶ τὸν οὐκ ἐκλύσεται,   [ἀντ. γ
  ὑπὸ δὲ γᾶν φυγών   175
  οὔποτ' ἐλευθεροῦται,
  ποτιτρόπαιος δ' ὢν † ἕτερον ἐν κάρᾳ
  μιάστορ' ἐκείνου πάσεται †

Απ. ἔξω, κελεύω, τῶνδε δωμάτων τάχος
     χωρεῖτ', ἀπαλλάσσεσθε μαντικῶν μυχῶν,   180
     μὴ καὶ λαβοῦσα πτηνὸν ἀργηστὴν ὄφιν
     χρυσηλάτου θώμιγγος ἐξορμώμενον

The mother-murderer you filched away – you, a god!
Which of these acts will anyone call 'just'?

Stanza 2

155 When the reproach came to me in my dream,
it struck me like a charioteer,
his goad grasped tightly,
into my heart,
into my guts.
160 One can feel from the dread public torturer
something heavy, very heavy and chilling.

Stanza 2'

Such are the actions of the younger gods
who exercise power completely beyond justice.
A throne dripping with gore
165 around its feet,
around its head,
one can see earth's navel bristling
with bloody deeds * and pollution upon it.

Stanza 3

Though a prophet, he stained his inmost shrine
170 with defilement at its hearth.
He did it himself, unbidden,
by honouring human concerns against the gods' law
and thereby destroying the Fates born long ago.

Stanza 3'

Yes, though he cause me distress also, Apollo will not
rescue him,
175 for even if Orestes flee to the Underworld
he will never be freed;
though a suppliant, * ...
...

(*Enter Apollo from the temple.*)

Ap. Out, I tell you! Out of this temple at once!
180 Go, get out of the recesses of this prophetic shrine,
lest you catch a winged, gleaming snake
sped from beatengold bowstring,

ἀνῇς ὑπ' ἄλγους μέλαν' ἀπ' ἀνθρώπων ἀφρόν,
ἐμοῦσα θρόμβους οὓς ἀφείλκυσας φόνου.
οὔτοι δόμοισι τοῖσδε χρίμπτεσθαι πρέπει,   185
ἀλλ' οὗ καρανιστῆρες ὀφθαλμωρύχοι
δίκαι σφαγαί τε, σπέρματος τ' ἀποφθορᾷ
παίδων κακοῦται χλοῦνις, ἠδ' ἀκρωνίαι
λευσμοί τε, καὶ μύζουσιν οἰκτισμὸν πολὺν
ὑπὸ ῥάχιν παγέντες. ἆρ' ἀκούετε   190
οἵας ἑορτῆς ἔστ' ἀπόπτυστοι θεοῖς
στέργηθρ' ἔχουσαι; πᾶς δ' ὑφηγεῖται τρόπος
μορφῆς· λέοντος ἄντρον αἱματορρόφου
οἰκεῖν τοιαύτας εἰκός, οὐ χρηστηρίοις
ἐν τοῖσι πλησίοισι τρίβεσθαι μύσος.   195
χωρεῖτ' ἄνευ βοτῆρος αἰπολούμεναι·
ποίμνης τοιαύτης οὔτις εὐφιλὴς θεῶν.

Χο.   ἄναξ Ἄπολλον, ἀντάκουσον ἐν μέρει·
αὐτὸς σὺ τούτων οὐ μεταίτιος πέλῃ,
ἀλλ' εἷς τὸ πᾶν ἔπραξας ὡς παναίτιος.   200
Απ.   πῶς δή; τοσοῦτο μῆκος ἔκτεινον λόγου.
Χο.   ἔχρησας ὥστε τὸν ξένον μητροκτονεῖν.
Απ.   ἔχρησα ποινὰς τοῦ πατρὸς πρᾶξαι· τί μήν;
Χο.   κἄπειθ' ὑπέστης αἵματος δέκτωρ νέου.
Απ.   καὶ προστραπέσθαι τούσδ' ἐπέστελλον δόμους.   205
Χο.   καὶ τὰς προπομποὺς δῆτα τάσδε λοιδορεῖς;
Απ.   οὐ γὰρ δόμοισι τοῖσδε πρόσφοροι μολεῖν.
Χο.   ἀλλ' ἔστιν ἡμῖν τοῦτο προστεταγμένον -
Απ.   τίς ἥδε τιμή; κόμπασον γέρας καλόν.
Χο.   τοὺς μητραλοίας ἐκ δόμων ἐλαύνομεν.   210
Απ.   τί γάρ; γυναικὸς ἥτις ἄνδρα νοσφίσῃ -
Χο.   οὐκ ἂν γένοιθ' ὅμαιμος αὐθέντης φόνος.
Απ.   ἦ κάρτ' ἄτιμα καὶ παρ' οὐδὲν ἠργάσω
Ἥρας Τελείας καὶ Διὸς πιστώματα·
Κύπρις δ' ἄτιμος τῷδ' ἀπέρριπται λόγῳ,   215
ὅθεν βροτοῖσι γίγνεται τὰ φίλτατα.
εἰνὴ γὰρ ἀνδρὶ καὶ γυναικὶ κόσμιος

and have to disgorge painfully the black froth from men,
vomiting up the clots of gore you sucked from them.

185   It is not fitting for you to approach this temple,
but rather where heads are lopped, eyes gouged,
condemnations and slittings of throat, and boys' virility spoiled
by destruction of their seed; where extremities are severed
and stonings occur, and men moan loud and pitifully,

190   impaled beneath the spine. Do you hear, then,
the kind of feast you're fond of, that makes you so abominated
by the gods? The whole manner of your appearance
explains why: such women as you are should more naturally
live in a blood-sucking lion's cave, not

195   rub off your defilement on shrines * conveniently near.
Go, you she-goats without a goatherd to tend you;
none of the gods is friendly to such a flock.

Ch-L.   Lord Apollo, listen to us in turn.
You not only share responsibility for these events,

200   you single-handedly did it all and bear total responsibility.

Ap.   What do you mean? Make a longer speech in explanation.

Cho.   You prophesied that the stranger should kill his mother.

Ap.   I prophesied that he should exact requital for his father, of course
I did.

Cho.   And then you undertook to be his shelterer, the blood still fresh.

Ap.   And ordered him to come as a suppliant to this shrine.

Cho.   And you abuse us, who did nothing more than escort him here?

Ap.   Yes, for you are not fit creatures to approach this shrine.

Cho.   But this has been assigned to us –

Ap.   What is this "honour"? Boast on about your fine privilege!

Cho.   We drive mother-murderers from their homes.

Ap.   Well, the sort of wife who slays her husband –

Cho.   That would not be murder of one who was like in blood and kin.

Ap.   In fact, you totally dishonour and have rendered null the
pledges of trust between Hera, Protectress of marriage, and Zeus.

215   Cyprian Aphrodite, too, has been cast away dishonoured by your
remark,
the goddess from whom humans' most intimate relations spring.
For the destined marriage-bond of a man and woman

ὅρκου 'στὶ μείζων, τῇ Δίκῃ φρουρουμένη.
εἰ τοῖσιν οὖν κτείνουσιν ἀλλήλους χαλᾷς
τὸ μὴ τίνεσθαι μηδ' ἐποπτεύειν κότῳ,   220
οὔ φημ' Ὀρέστην σ' ἐνδίκως ἀνδρηλατεῖν.
τῷ μὲν γὰρ οἶδα κάρτα σ' ἐνθυμουμένην,
τοῖς δ' ἐμφανῶς πράσσουσιν ἡσυχαιτέραν.
δίκας δὲ Παλλὰς τῶνδ' ἐποπτεύσει θεά.

Χο.   τὸν ἄνδρ' ἐκεῖνον οὔ τι μὴ λίπω ποτέ.   225
Απ.   σὺ δ' οὖν δίωκε καὶ πόνον πλέω τίθου.
Χο.   τιμὰς σὺ μὴ σύντεμνε τὰς ἐμὰς λόγῳ.
Απ.   οὐδ' ἂν δεχοίμην ὥστ' ἔχειν τιμὰς σέθεν.
Χο.   μέγας γὰρ ἔμπας πὰρ Διὸς θρόνοις λέγῃ·
      ἐγὼ δ' – ἄγει γὰρ αἷμα μητρῷον – δίκας   230
      μέτειμι τόνδε φῶτα κἀκκυνηγετῶ.
Απ.   ἐγὼ δ' ἀρήξω τὸν ἱκέτην τε ῥύσομαι·
      δεινὴ γὰρ ἐν βροτοῖσι κἀν θεοῖς πέλει
      τοῦ προστροπαίου μῆνις, εἰ προδῶ σφ' ἑκών.

Ορ.   ἄνασσ' Ἀθάνα, Λοξίου κελεύμασιν   235
      ἥκω· δέχου δὲ πρευμενῶς ἀλάστορα,
      οὐ προστρόπαιον οὐδ' ἀφοίβαντον χέρα,
      ἀλλ' ἀμβλὺν ἤδη προστετριμμένον τε πρὸς
      ἄλλοισιν οἴκοις καὶ πορεύμασιν βροτῶν.
      ὁμοῖα χέρσον καὶ θάλασσαν ἐκπερῶν,   240
      σῴζων ἐφετμὰς Λοξίου χρηστηρίους,
      πάρειμι δῶμα καὶ βρέτας τὸ σόν, θεά·
      αὐτοῦ φυλάσσων ἀναμενῶ τέλος δίκης.

Χο.   εἶέν· τόδ' ἐστὶ τἀνδρὸς ἐκφανὲς τέκμαρ·
      ἕπου δὲ μηνυτῆρος ἀφθέγκτου φραδαῖς·   245

is greater than any oath, and has Justice as its guardian.
If against those who slay their mates you slacken
220   in exacting vengeance and supervising angrily,
I say that you are unjust in your prosecution of Orestes.
For in his case, I know, you are very concerned,
while in the case of ones who act openly, you're rather relaxed.
But decision about rights in this case the goddess Pallas Athena
    will supervise.

Cho.   I shall never leave that man, never.
Ap.   Well, then, keep on pursuing; make more trouble for yourself.
Cho.   Don't try to curtail my privileges by your reasoning.
Ap.   I wouldn't take your "privileges" as a gift.
Cho.   No, for you are reputed to be great at Zeus' throne even without
    them.
230   I on the other hand – for a mother's blood leads me on – shall go
and seek justice from this man, and am already on the track.
Ap.   I for my part will aid and rescue my suppliant,
for dreadful both among men and gods
is a suppliant's wrath, if I betray him willingly.

(*Apollo returns into his temple. The Chorus depart along the eastern [stage-right] parodos, leaving the stage empty. The scene changes to Athens, almost certainly the Acropolis. Orestes enters, probably along the eastern parodos. He speaks first from a distance.*)

ORESTES
235   Queen Athena, by Loxias Apollo's instructions
I have come; receive the accursed wretch graciously –
not as a polluted suppliant, nor uncleansed of hand,
but with guilt blunted and worn away at
other shrines and through dealings with men.
240   Crossing land and sea alike,
observing Loxias Apollo's oracular commands,
I am here at your shrine and statue, goddess;
(*He moves towards Athena's statue.*)
keeping watch here I await the outcome of justice.

(*The Chorus enter by the same parodos as Orestes had used, but at first they do not see him, for he is perhaps crouching behind Athena's statue.*)

Ch-L.   Well, here is a manifest sign of the man.
245   Follow the silent informer's clues,

τετραυματισμένον γὰρ ὡς κύων νεβρὸν
πρὸς αἷμα καὶ σταλαγμὸν ἐκματεύομεν.
πολλοῖς δὲ μόχθοις ἀνδροκμῆσι φυσιᾷ
σπλάγχνον· χθονὸς γὰρ πᾶς πεποίμανται τόπος,   250
ὑπέρ τε πόντον ἀπτέροις ποτήμασιν
ἦλθον διώκουσ' οὐδὲν ὑστέρα νεώς.
καὶ νῦν ὅδ' ἐνθάδ' ἐστί που καταπτακών·
ὀσμὴ βροτείων αἱμάτων με προσγελᾷ.

ὅρα, ὅρα μάλ' αὖ·
πάντα λεῦσσε μὴ   255
λάθῃ φύγδα βὰς ματροφόνος ἀτίτας.   256/7
ὁ δ' † αὖτε γοῦν † ἀλκὰν ἔχων
περὶ βρέτει πλεχθεὶς θεᾶς ἀμβρότου
ὑπόδικος θέλει γενέσθαι χρεῶν.   260
τὸ δ' οὐ πάρεστιν. αἷμα μητρῷον χαμαὶ
δυσαγκόμιστον, παπαῖ·
τὸ διερὸν πέδοι χύμενον οἴχεται.
ἀλλ' ἀντιδοῦναι δεῖ σ' ἀπὸ ζῶντος ῥοφεῖν
ἐρυθρὸν ἐκ μελέων πελανόν· ἀπὸ δὲ σοῦ   265
φεροίμαν βοσκὰν πώματος δυσπότου.
καὶ ζῶντά σ' ἰσχνάνασ' ἀπάξομαι κάτω,
ἀντίποιν' ὡς τίνῃς ματροφόνου δύας·
ὄψῃ δὲ κεἴ τις ἄλλος ἤλιτεν βροτῶν
ἢ θεὸν ἢ ξένον τιν' ἀσεβῶν   270
ἢ τοκέας φίλους,
ἔχονθ' ἕκαστον τῆς δίκης ἐπάξια.
μέγας γὰρ Ἅιδης ἐστὶν εὔθυνος βροτῶν
ἔνερθε χθονός,
δελτογράφῳ δὲ πάντ' ἐπωπᾷ φρενί.   275

Ορ.   ἐγὼ διδαχθεὶς ἐν κακοῖς ἐπίσταμαι
πολλοὺς καθαρμοὺς καὶ λέγειν ὅπου δίκη
σιγᾶν θ' ὁμοίως· ἐν δὲ τῷδε πράγματι
φωνεῖν ἐτάχθην πρὸς σοφοῦ διδασκάλου.

for like a dog on the trail of a wounded fawn
we're tracking him down along the drops of blood.
He's gasping out his guts with many man-crushing labours,
for he's been driven like a sheep over the whole surface of earth;
250   and over sea as well, flying without wings
I came in pursuit as fast as any ship.
And now he's here somewhere, cowering with fear:
the smell of human blood smiles at me in welcome.

Cho.   (*perhaps individual members or groups in turn*)
Look, look again!
255   Look everywhere lest
the mother-slayer escape unnoticed, get off unpunished.
(*They catch sight of him*)
  * He's found protection;
with his arms twined round the immortal goddess' statue
260   he is willing to stand trial for his debts.
But that cannot be. A mother's blood once fallen
cannot be recovered – O!
The liquid, once spilt on the ground, is gone.
But you must let us in exchange suck
265   the red clots from your limbs, your living flesh; it's from you
that I hope to have the fodder of a vile drink,
and I shall shrivel you and take you down alive
so you may pay requital for your mother's death-agonies.
You will see that if any other mortal sins
270   by failing to reverence god or guest
or dear parents,
each receives the dues of justice;
for Hades is a mighty corrector of men
beneath the earth,
275   and supervises all things with his recording mind.

Or.   My sufferings have taught me and so I know
a variety of purifications: when it is right to speak,
when also to be silent, and in this affair
it was a wise teacher who instructed me to speak.

βρίζει γὰρ αἷμα καὶ μαραίνεται χερός,   **280**
μητροκτόνον μίασμα δ' ἔκπλυτον πέλει·
ποταίνιον γὰρ ὂν πρὸς ἑστίᾳ θεοῦ
Φοίβου καθαρμοῖς ἠλάθη χοιροκτόνοις.
πολὺς δέ μοι γένοιτ' ἂν ἐξ ἀρχῆς λόγος,
ὅσοις προσῆλθον ἀβλαβεῖ ξυνουσίᾳ   **285**
– χρόνος καθαίρει πάντα γηράσκων ὁμοῦ –
καὶ νῦν ἀφ' ἁγνοῦ στόματος εὐφήμως καλῶ
χώρας ἄνασσαν τῇσδ' Ἀθηναίαν ἐμοὶ
μολεῖν ἀρωγόν· κτήσεται δ' ἄνευ δορὸς
αὐτόν τε καὶ γῆν καὶ τὸν Ἀργεῖον λεὼν   **290**
πιστὸν δικαίως ἐς τὸ πᾶν τε σύμμαχον.
ἀλλ' εἴτε χώρας ἐν τόποις Λιβυστικοῖς
Τρίτωνος ἀμφὶ χεῦμα γενεθλίου πόρου
τίθησιν ὀρθὸν ἢ κατηρεφῆ πόδα
φίλοις ἀρήγουσ', εἴτε Φλεγραίαν πλάκα   **295**
θρασὺς ταγοῦχος ὡς ἀνὴρ ἐπισκοπεῖ,
ἔλθοι, κλύει δὲ καὶ πρόσωθεν ὢν θεός,
ὅπως γένοιτο τῶνδ' ἐμοὶ λυτήριος.

Χο. οὔτοι σ' Ἀπόλλων οὐδ' Ἀθηναίας σθένος
ῥύσαιτ' ἂν ὥστε μὴ οὐ παρημελημένον   **300**
ἔρρειν, τὸ χαίρειν μὴ μαθόνθ' ὅπου φρενῶν,
ἀναίματον βόσκημα δαιμόνων, σκιάν.
 οὐδ' ἀντιφωνεῖς, ἀλλ' ἀποπτύεις λόγους,
ἐμοὶ τραφείς τε καὶ καθιερωμένος;
καὶ ζῶν με δαίσεις οὐδὲ πρὸς βωμῷ σφαγείς.   **305**
ὕμνον δ' ἀκούσῃ τόνδε δέσμιον σέθεν·

   ἄγε δὴ καὶ χορὸν ἅψωμεν, ἐπεὶ
   μοῦσαν στυγερὰν
   ἀποφαίνεσθαι δεδόκηκεν,
   λέξαι τε λάχη τὰ κατ' ἀνθρώπους   **310**
   ὡς ἐπινωμᾷ στάσις ἀμή.
   εὐθύδικοι θ' αἵδ' οἰόμεθ' εἶναι·
   τοὺς μὲν καθαρὰς χεῖρας ἔχοντας

280 For the blood is drowsy and withers from my hand,
and the miasma of matricide has been washed away,
for, while it was still fresh, at the hearth of the god
Phoebus Apollo himself it was driven out with purifications of
slain swine.
I could go back to the beginning and make a long story
285 of the many men I approached and mixed with, without causing
harm,
for time, as it joins in growing old, purifies all things.
So, too, now with holy lips and propitiously I call
upon the Queen of this land, Athena, to come to me
as my defender; without compulsion of arms she will acquire
290 myself, my country, and the populace of Argos
as trusty allies in justice and for all time.
Whether in Libyan regions of the earth,
at the flowing stream of Triton where she was born,
she is seated in repose or standing,
295 giving aid to her friends, or whether she is overseeing
the Phlegraean plain like a bold commander,
I pray that she come (a god can hear even from afar)
in order that she may release me from these creatures here.

Ch-L. Neither Apollo nor Athena's strength
300 can save you from going, abandoned,
to perdition, with not even an inkling of joy in your soul,
bloodless fodder for spirits, a shade.
(*The leader pauses for a reply.*)
You say nothing in response? You spit at my words?
You, nurtured as a victim consecrated to me?
305 While still alive, not slain at any altar, you'll make a feast for
me;
you shall hear this song, your binding-spell.

Choral Ode

Prelude

Come, then, let us also join in a circle to dance, since
we are determined to display
our frightening Muse,
310 and to tell how our company
discharges its assigned offices among men.
Indeed, we think we dispense straight judgements:
against those who have clean hands

οὖτις ἐφέρπει μῆνις ἀφ' ἡμῶν,
ἀσινὴς δ' αἰῶνα διοιχνεῖ·   315
ὅστις δ' ἀλιτὼν ὥσπερ ὅδ' ἀνὴρ
χεῖρας φονίας ἐπικρύπτει,
μάρτυρες ὀρθαὶ τοῖσι θανοῦσιν
παραγιγνόμεναι πράκτορες αἵματος
αὐτῷ τελέως ἐφάνημεν.   320

μᾶτερ ἅ μ' ἔτικτες, ὦ μᾶτερ   [στρ. α
Νύξ, ἀλαοῖσι καὶ δεδορκόσιν
ποινάν, κλῦθ'· ὁ Λατοῦς γὰρ ἶ-
νίς μ' ἄτιμον τίθησιν
τόνδ' ἀφαιρούμενος   325
πτῶκα, ματρῷον ἅγ-
νισμα κύριον φόνου.

ἐπὶ δὲ τῷ τεθυμένῳ   [μεσῳδ. α
τόδε μέλος, παρακοπά,
παραφορὰ φρενοδαλής,   330
ὕμνος ἐξ Ἐρινύων
δέσμιος φρενῶν, ἀφόρ-
μικτος, αὐονὰ βροτοῖς.

τοῦτο γὰρ λάχος διανταία   [ἀντ. α
Μοῖρ' ἐπέκλωσεν ἐμπέδως ἔχειν,   335
† θανάτων τοῖσιν αὐτουργίαις
ξύμπας ωσι(ν) μάταιοι †
τοῖς ὁμαρτεῖν ὄφρ' ἂν
γᾶν ὑπέλθῃ· θανὼν δ'
οὐκ ἄγαν ἐλεύθερος.   340

[ἐπὶ δὲ τῷ τεθυμένῳ
τόδε μέλος, παρακοπά,
παραφορὰ φρενοδαλής,
ὕμνος ἐξ Ἐρινύων

no wrath from us advances
315 and he lives his life through without suffering.
But for the sinner who, like this man,
tries to hide hands that are steeped in blood,
we stand by, true witnesses for those who are dead,
and show him that we have full authority
320 to collect the fine – his blood.

Stanza 1

Mother, O mother Night! You bore me
to be a requital for dead and living alike;
hear me! For Leto's son Apollo
is bringing dishonour upon me
325 by trying to take from me
this cowering hare, who must rightfully
atone for his mother's blood.

Mesode

Over the victim
this is our song to bring delirium,
330 derangement destroying the brain,
a song from the Erinyes
binding the brain, not played
to the lyre, a withering death for mortals.

Stanza 1'

For this was the office that Moira relentlessly
335 spun out to be firmly implanted for all time,
that * upon those who blindly fall in
with acts of sinful self-will
I should attend always until
he goes below ground; and even in death
340 he is not unduly free.

[vv. 341 – 46 = 328 – 33]

δέσμιος φρενῶν, ἀφόρ-   345
μικτος, αὐονὰ βροτοῖς.]

γιγνομέναισι λάχη τάδ' ἐφ'   [στρ. β
ἁμὶν ἐκράνθη·
ἀθανάτων δ' ἀπέχειν χέρας,
οὐδέ τις ἐστὶ   350
συνδαίτωρ μετάκοινος.
παλλεύκων δὲ πέπλων ἄκληρος ἄμοιρος
                              ἐτύχθην   352/3
<- ˘ - ˘ - ˘ ->   353a

δωμάτων γὰρ εἱλόμαν   [μεσῳδ. β
ἀνατροπάς, ὅταν Ἄρης   355
τιθασὸς ὢν φίλον ἕλῃ,
ἐπὶ τὸν ὧδ' ἱέμεναι
κρατερὸν διθ' ὁμοίως
μαυροῦμεν ὑφ' αἵματος νέου.

σπεύδομεν αἵδ' ἀφελεῖν τινα   [ἀντ. β
τᾶσδε μερίμνας   361
θεούς τ' ἀτέλειαν ἐμαῖσι λιτ-
αῖς ἐπικραίνειν,
μηδ' εἰς ἄγκρισιν ἐλθεῖν·
Ζεὺς δ' αἱμοσταγὲς ἀξιόμισον ἔθνος τόδε
                              λέσχας   365/6
ἃς ἀπηξιώσατο.

δόξαι δ' ἀνδρῶν καὶ μάλ' ὑπ' αἰθέρι σεμναί   [στρ. γ
τακόμεναι κατὰ γᾶς μινύθουσιν ἄτιμοι
ἁμετέραις ἐφόδοις μελανείμοσιν   370
ὀρχησμοῖς τ' ἐπιφθόνοις ποδός·

At our birth these offices
were guaranteed to us;
it was guaranteed, too, that the gods keep their hands away,
350 nor does any god
join in and partake of our feast.
I in turn have no share or allotment in white-robed
festivals...

Mesode

For I chose as my mission the overthrow
355 of homes when the War-god, tamed and kept
in the house, turns wild and slays a loved one.
Upon such a slayer, however powerful he may be,
we thus hurl ourselves and * drain away
his fresh blood.

Stanza 2'

360 * Here we are, eager to remove someone
from this worrisome task,
eager, too, that the gods guarantee immunity
to my prayers
and not even come to a test.
365/6 But Zeus banished our tribe from his company,
as being (he said) 'blood-stained,' 'worthy of hate.'

Stanza 3

Men's solemn pretensions, though they may touch the sky,
melt beneath the earth, waste to nothing, are dishonoured
370 at our assaults in our black robes
and our angry dancing-kicks.

μάλα γὰρ οὖν ἁλομένα   [μεσῳδ. γ
ἀνέκαθεν βαρυπετῆ
καταφέρω ποδὸς ἀκμάν,
σφαλερὰ <καὶ >τανυδρόμοις   375
κῶλα, δύσφορον ἄταν.

πίπτων δ' οὐκ οἶδεν τόδ' ὑπ' ἀφρονι λύμᾳ·   [ἀντ. γ
τοῖον ἐπὶ κνέφας ἀνδρὶ μύσος τε ποτᾶται,
καὶ δνοφερὰν τιν' ἀχλὺν κατὰ δώματος
αὐδᾶται πολύστονος φάτις.   380

μένει γάρ· εὐμήχανοι   [στρ. δ
δὲ καὶ τέλειοι κακῶν
τε μνήμονες, Σεμναὶ
καὶ δυσπαρήγοροι βροτοῖς,
ἄτιμ' ἀτίετα διόμεναι λάχη   385
θεῶν διχοστατοῦντ' ἀνηλίῳ λάπᾳ,
δυσοδοπαίπαλα δερκομένοισι
καὶ δυσομμάτοις ὁμῶς·

                             [? μεσῳδ. δ

τίς οὖν τάδ' οὐχ ἄζεταί   [ἀντ. δ
τε καὶ δέδοικεν βροτῶν,   390
ἐμοῦ κλύων θεσμόν,
τὸν Μοιρόκραντον ἐκ θεῶν
δοθέντα τέλεον; ἔτι δέ μοι <μένει >
γέρας παλαιόν, οὐδ' ἀτιμίας κυρῶ,
καίπερ ὑπὸ χθόνα τάξιν ἔχουσα   395
καὶ δυσήλιον κνέφας.

ΑΘΗΝΑ

πρόσωθεν ἐξήκουσα κληδόνος βοὴν
ἀπὸ Σκαμάνδρου γῆν καταφθατουμένη,
ἣν δῆτ' Ἀχαιῶν ἄκτορές τε καὶ πρόμοι,
τῶν αἰχμαλώτων χρημάτων λάχος μέγα,   400

For, taking a long leap from above,
I come down hard,
land on my toes
375   and tumble my victim, however nimble
his limbs – unbearable ruin for him!

Stanza 3'

He falls, but does not know why, for his brain is destroyed:
such darkness and defilement flutter over the man,
and report with many a sigh declares
380   a murky mist is settling on his house.

Stanza 4

For fulfillment awaits. We are versatile,
we accomplish our ends, we are mindful
of wrongs, we are august and hard
for men to appease.
385   The offices we practice are 'dishonoured,'
sundered from the gods by sunless slime,
rough and rocky for sighted
and sightless alike.

(? Mesode)
Stanza 4'

How, then, can human beings not respect
390   and fear my role,
when they hear from me the ordinance
guaranteed by Moira and granted by the gods
as fully effective? There yet remains to me
an ancient privilege. I am not dishonoured,
395   even though I keep my station in the
sunless gloom beneath the earth.

(Enter Athena in a horse-drawn chariot, along the eastern parodos.)

ATHENA

I heard the sound of your call from afar,
from Scamander, where I was taking control of land
which in fact the leaders and chiefs of the Achaeans
400   assigned, a handsome share of the spoils of war,

ἔνειμαν αὐτόπρεμνον ἐς τὸ πᾶν ἐμοί,
ἐξαίρετον δώρημα Θησέως τόκοις·
ἔνθεν διώκουσ' ἦλθον ἄτρυτον πόδα
[πτερῶν ἄτερ ῥοιβδοῦσα κόλπον αἰγίδος]
πώλοις ἀκμαίοις τόνδ' ἐπιζεύξασ' ὄχον.   405
καὶ νῦν δ' ὁρῶσα τήνδ' ὁμιλίαν χθονὸς –
ταρβῶ μὲν οὐδέν, θαῦμα δ' ὄμμασιν πάρα.
τίνες ποτ' ἐστέ; πᾶσι δ' ἐς κοινὸν λέγω,
βρέτας τε τοὐμὸν τῷδ' ἐφημένῳ ξένῳ·
ὑμᾶς θ' ὁμοίας οὐδενὶ σπαρτῶν γένει,   410
οὔτ' ἐν θεαῖσι πρὸς θεῶν ὁρωμέναις,
οὔτ' οὖν βροτείοις ἐμφερεῖς μορφώμασιν –
λέγειν δ' ἄμορφον ὄντα τοὺς πέλας κακῶς
πρόσω δικαίων, ἠδ' ἀποστατεῖ Θέμις.

Χο.   πείσῃ τὰ πάντα συντόμως, Διὸς κόρη·   415
      ἡμεῖς γάρ ἐσμεν Νυκτὸς αἰανῆς τέκνα,
      Ἀραὶ δ' ἐν οἴκοις γῆς ὑπαὶ κεκλήμεθα.

Αθ.   γένος μὲν οἶδα κλῃδόνας τ' ἐπωνύμους
Χο.   τιμάς γε μὲν δὴ τὰς ἐμὰς πείσῃ τάχα.
Αθ.   μάθοιμ' ἂν εἰ λέγοι τις ἐμφανῆ λόγον.   420
Χο.   βροτοκτονοῦντας ἐκ δόμων ἐλαύνομεν.
Αθ.   καὶ τῷ κτανόντι ποῦ τὸ τέρμα τῆς φυγῆς;
Χο.   ὅπου τὸ χαίρειν μηδαμοῦ νομίζεται.
Αθ.   ἦ καὶ τοιαύτας τῷδ' ἐπιρροιζεῖς φυγάς;
Χο.   φονεὺς γὰρ εἶναι μητρὸς ἠξιώσατο.   425
Αθ.   ἄλλης ἀνάγκης οὔτινος τρέων κότον;
Χο.   ποῦ γὰρ τοσοῦτο κέντρον ὡς μητροκτονεῖν;
Αθ.   δυοῖν παρόντοιν ἥμισυς λόγου πάρα.
Χο.   ἀλλ' ὅρκον οὐ δέξαιτ' ἄν, οὐ δοῦναι θέλει.
Αθ.   κλύειν δίκαιος μᾶλλον ἢ πρᾶξαι θέλεις.   430
Χο.   πῶς δή; δίδαξον· τῶν σοφῶν γὰρ οὐ πένῃ.
Αθ.   ὅρκοις τὰ μὴ δίκαια μὴ νικᾶν λέγω.
Χο.   ἀλλ' ἐξέλεγχε, κρῖνε δ' εὐθεῖαν δίκην.
Αθ.   ἦ κἀπ' ἐμοὶ τρέποιτ' ἂν αἰτίας τέλος;
Χο.   πῶς δ' οὔ; σέβουσαί γ' ἄξι' ἀντ' ἐπαξίων.   435

to be mine totally and for all time,
a choice gift for Theseus' sons.
From there I came with speed, but effortlessly,
[without wings, merely swishing the folds of my aegis]
405 once I had yoked this car to vigorous horses.
(*She descends and notices the chorus of Erinyes.*)
And now as I see this strange group of visitors to my land –
I'm not afraid, but my eyes are filled with wonder.
Who in the world are you? I speak to all alike
and to this stranger seated at my statue;
410 but as for you who are clearly like no other race of creatures,
neither among sights seen by gods
nor again resembling any human shapes –
still, for neighbours to speak ill of a person because he is
unsightly
is far removed from justice, and Right stands aside.

Cho. 15 You shall learn the whole matter in short order, daughter of Zeus:
We, indeed, are the children of endless Night,
and are named 'Curses' in our homes beneath the earth.

Ath. I now know your lineage and designated names

Cho. but you shall soon learn my prerogatives as well.

Ath. 20 I shall understand, if someone should give a clear account.

Cho. We drive murderers from their homes.

Ath. And for the killer, where is the limit of your pursuit?

Cho. Where joy has no currency whatever.

Ath. You cry this man on to such an endless flight?

Cho. 25 Yes, for he saw fit to be his mother's murderer.

Ath. Did he not perhaps fear the wrath brought by some other
compulsion?

Cho. No, for what could possibly goad anyone to matriqide?

Ath. (*turning to Orestes*)
There are two sides; we've heard only half the story.

Cho. (*insistently*) But he would not accept an oath, nor is willing to
give one.

Ath. 30 You wish to be reputed just, but not to act so.

Cho. What do you mean? Instruct me, for you are not poor in wisdom.

Ath. I mean, don't try to win an unjust victory merely through oaths. 431

Cho. Well, begin the interrogation, and reach a decision by a regular
trial.

Ath. You mean you would turn over to me the issue and completion of
this case?

Cho. 435 Certainly, for we at any rate reverence a 'worthy return for

Αθ.　τί πρὸς τάδ' εἰπεῖν, ὦ ξέν', ἐν μέρει θέλεις;
λέξας δὲ χώραν καὶ γένος καὶ ξυμφορὰς
τὰς σάς, ἔπειτα τῶνδ' ἀμυναθοῦ ψόγον·
εἴπερ πεποιθὼς τῇ δίκῃ βρέτας τόδε
ἧσαι φυλάσσων ἑστίας ἐμῆς πέλας,　　　　　　440
σεμνὸς προσίκτωρ ἐν τρόποις Ἰξίονος,
τούτοις ἀμείβου πᾶσιν εὐμαθές τί μοι.

Ορ.　ἄνασσ' Ἀθάνα, πρῶτον ἐκ τῶν ὑστάτων
τῶν σῶν ἐπῶν μέλημ' ἀφαιρήσω μέγα·
οὐκ εἰμὶ προστρόπαιος, οὐδ' ἔχων μύσος　　　445
πρὸς χειρὶ τἠμῇ τὸ σὸν ἐφεζόμην βρέτας.
τεκμήριον δὲ τῶνδέ σοι λέξω μέγα·
ἄφθογγον εἶναι τὸν παλαμναῖον νόμος,
ἔστ' ἂν πρὸς ἀνδρὸς αἵματος καθαρσίου
σφαγαὶ καθαιμάξωσι νεοθηλοῦς βοτοῦ.　　　450
πάλαι πρὸς ἄλλοις ταῦτ' ἀφιερώμεθα
οἴκοισι καὶ βοτοῖσι καὶ ῥυτοῖς πόροις.
ταύτην μὲν οὕτω φροντίδ' ἐκποδὼν λέγω,
γένος δὲ τοὐμὸν ὡς ἔχει πεύσῃ τάχα.
Ἀργεῖός εἰμι, πατέρα δ' ἱστορεῖς καλῶς,　　455
Ἀγαμέμνον', ἀνδρῶν ναυβατῶν ἁρμόστορα,
ξὺν ᾧ σὺ Τροίαν ἄπολιν Ἰλίου πόλιν
ἔθηκας. ἔφθιθ' οὗτος οὐ καλῶς μολὼν
ἐς οἶκον· ἀλλά νιν κελαινόφρων ἐμὴ
μήτηρ κατέκτα ποικίλοις ἀγρεύμασιν　　　　460
κρύψασ', ἃ λουτρῶν ἐξεμαρτύρει φόνον.
κἀγὼ κατελθών, τὸν πρὸ τοῦ φεύγων χρόνον,
ἔκτεινα τὴν τεκοῦσαν, οὐκ ἀρνήσομαι,
ἀντικτόνοις ποιναῖσι φιλτάτου πατρός.
καὶ τῶνδε κοινῇ Λοξίας ἐπαίτιος　　　　　465
ἄλγη προφωνῶν ἀντίκεντρα καρδίᾳ,
εἰ μή τι τῶνδ' ἔρξαιμι τοὺς ἐπαιτίους.
σὺ δ' εἰ δικαίως εἴτε μὴ κρῖνον δίκην·
πράξας γὰρ ἐν σοὶ πανταχῇ τάδ' αἰνέσω.

Αθ.　τὸ πρᾶγμα μεῖζον, εἴ τις οἴεται τόδε　　　470

worthy acts'.

Ath.   (*to Orestes*) Stranger, what do you wish to say to these charges in
turn?
Begin by telling your country, your family and your
circumstances; then defend yourself against these women's
reproaches.
If it really is with full confidence in justice that you sit
440   keeping watch at this statue near my hearth,
a solemn suppliant in the manner of Ixion,
then make me a comprehensible reply to all these allegations.

Or.   Queen Athena, I shall begin by trying to dispel the great
concern betokened by your final words:
445   I am not a polluted suppliant, nor with defilement
on my hand did I take my seat at your statue.
And I shall tell you a mighty proof of this fact:
the law is that a guilty individual be silent
until the blood of a slaughtered young animal
450   has been sprinkled on him by a man who can purify from blood-
guilt.
Long since have these expiatory rites been performed on me
at other houses, with a variety of animals and flowing streams.
Thus, I bid good-riddance to this concern at least.
But my family background you shall learn at once:
455   I am an Argive; my father you know full well,
Agamemnon, organizer of a force of sailors
with whom you made Troy and Ilium a non-city.
He, however, perished ingloriously after he had
come home; my black-souled mother
460   slew him after covering him with a net of cunning design
which gave open witness to the murder in the bath.
I for my part returned, since before this I was an exile,
and killed the mother who bore me, I'll not deny it,
a killing in requital for my beloved father.
465   Loxias, too, is answerable in common for these deeds,
since he kept proclaiming anguish to goad the heart
unless I took some action against those answerable for these
events.
But whether I acted justly or not – it's for you to decide the case;
however I fare at your hands, I shall be content.

Ath.   The matter is too great, if any mortal thinks he can

βροτὸς δικάζειν· οὐδὲ μὴν ἐμοὶ θέμις
φόνου διαιρεῖν ὀξυμηνίτου δίκας,
ἄλλως τε καὶ σὺ μὲν † κατηρτυκὼς ὅμως †
ἱκέτης προσῆλθες καθαρὸς ἀβλαβὴς δόμοις,
[ὅμως δ' ἄμομφον ὄντα σ' αἱροῦμαι πόλει]   475
αὗται δ' ἔχουσι μοῖραν οὐκ εὐπέμπελον,
καὶ μὴ τυχοῦσαι πράγματος νικηφόρου,
χωρεῖ μεταῦθις ἰὸς ἐκ φρονήματων
πέδοι πεσὼν ἄφερτος, αἰανὴς νόσος.

    τοιαῦτα μὲν τάδ' ἐστίν· ἀμφότερα, μένειν   480
† πέμπειν δὲ δυσπήματ' ἀμηχάνως ἐμοί †
ἐπεὶ δὲ πρᾶγμα δεῦρ' ἐπέσκηψεν τόδε,
φόνων δικαστὰς ὁρκίων αἱρουμένη
<   >
θεσμόν, τὸν εἰς ἅπαντ' ἐγὼ θήσω χρόνον.
ὑμεῖς δὲ μαρτύριά τε καὶ τεκμήρια   485
καλεῖσθ', ἀρωγὰ τῆς δίκης ὁρκώματα.
κρίνασα δ' ἀστῶν τῶν ἐμῶν τὰ βέλτατα
ἥξω διαιρεῖν τοῦτο πρᾶγμ' ἐτητύμως.

[ὅρκον πορόντας μηδὲν ἔκδικον φρεσίν]

Χο.   νῦν καταστροφαὶ νέων   [στρ. α
          θεσμίων, εἰ κρατή   491
          σει δίκα <τε >καὶ βλάβα
          τοῦδε μητροκτόνου·
          πάντας ἤδη τόδ' ἔργον εὐχερεί-
          ᾳ συναρμόσει βροτούς.   495
          πολλὰ δ' ἔτυμα παιδότρωτα
          πάθεα προσμένει τοκεῦ-
          σιν μεταῦθις ἐν χρόνῳ.

          οὐδὲ γὰρ βροτοσκόπων   [ἀντ. α
          μαινάδων τῶνδ' ἐφέρ-   500
          ψει κότος τις ἐργμάτων·

adjudicate it; not even for me would it be right
to discriminate claims to justice for a slaying that arouses sharp
  wrath,
especially since you have come, *thoroughly inured to suffering,
474 a suppliant purified, causing no harm to this abode,
476 and these women for their part have an allotted office not easily
  dispensed with,
and if they do not obtain victory in the proceedings—
there comes in after time a poison from their ill intent
seeping into the ground intolerably, an everlasting blight.
480 Such, then, is the situation. Both alternatives, retention
or dismissal, * bring suffering and are unmanageable for me.
But since this business landed here like a lightning bolt,
after I have chosen judges of homicide under oath,
[...]
an ordinance which I shall institute for all time to come.
(*She addresses directly both Orestes and the Chorus.*)
485 You, now, call witnesses, marshal evidence,
safeguards under oath of the justice of the case.
After I have selected the best of my citizens,
I shall return to make a true determination of this matter.

[not offering any unjust oath with their minds]
(*Exit Athena, probably accompanied by Orestes.*)

Second Choral Ode

Stanza 1

Cho.   Now will Athena's new ordinances
cause a revolution,
if this matricide's malicious plea
shall prevail.
This deed will quickly make all men
495 quite ready to undertake crime
and many genuine sufferings from wounds
dealt by their children await parents
in time to come.

Stanza 1'

For there will be no onslaught of anger at wrongdoing
00 from these maenad watchers-of-men;

πάντ' ἐφήσω μόρον.
πεύσεται δ' ἄλλος ἄλλοθεν † προφωνῶν † τὰ τῶν πέλας κακά,
λήξειν ὑπόδοσίν τε μόχθων·   505
ἀκεά δ' οὐ βέβαια τλά-
μων μάταν παρηγορεῖ.

μηδέ τις κικλησκέτω   [στρ. β
ξυμφορᾷ τετυμμένος
τοῦτ' ἔπος θροούμενος,   510
Ὦ Δ ί κ α,
ὦ θ ρ ό ν ο ι τ' Ἐ ρ ι ν ύ ω ν·
ταῦτά τις τάχ' ἂν πατὴρ
ἢ τεκοῦσα νεοπαθὴς
οἶκτον οἰκτίσαιτ', ἐπει-   515
δὴ πίτνει δόμος Δίκας.

ἔσθ' ὅπου τὸ Δεινὸν εὖ   [ἀντ. β
καὶ φρενῶν ἐπίσκοπον
δεῖ μένειν καθήμενον·
ξυμφέρει   520
σωφρονεῖν ὑπὸ στένει.
τίς δὲ μηδὲν † ἐν φάει
καρδίαν ἀνατρέφων †
ἢ πόλις βροτός θ' ὁμοί-
ως ἔτ' ἂν σέβοι Δίκαν;   525

μήτ' ἄναρκτον βίον   [στρ. γ
μήτε δεσποτούμενον
αἰνέσῃς·
παντὶ μέσῳ τὸ κράτος θεὸς
ὤπασεν, ἀλλ' ἄλλα δ' ἐφορεύει.   530/1
ξύμμετρον δ' ἔπος λέγω·
Δυσσεβίας μὲν Ὕβρις τέκος
ὡς ἐτύμως,

I shall allow every kind of murder
and a man shall enquire of another,
as he * sees the wrongs done to his neighbours,
505   where he may find an abatement or remission of sufferings;
poor wretch, he can only offer uncertain remedies
as a vain consolation.

                                                       Stanza 2

Let no one, when he is struck
by disaster, plaintively
510   call out these words:
"O Justice !
O thrones of the Erinyes ! "
Some father
or mother, newly stricken,
515   might raise a pitiful lament,
since Justice's house is falling.

                                                    Stanza 2'

There is a place where Fear is good
and ought to abide seated majestically,
overseeing men's thoughts.
520   There is an advantage
in learning prudence under duress.
What city, and in like manner
what man * whose heart was never diverted
by fear would any longer
525   show reverence for Justice?

                                                   Stanza 3

Give approval
to a life that is neither anarchic
nor ruled by a despot.
God grants
530   mastery always to the middle way,
but his manner of surveillance differs at different times.
'Be moderate' is my advice:
truly Impiety's offspring
is Hybris,

ἐκ δ' Ὑγιείας   535
φρενῶν ὁ πᾶσιν φίλος
καὶ πολύευκτος Ὄλβος.

ἐς τὸ πᾶν σοι λέγω,   [ἀντ. γ
βωμὸν αἴδεσαι Δίκας,
μηδέ νιν   540
κέρδος ἰδὼν ἀθέῳ ποδὶ
λὰξ ἀτίσῃς· Ποινὰ γὰρ ἐπέσται.   542/3
κύριον μένει Τέλος.
πρὸς τάδε τις τοκέων σέβας   545
εὖ προτίων
καὶ ξενοτίμους
ἐπιστροφὰς δωμάτων
αἰδόμενός τις ἔστω.

ἑκὼν δ' ἀνάγκας ἄτερ δίκαιος ὢν   [στρ. δ
οὐκ ἄνολβος ἔσται,   551
πανώλεθρος <δ' >οὔποτ' ἂν γένοιτο.
τὸν ἀντίτολμον δέ φαμι παρβάδαν
ἄγοντα πολλὰ παντόφυρτ' ἄνευ δίκας
βιαίως ξὺν χρόνῳ καθήσειν   555
λαῖφος, ὅταν λάβῃ πόνος,
θραυομένας κεραίας.

καλεῖ δ' ἀκούοντας οὐδὲν <ἐν >μέσᾳ   [ἀντ. δ
δυσπαλεῖ τε δίνᾳ·
γελᾷ δὲ δαίμων ἐπ' ἀνδρὶ θερμῷ,   560
τὸν οὔποτ' αὐχοῦντ' ἰδὼν ἀμηχάνοις
δύαις λαπαδνὸν οὐδ' ὑπερθέοντ' ἄκραν·
δι' αἰῶνος δὲ τὸν πρὶν ὄλβον
ἕρματι προσβαλὼν Δίκας
ὤλετ' ἄκλαυτος, ἄιστος.   565

Αθ.   κήρυσσε, κῆρυξ, καὶ στρατὸν κατειργαθοῦ,

535 while from Health-of-mind
is born Prosperity beloved by all
and frequent object of prayer.

Stanza 3'

For all time to come, then, I tell you,
show respect for Justice's altar
540 and do not,
with an eye to profit,
dishonour it with a godless kick;
for Requital will take charge.
The appointed End awaits.
545 Therefore, let a man show reverence and honour
for parents and be
respectful to guests
and give them honourable welcome
in his home.

Stanza 4

550 And the one who is just voluntarily, not under compulsion,
will not be without prosperity,
nor will he ever be totally ruined.
But I say that the one who, by contrast, boldly
and sinfully plunders extensively without justice
555 will eventually be forced to lower
his sail when trouble overtakes him
and his ship's yard-arm is smashed.

Stanza 4'

He calls, but they do not hear him as he wrestles
in the midst of the vortex;
560 the divinity laughs at a man hot for crime,
laughs to look upon the man who, foolishly counting himself safe,
is now weak with unmanageable sufferings and cannot surmount
    the wave's crest.
Thus he lets his lifelong prosperity
strike Justice's reef
565 and perishes unlamented, unseen.

*(Enter Athena, who has made the necessary arrangements regarding jurors
and these, probably ten in number, now accompany her, along with one or
more of the usual court officials, including a Herald.)*

Ath.   Herald, make your proclamation and keep the people back

εἰς οὐρανὸν δὲ διάτορος Τυρσηνικὴ
σάλπιγξ βροτείου πνεύματος· πληρουμένη
ὑπέρτονον γήρυμα φαινέτω στρατῷ·
πληρουμένου γὰρ τοῦδε βουλευτηρίου   570
σιγᾶν ἀρήγει καὶ μαθεῖν θεσμοὺς ἐμοὺς
πόλιν τε πᾶσαν εἰς τὸν αἰανῆ χρόνον
καὶ τούσδ', ὅπως ἂν εὖ καταγνωσθῇ δίκη.

    ἄναξ Ἄπολλον, ὧν ἔχεις αὐτὸς κράτει·
τί τοῦδε σοὶ μέτεστι πράγματος λέγε.   575

Απ. καὶ μαρτυρήσων ἦλθον – ἔστι γὰρ νόμῳ
ἱκέτης ὅδ' ἀνὴρ καὶ δόμων ἐφέστιος
ἐμῶν, φόνου δὲ τῷδ' ἐγὼ καθάρσιος –
καὶ ξυνδικήσων αὐτός. αἰτίαν δ' ἔχω
τῆς τοῦδε μητρὸς τοῦ φόνου. σὺ δ' εἴσαγε   580
ὅπως <τ' >ἐπίστᾳ τήνδε κύρωσον δίκην.

Αθ. ὑμῶν ὁ μῦθος, εἰσάγω δὲ τὴν δίκην.
ὁ γὰρ διώκων πρότερος ἐξ ἀρχῆς λέγων
γένοιτ' ἂν ὀρθῶς πράγματος διδάσκαλος.

Χο. πολλαὶ μέν ἐσμεν, λέξομεν δὲ συντόμως.   585
ἔπος δ' ἀμείβου πρὸς ἔπος ἐν μέρει τιθείς·
τὴν μητέρ' εἰπὲ πρῶτον εἰ κατέκτονας.

Ορ. ἔκτεινα. τούτου δ' οὔτις ἄρνησις πέλει.

Χο. ἐν μὲν τόδ' ἤδη τῶν τριῶν παλαισμάτων.

Ορ. οὐ κειμένῳ πω τόνδε κομπάζεις λόγον.   590

Χο. εἰπεῖν γε μέντοι δεῖ σ' ὅπως κατέκτανες.

Ορ. λέγω· ξιφουλκῷ χειρὶ πρὸς δέρην τεμών.

Χο. πρὸς τοῦ δ' ἐπείσθης καὶ τίνος βουλεύμασιν;

Ορ. τοῖς τοῦδε θεσφάτοισι. μαρτυρεῖ δέ μοι.

Χο. ὁ μάντις ἐξηγεῖτό σοι μητροκτονεῖν;   595

Ορ. καὶ δεῦρό γ' ἀεὶ τὴν τύχην οὐ μέμφομαι.

Χο. ἀλλ' εἴ σε μάρψει ψῆφος, ἀλλ' ἐρεῖς τάχα.

Ορ. πέποιθ', ἀρωγὰς δ' ἐκ τάφου πέμπει πατήρ.

Χο. νεκροῖσί νυν πέπισθι μητέρα κτάνων.

and let the air-borne note of the shrill Etruscan
trumpet, filled with human breath,
make plain its high-pitched voice to the people.

     (Trumpet sounds.)

570 For while this council-chamber is being filled
it is beneficial that the whole city and *these men assembled
be silent and learn my ordinances for all time to come,
so that a just determination may be made of the case.

     (She turns to Apollo.)

My lord Apollo, exercise control over your own sphere of
  authority:

575 tell what part you have in this affair.

Ap. Indeed, I have come to testify for this man is by usage and law
a suppliant and one who came to my temple
for asylum, but I purified him from the taint of murder
and I myself will be his advocate. Yes, I take reponsibility

580 for his mother's murder. You for your part begin the proceedings
and deal authoritatively with this lawsuit as you know how to do.

     (Athena turns to the Erinyes.)

Ath. It is yours to speak – I am beginning the proceedings;
for the plaintiff, by telling the story from the beginning,
can give accurate instruction in the matter.

Cho.585 We are many, but we shall speak succinctly.

     (The Chorus-leader addresses Orestes.)

Respond by making a statement in reply to mine:
say first whether or not you killed your mother.

Or. I killed her; there is no denying this.

Cho. The first of three falls has gone to us.

Or. 590 You make a boastful statement, but I am not yet on the ground.

Cho. And yet you must say how you committed the killing.

Or. I tell you, I slit her throat with a sword held in my hand.

Cho. By whom were you persuaded, and by whose suggestion?

Or. *(points to Apollo)* By this god's oracular pronouncements – and
  he is my witness.

Cho. The prophetic god expounded to you that you kill your mother?

Or. 595 Yes, and thus far I have no complaint about what has happened to
  me.

Cho. But if the vote of condemnation catches hold of you, you'll soon
  change your story.

Or. I have confidence, and my father sends means of assistance from
  the grave.

Cho. Have confidence, then, in the dead – after killing your mother!

Ορ.   δυοῖν γὰρ εἶχε προσβολὰς μιασμάτοιν.   600
Χο.   πῶς δή; δίδαξον τοὺς δικάζοντας τάδε.
Ορ.   ἀνδροκτονοῦσα πατέρ' ἐμὸν κατέκτανε.
Χο.   τί γάρ; σὺ μὲν ζῇς, ἡ δ' ἐλευθέρα φόνῳ.
Ορ.   τί δ' οὐκ ἐκείνην ζῶσαν ἤλαυνες φυγῇ;
Χο.   οὐκ ἦν ὅμαιμος φωτὸς ὃν κατέκτανεν.   605
Ορ.   ἐγὼ δὲ μητρὸς τῆς ἐμῆς ἐν αἵματι;
Χο.   πῶς γάρ σ' ἔθρεψεν ἐντός, ὦ μιαιφόνε,
        ζώνης; ἀπεύχῃ μητρὸς αἷμα φίλτατον;
Ορ.   ἤδη σὺ μαρτύρησον, ἐξηγοῦ δέ μοι,
        Ἄπολλον, εἴ σφε σὺν δίκῃ κατέκτανον.   610
        δρᾶσαι γάρ, ὥσπερ ἔστιν, οὐκ ἀρνούμεθα·
        ἀλλ' εἰ δίκαιον εἴτε μὴ τῇ σῇ φρενὶ
        δοκεῖ τόδ' αἷμα, κρῖνον, ὡς τούτοις φράσω.
Απ.   λέξω πρὸς ὑμᾶς, τόνδ' Ἀθηναίας μέγαν
        θεσμόν, δικαίως, μάντις ὢν δ' οὐ ψεύσομαι.   615
        οὐπώποτ' εἶπον μαντικοῖσιν ἐν θρόνοις,
        οὐκ ἀνδρός, οὐ γυναικός, οὐ πόλεως πέρι,
        ὃ μὴ κελεύσαι Ζεὺς Ὀλυμπίων πατήρ.
        τὸ μὲν δίκαιον τοῦθ' ὅσον σθένει μάθε.
        βουλῇ πιφαύσκω δ' ὕμμ' ἐπισπέσθαι πατρός.   620
        ὅρκος γὰρ οὔτι Ζηνὸς ἰσχύει πλέον.
Χο.   Ζεύς, ὡς λέγεις σύ, τόνδε χρησμὸν ὤπασε
        φράζειν Ὀρέστῃ τῷδε, τὸν πατρὸς φόνον
        πράξαντα μητρὸς μηδαμοῦ τιμὰς νέμειν;
Απ.   οὐ γάρ τι ταὐτὸν ἄνδρα γενναῖον θανεῖν   625
        διοσδότοις σκήπτροισι τιμαλφούμενον,
        καὶ ταῦτα πρὸς γυναικός, οὔ τι θουρίοις
        τόξοις ἐκηβόλοισιν ὥστ' Ἀμαζόνος,
        ἀλλ' ὡς ἀκούσῃ, Παλλάς, οἵ τ' ἐφήμενοι
        ψήφῳ διαιρεῖν τοῦδε πράγματος πέρι.   630
        ἀπὸ στρατείας γάρ νιν † ἠμποληκότα †
        τὰ πλεῖστ' ἄμεινον εὔφροσιν δεδεγμένη
        † δροίτῃ περῶντι λουτρὰ κἀπὶ τέρματι †
        φᾶρος περεσκήνωσεν, ἐν δ' ἀτέρμονι

Or.	I did it because she was afflicted by a double defilement.
Cho.	How so? You'd better instruct the jurors of your meaning.
Or.	She killed her husband, and the man she killed was my father.
Cho.	But consider this: you are still alive, while death has absolved her.
Or.	Well, why didn't you hound her down by pursuing her when she was still alive?
Cho.	She was no blood relation of the man she killed.
Or.	And am I then my mother's child by blood?
Cho.	How otherwise did she nourish you in her womb, you foul murderer? Do you abjure your mother's dearest blood?

Or. (*appeals to Apollo*) Now testify, and expound for me,
610   Apollo, whether I killed her with justice.
For that I did the deed, as is the case, I do not deny;
but whether this bloodshed seems to your way of thinking to have been just or not,
decide, so that I may tell these men.

Ap. (*addresses the jury directly*) I shall tell you, the court set up by Athena's great
615   ordinance – it was done justly. I am a prophet and shall not lie.
Never on any occasion did I speak from my prophetic throne, concerning man or woman or city,
what Zeus, father of Olympians, did not command me to say.
Understand, then, how strong this justice is.
620   I bid you to attend to the will of the father,
for an oath does not have any greater strength than Zeus.

Cho. Did Zeus, as you allege, bestow the utterance of this oracle
to Orestes here, that in exacting the penalty of his father's murder,
he should totally ignore his mother's claims?

Ap. Certainly, for it is not by any means the same thing when a man dies, one of noble birth
and honoured because of his royal, god-given authority –
and that at his wife's hands, and not by the furious
far-ranging arrows of some Amazon,
but in the way that you will hear, Pallas, and those seated
630   here to decide about this matter by vote.
As he was returning from the expedition after * trafficking
for the most part successfully, she, receiving him with cheerful ...
as he was finishing in the bath and at the end
she covered him round with a cloth and in the endless

κόπτει πεδήσασ' ἄνδρα δαιδάλῳ πέπλῳ.   635
ἀνδρὸς μὲν ὑμῖν οὗτος εἴρηται μόρος
τοῦ παντοσέμνου, τοῦ στρατηλάτου νεῶν·
ταύτην τοιαύτην εἶπον, ὡς δηχθῇ λεώς,
ὅσπερ τέτακται τήνδε κυρῶσαι δίκην.

Χο. πατρὸς προτιμᾷ Ζεὺς μόρον τῷ σῷ λόγῳ,   640
αὐτὸς δ' ἔδησε πατέρα πρεσβύτην Κρόνον·
πῶς ταῦτα τούτοις οὐκ ἐναντίως λέγεις;
ὑμᾶς δ' ἀκούειν ταῦτ' ἐγὼ μαρτύρομαι.

Απ. ὦ παντομισῆ κνώδαλα, στύγη θεῶν,
πέδας μὲν ἂν λύσειεν, ἔστι τοῦδ' ἄκος   645
καὶ κάρτα πολλὴ μηχανὴ λυτήριος·
ἀνδρὸς δ' ἐπειδὰν αἷμ' ἀνασπάσῃ κόνις
ἅπαξ θανόντος, οὔτις ἔστ' ἀνάστασις.
τούτων ἐπῳδὰς οὐκ ἐποίησεν πατὴρ
οὑμός, τὰ δ' ἄλλα πάντ' ἄνω τε καὶ κάτω   650
στρέφων τίθησιν οὐδὲν ἀσθμαίνων μένει.

Χο. πῶς γὰρ τὸ φεύγειν τοῦδ' ὑπερδικεῖς ὅρα·
τὸ μητρὸς αἷμ' ὅμαιμον ἐκχέας πέδοι
ἔπειτ' ἐν Ἄργει δώματ' οἰκήσει πατρός;
ποίοισι βωμοῖς χρώμενος τοῖς δημίοις;   655
ποία δὲ χέρνιψ φρατέρων πρόσδεξεται;

Απ. καὶ τοῦτο λέξω, καὶ μάθ' ὡς ὀρθῶς ἐρῶ·
οὐκ ἔστι μήτηρ ἡ κεκλημένη τέκνου
τοκεύς, τροφὸς δὲ κύματος νεοσπόρου·
τίκτει δ' ὁ θρῴσκων, ἡ δ' ἅπερ ξένῳ ξένη   660
ἔσωσεν ἔρνος, οἷσι μὴ βλάψῃ θεός.
τεκμήριον δὲ τοῦδέ σοι δείξω λόγου·
πατὴρ μὲν ἂν γείναιτ' ἄνευ μητρός· πέλας
μάρτυς πάρεστι παῖς Ὀλυμπίου Διός,
οὐκ ἐν σκότοισι νηδύος τεθραμμένη,   665
ἀλλ' οἷον ἔρνος οὔτις ἂν τέκοι θεά.
ἐγὼ δέ, Παλλάς, τἄλλα θ' ὡς ἐπίσταμαι
      <   >
τὸ σὸν πόλισμα καὶ στρατὸν τεύξω μέγαν·

635   folds of the embroidered robe she fettered her husband and
        struck.
    This death has been narrated to you of a man
    totally august, commander of a fleet.
    Such a speech I have made in order that the people, whose task it
        is
    to deal authoritatively with this case, might be stung to action.

Cho.   According to your argument, Zeus has preferential regard for a
        father's death,
    but he himself bound his aged father, Kronos:
    can you deny that this contradicts your recent argument?
    (*The Chorus-leader turns to the jury.*)
    I call upon you, jurors, as witnesses that you hear this.

Ap.   O beasts completely hateful, objects of loathing to the gods,
645   one can unlock fetters – there is a remedy for this
    and a great range of devices to undo the wrong;
    but once a man has died and the dust draws in
    his blood, for him there is no resurrection.
    To achieve this my father did not fashion any spells,
650   even though all other things he can turn upside down
    at will, and not even pant from the exertion.

Cho.   In that case be careful how you plead for this man's acquittal;
    after spilling to the ground his mother's kindred blood,
    will he then dwell within his father's halls at Argos?
655   What public altars could he use?
    What purifying water of his brotherhood will accept him?

Ap.   I will tell you this also, and note how correctly I shall speak.
    The mother so-called is not the child's
    begetter, but only nurse of the new-sown embryo;
660   the one who mounts, the male, engenders, whereas *she*, unrelated,
        merely preserves the shoot
    for one unrelated to her, unless some heaven-sent miscarriage
        occurs.
    I shall show you a proof of this assertion:
    a father could give birth without a mother; near to hand
    there is one to bear witness – the daughter of Olympian Zeus,
665   who was not nurtured in a womb's darkness
    but is the kind of shoot that no goddess could give birth to.
    (*He turns to Athena.*)
    * Pallas, both in other respects as I know how, I ...
    shall make your city and its people great;

καὶ τόνδ' ἔπεμψα σῶν δόμων ἐφέστιον,
ὅπως γένοιτο πιστὸς ἐς τὸ πᾶν χρόνου.   670
καὶ τόνδ' ἐπικτήσαιο σύμμαχον, θεά,
καὶ τοὺς ἔπειτα, καὶ τάδ' αἰανῶς μένοι,
στέργειν τὰ πιστὰ τῶνδε τοὺς ἐπισπόρους.

Αθ.   ἤδη κελεύω τούσδ' ἀπὸ γνώμης φέρειν
ψῆφον δικαίαν, ὡς ἅλις λελεγμένων;   675

Απ.   ἡμῖν μὲν ἤδη πᾶν τετόξευται βέλος,
μένω δ' ἀκοῦσαι πῶς ἀγὼν κριθήσεται.

Αθ.   τί γάρ; πρὸς ὑμῶν πῶς τιθεῖσ' ἄμομφος ὦ;

Χο.   ἠκούσαθ' ὧν ἠκούσατ', ἐν δὲ καρδίᾳ
ψῆφον φέροντες ὅρκον αἰδεῖσθε, ξένοι.   680

Αθ.   κλύοιτ' ἂν ἤδη θεσμόν, Ἀττικὸς λεώς,
πρώτας δίκας κρίνοντες αἵματος χυτοῦ.
ἔσται δὲ καὶ τὸ λοιπὸν Αἰγέως στρατῷ
αἰεὶ δικαστῶν τοῦτο βουλευτήριον.
πάγον δ' Ἄρειον τόνδ', Ἀμαζόνων ἕδραν   685
σκηνάς θ', ὅτ' ἦλθον Θησέως κατὰ φθόνον
στρατηλατοῦσαι, καὶ πόλιν νεόπτολιν
τήνδ' ὑψίπυργον ἀντεπύργωσαν τότε,
Ἄρει δ' ἔθυον, ἔνθεν ἔστ' ἐπώνυμος
πέτρα πάγος τ' Ἄρειος· ἐν δὲ τῷ σέβας   690
ἀστῶν φόβος τε ξυγγενὴς τὸ μὴ ἀδικεῖν
σχήσει τό τ' ἦμαρ καὶ κατ' εὐφρόνην ὁμῶς,
αὐτῶν πολιτῶν μὴ 'πικαινούντων νόμους·
κακαῖς ἐπιρροαῖσι βορβόρῳ θ' ὕδωρ
λαμπρὸν μιαίνων οὔποθ' εὑρήσεις ποτόν.   695
τὸ μήτ' ἄναρχον μήτε δεσποτούμενον
ἀστοῖς περιστέλλουσι βουλεύω σέβειν,
καὶ μὴ τὸ δεινὸν πᾶν πόλεως ἔξω βαλεῖν·
τίς γὰρ δεδοικὼς μηδὲν ἔνδικος βροτῶν;
τοιόνδε τοι ταρβοῦντες ἐνδίκως σέβας   700
ἔρυμά τε χώρας καὶ πόλεως σωτήριον
ἔχοιτ' ἂν οἷον οὔτις ἀνθρώπων ἔχει,
οὔτ' ἐν Σκύθῃσιν οὔτε Πέλοπος ἐν τόποις.

	in fact, I sent this man (*he motions to Orestes*) to be a suppliant at your temple,
70	that he might be a trusted friend for all time to come
	and so that you might acquire him as an ally, goddess,
	and those who come after, and that this might endure everlastingly,
	namely, that their descendants cherish the pledges of trust.
Ath.	Am I now to command these jurors to cast a just vote
75	in accordance with their judgement, on grounds that the arguments have been sufficient?
Ap.	All our bolts have already been shot,
	but I am waiting to hear how the contest will be decided.
Ath.	(*She turns to the Chorus-leader.*)
	Well, then, what can I do to escape your blame?
Cho.	(*Ignoring her, but turning to the jury.*)
	You heard what you heard and, as you cast your votes,
680	show respect in your hearts for the oath, strangers.
Ath.	Hear now my ordinance, people of Athens,
	as you decide this first lawsuit for shed blood.
	There will always exist, even in future time, for Aegeus' people
	this deliberative council of jurors;
85	this "Areopagus" hill, the Amazons' position
	and camp, when they came because of a grudge against Theseus,
	leading an attacking army and at that time raised up
	this new city and built its opposing ramparts high –
	they sacrificed to Ares, and for that reason the rock and hill
90	are called after him "Ares'." Reverence for this court
	by the citizens and an in-born fear will deter them
	from criminal acts, both by day and night alike,
	so long as the citizens themselves make no innovations in the laws;
	if by evil in-pourings and mud
95	you pollute bright water, you'll never find a drink.
	I counsel my citizens to cherish and revere
	neither anarchy nor despotism
	and not to expel fear entirely from the city,
	for what man who fears nothing can be just?
00	If you manifest a just fear toward such a reverend body,
	you would have a bastion to bring safety to the land and city
	such as no one on earth possesses,
	neither among the Scythians nor in the Peloponnese.

κερδῶν ἄθικτον τοῦτο βουλευτήριον,
αἰδοῖον, ὀξύθυμον, εὑδόντων ὕπερ   705
ἐγρηγορὸς φρούρημα γῆς καθίσταμαι.

    ταύτην μὲν ἐξέτειν' ἐμοῖς παραίνεσιν
ἀστοῖσιν ἐς τὸ λοιπόν· ὀρθοῦσθαι δὲ χρὴ
καὶ ψῆφον αἴρειν καὶ διαγνῶναι δίκαν
αἰδουμένους τὸν ὅρκον. εἴρηται λόγος.   710

Χο.   καὶ μὴν βαρεῖαν τήνδ' ὁμιλίαν χθονὸς
ξύμβουλός εἰμι μηδαμῶς ἀτιμάσαι.

Απ.   κἄγωγε χρησμοὺς τοὺς ἐμούς τε καὶ Διὸς
ταρβεῖν κελεύω μηδ' ἀκαρπώτους κτίσαι.

Χο.   ἀλλ' αἱματηρὰ πράγματ' οὐ λαχὼν σέβεις,   715
μαντεῖα δ' οὐκέθ' ἁγνὰ μαντεύσῃ νέμων.

Απ.   ἦ καὶ πατήρ τι σφάλλεται βουλευμάτων
πρωτοκτόνοισι προστροπαῖς Ἰξίονος;

Χο.   λέγεις· ἐγὼ δὲ μὴ τυχοῦσα τῆς δίκης
βαρεῖα χώρᾳ τῇδ' ὁμιλήσω πάλιν.   720

Απ.   ἀλλ' ἔν τε τοῖς νέοισι καὶ παλαιτέροις
θεοῖς ἄτιμος εἶ σύ· νικήσω δ' ἐγώ.

Χο.   τοιαῦτ' ἔδρασας καὶ Φέρητος ἐν δόμοις·
Μοίρας ἔπεισας ἀφθίτους θεῖναι βροτούς.

Απ.   οὔκουν δίκαιον τὸν σέβοντ' εὐεργετεῖν,   725
ἄλλως τε πάντως χὤτε δεόμενος τύχοι;

Χο.   σύ τοι παλαιὰς διανομὰς καταφθίσας
οἴνῳ παρηπάτησας ἀρχαίας θεάς.

Απ.   σύ τοι τάχ' οὐκ ἔχουσα τῆς δίκης τέλος
ἐμῇ τὸν ἰὸν οὐδὲν ἐχθροῖσιν βαρύν.   730

Χο.   ἐπεὶ καθιππάζῃ με πρεσβῦτιν νέος,
δίκης γενέσθαι τῆσδ' ἐπήκοος μένω,

I establish this deliberative council to be uncorrupted by thought
    of profit,

705   worthy of respect, quick to wrath, on behalf of those who sleep
an ever-wakeful guard-post of the land.
This rather lengthy advice I have given to my
citizens for the future, but now

        (*She beckons to the jurymen.*)
           you must arise,
take a pebble and decide the case,

710   showing respect for the oath. My speech is finished.

(*The jurors stand up and proceed to the table on which are placed two
urns [cf. v. 742], one to receive votes of condemnation, the other of
acquittal. Possibly one juror casts his vote after each of the couplets
which follow.*)

Ch-L.   (*to the jurors*) Indeed, I advise you not to make our visitation to
        the country oppressive
by dishonouring us in any way.

Ap.   And I bid you fear my oracles and Zeus'
and not make them fruitless.

Cho.   (*to Apollo*) But you reverence deeds of blood, though not within
        your allotted office,
and the oracles you assign when you prophesy will no longer be
        holy.

Ap.   Oh, I suppose the plans of father Zeus went awry
at the time when Ixion supplicated him for the primal slaying?

Cho.   You say so, but if I don't win the case

720   I shall be an oppressive visitor to this land in future.

Ap.   But both among the young and elder
gods you are without honour; I shall win.

Cho.   That's exactly what you did in Pheres' palace, too:
you persuaded the Fates to make men immortal.

Ap.   Wasn't it right for me to do a good turn to that pious man,
especially when he happened to be in such need?

Cho.   You destroyed age-old arrangements
and led ancient goddesses astray with wine.

Ap.   And you will soon, if you do not get total victory in the suit,

730   vomit out your poison – but one not at all oppressive to your
        enemies.

Cho.   Since you, youngster, ride roughshod over me your elder,
I am waiting to hear the judgement,

ὡς ἀμφίβουλος οὖσα θυμοῦσθαι πόλει.

Αθ. ἐμὸν τόδ' ἔργον, λοισθίαν κρῖναι δίκην·
ψῆφον δ' Ὀρέστῃ τήνδ' ἐγὼ προσθήσομαι· 735
μήτηρ γὰρ οὔτις ἐστὶν ἥ μ' ἐγείνατο,
τὸ δ' ἄρσεν αἰνῶ πάντα, πλὴν γάμου τυχεῖν,
ἅπαντι θυμῷ, κάρτα δ' εἰμὶ τοῦ πατρός.
οὕτω γυναικὸς οὐ προτιμήσω μόρον
ἄνδρα κτανούσης δωμάτων ἐπίσκοπον. 740
νικᾷ δ' Ὀρέστης κἂν ἰσόψηφος κριθῇ.
ἐκβάλλεθ' ὡς τάχιστα τευχέων πάλους,
ὅσοις δικαστῶν τοῦτ' ἐπέσταλται τέλος.

Ορ. ὦ Φοῖβ' Ἄπολλον, πῶς ἀγὼν κριθήσεται;
Χο. ὦ Νύξ, μέλαινα μῆτερ, ἆρ' ὁρᾷς τάδε; 745
Ορ. νῦν ἀγχόνης μοι τέρματ', ἢ φάος βλέπειν.
Χο. ἡμῖν γὰρ ἔρρειν, ἢ πρόσω τιμὰς ἔχειν·
πεμπάζετ' ὀρθῶς ἐκβολὰς ψήφων, ξένοι,
τὸ μὴ ἀδικεῖν σέβοντες ἐν διαιρέσει.

Ορ. γνώμης δ' ἀπούσης πῆμα γίγνεται μέγα, 750
πεσόντα τ' οἶκον ψῆφος ὤρθωσεν μία.

Αθ. ἀνὴρ ὅδ' ἐκπέφευγεν αἵματος δίκην·
ἴσον γάρ ἐστι τἀρίθμημα τῶν πάλων.

Ορ. ὦ Παλλάς, ὦ σώσασα τοὺς ἐμοὺς δόμους,
γαίας πατρῴας ἐστερημένον σύ τοι 755
κατῴκισάς με. καί τις Ἑλλήνων ἐρεῖ
Ἀργεῖος ἀνὴρ αὖθις, ἔν τε χρήμασιν
οἰκεῖ πατρῴοις, Παλλάδος καὶ Λοξίου
ἕκατι καὶ τοῦ πάντα κραίνοντος τρίτου
Σωτῆρος· – ὃς πατρῷον αἰδεσθεὶς μόρον 760
σῴζει με, μητρὸς τάσδε συνδίκους ὁρῶν.
ἐγὼ δὲ χώρᾳ τῇδε καὶ τῷ σῷ στρατῷ
τὸ λοιπὸν εἰς ἅπαντα πλειστήρη χρόνον

	for I am in doubt whether to be angry towards the city.
Ath.	It is my function to judge the case last –

(She holds up her pebble.)

735 and I shall add this vote for Orestes' benefit,
for there is no mother who gave birth to me
and I approve the male principle in all things and with all my
    heart
– except in the matter of marriage, and am very much my father's
    child.
740 So I shall not have preferential regard for the death of a woman
who killed her husband, the overseer of the household.
Orestes wins, even if his case is decided with equality of votes.

(She turns and addresses the jurymen.)

Turn out with all speed the ballots from the urns
you of the jurors to whom this function has been assigned.

(The counting begins.)

Or.	O Phoebus Apollo, how will the contest be decided?
Ch.-L.	O black Night my mother, can you see what's going on?
Or.	The end for me now is hanging, or to look upon the light.
Cho.	And for us to go to perdition, or continue hereafter in possession of honours.

(Athena proceeds to the spot where the urns have been turned out, to verify the count.)

Make sure to count correctly the votes cast, strangers,
reverencing the principle of justice in your division of them.

Or.	When a vote for acquittal is lacking, great misery occurs, and when a house has fallen, a single vote can set it up again.

(After examining the votes Athena, in her capacity as presiding magistrate, announces the verdict.)

Ath.	This man has been acquitted in the trial for bloodshed, for the number of votes is equal.
Or.	O Pallas, who saved my house,

755 you have re-settled me in the land of my fathers
of which I had been deprived. And some Greek will say,
"This man is an Argive again, and he dwells in his ancestral
property, thanks to Pallas and Loxias
and the Third, who guarantees all,
760 Zeus Saviour." He, out of respect for a father's death,
keeps me safe, as he looks upon these female advocates of my
    mother.
But to this land and with your people
for all the fulness of time to come

ὁρκωμοτήσας νῦν ἄπειμι πρὸς δόμους,
μή τοί τιν' ἄνδρα δεῦρο πρυμνήτην χθονὸς   765
ἐλθόντ' ἐποίσειν εὖ κεκασμένον δόρυ.
αὐτοὶ γὰρ ἡμεῖς ὄντες ἐν τάφοις τότε
τοῖς τἀμὰ παρβαίνουσι νῦν ὀρκώματα
† ἀμηχάνοισι πράξομεν δυσπραξίαις †
ὁδοὺς ἀθύμους καὶ παρόρνιθας πόρους   770
τιθέντες, ὡς αὐτοῖσι μεταμέλῃ πόνου·
ὀρθουμένοις δὲ καὶ πόλιν τὴν Παλλάδος
τιμῶσιν ἀεὶ τήνδε συμμάχῳ δορὶ
αὐτοὶ σφιν ἡμεῖς ἐσμεν εὐμενέστεροι.

    καὶ χαῖρε καὶ σὺ καὶ πολισσοῦχος λεώς·   775
πάλαισμ' ἄφυκτον τοῖς ἐναντίοις ἔχοις,
σωτήριόν τε καὶ δορὸς νικηφόρον.

Χο.   ἰὼ θεοὶ νεώτεροι, παλαιοὺς νόμους   [στρ. α
        καθιππάσασθε κἀκ χερῶν εἵλεσθέ μου·
        ἐγὼ δ' ἄτιμος ἁ τάλαινα βαρύκοτος   780
        ἐν γᾷ τᾷδε, φεῦ,
        ἰὸν ἰὸν ἀντιπενθῆ μεθεῖσα καρδίας
        χθονὶ σταλαγμὸν
        ἄφορον, ἐκ δὲ τοῦ
        λειχὴν ἄφυλλος ἄτεκνος, ὦ Δίκα Δίκα,   785
        πέδον ἐπισύμενος
        βροτοφθόρους κηλῖδας ἐν χώρᾳ βαλεῖ.
        στενάζω· τί ῥέξω;
        γελῶμαι· δύσοιστ' ἐν
        πολίταις ἔπαθον.   790
        ἰὼ μεγάλατοι
        κόραι δυστυχεῖς
        Νυκτὸς ἀτιμοπενθεῖς.

Λθ.   ἐμοὶ πίθεσθε μὴ βαρυστόνως φέρειν·
        οὐ γὰρ νενίκησθ', ἀλλ' ἰσόψηφος δίκη   795
        ἐξῆλθ' ἀληθῶς οὐκ ἀτιμίᾳ σέθεν·

I swear an oath now, before returning home,
765 that never shall any steersman of my land
come against you as leader of a formidable band of spearmen.
For I myself, though then in my grave,
on any who transgress my present oaths
* shall wreak horrible catastrophes by making
770 their journey hither dispirited and ill-omened,
so that they regret the effort they have made;
but if they keep their oaths and continuously honour
this city of Pallas with an army bound by alliance,
I myself am favourably disposed to them.
775 And so farewell to you and to the city's people;
may you hold your enemies in a wrestling-grip with no escape,
one that brings salvation and in battle victory.

(Orestes exits by the audience's left-hand, i.e. the eastern, parodos. Possibly Apollo accompanies him.)

Third Choral Ode

Stanza 1

Cho.   O younger gods, you have ridden roughshod
over ancient laws and snatched the prey from my hands.
780 But I am dishonoured and miserable and oppressively angry
in this land – oh ! –
as I emit my heart's poison, a poison in payment for grief,
trickling in drops to the ground,
unbearable, and from it
785 blight killing crops, killing children; O Justice Justice,
rapidly assaulting the soil
will fling deadly plague-spots in the land.
I groan. What should I do?
I am being mocked. I was treated
790 intolerably by the citizens.
How greatly afflicted are we,
the ill-fated maiden daughters
of Night, dishonoured and full of grief.

Ath.   Take my advice: do not bear it with such heavy groans !
795 It was not a defeat for you, but a true outcome of a trial
in which the votes were equal, no dishonour to you;

ie if not for Aa, they would have won – and (overleaf) Zeus + Ap were on Or's side

ἀλλ' ἐκ Διὸς γὰρ λαμπρὰ μαρτύρια παρῆν,
αὐτός θ' ὁ χρήσας αὐτὸς ἦν ὁ μαρτυρῶν
ὡς ταῦτ' Ὀρέστην δρῶντα μὴ βλάβας ἔχειν.
ὑμεῖς δὲ μήτε τῇδε γῇ βαρὺν κότον   800
σκήψητε, μὴ θυμοῦσθε, μηδ' ἀκαρπίαν
τεύξητ' ἀφεῖσαι † δαιμόνων † σταλάγματα,
βρωτῆρας αἰχμὰς σπερμάτων ἀνημέρους.
ἐγὼ γὰρ ὑμῖν πανδίκως ὑπίσχομαι
ἕδρας τε καὶ κευθμῶνας ἐνδίκου χθονὸς   805
λιπαραθρόνοισιν ἡμένας ἐπ' ἐσχάρας
ἕξειν ὑπ' ἀστῶν τῶνδε τιμαλφουμένας.

Χο.   ἰὼ θεοὶ νεώτεροι, παλαιοὺς   [ἀντ. α
           καθιππάσασθε κἀκ χερῶν εἵλεσθέ μου·
           ἐγὼ δ' ἄτιμος ἁ τάλαινα βαρύκοτος   810
           ἐν γᾷ τᾷδε, φεῦ,
           ἰὸν ἰὸν ἀντιπενθῆ μεθεῖσα καρδίας
           χθονὶ σταλαγμὸν
           ἄφορον, ἐκ δὲ τοῦ
           λειχὴν ἄφυλλος ἄτεκνος, ὦ Δίκα Δίκα,   815
           πέδον ἐπισύμενος
           βροτοφθόρους κηλῖδας ἐν χώρᾳ βαλεῖ.
           στενάζω· τί ῥέξω;
           γελῶμαι· δύσοιστ' ἐν
           πολίταις ἔπαθον.   820
           ἰὼ μεγάλατοι
           κόραι δυστυχεῖς
           Νυκτὸς ἀτιμοπενθεῖς.

Ἀθ.   οὐκ ἔστ' ἄτιμοι, μηδ' ὑπερθύμως ἄγαν
      θεαὶ βροτῶν κτίσητε δύσκηλον χθόνα.   825
      κἀγὼ πέποιθα Ζηνί, καὶ τί δεῖ λέγειν;
      καὶ κλῇδας οἶδα δώματος μόνη θεῶν
      ἐν ᾧ κεραυνός ἐστιν ἐσφραγισμένος.
      ἀλλ' οὐδὲν αὐτοῦ δεῖ. σὺ δ' εὐπιθὴς ἐμοὶ

the reason was, Zeus was the source of the shining clear testimony
and the very one who prophesied was the one himself testifying
that Orestes, although he did the deed, should not be harmed.

800 And you for your part do not hurl your oppressive anger
against this land, nor continue in anger, nor create
sterility of crops by emitting (...) drops,
savage lances that devour seeds.
For I promise you with total justice that you will have
805 a place to settle in the recesses of this just land,
enthroned at lustrous hearths
and receiving full honours from these citizens.

*compromise/
reward*

Stanza 1

Cho. O younger male gods, you rode roughshod
over ancient laws and snatched the prey from my hands.
810 But I am dishonoured and miserable and oppressively angry
in this land – oh ! –
as I emit my heart's poison, a poison in payment for grief,
trickling in drops to the ground,
unbearable, and from it
815 blight killing crops, killing children, O Justice Justice,
rapidly assaulting the soil
will fling deadly plague-spots in the land.
I groan. What should I do?
I am being mocked. I was treated
820 intolerably by the citizens.
How greatly afflicted are we,
the ill-fated maiden daughters
of Night, dishonoured and full of grief.

Ath. You are not dishonoured, and do not in an excess of anger,
825 goddesses, put the land of these mortals beyond cure.
I also place my trust in Zeus – what need to say this explicitly? –
and I alone of the gods know the keys of the chamber
in which his thunderbolt is safely sealed.
But no need of that. Let me persuade you:

*double-edged
she's not stupid!*

γλώσσης ματαίας μὴ 'κβάλῃς ἔπη χθονί,   830
καρπὸν φέροντα πάντα μὴ πράσσειν καλῶς.
κοίμα κελαινοῦ κύματος πικρὸν μένος,
ὡς σεμνότιμος καὶ ξυνοικήτωρ ἐμοί.
πολλῆς δὲ χώρας τῆσδε τἀκροθίνια
θύη πρὸ παίδων καὶ γαμηλίου τέλους   835
ἔχουσ' ἐς αἰεῖ τόνδ' ἐπαινέσεις λόγον.

Χο.   ἐμὲ παθεῖν τάδε, φεῦ,   [στρ. β
        ἐμὲ παλαιόφρονα κατά τε γᾶν οἰκεῖν,
        ἀτίετον μύσος· (φεῦ)
        πνέω τοι μένος <θ' >ἅπαντά τε κότον·   840
        οἰοῖ δᾶ, φεῦ·
        τίς μ' ὑποδύεται
        πλευρὰς ὀδύνα;
        ἄιε μᾶτερ Νύξ·
        ἀπό με γὰρ τιμᾶν   845
        δαναιᾶν θεῶν
        δυσπάλαμοι παρ' οὐδὲν ἦραν δόλοι.

Αθ.   ὀργὰς ξυνοίσω σοι· γεραιτέρα γὰρ εἶ,
[καίτοι μὲν σὺ κάρτ' ἐμοῦ σοφωτέρα]
φρονεῖν δὲ κἀμοὶ Ζεὺς ἔδωκεν οὐ κακῶς.   850
ὑμεῖς δ' ἐς ἀλλόφυλον ἐλθοῦσαι χθόνα
γῆς τῆσδ' ἐρασθήσεσθε. προυννέπω τάδε·
οὑπιρρέων γὰρ τιμιώτερος χρόνος
ἔσται πολίταις τοῖσδε, καὶ σὺ τιμίαν
ἕδραν ἔχουσα πρὸς δόμοις Ἐρεχθέως   855
τεύξῃ παρ' ἀνδρῶν καὶ γυναικείων στόλων
ὅσ' ἂν παρ' ἄλλων οὔποτ' ἂν σχέθοις βροτῶν.
σὺ δ' ἐν τόποισι τοῖς ἐμοῖσι μὴ βάλῃς
μήθ' αἱματηρὰς θηγάνας, σπλάγχνων βλάβας
νέων, ἀοίνοις ἐμμανεῖς θυμώμασιν,   860
μήτ' ἐξελοῦσ' ὡς καρδίαν ἀλεκτόρων
ἐν τοῖς ἐμοῖς ἀστοῖσιν ἱδρύσῃς, Ἄρη

830   do not from a foolish tongue fling at the land words
that bear fruit of total disaster for all things.
Lull to sleep the black wave's sharp force,
aware that you are held in honour and co-resident with me.
As you eternally receive this vast country's firstfruits,
835   sacrificial offerings on behalf of children and the rite of marriage,
you will approve this speech I've made.

Stanza 2

Cho.   That I should have such treatment – Oh ! –
for all my wisdom and years, and take up residence in the land
is an affront to my honour, a defilement. Oh !
840   See how I breathe force and total anger.
Oh ! Ah !
What is this pain that seeps into
and fills me?
Hear, mother Night !
845   I was no match for the gods' tricks:
they undid me, stripped from me
my ancient honours.

Ath.   I shall bear with your rages for you are older,
[and yet you, very wiser than I]
850   though to me also Zeus has granted some good sense.
If you go to some foreign land
you will grow passionately fond of this country. I tell you this
       solemnly;
for time in its forward flow will bring ever greater honours
to these citizens, and you will have an honourable
855   place close to the palace of Erechtheus,
and you shall obtain from men and companies of women
such honours as you never would have from any other mortals.
But you must neither cast within my territory
incitements to bloodshed, such as do damage
860   to young men's guts by maddening them with a kind of drunken
      rage
nor take out and fix in my citizens
the heart as it were of fighting cocks, a war-spirit

ἐμφύλιόν τε καὶ πρὸς ἀλλήλους θρασύν.
ἐνοικίου δ' ὄρνιθος οὐ λέγω μάχην·   866
θυραῖος ἔστω πόλεμος, † οὐ μόλις παρών   864
ἐν ᾧ † τίς ἐστι δεινὸς εὐκλείας ἔρως.   865
    τοιαῦθ' ἑλέσθαι σοι πάρεστιν ἐξ ἐμοῦ,   867
εὖ δρῶσαν, εὖ πάσχουσαν, εὖ τιμωμένην
χώρας μετασχεῖν τῆσδε θεοφιλεστάτης.

Χο.   ἐμὲ παθεῖν τάδε, φεῦ,   [ἀντ. β
            ἐμὲ παλαιόφρονα κατά τε γᾶν οἰκεῖν,   871
            ἀτίετον μύσος· (φεῦ)
            πνέω τοι μένος < θ' >ἅπαντά τε κότον·
            οἰοῖ δᾶ, φεῦ·
            τίς μ' ὑποδύεται   875
            πλευρὰς ὀδύνα;
            ἄιε μᾶτερ Νύξ·
            ἀπό με γὰρ τιμᾶν
            δαναιᾶν θεῶν
            δυσπάλαμοι παρ' οὐδὲν ἦραν δόλοι.   880

Αθ.   οὔτοι καμοῦμαί σοι λέγουσα τἀγαθά,
       ὡς μήποτ' εἴπῃς πρὸς νεωτέρας ἐμοῦ
       θεὸς παλαιὰ καὶ πολισσούχων βροτῶν
       ἄτιμος ἔρρειν τοῦδ' ἀπόξενος πέδου.
       ἀλλ' εἰ μὲν ἁγνόν ἐστί σοι Πειθοῦς σέβας,   885
       γλώσσης ἐμῆς μείλιγμα καὶ θελκτήριον,
       σὺ δ' οὖν μένοις ἄν· εἰ δὲ μὴ θέλεις μένειν,
       οὔ τἂν δικαίως τῇδ' ἐπιρρέποις πόλει
       μῆνίν τιν' ἢ κότον τιν' ἢ βλάβην στρατῷ·
       ἔξεστι γάρ σοι τῆσδε γαμόρῳ χθονὸς   890
       εἶναι δικαίως ἐς τὸ πᾶν τιμωμένῃ.
Χο.   ἄνασσ' Ἀθάνα, τίνα με φὴς ἔχειν ἕδραν;
Αθ.   πάσης ἀπήμον' οἰζύος· δέχου δὲ σύ.
Χο.   καὶ δὴ δέδεγμαι· τίς δέ μοι τιμὴ μένει;
Αθ.   ὡς μή τιν' οἶκον εὐθενεῖν ἄνευ σέθεν.   895

inbred and a boldness against kin.
866) For I say there is no place for a domestic cock-fight !
864) Let whatever war there is be foreign, and * that comes easily
865) when one feels a terrible passion for renown.
    Such, then, is the choice I am offering you to make: *makes it found v.v. good.*
that, bestowing good, receiving good, in goodly honour,
you have a share in this land so beloved by the gods.

Stanza 2

Cho. That I should have such treatment – Oh ! –
for all my wisdom and years, and take up residence in the land,
is an affront to my honour, a defilement. Oh !
See how I breathe force and total anger.
Oh ! Ah !
875 What is this pain that seeps into
and fills me?
Hear, mother Night !
I was no match for the gods' tricks:
they undid me, stripped from me
880 my ancient honours.

Ath. I shall not weary of describing benefits to you   *NB patience*
so that you may never say that by me, a younger goddess,
and by the ciy's people, you an aged divinity
went to perdition, dishonoured and banished from this land.
885 But if the reverence due to Persuasion is sacred to you –
if my tongue has power to soothe and cast a spell –
you will stay; but if you do not wish to stay,
still you could not in justice weigh out against the city
any measure of wrath or anger or harm against the people,
890 for it is open to you to have landholder's status in this country
and receive a just share of honour for all time to come.
Cho. Queen Athena, what place do you say that I have here?
Ath. One that is free of all pain and suffering; accept it.
Cho. Let's say I accept: what honour awaits me in that case?
Ath. That no household shall flourish without you.

*Chorus is interested but still hesitant –
He still patient + generous
+ gentle.
She led the worse to water + is now saying
it's OK, fresh nice water.
The gate to field is wide open*

Χο. σὺ τοῦτο πράξεις, ὥστε με σθένειν τόσον;
Αθ. τῷ γὰρ σέβοντι συμφορὰς ὀρθώσομεν.
Χο. καί μοι πρόπαντος ἐγγύην θήσῃ χρόνου;
Αθ. ἔξεστι γάρ μοι μὴ λέγειν ἃ μὴ τελῶ.
Χο. θέλξειν μ' ἔοικας, καὶ μεθίσταμαι κότου.   900
Αθ. τοιγὰρ κατὰ χθόν' οὖσ' ἐπικτήσῃ φίλους.
Χο. τί οὖν μ' ἄνωγας τῇδ' ἐφυμνῆσαι χθονί;
Αθ. ὁποῖα νίκης μὴ κακῆς ἐπίσκοπα,
    καὶ ταῦτα γῆθεν ἔκ τε ποντίας δρόσου
    ἐξ οὐρανοῦ τε, κἀνέμων ἀήματα   905
    εὐηλίως πνέοντ' ἐπιστείχειν χθόνα,
    καρπόν τε γαίας καὶ βοτῶν ἐπίρρυτον
    ἀστοῖσιν εὐθενοῦντα μὴ κάμνειν χρόνῳ,
    καὶ τῶν βροτείων σπερμάτων σωτηρίαν·
    τῶν δυσσεβούντων δ' ἐκφορωτέρα πέλοις.   910
    στέργω γάρ, ἀνδρὸς φιτυποίμενος δίκην,
    τὸ τῶν δικαίων τῶνδ' ἀπένθητον γένος.
    τοιαῦτά σοὔστι. τῶν ἀρειφάτων δ' ἐγὼ
    πρεπτῶν ἀγώνων οὐκ ἀνέξομαι τὸ μὴ οὐ
    τήνδ' ἀστύνικον ἐν βροτοῖς τιμᾶν πόλιν.   915

Χο.   δέξομαι Παλλάδος ξυνοικίαν,   [στρ. α
             οὐδ' ἀτιμάσω πόλιν
             τὰν καὶ Ζεὺς ὁ παγκρατὴς Ἄρης τε
             φρούριον θεῶν νέμει,
             ῥυσίβωμον Ἑλλάνων ἄγαλμα δαιμόνων·   920

             ἅ τ' ἐγὼ κατεύχομαι
             θεσπίσασα πρευμενῶς
             ἐπισσύτους [βίου] τύχας ὀνησίμους
             γαίας ἐξαμβρῦσαι   924/5
             φαιδρὸν ἁλίου σέλας.

Αθ.   τάδ' ἐγὼ προφρόνως τοῖσδε πολίταις
             πράσσω, μεγάλας καὶ δυσαρέστους

Cho.	You will do this, so that I shall have such strength?
Ath.	Yes, for I shall direct aright the fortunes of all who revere you.
Cho.	And will you make me a pledge of that in perpetuity?
Ath.	Yes, for I could just as well keep silent about what I shall not fulfill.
Cho.	900 It seems that you will cast a spell on me: I am indeed departing from my anger.
Ath.	Therefore as residents in the land you will acquire additional friends.
Cho.	What blessings, then, do you bid me pray for in my song?
Ath.	Such as look to no base victory,

and that these benefits accrue from earth and from watery deep
905   and from sky, and that winds' blowing
come with sunny breath upon the land,
and that earth's fruit and flocks' offspring flourish
in floods for the citizens and be unwearied by the passage of
    time,
and that the seed of human generation remain forever safe;
910   the impious, however, I urge you to extirpate.
For I, like a careful gardener, love
and will preserve from grief the race of these just men.
(*Her sweeping gesture includes not only the Areopagites but the whole audience.*)
Such blessings are yours to give, while I for my part
shall not fail to honour this city among men
915   by bringing her victory in the glorious contests of war.

Choral Exodos

Stanza 1

Cho.	I shall accept co-residency with Pallas Athena

and will not dishonour the city
that even Zeus All-prevailing and Ares
direct as the gods' watch-post
920   and glorious defender of the altars of Greece's divinities;
for her I make my prayer
in kindly prophecy,
that the sun's radiant gleam
924/5   bring a flood of benefits
bursting luxuriantly from the soil.

Ath.	It is with good intent to these citizens of mine

that I am doing this, by having established in residence here

δαίμονας αὐτοῦ καταναασαμένη·
πάντα γὰρ αὗται τὰ κατ' ἀνθρώπους   930
ἔλαχον διέπειν.
ὅ γε μὴν κύρσας βαρεῶν τούτων
οὐκ οἶδεν ὅθεν πληγαὶ βιότου·
τὰ γὰρ ἐκ προτέρων ἀπλακήματά νιν
πρὸς τάσδ' ἀπάγει· σιγῶντ' ὄλεθρος   935
καὶ μέγα φωνοῦντ'
    ἐχθραῖς ὀργαῖς ἀμαθύνει.

Χο.   δενδροπήμων δὲ μὴ πνέοι βλάβα,   [ἀντ. α
       τὰν ἐμὰν χάριν λέγω,
       φλογμοὺς ὀμματοστερεῖς φυτῶν τὸ   940
       μὴ περᾶν ὅρον τόπων,
       μηδ' ἄκαρπος αἰανὴς ἐφερπέτω νόσος,
       μῆλά τ' εὐθενοῦντα Πὰν
       ξὺν διπλοῖσιν ἐμβρύοις
       πόροι χρόνῳ τεταγμένῳ· γόνος   945
       πλουτόχθων ἑρμαίαν
       δαιμόνων δόσιν πόροι.

Αθ.   ἦ τάδ' ἀκούετε, πόλεως φρούριον,
       οἷ' ἐπικραίνει;
       μέγα γὰρ δύναται πότνι' Ἐρινὺς   950
       παρά τ' ἀθανάτοις τοῖς θ' ὑπὸ γαῖαν,
       περί τ' ἀνθρώπων φανεραὶ τελέως
       διαπράσσουσιν, τοῖς μὲν ἀοιδάς,
       τοῖς δ' αὖ δακρύων
           βίον ἀμβλωπὸν παρέχουσαι.   955

Χο.   ἀνδροκμῆτας δ' ἀώ-   [στρ. β
       ρους ἀπεννέπω τύχας·
       νεανίδων δ' ἐπηράτων
       ἀνδροτυχεῖς βιότους δότε, κύρι' ἔχοντες, 959/60
       θεαί τ', ὦ Μοῖραι

great and implacable divinities.
930 For these goddesses have been allotted the task
of managing all things in human affairs.
Indeed, anyone who encounters them as oppressive adversaries
does not know what has knocked his life to pieces,
for the sins of his ancestors hale him off
935 to trial before these goddesses; whether he is silent
or shouts loudly, destruction
pulverizes him with an enemy's rage.

Stanza 1'

Cho. And may no blight blow upon and ruin the trees
– I mention a favour I can grant;
940 may scorching heat that sears the buds from plants
not cross the borders of the land;
may everlasting sterility of crops not assail it,
but may Pan rear the flocks and
make them flourish with twin offspring
945 at the appointed time;
and may earth's rich progeny of metals honourably
provide the gods' gift of a "lucky strike."

Ath. Do you hear this, my city's watch-post?
Do you hear what benefits she is guaranteeing?
950 For the reverend Erinys has great power
both among the immortals and those beneath the earth;
in human affairs, too, they achieve their ends
manifestly and completely.
For some they provide reasons for song,
955 for others again a life darkened *by tears.

Stanza 2

Cho. I banish forever the killing of men
before their time.
Instead, grant to lovely young girls
959/60 lives spent in felicity with their husbands;
grant it, you gods who hold authority, and grant it O Fates,

now He's telling all that they are are — convincing any doubting human.

All is calm + peaceful — reconciled.

ματροκασιγνῆται,
δαίμονες ὀρθονόμοι,
παντὶ δόμῳ μετάκοινοι,
παντὶ χρόνῳ δ' ἐπιβριθεῖς,   965
ἐνδίκοις ὁμιλίαις
παντᾷ τιμιώταται θεῶν.

Αθ.   τάδε τοι χώρᾳ τἠμῇ προφρόνως
ἐπικραινομένων
γάνυμαι. στέργω δ' ὄμματα Πειθοῦς,   970
ὅτι μοι γλῶσσαν καὶ στόμ' ἐπωπᾷ
πρὸς τάσδ' ἀγρίως ἀπανηναμένας.
ἀλλ' ἐκράτησε Ζεὺς Ἀγοραῖος,
νικᾷ δ' ἀγαθῶν
    Ἔρις ἡμετέρα διὰ παντός.   975

Χο.   τὰν δ' ἄπληστον κακῶν   [ἀντ. β
μήποτ' ἐν πόλει Στάσιν
τᾷδ' ἐπεύχομαι βρέμειν,
μηδὲ ποῦσα κόνις μέλαν αἶμα πολιτᾶν   979/80
δι' ὀργὰν ποινὰς
ἀντιφόνους Ἄτας
ἁρπαλίσαι πόλεως,
χάρματα δ' ἀντιδιδοῖεν
κοινοφιλεῖ διανοίᾳ   985
καὶ στυγεῖν μιᾷ φρενί·
πολλῶν γὰρ τόδ' ἐν βροτοῖς ἄκος.

Αθ.   ἆρα φρονοῦσιν γλώσσης ἀγαθῆς
ὁδὸν εὑρίσκειν;
ἐκ τῶν φοβερῶν τῶνδε προσώπων   990
μέγα κέρδος ὁρῶ τοῖσδε πολίταις·
τάσδε γὰρ Εὔφρονας εὔφρονες ἀεὶ
μέγα τιμῶντες καὶ γῆν καὶ πόλιν
ὀρθοδίκαιον

my sisters by the same mother, Night,
divine dispensers of right
who have a common share in every household
65 but can weigh heavily at any time,
everywhere most honoured of all goddesses
because your visitations are just.

Ath. Because they are guaranteeing these benefits
for my country with such good intent,
70 I rejoice. For I love Persuasion's face
because she supervised my lips and speech
when these goddesses were saying "No" so savagely.
But Zeus, Protector of assemblies, prevailed
and the victory goes
975 to our joint and permanent striving for good.

Stanza 2'

Cho. I pray in addition that the growling of Factional Strife,
hungry for evil,
never be heard in this city,
79/80 and that the earth not drink citizens' black blood,
angrily snatching up mutual slaughter
as Atē's requital exacted from the city.
Rather, may the citizens enjoy
shared pleasures,
85 a unanimity of thought in their loves
and hatreds;
for this cures many ills in human life.

Ath. Do they intend to find
the path of blessing?
90 Then from these frightening visages
I see great profit accruing to these citizens,
for if you are kindly to these Kindly Ones,
always honouring them greatly, you will surely be shining
examples
of men who manage both land and city

πρέψετε πάντως διάγοντες.   995

Χο.   < χαίρετε > χαίρετ' ἐν αἰσιμίαισι πλούτου,   [στρ. γ
χαίρετ', ἀστικὸς λεώς,
ἴκταρ ἡμένας Διὸς
παρθένου φίλας φίλοι,
σωφρονοῦντες ἐν χρόνῳ·   1000
Παλλάδος δ' ὑπὸ πτεροῖς
ὄντας ἅζεται πατήρ.

Αθ.   χαίρετε χὑμεῖς, προτέραν δ' ἐμὲ χρὴ
στείχειν θαλάμους ἀποδείξουσαν
πρὸς φῶς ἱερὸν τῶνδε προπομπῶν.   1005
ἴτε καὶ σφαγίων τῶνδ' ὑπὸ σεμνῶν
κατὰ γῆς σύμεναι τὸ μὲν ἀτηρὸν
χώρας ἀπέχειν, τὸ δὲ κερδαλέον
    πέμπειν πόλεως ἐπὶ νίκῃ.
ὑμεῖς δ' ἡγεῖσθε, πολισσοῦχοι   1010
παῖδες Κραναοῦ, ταῖσδε μετοίκοις·
εἴη δ' ἀγαθῶν
    ἀγαθὴ διάνοια πολίταις.

Χο.   χαίρετε, χαίρετε δ' αὖθις, ἐπανδιπλοίζω,   [ἀντ. γ
πάντες οἱ καὶ ἀ πτόλιν   1015
δαίμονές τε καὶ βροτοὶ
Παλλάδος πόλιν νέμον-
τες, μετοικίαν δ' ἐμὴν
εὐσεβοῦντες οὔτι μέμ-
ψεσθε συμφορὰς βίου.   1020

Αθ.   αἰνῶ τε μύθους τῶνδε τῶν κατευγμάτων
πέμψω τε φέγγει λαμπάδων σελασφόρων
εἰς τοὺς ἔνερθε καὶ κάτω χθονὸς τόπους
ξὺν προσπόλοισιν αἵτε φρουροῦσιν βρέτας

995 in a just and upright way.

Cho. Farewell, may you fare well in the destined enjoyment of wealth,
farewell, people of the city,
friends of the friendly Virgin Goddess
seated near Zeus,
1000 and men wise with the passage of time;
and since you are under Pallas Athena's wings
Father Zeus has respect for you.

(*Enter a subsidiary chorus of Escorts carrying torches and
leading sacrificial victims. Possibly the Areopagites join them to
sing the Finale.*)

Ath. Farewell to you, too, but I must go first
to show the deep dwelling-places
1005 by the sacred light which these escorts are carrying.
Go, then, and may these august victims for sacrifice accompany
you
(*She motions to the sacrificial offerings carried by some of the
Escorts.*)
as you hasten beneath the earth, to keep in check what might
bring ruin
to the country, but send instead whatever is advantageous
to the city's profit in gaining victory.
1010 And you who are in charge of the city,
Kranaos' sons, lead the way for these new residents;
and may there be good intent on the citizens' part
for the good done to them.

Cho. Farewell again, fare well — I redouble my wish,
1015 all you throughout the city,
divinities and mortals
who inhabit Pallas' city,
and if you show reverence for my residency
you will have no fault to find
1020 with what befalls you in life.

Ath. I approve the utterance of these prayers
and shall send you to the regions below and underneath the earth
by the light of radiant torches
with female attendants who guard

τοὐμὸν δικαίως· ὄμμα γὰρ πάσης χθονὸς   1025
Θησῇδος ἐξίκοιτ' ἄν, εὐκλεὴς λόχος
παίδων γυναικῶν, καὶ στόλος πρεσβυτίδων
<   >
φοινικοβάπτοις ἐνδυτοῖς ἐσθήμασι
τιμᾶτε, καὶ τὸ φέγγος ὁρμάσθω πυρός,
ὅπως ἂν εὔφρων ἥδ' ὁμιλία χθονὸς   1030
τὸ λοιπὸν εὐάνδροισι συμφοραῖς πρέπῃ.

ΠΡΟΠΟΜΠΟΙ

βᾶτε δόμῳ μεγάλαι φιλότιμοι   [στρ. α
Νυκτὸς παῖδες ἄπαιδες ὑπ' εὔφρονι πομπᾷ. 1033/4
εὐφαμεῖτε δέ, χωρῖται.   1035

γᾶς ὑπὸ κεύθεσιν ὠγυγίοισιν   [ἀντ. α
τιμαῖς καὶ θυσίαις περίσεπται † τύχαι τε †
εὐφαμεῖτε δὲ πανδαμεί.

ἵλαοι δὲ καὶ εὐθύφρονες γᾷ   [στρ. β
δεῦρ' ἴτε Σεμναὶ <Θεαὶ> πυριδάπτῳ   1040/1
λαμπάδι τερπόμεναι καθ' ὁδόν· ὀλολύξατε νῦν
                ἐπὶ μολπαῖς.   1042/3

σπονδαὶ δ' † ἐς τὸ πᾶν ἔνδαιδες οἴκων † [ἀντ. β
Παλλάδος ἀστοῖς· Ζεὺς Παντόπτας   1045
οὕτω Μοῖρά τε συγκατέβα· ὀλολύξατε νῦν
                ἐπὶ μολπαῖς.

my statue in justice. For the eye of the whole land
of Theseus will come forth, a celebrated troop
of children, women, and a company of old women
...
pay honour to them who are dressed in scarlet-dyed
attire, and let the blaze of torch-fire move forward
(*The procession begins to file out, probably through the western parodos.*)
in order that these visitors to my country may show their good will

in future by conspicuously inspiring her men with courage.

will also make Athenians proud + to mindful of their advantages/benefits.

Choral Song
ESCORTS

Stanza 1

Go home, you great, proud
children of Night (yet not children), with us as escorts of good
intent—
and you, inhabitants of the land, keep auspicious silence.

Stanza 1'

Under earth's primeval caverns
*you shall be greatly reverenced with honours and sacrifices—
and you, the city's whole population, keep auspicious silence.

Stanza 2

Propitiously and with straight intent for our country
come here, you August Goddesses,
(*The Eumenides now join the procession.*)
accompanied by fiercely blazing
torch-light and taking pleasure along the way;
raise a joyful shout, now, to accompany our songs.

Stanza 2'

A treaty *has been sealed for all time
with Pallas Athena's citizens; Zeus All-seeing
and Fate in this way came down to join them;
raise a joyful shout, now, to accompany our songs.

(*All exit.*)

This section it The end of this play is pervaded by good will + generosity, + that balm it is so pt that the audic is filled w. the same goodness; all can wallow in this balm, which originates fr Aa.

Vatican, Museo Gregoriano Profano inv. 10450; Roman marble sarcophagus c. 150 A.D.: from left to right, Orestes and Pylades at the grave of Agamemnon, Orestes slaying Aegisthus, then Clytemnestra, Orestes proceeding from Delphi with drawn sword; Erinyes asleep at either side and, at centre-right, holding a winding-sheet. See pp. 31 & 32. (photo courtesy of the German Archaeological Institute, Rome).

COMMENTARY

Action

The Delphic priestess, or Pythia, enters the acting-area either through the temple doors or along one of the side entrance-ways or "parodoi"; probably she enters by the west, or stage-left parodos, which was conventionally used by those arriving from the city (see Intro, p. 14). She stands before the main door of the temple and offers her ritual prayer, invoking the divinities of the place to look propitiously upon her and the faithful who have come to this, the most celebrated of Greece's oracular shrines. Her language is calm and dignified and the whole scene (until the rude shock of vv. 34 ff.) is pervaded by a feeling of serenity and holy peace; we may compare the similarly bright but almost wistful opening of Euripides' *Ion*, which is also set at Delphi.

1–2 first ... primeval: the repetition makes an impressive beginning and underlines the antiquity of Delphi as a prophetic shrine. There were other versions of the succession of tenants at Delphi, but Aesch. introduces several additional stages. The effect is to enhance Apollo's position when he finally takes over. "The object of Aeschylus was to point out the dignity and authority of Apollo and his oracle, and to show that no violence nor injustice had been committed in the transfer of it to its successive possessors" (Paley). Note, however, that the effect will be to throw into high relief the ineffectualness of traditional (Olympian) formulae and rituals in the face of the darker and psychologically deeper-rooted vengefulness of the (chthonic) Erinyes.

2 There was a shrine to Earth at Delphi even in Plutarch's day c. 100 A.D. (*Mor.* 402 C–D). **Earth ... Themis:** although these two goddesses were sometimes identified (*P.V.* 209–10), the usual genealogy made Themis daughter of Earth and Heaven (Hesiod, *Theog.* 135–6), and thus one of the race of Titans (hence the ref. in v. 6 to "another Titaness"). Her name signifies "arrangement, ordering," and, when not personified, it is an early Greek synonym for "law." At Hes. *Theog.* 901 ff. she becomes Zeus' consort and gives birth to the "Hours," Good Order, Justice and Peace. In the *Homeric Hymn to Apollo* (III) 123–5, Themis, much to Leto's pleasure, acts as nanny to Apollo.

4 so the story goes: There is no note of skepticism in the phrase, which is "factual and simply marks an affirmation as being beyond the speaker's direct knowledge" (Friis Johansen & Whittle on Aesch. *Suppl.* 230); cf. *Sept.* 225.

5–8 The smooth and peaceable nature of the transition is emphasized (so different from that in the house of Atreus); just as Phoebe received proprietorship of the shrine from Themis, she passed it on to Apollo – as a birthday gift (v. 7). We hear nothing of Apollo's wresting control of the sanctuary by force, which was the more common myth, nothing of his having to slay the Python; contrast Eur. *I.T.* 1244 ff. where some of the same divinities occur in a more violent context and Apollo has to persuade Zeus to discontinue Themis' emission of prophetic dreams.

6 The Titans – children of Ouranos and Gaia (Heaven and Earth) – were the race of gods preceding the Olympians. For the ten-year struggle between the newer and the older races of gods, see n. on v. 641 below.

7 Phoebe, sister of Themis also in Hesiod (*Theog.* 135–36), was either Leto's sister (Schol. on *Eum.* 3a) or her mother (Hes. *Theog.* 404 ff.). In either case, her introduction here makes the succession longer and so more venerable, and it becomes almost a domestic matter. A birthday present was brought to a new-born infant at a family celebration, which was held five or ten days after the birth, and it was on this occasion that the child was given his or her name.

8 It is noteworthy that the stem *Phoeb-*, which signifies 'bright', occurs three times in two lines. *Phoebus*, which "probably has its origin in an epithet" (West on Hes. *Theog.* 136), is therefore a significant name. Plutarch remarks that Apollo, after his return from exile for slaying the Python and purification for his final investiture at Delphi, was "truly the 'radiant one'" (*de defect. orac.* 421 C).

9 **The lake on Delos** is often mentioned, from Theognis 7 on, as a conspicuous feature in the island's landscape; Leto gave birth to Apollo while gripping a palm-tree which grew on the shore of the lake. The **ridge of rock** seems to refer specifically to Mt. Kynthos.

10 This version of Apollo's journey appears to be invented to give special honour to Athens (so the schol. on v. 11). Another – perhaps the standard – account had Apollo come to Delphi from Delos via Mt. Olympos and Thessaly, thence to Euboia, across the Euripus and through Boeotia (*Hymn to Apollo* [III] 186, 214 ff.), by-passing Athens entirely. As a memorial of his journey, Apollo had a shrine at Delium in southern Boeotia (Thuc. 4. 76. 4).

11 Again, the solemnity is enhanced by the very full expression.

13 The Scholiast here identifies the **builders of roads** as Athenians. Some commentators see a reference to them as well in the phrase **Hephaestus' sons**, since the Athenians believed themselves to be descended from Erichthonios, son of Hephaestus and Earth, but the phrase is probably only a periphrasis for "craftsmen." There was a story that Hephaestus and Athena built the third, brazen, temple at Delphi (Pind. *Paean* VIII [fr. 52 i, Snell], vv. 65–71).

14 The translation cannot capture the sonorous three-word line (see M. Marcovich, *Three-Word Trimeter in Greek Tragedy* [Königstein: Hain, 1984] 35). The scholia here record the useful information that, when a sacred embassy went from Athens to Delphi, it was preceded by a troop of men carrying axes "as if to civilize the land" (cf. A. Plassart, "Eschyle et le fronton est du temple delphique des Alcméonides," *Revue des études anciennes* 42 [1940] 293–99).

15 Epicharmus was said to have mocked Aesch. for overusing the word translated here as "honour" (Schol. *Eum.* 626). Cf. vv. 626, 807 below, *Ag.* 922, where Fraenkel suggests that it "once belonged to the language of religious ceremonies."

16 **Delphos**, son of Poseidon and the Earth-goddess-figure Melaina or Melantho, was a convenient namesake of the people of Delphi. He may be one of the naked male figures depicted on the east pediment of the 6th cent. Delphic temple which was partially financed by the noble Alkmeonid family of Athens.

Apollo's reception is diplomatically correct, even regal. The nautical image **steersman of this land** is appropriate to the context, since the stem *delph-* signifies "dolphin;" it will recur in v. 765 below.

17 **Zeus** is guarantor of Apollo's prophetic skill, a point that will be repeated several times later (vv. 229, 616 ff., 713, 797) and which is as old as *Hymn to Apollo* (III) 132 and *Hymn to Hermes* (IV) 535–38.

19 Repetition of the point already made in v. 17 reinforces Apollo's claim to be the authoritative tenant of Greece's most venerable oracular shrine. The exact sense of the title 'Loxias' is uncertain. It seems to designate Apollo as a god of prophecy. It is allegedly derived from *loxos*, 'slanting,' and is sometimes explained as referring to the ambiguity of oracles, or to the sun's journey across the ecliptic. As with many divine epithets (e.g. Lukeios), the 'real' meaning may be lost.

20 The **prelude** was the introductory section of a musical composition or speech and was the generic title given in antiquity to the "Homeric Hymns." Compare Agamemnon's remark, some twenty lines into his speech after his return from Troy, "to the gods I have drawn out this prelude" (*Ag.* 829).

21 If the line is authentic, Athena is given her title 'Pronaia' because of the position of her sanctuary *before* and on the road leading to the main entrance to the shrine. Although it is appropriate to find Athena associated with Apollo at Delphi, just as he will be with her at Athens later in the play, I suggest that v.21 is interpolated here from another context. In the account is clumsy and given pride of place (*presbeuetai*) is an awkward repetition from v.1.

22–23 The Corycian grotto, on the heights above the shrine, was a well known haunt of the Nymphs, who are often associated in art and cult with both Apollo and Dionysus (v. 24). Herodotus tells (8. 32) how most of the Delphians took frightened refuge there when they learned of the impending Persian invasion of their territory in 480 B.C. Aesch.'s description in v. 23 suggests something remote, mysterious, sacred. The word translated here **haunt** also suggests the wheeling motion of birds in flight; spiritual beings are as little earthbound as the birds in whose company they are here found.

delight ... divine: I have taken over Weir Smyth's trans.

24 **Bromios** ("Roarer") was a title of Dionysus, probably derived from his bull-embodiment (see Dodds on Eur. *Bacch.* 65–67); he is also regularly associated with the Nymphs of Parnassus (Soph. *Ant.* 1126 ff.). In later times Dionysus was thought to be in residence at Delphi during Apollo's absence in the three winter months, but it is not certain that this belief was held in the fifth century (see, in general, H.W. Parke, *Greek Oracles* [London: Hutchinson, 1967] 39 f.).

25–26 Eur. was to make this story the subject of his *Bacchae* (as perhaps already in Aesch.'s *Pentheus;* in Aesch.'s *Xantriai*, as we learn from Schol. *Eum.* 26 c, Dionysus' attack on Pentheus took place, as in Eur., on Mt. Cithaeron). Eur. has his Dionysus use the same military metaphor of "leading an army" against his opponents at *Bacch.* 52. Perhaps the point Aesch. is making here is that Dionysus has earned a place in religious rites at Delphi by his killing of Pentheus. Schol. *Eum.* 26 a,b take the point of the comparison to be that Pentheus did not withstand his aggressor, and so made an easy prey. In any case, Dionysus is frequently placed in a Delphic setting (Eur. *Bacch.* 306–7, *I.T.* 1243).

27 **Pleistos** is the river-gorge below Delphi; in personified form, he was the father of the Corycian nymphs (Apol. Rhod. 2. 711). There was a tradition that Poseidon had originally shared the Delphic shrine with Earth, but that when Apollo took over, he gave Poseidon the island of Calauria off Trozen in exchange; Paus. noted (10. 24. 4) that "in the temple [of Apollo at Delphi] there is an altar of Poseidon, because the possession of the oldest oracle was shared by Poseidon." Poseidon was also the father of Delphos (n. on v. 16 above).

28 The epithet **Fulfiller** is probably meant to recall Clytemnestra's chilling cry at *Ag.* 973, "Zeus, Zeus Fulfiller, fulfil my prayers." The Erinyes will later apply the notion of completion or fulfilment to themselves (vv. 320, 382, 393 below). There was an altar to Zeus "on High" (*Hypatos*; cf. *Ag.* 55) in front of the Erechtheum, at which only wineless libations were offered (Paus. 1. 26. 5); cf. v. 107 below.

29 **prophetess:** the same word as she had applied to Apollo (v. 18) and one cognate with that used of Earth (v. 2). She thus claims to speak with the god's authoritative voice. Her actual prophecies were uttered from behind a curtain as she sat on a tripod in an inner room, and it is this posture to which she seems to be referring here.

30 The Pythia's prayer for a successful consultation bears a palpable irony, as we shall soon learn.

32 Certain groups (among them Greeks, according to the present passage; we are reminded of Delphi's status as an international shrine) were given "right of priority" in consulting the oracle. The specific order of individual consultation was determined by lot. (See Parke and Wormell, *The Delphic Oracle* [Oxford: Basil Blackwell, 1956] I. 31.)

33 in whatever way ...: she is merely the instrument, or "mouthpiece," of Apollo.

36 have no strength ... cannot raise: Aesch. here uses two exceedingly rare words for which the lexicographer Hesychius offers more familiar equivalents. It is possible that the poet has the Pythia lapse into a formal, even antiquated, mode of expression to mark her discomposure.

37–38 The language emphasizes her sudden terrified enfeeblement. Whether she is actually down on the ground or merely crouching low as she supports herself on the doorframe of the temple-entrance is unclear (according to Mills [see General Bibliography, "Texts"], "the priestess holds on with her hands to the walls to prevent herself from falling"); in any case, the effect will have been one of operatic exaggeration, without any trace of the comic. The phrasing of v. 38 seems intended to echo the Argive elders at the opening of *Ag.* (74–75), "plying our staves with strength equal to a child's" (*anti*- and *iso*- in compounds are favourite Aeschylean ways of saying "no better than - "; Electra calls herself *antidoulos*, "no better than a slave," at *Cho.* 135).

39 Neither ancient descriptions nor archaeological discoveries have enabled scholars to reconstruct with any assurance the exact physical arrangements of the interior of the shrine; the term *muchos* (also at v. 170 below; possibly from *muo* "to be shut tight") designated the innermost portion, to which the Pythia "descended" (according to several sources) and took up her trance-posture and from which she uttered her prophecies for the temple-staff, and perhaps also the enquirers, to hear. From the view of these latter she was cut off by some kind of curtain or screen. The ref. to garlands is confirmed by a schol. on Ar. *Plutus* 39, who reports that "the tripods and the priestess were wreathed with bay," and garlands in connection with Delphi are mentioned also at Eur. *Ion* 224 and 1310.

40 The vase paintings as well as ancient descriptions give prominence to the large bulbous "navel-stone" which was the shrine's most prominent feature. It was roughly the shape of an elongated egg, decorated with fillets, or, in some representations, a hunting-net, and reputedly marked the centre of the world, the spot where two eagles, released by Zeus from the ends of the earth in opposite directions, met. The story was told in a celebrated *Paean* by Pindar, now lost, and there were golden statues of the eagles near the stone itself (Strabo 9. 3. 6 C419–20, Paus. 10. 16. 3, Plut. *Mor.* 409 E). See, in general, A.B. Cook, *Zeus* II (Cambridge: Cambridge University Press, 1925; repr. New York, 1965) 169 ff. The impressive compound **god-polluted** will be expanded upon by the Erinyes later (vv. 169 ff.).

41 The word translated **suppliant** could designate either one who "turns towards" a god for assistance (cf. vv. 205, 234, 718 below), or one in need of purification, hence, one polluted or under a curse (vv. 237, 445; v. 177 is ambiguous). Cf. Fraenkel on *Ag.* 1587; Friis Johansen & Whittle on *Suppl.* 362; Garvie on *Cho.* 287.

41–42 Whose blood is dripping from Orestes' hands? Some commentators think it is the blood of the animal slaughtered in the Delphic rite of purification, but in light of the Chorus' reference at *Ag.* 1351 to the killer's 'fresh-drawn sword' and the emphasis given to Orestes' blood- stained hands at *Cho.* 1055 (see Garvie's n. on *Cho.* 1055–6), I prefer H.J. Rose's explanation, that the Pythia "... transcends time and space for a moment and sees Orestes, not as he actually is, but as he was just after murdering his mother" (*Commentary* II, p. 233). This was essentially the explanation of the schol. here (42a) and is supported by vv. 247 and 317 below.

fresh-drawn: the murders are pictured so vividly that it is as if they have just been committed.

43 At the end of the preceding play Orestes set out for Apollo's shrine equipped with "festooned branch," the usual emblem of a suppliant (*Cho.* 1035 with Garvie's n.), and this is how the Pythia has discovered him. The branch is "tall," the garlanding "modest," the fleece "bright": the details add solemnity, but they also mark Aesch.'s high-flown style which Aristoph. could not resist mocking. (The text of vv. 44–5 has suffered corruption by the intrusion of an explanatory gloss; I translate my own rather drastic re-arrangement.)

46 The Pythia now goes on to describe the rest of the scene which, she implies, has so shocked and confused her that she cannot vouch for any of the details; she adduces a string of parallels only to reject each as falling short of *this* appalling sight. **company** is a military metaphor; these strange creatures represent a serious threat.

47 That they should be both asleep and **sitting on chairs** seems peculiar and uncomfortable; see Intro. p. 12.

48 ff. The Pythia, striving to make the unparalleled somehow more comprehensible, grasps at a comparison ready-to-hand, one that in fact Orestes had already used (*Cho.* 1048): the Gorgons also were snaky-locked (often in archaic art and *Orph. Hymn* 69. 16). She then tries for a more precise comparison, to the Harpies, but, frightened almost to distraction, she remembers what strikes her as a significant difference: these creatures, unlike conventional representations of Harpies, have no wings. (The Erinyes are in fact depicted with wings in some vase-representations and so described at Eur. *Or.* 317). The Pythia's disconnected speech reflects her confusion of mind.

49 It seems to me unnecessary to postulate a lacuna after this line (so Page, following Wakefield), in which the Pythia would have named the Harpies and made the pedantic point that they, too, like the Gorgons (but unlike the creatures she has been trying to describe) were winged. (A.L. Brown points out to me that the omission of a noun in the fem. acc. pl. in vv. 50–1 is awkward; *gegrammenas* must be taken as "pictures of women.")

50 **Phineus** was punished by the gods for blinding his sons on the false information of their stepmother; in another version of the story (Soph. *Ant.* 971 ff.), it was Phineus' second wife herself who blinded them. For this, or some other, crime, he was himself blinded and afflicted by the "Harpies" (lit., "Snatchers"). "These were winged female creatures, and when a table was laid for Phineus, they flew down from the sky and snatched up most of the victuals, and what little they left stank so that nobody could touch it" ("Apollodorus" 1.9.21, trans. J.G. Frazer). Virgil makes one of the Harpies refer to herself as "oldest of the Furies" (*Aen.* 3. 252). The Harpies were referred to in plays by Sophocles and Aeschylus titled *Phineus*, and Aeschylus' version was part of the trilogy along with *Persians* that won first prize in 472 B.C.

52 The Erinyes are black also at *Ag.* 462–63 and "black-robed" at v. 370 below (cf. v. 352). At *Cho.* 1049 they wear "gray chitons" (a colour particularly associated with mourning, as Garvie remarks in his n. there). They are "black-skinned" at Eur. *Or.* 321 and *Elec.* 1345 (see Denniston's n. there). The phrase here translated **thoroughly** (also at *Ag.* 682) is almost an Aeschylean mannerism (H.W. Miller, *Classical Journal* 32 [1937] 228–9). Usually in Aesch. it means "for all time" (below vv. 83, 291, 401, 538, 670, 891, and perhaps 1044).

53 **they snore**: The Greek word which Aesch. uses, like its English equivalent, tends not to occur in dignified contexts. Clytemnestra's ghost will later return to the subject of their noxious breath (vv. 137–38 below).

54 drip from their eyes etc.: At the close of the preceding play Orestes used similar language to describe the creatures which were then only his hallucination: "They distil hateful blood from their eyes" (*Cho.* 1058).

56 For the first time a note is sounded which will recur frequently in the play: the gulf that separates the Erinyes from the Olympian gods. Here, their repulsive appearance and outlandish 'get-up' (for that is what *kosmos* means, no more) cuts them off from human converse as well. Such is the measure of the distance both sides must travel before any reconciliation can be effected.

57 ff. The Greek word-order is slightly cumbersome, but intelligible. The Pythia puts the crowning touch on her narration: the Erinyes, like deformed and noxious offspring, would make any "mother-" land that bore them regret it.

60 ff. The Pythia is content to leave it to her master to deal with these creatures, and the way is thus prepared for Apollo's entrance. Here, the use of the adj. **mighty** in v. 61 is more than complimentary; it suggests that he will need all his might to cope with the situation (the compound adj. in the same line-position applied to "Loxias' mighty oracle" at *Cho.* 269).

63 purifier of others' houses: For Apollo's purification of Orestes, see n. on v. 283 below.

Many editors propose to deviate from the MSS and insert vv. 85–87 or 85–88 after v. 63, but the improvement in sense and dramatic effect is negligible. See n. on v. 85 below.

Action

After v. 63 the Pythia leaves the stage probably using the same (west) entrance-way as that by which she entered. The interior of the temple is then revealed by means of the wheeled platform or *ekkyklema* (so the scholiast on v. 64b and c), or the two actors playing Orestes and Apollo (with probably the mute Hermes) "simply enter from the temple" (Verrall; so also Hammond, "Conditions" 439). There is a further problem about when and how the Chorus of Erinyes first appear, but a case can be made for the presentation of at least a few of them now, asleep in a circle about Orestes. See Intro. pp. 12–13.

64 I shall not betray you: Orestes had used a similar phrase in *Cho.* to express confidence that "Loxias' mighty oracle" (see n. on vv. 60 ff. above) would not betray him (*Cho.* 269).

65 The gods were noted for their ability to hear worthy suppliants **even from afar** (vv. 297, 397 below; *Ag.* 952).

66 I shall not be gentle: Apollo's promise is more than fulfilled by his language and whole manner towards the Erinyes later.

67–68 Apollo is offering a proof of his power to protect Orestes; the implication is that he has cast upon Orestes' pursuers a supernatural sleep. Previously they had been (apparently) sitting watchfully in a circle about Orestes (v. 47); now, whether or not the god has acted upon them directly, they have become quiescent.

these savage women: use of the deictic "these" strongly implies that some of the sleeping Erinyes are there for Orestes, and the audience, to see. **savage**: Apollo uses a strong word, elsewhere applied to the war-god, Ares.

68 the abominable maidens: since "maidens" was a term usually used of attractive young women (e.g. the archaic statues known as *korai*), the juxtaposition is intentionally striking; **abominable**: Apollo uses a cognate term at v. 191 below.

69 aged antique children: "a bold and contemptuous oxymoron" (Sidgwick), like "abominable maidens" just above. The phrase "long-lived maidens" at *P.V.* 794 is similar, but tamer (there it is the Graiai, "Aged Ones," who are being described).

with whom no one ever consorts: this note of complete quarantine it is in Apollo's interest to emphasize (perhaps overemphasize: cf. vv. 191 ff., 721–22). The Erinyes themselves sometimes echo this kind of language (vv. 352–53, 360 ff., 385–86) but, since there will eventually be a rapprochement between the opposing sides, they must even now possess a capacity for reform which Apollo ignores, or at least depreciates.

71–72 evil darkness ... is their abode: an interesting turn of phrase, since Darkness personified (*Skotos*) was sometimes named as the Erinyes' father (Soph. *O.C.* 40).

73 objects of hatred: Aesch. uses a form of words (the abstract neut. pl.) that conveys utter contempt. Similarly, Eteocles calls the frightened females of the Chorus at *Sept.* 186 "objects of hatred to moderate men"; cf. v. 644 below, "objects of loathing to the gods."

74 Nevertheless ...: that is, because the sleep cast upon them (67 f.) is only temporary and they will soon resume the pursuit.

75–76 Apollo emphasizes the lengthy and exhausting journey that lies ahead, a point that Orestes and his pursuers later corroborate (vv. 240, 249 ff.)

78 your tendance: The metaphor is from tending cattle which, though a little strange, occurs elsewhere in Aesch. (*Ag.* 669, *Suppl.* 929), where the language makes clear that what is meant is "tend in one's thoughts, give careful attention to."

80 her ancient statue: the ancient olivewood statue of Athena, which later stood in the Erechtheum. It was this statue that was ceremonially garbed at the Great Panathenaia.

81 there we shall get us judges: this is similar to the technique used by Euripides in his prologues of providing the audience with a very general outline of the action to follow. Occasionally (as in *Ion*), the Prologue-prophecy is misleading; not so here, where Apollo's prophetic skills are proved by what happens later in the play.

81–82 words that cast a spell: Athena will use similar language in describing the almost magical powers of persuasion at vv. 885–86 below (similarly, *Suppl.* 447).

83 once for all: see n. on v. 52 above. The finality of the release from toils now being promised by Apollo is worth noting. As A.L. Brown has pointed out to me, characters earlier in the trilogy (the watchman, the army's messenger, Clytemnestra, Agamemnon's children) had prayed for a release from their troubles, or mistakenly believed that these were past. Now the prospect seems genuinely within reach.

84 For I in fact: so far from sweeping under the carpet his role in Clytemnestra's killing, Apollo here reaffirms it strongly, nor does he shrink from admitting it during the trial (vv. 579–80 below). **persuaded:** cf. v. 593 below (although it may be thought that "persuade" is too pale an expression in view of Apollo's threats of punishment if Orestes had disobeyed him: *Cho.* 270 ff.; cf. *Cho.* 1032–33 and *Eum.* 466–67 below).

85 ff. Some editors, following Burges, have transposed vv. 85–87 (Maas added 88) to follow v. 63, but the lines make satisfactory sense as they appear in the MSS. (For a defence of the MSS order, see Deborah Roberts, *Apollo and his Oracle* 49 n. 23). (Full details of works cited by author and title, or short title, only can be found in the General Bibliography at the end.)

86 learn as well: Orestes' nerves are frayed by his ordeals, past and to come, and his language betrays the strain he is under. This, as Prof. Scott points out, parallels the annoyance that Clytemnestra's ghost feels at *her* supernatural allies, the Erinyes, for failing to look after her interests, although her reaction is (as we shall see) much more pronounced.

87 a pledge: the Chorus-leader uses a cognate term at v. 898 below. There is perhaps a residual legal, or semi-legal, sense: the bond or surety put up as a guarantee of (say) a betrothal (see G. Hutchinson's n. on *Sept.* 396).

89 As for you: this direct address suggests that there was a mute character representing Hermes on the stage. He came out with Orestes and Apollo before v. 64, or, less likely, emerged from the temple just in time to be given this command by his brother. The audience would be bewildered if there was no actual recipient of Apollo's elaborate address. (Appeals to Hermes figure fairly prominently in *Cho.*: vv. 1, 124b, 727.)

my own brother in blood and of a common father: since, by the restrictive definition of "blood kinship" which Apollo himself will propound later (vv. 658 ff.), only the father is the "true parent," this is something of a redundancy. This may be a bit of foreshadowing by the poet.

90 live up to your title: Aesch. uses a similar phrase at *Sept.* 658 ("Polyneices" = "Causer of much Strife"). Which of Hermes' titles is in question here? The scholiast on v. 91 says it was "Hodios," "Protector of Wayfarers," but the next verse suggests the title "Pompaios," "Escorter" (although the epithet was usually applied to Hermes in virtue of his function of "escorting" dead souls to the underworld).

91 shepherding this suppliant: the metaphor is easier to understand than "tendance" in v. 78, since actual protective escort is involved. This is the first, and also among the mildest, of many occurrences of animal imagery in the play; see n. on v. 130 below.

92–93 outcasts who are sent: I have translated Blaydes' conjecture, which makes the participle "sent" agree not with the Greek noun that immediately precedes, "sanctity," but with "outcasts." (Compare for the phrase *Cho.* 940–1, Soph. *El.* 69–70.) (A.L. Brown, however, remarks on the difficulty of construing with the dat. "to men." If the MS reading be retained, Mills' interpretation seems best: "Zeus reveres this reverence due to outlaws, when it comes to men with the fortune of good guidance.")

Action

Apollo returns into the temple, from which he will emerge again rather agitatedly at v. 179. Orestes steps over the sleeping Erinyes and he and Hermes depart, probably along the eastern, stage-right, parodos, which conventionally signified the direction of the countryside (see n. on v. 231). Clytemnestra's ghost appears, exactly how or from where is uncertain: either by a trap door on the stage, if such were available (Pollux 4. 127, 132, who calls it *anapiesma*), or by a parodos. But no suggestion is completely free of difficulties; see Intro. p. 12.

94 Without any advance warning Clytemnestra's lurid epiphany must have astonished the audience. Also noteworthy is the poet's bold inventiveness in presenting her as a dream to a collection rather than to a single individual. Although Aesch. no doubt had in mind and was influenced by Homer's *Iliad* XXIII. 65 ff., where the dead Patroclus chides Achilles, "You sleep and have forgotten me ...", this is quite beyond the epic – that is to say, the traditional – conception of dream-apparitions to individuals. (See, in general, Robert Lennig, *Traum und Sinnestäuschung bei Aischylos, Sophokles, Euripides* [diss. Tübingen, 1969] 77–80; Ed. Lévy, *"Le théâtre et le rêve"* [see General Bibliography].)

The spectre's speech is full of fire and rage, and its thunderous vigour can be appreciated in spite of serious difficulties in the text and the possibility of disarrangement of verses (see below). She begins by emphasizing her outrageous treatment in the Underworld; the Erinyes' neglect of their obligations to her simply compounds her feeling of being victimized. At vv. 106 ff. the temperature rises considerably and she employs the usual prayer-formula, the *quid pro quo*, to drive home her point. Her final thrust is to emphasize the ease, almost effortlessness, of Orestes' escape, a particularly venomous way of taking the Erinyes to task for dereliction of duty.

Sleep on, then!: this form is usually a mild imperative or polite request; here, with heavy irony: "Don't let me interfere with your sleep" (cf. Soph. *El.* 1491, *Ant.* 444, where Jebb comments that the phrase "gives a contemptuous permission").

The word here translated **You, there!** was "used to attract attention" (Seaford on Eur. *Cycl.* 51) and was, as we learn from Xenophon, *Cyneg.* 6. 19, a hunting call (for hunting language generally, cf. Thomson on vv. 130–9). The bare feminine participle "sleeping (women)" also contains a note of disparagement.

95 ff. Although the gist of Clytemnestra's complaint is clear enough, the language in which she states it is incoherent with the text as it stands. Edd. have suggested rearranging these verses in various ways, often with additions or deletions of connective particles, but I believe the order which I adopt has the double virtue of restoring a semblance of logical sequence to Clytemnestra's argument, and of requiring no alterations in individual words. (I had arrived at this conclusion independently, only to discover that it had already been proposed by Samuel Musgrave in his marginal notes in a 1745 ed. of Stanley's *Aeschylus*, which I was able to examine in the British Library.)

96, 99 among the other corpses ... blame from them: among the other dead she suffers "dishonour" for her inability to get the Erinyes to execute vengeance for her; on top of that, the dead among whom she now dwells reproach her because of the murder she herself committed.

97 reproaches do not cease: with my re-arrangement, the reference of these "reproaches" is left purposely ambiguous. Not only do the other dead reproach her, but also – and especially – she will continue to cast reproaches at the Erinyes. The picture of Clytemnestra surrounded by other shades in the Underworld recalls in a general way the scene in *Od.* 24, where first the shades of Achilles and Agamemnon, then of Agamemnon and the newly- arrived Amphimedon, engage in conversation. For the "reproaches" of the dead, see Homer *Il.* XXIII. 69 ff. (Patroclus to Achilles), *Od.* 11. 66 ff. (Elpenor to Odysseus).

100 treated so terribly: she perhaps points to the slash-marks at her neck (see v. 592 below). She insistently returns to the subject at v. 103.

loved ones: a "poetic" plural (unless she has Electra's complicity in mind). The word is used frequently in Gk. poetry to denote any close bond: parent–child (here and v. 608 below, *Cho.* 234, where Orestes refers to "loved ones ... who have become hateful"), man–wife (*Cho.* 893, Clytemnestra of the dead Aegisthus), brother–sister, or any close friends. (Use of the term does not entail that there is a "loving" relationship between the individuals in question.)

102 a mother-killer's hands: Aesch. is fond of compounds of this type, and of this one in particular (vv. 202, 281, 427, 493, 595; cf. v. 283 below, "purifications of slain swine," with Denniston-Page's n. on *Ag.* 1511–12 for this kind of "shorthand" adjectival formation).

103–105 These lines have been the subject of almost unending, and largely fruitless, dispute. V. 105, or both 104 and 105, have been condemned by many edd. In spite of a certain clumsiness, or at least ambiguity, of expression, I believe they are genuine; a full defense can be found in my article "The *Phrēn* Asleep: Aeschylus, *Eumenides* 103–105", in M. Cropp and others, edd., *Greek Tragedy and its Legacy: Essays presented to D.J. Conacher* (Calgary: Univ. of Calgary Press, 1986) 35–42 (I now believe v. 103 should be punctuated as a question.)

103 **in your heart:** they cannot literally "see" her wounds, because they are asleep. There is the added consideration that they are to feel her painful wounds as she feels them. The scholiast makes the useful if not particularly recondite comment that it is "quite tragic" for the marks of Clytemnestra's murder still to be visible.

104 **the sleeping mind:** *Phrēn* is more than "mind"; it is the organ of "undifferentiated psychic activity" (R. B. Onians, *The Origins of European Thought about the body, etc.* [2nd ed., Cambridge: Cambridge University Press, 1954] 14). The point she is making is paradoxical, and based on a rather abstruse psychological theory. She is asking them to "see" her wounds not with their "real" eyes (which they would be unable to do in any case, since they are asleep), but with their "mind's eye", which, paradoxically, will allow them an even "brighter" (*i.e.* clearer and more truthful) vision than they have if they were awake. (There is perhaps the added suggestion that the *phrēn's* powers of insight, as well as foresight, are greater because sleep is a time when the *phrēn* is free of the confused and distracting impressions experienced during waking hours.) The word "bright" is regularly used by scientific researchers like Alcmeon of Croton and Anaxagoras before Aesch., and the writers of the Hippocratic corpus afterwards, to explain the physiology of sight. Aeschylus elsewhere commends oracles and prophetic visions as being "bright," *i.e.* truthful, and not enigmatic or misleading (*Ag.* 1178–80, *P.V.* 833, perhaps *Cho.* 285, although the passage is obscure).

105 It is considerably more difficult to defend this verse than the preceding. In its justification one could point out that (a) general maxims of this kind are more often expressed in two lines, and with antithesis, than in one; and (b) the irrelevant or slightly illogical is no stranger to Aeschylus' text. The excuse for Clytemnestra's proceeding from insight (which she is insisting the Erinyes manifest in her case) to foresight rests on considerations put forward in the preceding note: these two cognitive powers were often not kept entirely distinct, and the clarity and veracity of prophetic visions were often described in terms of "brightness."

Finally, a reference to "mortals" here (**man's lot** in my trans.) seems markedly out of place, since a ghost is addressing divine, or at least semi-divine, beings. Commentators have characterized this as inept, or even impossible, but this is really a quibble; the reference to humans is quite natural in this kind of universal maxim and "merely generalises the sentiment" (as Paley remarks).

106 This is the bargain struck between dedicant and divine recipient of prayers and offerings, the *quid pro quo* (moderns, if they pray at all, are less hard-nosed).

you lapped up: she uses a word more appropriately applied to animals (thus, of the "Argive lion" at Troy, *Ag.* 828); it is not entirely out of place – Apollo alludes offensively later to their semi-animal nature (vv. 192 ff.) – but a coarse expression, and perhaps intentionally insulting. The fullness of the description of the sacrifices recalls the offerings of Queen Atossa at *Pers.* 609 ff. (cf. also Eur. *Erechtheus,* fr. 65 Austin [*Nova Fragmenta Euripidea*] vv. 83 ff.).

107 **wineless libations, appeasements for the sober:** The evidence for this aspect of the cult of the Erinyes and related beings is collected and analyzed by A. Henrichs, "The 'Sobriety' of Oedipus: Sophocles *O.C.* 100 Misunderstood," *Harvard Studies in Classical Philology* 87 (1983) 87–100 (pp. 96–97 for a "catalogue of wineless libations and their attested recipients in Attica"). For details of the actual ritual, in so far as it can be reconstructed, see Dietrich, *Death, Fate and the Gods* (London: Athlone Press, 1967) 114 ff. (offerings of water and milk, sometimes honey, along with gruel and cakes, as well as, on occasion, animal victims [*Eum.* 108, 1007], black sheep and piglets, the liquid being poured into the ground through a tube).

appeasements: a cognate term appears also in Atossa's account, mentioned above (*Pers.* 610).

108 hearth-fire: Clytemnestra uses the word *eschara*, which designated a kind of hollowed-out pit (in modern Greek, a barbecue), at which sacrifices were made to divinities of the Underworld and to heroes. The Olympians were worshipped at a *bōmos*, or free-standing altar.

109 sanctified by night: offerings are appropriately made at night to creatures who claim to be Night's children (vv. 416, 1034 below). We remember, too, that according to one source, judicial proceedings before the Areopagus were held "at night and in the dark" (Lucian, *Hermotimos* 64).

a time not shared: once again, the Erinyes' exclusiveness is emphasized (cf. v. 69 above, "with whom no one ever consorts").

110 these offerings now being trampled on: the Chorus in the preceding play had warned against the sin of "trampling justice to the ground" (*Cho.* 641–42), and the Erinyes later will use similar imagery (vv. 539 ff. below). For the implications of the word here translated "trample", see Fraenkel on *Ag.* 372 and Garvie on *Cho.* 639–45 ("it is regularly something holy or precious that is trampled and destroyed," p. 221).

111 like a fawn: the fawn was a favourite prey, no doubt in real as in fictional hunts (Homer, *Il.* XXII. 189 ff.; Eur. *Bacch.* 866 ff.). The Chorus pick up the hunt image at v. 147 below and elaborate upon the simile at vv. 246–47.

112 with no effort at all: Clytemnestra exaggerates to increase the Erinyes' chagrin.

112–113 he leapt out lightly from inside the nets: Orestes' defiance of his pursuers is made to sound almost jaunty, and his feat the more incredible because he had seemed so tightly enmeshed; cf. the phrase "light leap" at *Pers.* 305. The term used here for "net" denoted "a hunting tunnel-net, ending in a pouch" (Jebb on Soph. *El.* 1476, citing Xenophon, *Cynegeticus* 6.7). The advice given at Xen. *Cyneg.* 6.8 is relevant: "the net-keeper should set up his net-poles long and high, in order that the hare not jump over." After the murder of her husband, Clytemnestra gloatingly says that she has fenced "the nets of harm to a height past overleaping" (*Ag.* 1375–76, Fraenkel's trans.).

113 having thumbed his nose: not exactly what the Greek says, but a near modern equivalent (lit., "screw up the eyes in mockery").

114–115 about my very being: lit., "about my life"; her son's capture and punishment are of the utmost moment to her (Lloyd-Jones renders, "my whole existence").

116 I, a dream, Clytemnestra: The line is a magnificently formal conclusion to what has been (from v. 106 on, at any rate), a strong piece of rhetoric. The Ghost caps her command by announcing her name in an imperious and almost heroic way, much in the way Odysseus does when he has finally got away from the Cyclops' clutches (*Od.* 9. 504). Dr. Ireland draws to my attention the later use of this technique at Men. *Aspis* 148, where Tychē ("Chance") identifies herself after a speech of some fifty lines.

117 (snorting): the word *mugmos* here and at vv. 120 and 129 below, and *ōgmos* ("whimpering," vv. 123, 126), are descriptions of the noises the Chorus is supposed to make. The scholiast notes them as stage-directions inserted by the poet; as such, they are rather rare but not for that reason to be excised (for a different view, O. Taplin, "Did the Greek dramatists write stage instructions?", *Proceedings of the Cambridge Philological Society* 203 n.s. 23 [1977] 121–32). I take it that some, at least, of the Erinyes are in view to receive Clytemnestra's rebukes; Taplin, however, thinks that none are as yet visible (see Intro. pp. 12–13).

118 snort on, then: the same rather heavy-handed irony as at v. 94 above, "sleep on, then!"

119 For he has friends etc.: my trans. gives the general sense that I believe this line must have had, but Aesch.'s exact wording seems to me irrecoverable.

125 Cf. v. 71, "their coming to birth was for evil's sake."

127 the arch-plotters: it is not clear why they are called "arch-" (the Greek word means "with legal authority"; see n. on v. 544 below). Compare, for the image *Ag.* 650–1, "fire and sea, though worst enemies before, joined a conspiracy" to wreck the Greek fleet on its way from Troy, and for the sense, Odysseus' comment, "sweet sleep came upon me in my weariness" and overcame his watchfulness against his comrades' inquisitiveness regarding Aeolus' gift (*Od.* 10. 31.).

128 Who is the dread dragoness? Principally the Erinyes (cf. Orestes' description of them as "thickly entwined with snakes" at *Cho.* 1049–50), but use of the singular may show that Clytemnestra is also hinting at herself, for at *Cho.* 249 Orestes calls her a "dread viper."

force: an epic word, "life force," élan vital; cf. vv. 832 and 840 below.

130 Catch, catch …: cf. Ar. *Ach.* 281. It is uncertain whether only the Chorus-leader spoke this unmetrical line or whether, as Wilamowitz proposed, "the Furies emit these words not in unison but as each stirs in her dream" (scholion 130a assumes multiple speakers). In either case the language is clearly that of the hunt and the metaphor, already introduced by Clytemnestra (v. 111 above), begins to take on the vividness of reality: the Erinyes are the hunters and Orestes is their prey. The vocabulary of hunting will recur frequently (vv. 139, 147 ff.), reaching its climax at vv. 246–47. For the technical language of the hunt, see Thomson's full note on 130–39. For hunting imagery in Aesch., P. Vidal-Naquet, "Hunting and Sacrifice in Aeschylus' *Oresteia*," in J.-P. Vernant and P. Vidal-Naquet, *Tragedy and Myth in Ancient Greece* (Engl. trans. Brighton: Harvester Press, and Atlantic Highlands: Humanities Press, 1981) 150 ff. (162 ff. for *Eum.*); E. Petrounias, *Funktion u. Thematik der Bildern bei Aeschylos* ([*Hypomnemata* 48] Göttingen: Vandenhoeck and Ruprecht, 1976) 173 ff. There is a good analysis of how this hunt-imagery is calculated to inspire terror in J. de Romilly, *La crainte et l'angoisse dans le théâtre d' Eschyle* (Paris: Les belles lettres, 1958) 88 f., 91 f. She remarks that the Erinyes seem less interested in catching Orestes than in making him feel "indefinitely and cruelly hunted."

Catch: I follow Thomson in interpreting this as "Catch his scent" rather than "Seize him."

Bar him: I have translated M.L. West's emendation for the word offered by the MSS, which must mean "Be careful!" (*Bulletin of the Institute of Classical Studies, Univ. of London* 24 [1977] 100).

131 you're baying: the noun from which this verb is formed is regularly used in descriptions of hounds during a hunt (Xen. *Cyneg.* 4.5, 5.19, 6.17 and 23).

132 –133 … its troublesome task … don't let toil: I retain the MS reading at the end of both lines (with 132 compare *Ag.* 1530–1, *phrontidos … merimnan*). (To be noted, however, is Dawe's change of *ponou* in v. 132 to *phonou*, which is accepted by Page and A.L. Brown; the meaning will presumably be, "its concern (to follow the trail) of blood.")

133 gain a victory over: compare v. 88 above for a similar expression.

134 do not … ignore my misery: she means the wrong being done to her by the Erinyes in letting Orestes escape, rather than her murder at Orestes' hands.

make you soft: compare v. 74 above, "show no softness."

135 let your insides ache: lit., "feel pain in your liver" (at v. 466 below "heart" replaces "liver"). A deep or genuine impression made on one's inmost sensibilities is said to "touch" or "approach" the liver at *Ag.* 432, 792, cf. *Cho.* 272 (see J. Dumortier, *Le vocabulaire médicale d'Eschyle et les écrits hippocratiques* [Paris: Les belles lettres, 1935] 19; Hipp. *Morb*. II.4; de Romilly, *La crainte et l'angoisse* [n. on v. 130 above] 28–29). Compare v. 158 below, with n. there. **my just reproaches** picks up her reference to "reproaches" in v. 97 above.

137 **Send someone**: Not without misgivings, I accept Wakefield's change of the final word to the "ominous" indef. pron. They are to send "someone", that is, Orestes, on his way, fill his sails (there is a similar nautical metaphor at *Cho*. 317 and 927, with Hermann's emendation) with a **gale of blood**. There is perhaps an additional point, since the Pythia had warned of the Erinyes' "unapproachable exhalations" (v. 53 above).

138 **shrivelling him up**: similar expressions of physiological detail can be found in the Hippocratic corpus.

the belly's fire: their scorching, withering breath comes from deep within them (I see no need to weaken the meaning of the word translated here as "belly" [or "womb"; cf. v. 665 below], as Dumortier attempts to do [*Le vocabulaire médical d'Eschyle* (n. on v. 135 above) p. 17: "poitrine"]).

139 **wither him**: the vb. recurs in v. 280 below.

by renewing your pursuit: lit., "with second pursuits." If this is supposed to mean "a second stage of pursuing" (the first presumably being that as far as Delphi), the expression seems oddly obscure. After speaking this line the Ghost departs, presumably by the same way by which she entered (see n. on 93 *Action* above).

140 The writer of the M-scholia adds to the designation of speaker that this line is spoken by only one member of the Chorus, which the context makes probable enough.

141 **kick off sleep**: the metaphor, that of a bucking horse, is not uncommon. The compound form of the vb. occurs again at *P.V*. 651–2 in the rather odd phrase "Don't kick off (i.e. spurn) the bed of (i.e. marriage with) Zeus."

142 **our dream prelude**: in music and the recitation of epic poetry, the introductory section to a longer work was designated by this term. Later, it came to have a technical sense in rhetoric, "exordium." Cf. v. 20 above, "by way of prelude."

143–178 The Chorus' entry-song, or "Parodos," which derives its technical designation from the fact that it was usually sung as the chorus entered the orchestra along the parodoi, or side entranceways. Since so much obscurity attends the timing and manner of the Chorus' entry in this play, it is impossible to be sure how many chorus-members were "in place" for the singing of this song (see Intro. pp. 12–13). A time-interval might therefore be postulated between vv. 142 and 143, to allow the Chorus-members to "awaken," *i.e.*, step from the platform or from inside the temple, take up a regular formation, and sing the "Parodos" in the manner of an ordinary ode.

The Chorus respond to and corroborate Clytemnestra's charges. They share her suffering (vv. 143–45 with 121), the intolerable chagrin at having had their prey escape; and the sting of her reproaches has reached home (vv. 156–9 with 136). More to the point, however, for the subsequent action, they lay blame upon Apollo (although the designation "younger gods" in v. 162 is ominously general; we remember that Athena will come in for her share of condemnation later); though a god, he has condoned godless behaviour (vv. 151, 153, 172), and has thereby defiled the sanctity of his own shrine (vv. 164–70), and contravened justice (vv. 154, 163). The song ends with their insistence for the first (but by no means the last) time on the inexorability of their pursuit of Orestes (vv. 174–8).

The metre is a mixture of dochmiac (generally taken as denoting high excitement) and iambic (see Appendix III, below). Scholars disagree about whether or how much of the song was divided among individual choristers, perhaps as each was aroused to full wakefulness. Some commentators have suggested that the Chorus divided and sang alternating stanzas antiphonally, as semi-choruses (thus, "me ... also" in v. 174).

143–145 we have suffered.... I have suffered.... We suffered....: this rather disjointed sequence, with the change from pl. to sing. and back to pl. again and postponement of the direct object to v. 145, suggests an interruption of one singer by another.

144 in vain: because their labour in pursuing Orestes as far as Delphi seems to have been wasted, since he has got away. V. 144 and its corresponding v. 150 as well as 147 = 153, 155 = 162, and 169 = 174 are iambic trimeters, normally the metre of spoken dialogue. If these were delivered in a kind of recitative, it is perhaps an indication that that particular chorus-member was just "coming to" from her comatose inactivity.

147–148 A return to the hunting imagery; see n. on v. 130 above (for the net see n. on v. 112–113 above).

149 you're a thief: they set up a slight conundrum, which they proceed to explain in v. 153 below, "you filched away."

150 The Erinyes make two points against Apollo: (1) he is younger than they and should be showing deference to his elders, and (2) they are females and as a male he should respect them. The themes will recur frequently; Petrounias (cited in n. on v. 130 above) 280 ff. cites vv. 150, 731 (where it is again combined with "trampling down"), 778 f.= 808 f., 838 = 871. **aged:** Apollo had used this epithet of them at v. 69 above. Besides being a description, it could also be a proper name, "The Aged Ones," who were sometimes identified with the Phorcides, female monsters, three in number, akin to the Gorgons and Echidna (Hesiod, *Theog.* 270 ff.), whose repulsive appearance is described at *P.V.* 794 ff. Aesch. wrote a separate play *Phorcides* (frs. 261–262 Radt). **you rode roughshod:** the term bears a hint of insouciant violence; it is repeated at vv. 731, 778 and 808 below, not elsewhere in Aesch.

151 reverencing ... godless: an effective contrast. Words cognate with this, denoting "reverence," are very frequent in this play, accounting for approximately one-third of the occurrences in Aesch.

152 cruel: lit. "sharp, bitter," although the metaphor is hardly felt.

153 mother-murderer: also at v. 210 below. Rose suggests that this, along with the term "father-murderer," were "the old legal or sacral words for one who assaults a 'parent,' the offense lying in the assault itself, apart from whether or not the results were fatal." If this is correct, the Erinyes may intentionally be using an emotionally charged word against their adversary.

filched away ... a god: strongly contrastive; gods ought to be (at least in Aesch.'s world-view) protectors of the moral order.

154 To this indignant question there is really no answer (these are similar forms of expression at *Ag.* 1487–8, *Cho.* 338); "justice" is thus shown to reflect different world-views, those of Apollo and the Erinyes being irreconcilable (for the time being, that is, until Athena bridges the gap).

155–168 Blass remarks that there are numerous correspondences (*Gleichklänge*) in this passage. These are sometimes exact verbal repetitions ("one can ..." in vv. 160 and 167), sometimes more subtle patterns involving phrases of similar syntactical and metrical shape ("into my heart, into my guts" v. 158–9 = "around its feet, around its head" v. 165–6). Fraenkel also comments on the "accurate symmetry" of the passage (*Aeschylus, Agamemnon* v. III, p. 515 n. 1).

155 This is a direct response to the Ghost's command at v. 135 above.

157 his goad grasped tightly: lit. "held in the middle" (perhaps to give greater force); the image is picked up from v. 136 above, "as sharp as goads." There may be an additional metaphor from wrestling since "held in the middle" suggests "a wrestling hold in which a man grasps his opponent around the waist and lifts him off the ground to throw him for a fall" (M.B. Poliakoff, *Studies in the Terminology of the Greek Combat Sports* [*Beiträge 3ur klassischen Philologie* Heft 146; Frankfurt/Main: Hain, 1986] 40; cf. ibid. 46–7).

158 into my heart: the *phrenes* (sing. *phrēn*; see v. 104 above), the major organ of perception and feeling, were conceived to have a specific physical location, which Aristotle describes as the diazoma, or "midriff," separating the heart and lungs from the liver, spleen and kidneys (*Parts of Animals* 672 b 11 ff.). In many passages, however, the term has a predominantly mental sense (see, in general, Onians, *Origins* [cited in n. on v. 104 above] 23 ff., 27–8 for Aesch.; Dumortier, *Le vocabulaire médical d'Eschyle* [n. on v. 135 above] 6–12).

into my guts: lit. "lobe of the liver" (see n. on v. 135 above).

160 torturer: Aesch. is fond of forming agent-nouns of this type, where the first part of the compound is itself a noun (in this case *mastix* = whip, scourge).

public: Aesch. uses the term denoting the slave who was the public executioner at Athens.

161 heavy, very heavy (similar are *Ag.* 215–6 and 1396). This term, which denotes something like "oppressive, threatening, dangerous," recurs frequently in the play as a kind of leitmotiv, the implication generally being that the Erinyes will be "oppressive" if they are not placated (see vv. 373, 711, 720, 730, 780 = 810, 794, 800, 932).

162 younger gods : as at v. 150 above.

164 ff. The phantasmagoric image of Apollo's throne and navel dripping with blood is effective, though certain minor points in the text remain obscure. Any "throne" at Delphi is most naturally taken as belonging to the god of the shrine or, by extension, to his priestess (cf. v. 616 below). It is not entirely clear, however, why this should be endowed with a head and feet, around which blood is pictured as dripping (I do not think Rose's interpretation is tenable: "presumably the foot and head, *i.e.* the whole person, of the deity occupying the seat"). The compound **dripping with gore**, which recurs at *Ag.* 1427, is a typical Aeschylean formation (analogously, *Sept.* 939, "flowing with blood," and cf. v. 367 below, "blood-stained").

168 I take the adj. *blosuron*, used by Homer in the sense of "shaggy, bristling", as modifying **navel** in the preceding line, with "blood" (Aesch. uses the plural form; perhaps something like "deeds of blood") as a kind of genit. of material dependent upon it: "the navel bristling with bloody deeds, having acquired a lasting pollution." For **pollution** Aesch. uses a strong word (*agos*) which denotes a ritual defilement whose effect might last in the minds of the superstitious for generations (one thinks of the *agos* of the Alcmeonid family, to which Pericles belonged; Thuc. 1. 126). The notion is picked up by **stained ... with defilement** in vv. 169–70. See in general R. Parker, *Miasma. Pollution and Purification in Early Greek Religion* (Oxford: Clarendon Press, 1983) 5–12.

171–2 he did it himself, unbidden: this constitutes the first part of the Erinyes' indictment against Apollo, that his protection of Orestes was spontaneous, and so the more reprehensible. **against the gods' law** in v. 172 lays the second part of the charge, and with the starkest of contrasts in the way the words for **human concerns** and **gods'** are juxtaposed: Apollo has aided his human protégé in contravention of a law which itself has the authority of the higher gods behind it. The phrasing is reminiscent of *P.V.* 29–30, "a god, not cowering before the anger of the gods, on mortals you bestowed honours beyond justice."

173 destroying the Fates: the audience would certainly have remembered the story, which Death in a similar scene from Euripides' *Alcestis* throws up to Apollo (v.

12), that the god cheated the Moirai by making them drunk; the Erinyes return to the tale in a more explicit way in vv. 727–8 below. It is to Aesch.'s advantage to remind his audience of this story for another reason: he will be concerned at various points in the play to enhance the status of the Erinyes by closely associating them with their more respectable half-sisters (vv. 334–5, 392, 1045–6, esp. 961–2; and compare *P.V.* 516). Cf. in general Garvie's n. on *Cho.* 306–8. Another reason for the Erinyes' invoking of the Fates here is the association of the latter goddesses with Dikē (*Ag.* 1535–6, with Fraenkel's n.).

        born long ago: cf. v. 150 above.

     174 me ... also: Although the phrase has been explained in other ways, the most natural interpretation is that it indicates a change of singer within the Chorus (so Murray and others).

     175 Even if Orestes flee to the Underworld: *i.e.*, not even death saves a sinner from punishment (evidently, in light of the whole "theology" surrounding the Erinyes; cf. vv. 338–40 below and *Suppl.* 228 ff., 414–416).

     177–178 Both the exact text and the meaning are obscure. The scholiast explains the word here translated **suppliant** (it certainly has that meaning at v. 41 above) as "accursed," and there are contexts where it must mean that (e.g. Eur. *H.F.* 1161, vv. 237 and 445 below; the scholiast on the latter also gives the meaning "accursed.") Furthermore, it is not clear whether the sentence refers to Orestes, who was the subject of the verb in the preceding verse, or Apollo, the subject of "rescue" in v. 174. Finally, it is uncertain what action is envisaged in v. 178. I mark the end of v. 177 and v. 178 as corrupt.

179 Action
Apollo emerges from his temple and gesticulates to the Chorus gathered in front of his precinct. His language is vehement, almost uncontrolled. He carries a bow (v. 181 and cf. Eur. *Alc.* 35, 39–40).

     I tell you!: Apollo is accustomed to giving commands (vv. 88 and 90 above, 235 below).

     180 recesses: the technically correct term for the "inmost recesses" of the temple, the *sanctum sanctorum*, to which, in some accounts, the Pythia retired to give her prophecies; cf. vv. 169–70 above. (Vv. 179–80 have sometimes been used to argue that some members of the chorus emerged from the temple just before Apollo's entry, but it seems to me likelier that he is simply ordering them to leave his entire precinct.)

     181 winged, gleaming snake: according as we are impressed or put off by the god's appearance and general manner, this will either be typically oracular circumlocution, or bombast (the latter not unusual in Aeschylean "high style" – e.g. dust the "thirsty sister of mud" at *Ag.* 494–5 or the "voiceless messenger of an army," *Suppl.* 180; fish as the "voiceless children of the unpolluted [mother]," *Pers.* 576–8 – and so perhaps not intended to characterize Apollo here). The verbal puzzle is solved by **bowstring** in the following line.

     182 Another resounding three-worder (in Greek; cf. v. 41 above, with n. there). With the compound translated here **beatengold** (also at *Sept.* 644) compare *Cho.* 290, "beatenbronze". Aristophanes could not resist a jibe at Aesch.'s "beatenbronze griffin-eagles and horsesteep phrases" (*Frogs* 929).

     183–184 disgorge ... black froth ... vomiting up the clots of gore: unpleasant language, but graphic and clinically precise. Apollo has a penchant for this kind of talk, which he will very shortly indulge more fully (vv. 186 ff.). In a sense, the physical process here described is the reverse of Clytemnestra's comment at v. 106

above, "you lapped up." With vomiting up compare v. 730 below. To be noted, too, is the detail of Clytemnestra's ominous dream: the snake to which she had given birth (= Orestes) drew from her breast a "clot of blood with the milk" (*Cho.* 533).

186 ff.   This list of brutal and degrading punishments kept the ancient commentators guessing, to judge from the number of lexicographers' notes and "glosses" that has survived.   After such exquisitely sadistic penalties, the ordinary Greek punishment of execution by stoning (v. 189) seems somewhat tame.

190   Impaled under the spine: there are few passages in Greek that come close to, let alone equal, the foregoing list for sheer blood-curdling horror; but we may compare the punishments which Orestes says he was threatened with by Apollo's oracle (*Cho.* 271 ff.).

191   so abominated: cf. v. 68 above.   In both cases the verbal root *-ptu* sounds like what it means, "to spit" (metaphorically also at v. 303 below).

192   the whole manner of your appearance: an ungallant comment, but not untypical of Apollo; Athena will be more polite (vv. 410 ff., a point she reverts to after the Erinyes' conversion and transformation into "Eumenides," v. 990).   There is a good parallel to this mode of insult at *P.V.* 78 (Hephaestus to Kratos), "your tongue's utterances are like your looks."

194   Lions stalk the house of Atreus (*Ag.* 141, 717, 827, 1224, 1259; *Cho.* 938); cf. in general, B.M.W. Knox, "The Lion in the House," *Classical Philology* 47 (1952) 17–25 = *Word and Action* (Baltimore: Johns Hopkins, 1979) 27–38; W. Whallon, *Problem and Spectacle* 40.   The adj. **blood-sucking** seems chosen by Apollo to give maximum offense; Clytemnestra had spoken, with greater boldness, of a "blood-licking lust," *Ag.* 1478.   The Erinyes echo and expand on this image at vv. 264–6 below.

195   rub off your defilement on strikes me as a vulgarism quite in keeping with Apollo's tone throughout the speech.

shrines you happen to be near: Page's caution led him to mark the transmitted text "suspect": rightly, in my opinion.

196   she-goats without a goatherd: perhaps another colloquialism, the "goat-" terminology adding an extra insult (Apollo can use this kind of metaphor very politely when he wants to: see vv. 78 "your tendance" and 91 "shepherding", with nn.).   The Erinyes will (verbally, at least) have the better of Apollo when they later remark that they have "shepherded" the whole earth in their pursuit of Orestes (v. 249).

198   Lord Apollo: by contrast to Apollo's vicious invective, the Erinyes are almost deferential (for a similar locution, see v. 574 below, where however, there is a problem of speaker-attribution).

199–200   not only share responsibility ... bear total responsibility: The point of the Erinyes' reproach against Apollo is that he has no one with whom to share the blame (not even Orestes!), but must bear the whole moral blame himself.   The chorus of elders in *Ag.* had used the term "totally responsible" as an epithet of Zeus (*Ag.* 1486).   The reference of these events in v. 199 is somewhat vague, like "these acts" in v. 154; they mean the whole situation. (See Fraenkel on *Ag.* 144.)

201   Continue ... so far: this may be sarcasm posing as politeness, a characteristic mode of Apolline speech in this play.

202–203 begin with the Greek vb. "prophesy," the next three vv. start with "and." It is angry and excited repartee, each side trying to get the better of the other (see in general S. Ireland, "Stichomythia in Aeschylus: the Dramatic Role of Syntax and Connecting Particles," *Hermes* 102 [1974] 509–24).

204   his shelterer: lit., "receiver;" for all that Aesch. likes – perhaps invents – this type of agent-noun (see v. 160 above, "torturer"), it is an odd phrase nonetheless.

206   who did nothing more than escort: they are being rather heavy-handedly ironical. The word **escort** perhaps prefigures, by the merest hint, the "escorts" who will accompany the Erinyes themselves at the end of the play (see vv. 1006, 1032 below).

208–209 The Erinyes proceed, with studied calm, to justify their presence at Delphi, and the debate opens out into a wider discussion of their function. Apollo, in his by now familiar caustic way, picks up their reference to "what has been assigned" and turns this in a direction of "honour" and "privilege." Little do we suspect at this point that upon a precise definition of their "honours" will depend the whole issue of their appeasement and absorption into the body politic of Athens. Formations on the *tim*-stem, which in the plural can mean "official functions," recur as a kind of leitmotif in the remainder of the play: vv. 227, 394, 419, 747, 807, 810, 824, 845 (847 in the trans.), 854, 868, 884, 894, 915, 967 (966 trans.); see, in general, E. Petrounias, *Funktion und Thematik der Bilder bei Aischylos* (n. on v. 130 above) 282.

209 Boast on: the Chorus had used the term, with a similar note of distaste, if not repugnance, just after Clytemnestra's long speech of exultation at her part in Agamemnon's death (*Ag.* 1399–1400).

your fine privilege: the word Aesch. employs here, like that for "honour," is Homeric, and it, too, often has a semi-concrete meaning, "(specific) privilege, perquisite." The Chorus will echo these terms proudly at the end of the First Choral Ode (vv. 393–4 below).

210 mother-murderers: see n. on v. 153 above.

212 The Chorus' reply, that only "murder of kin-blood" is within their sphere of prosecution, may seem to us rather lame; where were they, after all, when Agamemnon slew his daughter Iphigeneia? (Commentators have also detected a rather different notion of the Erinyes' functions at *Cho.* 283–4: Orestes claims that Apollo's oracle threatened him with "attacks arising from his father's spilt blood" if he were *not* to slay his mother. Garvie comments there, "At this stage [the Erinyes'] task is to punish Orestes if he *fails* to avenge his father. At the end of the play they will pursue him for *fulfilling* this duty ..." See on this inconsistency, which is underlined by Eur. at *Or.* 580–4, A.L. Brown, "The Erinyes in the *Oresteia*," 28–9, and Solmsen, *Hesiod and Aeschylus* 181–2 n. 16, with whose conclusion I agree: "... dramatic rather than religious reasons account for the restriction of the Erinyes' sphere of interest which we find in the *Eumenides*".) But it is precisely about the distinction which the Erinyes make here that the whole course of future events in the play revolves, and they revert to this very point in the trial scene later (see vv. 604–5). Apollo, the arch-Sophist, will take the topic to a new pitch of refinement in arguing that the Erinyes' pursuit of Orestes on grounds of a blood-bond between him and Clytemnestra is based on a physiological misconception: so-called "mother" and son have not this bond at all! (See on v. 657 below.) For the moment, however, he takes a different tack, and contents himself with introducing significant exemplars, or "paradigms," from the Olympian sphere to show that the sexual bond between a man and a woman, within or outside marriage (for that is the implication of vv. 215 – 216), deserves to be put on the same footing and must be considered just as sacrosanct as the alleged blood-bond between parents and children. The appeal to a persuasive example from elsewhere in the world of what we call "myth" is as old as Homer (see M.M. Willcock, "Mythological Paradeigmata in the *Iliad*," *Classical Quarterly* n.s. 14 [1964] 141–54) and is used frequently in the play (Ixion at vv. 441 and 717; Apollo himself and the Moirai [already noted on v. 173 above] at v. 724). For the time being, Apollo's argument remains unrefuted, but the Erinyes will get their own back later: it is all very well to cite Zeus' "pledges of trust" with his spouse, but his treatment of his father Kronos was less than exemplary (vv. 640–1 below).

213 **have rendered null:** the expression is closely paralleled by vv. 847 (= 880) below, and *Ag.* 229 (where see Fraenkel's n.).

214 **pledges of trust:** often used of marriage-vows (*Ag.* 878, *Cho.* 977). **Hera, Protectress of marriage:** the epithet *teleios* derives from the use of the word *telos* to designate a religious ritual and in particular the nuptial rite (cf. v. 835 below). Zeus Teleios (not in its more etymological sense, as at v. 28 above) and Hera Teleia, along with Aphrodite, were the gods specially invoked by a nuptial pair (Plut. *Mor.* 264 B), and Hera had a shrine under that cult-title at Stymphalos (Paus. 8. 22. 2, where it is implied that the title was awarded upon her marriage to Zeus).

216 **humans' most intimate relations:** the term *ta philtata* (see v. 100 above) here refers specifically to sexual intercourse, as the following lines show; the verse does not refer to "offspring of a marriage" (so Italie, *Index Aeschyleus*, p. 318: "used of the joys of love, not offspring").

217 **the destined marriage-bond ...:** cf. the cliché "marriages are made in Heaven" (although that of Clytemnestra and Agamemnon clearly was not). The Erinyes can hardly disagree with the sentiment (see below, vv. 958 ff.). Apollo seems to be combining two arguments (with a consequent loss of clarity): (1) the bond between marriage partners is every bit as sacred as that between parents and children; (2) it is inconsistent for the Erinyes to be exclusive in the prosecution of offenders against the latter but not the former, especially since that has physiological and genealogical priority.

218 **greater than any oath:** the language is similar to that in v. 621 below, but what point is Apollo trying to make? What is the "oath" involved in blood-ties? He must mean, in a general way, "more sacred even than the sacredness of an oath." (Dr. Ireland suggests to me that the expression "emphasise[s] the emotional bond rather than the more contractual aspect of marriage.")

219–220 The general sense is clear, although some minor textual and syntactical obscurities remain. (In 220 I accept, though unenthusiastically, Meineke's *tinesthai*, which most edd. adopt.)

220 **supervising angrily:** in his n. on *Ag.* 1270, Fraenkel called this a "remarkable phrase," for the vb. "supervise" generally denotes a benevolent activity by a higher being, as immediately below at v. 224, *Ag.* 1270 (already noted), *Cho.* 1, and elsewhere. The word "anger" is, as Garvie remarks in his n. on *Cho.* 924, "particularly associated with the Erinyes in *Eum.*;" cf. vv. 501 (499 in the trans.), 800, 840, 889 and 900.

222–223 The general sense is clear: Apollo points out a glaring inconsistency between the Erinyes' reaction to Orestes' murder of Clytemnestra and her murder of Agamemnon. But the exact text is uncertain. I accept Paley's suggestions and translate accordingly.

224 **decision about rights,** since the meaning of the word for "justice" in the plural is "pleas of right," as at *Ag.* 813, *Cho.* 461, *Suppl.* 231, and (apparently; the text has been questioned) v. 187 above. **in this case:** the vague pseudo-demonstrative, as at vv. 81 and 154 above (alternatively, "of these two opposing parties," Orestes and the Erinyes).

Apollo reaffirms his confidence in the fairness of Athena's judgement; cf. vv. 79 ff. above. This is an important step towards a final resolution of the conflict.

226 **Well, then:** I take this trans. from Sidgwick, who comments that the combination of particles is "impatient and contemptuous."

make more trouble may be a colloquialism = "toil to no avail."

227 **try to curtail:** really, since it is a pres. imperat. (as in the preceding verse), "keep on trying." I have taken the last word in the line as referring to the whole gist

of Apollo's preceding argument (so Paley, "your special pleading"), but other interpretations are possible (Verrall translates "by a word," and sees a reference to the term "trouble" in the preceding verse).

229 The Erinyes appear to mean, "You can highhandedly brush aside further privileges because your reputation in Olympian circles is so high." Since, however, in an exchange of this kind, the level of invective tends to increase, I think that the line must contain a more serious, if somewhat covert, criticism: "the way you are acting shows that your high reputation is undeserved."

230 ff. The scene ends as it began, with the two sides totally at odds. The Erinyes express their intent to take up again their hunt of the victim (see on v. 130 above). Apollo for his part will carry on with his mission, continued protection of the suppliant Orestes.

230 a mother's blood leads me on: the graphic immediacy of the language here and at v. 247 below seems to me to confirm the interpretation of the phrase "new-drawn sword" given in the n. on v. 42 above.

231 Action

The Chorus now leave the orchestra in a manner that "must have been quick and direct, quite likely at a run" (Taplin, *Stagecraft* 375) and in the same direction as Orestes had taken, that is, by the east parodos (see on v. 93 above). Apollo, at a more majestic pace, delivers the final three verses and then returns inside his temple. It is noteworthy that it is the Erinyes who take the lead; Apollo cannot stop them and does not try; he can only respond to their initiative.

234 a suppliant's wrath: the phrase brings out clearly that the suppliant is a sacrosanct person, for the term translated "wrath" is a strong one to use in this connection; it is a force that the Erinyes have in their own keeping to use against those with unclean hands (vv. 313–4, 889 below and *Il.* XXI. 523, where the phrase "wrath of the gods" occurs; also v. 101 above). In Aesch. Wrath is a mighty goddess-abstraction. She attracts powerful epithets: "remembering, child-avenging Wrath" (*Ag.* 155); "Wrath that-brings-her-thought-to-fulfilment" (*Ag.* 700, Fraenkel's trans.), and she has a hand, as those passages show, in the punishments of Paris and Agamemnon for their respective sins. (She also joins in forming striking compounds: "divinity of oppressive wrath" *Ag.* 1483; "murder that-arouses-sharp-wrath" v. 472 below).

The situation has in a sense been reversed. A divine being (Apollo) had threatened a human with terrible punishments for failure to obey his oracle; now the god must fear the wrath of the human for not protecting him from another set of divine forces, ones with whom he is at odds. As Dr. Ireland comments, "it is as if [Orestes] were now dictating the course of events".

235 Action

It does not happen very often in extant Greek drama that the Chorus leaves the orchestra, with a resulting vacancy of both acting and dancing space (see Taplin, *Stagecraft* 375–6, for the other instances). What effect might the poet have wanted to achieve? First, the inexorability of the Erinyes' pursuit of their victim is emphasized; Orestes had been told by his divine protector to roam the whole earth (vv. 75–7) and the huntresses are now shown ready to follow, undeterred, indefatigable (so Taplin, who notes their parting reference to the hunt-image at vv. 230–231). They are different from the choruses in the two preceding plays – and from what survives of Aeschylean drama except *Suppl.* – in that they are totally involved in the action and have a major stake in its outcome. At the level of stagecraft as well, it is immensely helpful to the dramatist to be able to bring Orestes on to an empty theatral space, for the audience is given to understand right from the beginning of the scene that the setting is now Athens. Since the text at vv. 242 and 259 makes clear that Orestes, upon instructions from Apollo (v. 80), addresses and embraces a statue of Athena, this must have been brought in during the interval after v. 234; whether it was placed in the orchestra or on stage is uncertain (see Intro. pp. 13–14). (Taplin [*Stagecraft* 377] entertains the possibility that the statue may have been in the orchestra from the beginning of the play, but this seems to me unlikely.) The presence of Athena's "ancient statue" seems intended to indicate that the scene has shifted not only to Athens but to a particular place in Athens, the Acropolis where, in later times, Athena's statue stood in the Erechtheum. It seems to be the Areopagus Hill at v. 566. Perhaps the reference to the shrine of Athena to which Orestes has now come is left purposely vague, precisely to obviate the need of a further scene-change. (So Thomson in his n. on v. 235: "... we are not told which shrine it is, nor in what part of the city. The situation is deliberately left undefined in order that we may pass on to the trial without further change of scene.")

235 by Loxias Apollo's instructions: here and at v. 241 Orestes is quick to present his *bona fides:* he has come to this solemn place and is now a suppliant at this most venerable statue, not out of any personal presumption, but only in obedience to a higher authority (vv. 79–80; cf. v. 224) and one which Athena herself is bound to acknowledge.

236 The word translated **accursed wretch** normally means "avenger." (See, for a similar shift of meaning, Soph. *Aj.* 373 with Jebb's n.) Other words which show this reciprocity in meaning (that is, both "active" and "passive" senses) are *prostropaios* (n. on v. 41), *miastor* (v. 178) and *palamnaios* (v. 448). See, in general, E. Tichy, *Glotta* 55 (1977) 171–2; Fraenkel's n. on *Ag.* 1501.

237 polluted suppliant: for the range of meanings of this word, see n. on v. 41 above.

uncleansed: given Aesch.'s fondness for significant names and other forms of word play, it seems likely that the Greek word he uses, *aphoibanton*, was chosen to remind us of Phoebus Apollo's role in Orestes' purification (v. 283 below; cf. also vv. 448 ff. below). The word occurs only here and at fr. 148 Radt from Aesch.'s *Neaniskoi* (see M.L. West, *Bulletin of the Institute of Classical Studies, Univ. of London* 30 [1983] 70 with n. 37).

238 ff. Taplin has noted the repeated emphasis in the play (vv. 75 ff. above; also 284 ff., 451–2) on the extent of Orestes' wanderings and the variety of purificatory procedures he claims he has already undergone (*Stagecraft* 379, 382–3). Why are the Erinyes not satisfied? Why do they continue to hound him, their lust for this blood unquenched? Apollo ordered the murder; Apollo purified the murderer, a point made repeatedly (*Cho.* 1059–60, *Eum.* 283 – with all its problems of interpretation from the point of view of cult –, 578; note especially that Athena accepts the fact of Orestes' ritual purity, v. 474 "purified, causing no harm to this abode"), but this makes not the least difference to them. No amount of merely "ritual" cleansing, no mere passage of time, no appeal to a higher authority such as Apollo's – indeed, the name of Orestes' protector seems merely to enflame their anger – can get them off his track. Thus the challenge to Athena is even greater to find a way where Apollo's pompous ritualism has failed. (See, on the connection between ritual-legal pollution attendant upon homicide and the action of *Eum.*, R. Parker, *Miasma* [n. on v. 168 above] 114, 386–7.)

Orestes' reference at v. 240 to **Crossing ... [the] sea** may indicate that he traveled by ship from Delphi's harbour (modern Itea) to the Isthmus of Corinth, and thence to

Athens by land; or perhaps he is simply indulging in overstatement.

238 blunted: the force of the metaphor can be seen clearly at *Sept.* 715, where Eteocles tells the Chorus, "I am whetted; you'll not blunt my edge with argument" (also *Sept.* 844, *P.V.* 866–7).

238–239 worn away ... dealings with men: the phrase reflects the belief widely held in fifth-century Greece that "the killer's exile is itself a form of purification" (Parker, *Miasma* [n. on v. 168 above] 386).

240 crossing ... 241 observing ...: normally these would be aorist participles indicating completed action. Present participles are used perhaps for vividness.

241 commands: the word used occurs in rather elevated contexts to denote solemn injunctions of gods or parents (*Cho.* 300, 685).

242 I am here: I translate my conjecture *pareimi* for the MSS' *proseimi*, "I shall approach".

243 the outcome of justice: the phrase is ambiguous (perhaps intentionally so) and could also mean "end of the case." It recurs at v. 729 below, and cf. v. 434 for a similar ambiguity. (See in general S. Goldhill, "Two Notes on *telos* and related words in the *Oresteia*," *Journal of Hellenic Studies* 104 [1984] 169–176, at 172.)

244 Action
The Chorus re-enter the orchestra in a second, or additional, parodos, almost certainly with a convincing dumb-show of agitated searching and bloodhound-like sniffing (v. 253). While they are thus engaged, the chorus-leader speaks the ten-line iambic introduction, as in the (first) Parodos (vv. 140–43). They then at v. 254 settle into their song, which is not symmetrically arranged in matching stanzas, but "astrophic" (W.C. Scott, *American Journal of Philology* 105 [1984] 158 ff.). Taplin, who notes similarly astrophic choral entrances, comments that the "lyric could well be split into parts and distributed among individuals or parts of the chorus" (*Stagecraft* 339). Various edd. attempt to indicate changes of singer with dashes (*paragraphoi*) scattered amongst the lines, but it is mostly guesswork. (The divisions in Thomson and Murray occur at lines 254, 258, 261, 264, 267, 269 and 273.) The metre, as in the Parodos (vv. 143–177), is a mixture of iambs (or equivalent) and dochmiacs; see Appendix III.

245 The leader speaks to her fellows in the manner of a hunter to his hounds, and uses a cryptic phrase of the type favoured by Aesch., although this is a rather tame example (see n. on v. 181 above). With **blood** in v. 247 the verbal puzzle is solved. The whole phrase is similar, as Groeneboom notes, to *Sept.* 82, where the dust raised by the attacking Argive army is referred to as "a voiceless, clear, genuine messenger."

246 See v. 111 above, with n. there.

247 The scholiast here calls the image of Orestes' sword still dripping with blood, after his long travels from Argos to Delphi and thence to Athens, "impossible." I prefer to see it as part of the eerie vividness, already noted on vv. 41–2 above, with which Aesch. portrays a murder so horrible that, for the Erinyes in their relentless pursuit at least, it is as if the trail of Clytemnestra's blood dripping from Orestes' sword had just been laid, and so with a potency still capable of drawing them on. (A more prosaic interpretation will confine the trail of dripping blood to the simile.) Verrall had the unusual idea that the blood was Orestes' own ("the phenomena of internal bleeding and the dripping of blood from the mouth, as marks of extreme physical exhaustion ..." [n. on his v. 244]).

248 gasping out his guts: a typically vivid physiological detail; cf. v. 138 above. The adj. **man-crushing** or "man-killing" (cf. v. 956 below; *Cho.* 889, Clytemnestra's call for a "man-killing axe;" *Suppl.* 678, a "man-killing plague") seems to me to count heavily against the usual interpretation of this line, which goes back to the scholiast here, that it is the Erinyes who are "gasping out their insides" because of their exertions in pursuing Orestes. Unless we are to justify their reference to a "man" along lines used to explain Clytemnestra's comment about "mortals" in v. 105 above (where see n.), the first part of the compound is meaningless (A.L. Brown suggests that the meaning is "deadly to their victims"). My interpretation rests in part on the similar language of *Ag*. 1388 ff. (the wounded Agamemnon "gasping out a sharp butchery of blood") and requires taking the word translated "guts" as the object, not the subject, of the vb. "gasp out," the subject (sc. "my victim") being supplied from what has preceded, esp. the reference to "the man" in v. 244. Cf. Soph. *Ant*. 1238.

249 driven like a sheep: the Greek says, more literally (and somewhat peculiarly), "the whole earth has been gone over as by a flock of sheep" (the vb. had been used at v. 91 above to imply "careful tendance," a sense that does not seem to be present here). In a manner of speaking, their image answers Apollo's insult at vv. 196–7: they are not goats, and do not need tending.

250 without wings: the phrase carries the same implication of effortless speed as Athena's entry "without wings" in the problematic v. 404 below; and of course they are, in actual fact, "wingless" (v. 51 above).

252 cowering with fear: they use a word whose stem recurs in the noun meaning "hare" at v. 326 below.

253 the smell of human blood smiles ...: a bold, chilling image, reminiscent of *Iliad* XIX. 362 ("the glitter of bronze rippled like laughter over the plain," Rieu), but its horror lies precisely in the repulsiveness of the object which is said to "smile in welcome" at the Erinyes. Cf. Eur. *Tro*. 1176–7, where Hecuba describes her dead grandson: "the gore of your broken bones smiles out."

255 In spite of some uncertainty about the exact text, the sense is hardly in doubt (the line must mean, in effect, "be sure to look all around" or "at everything").

256/257 mother-slayer: Aesch. uses a synonym for the term that occurs in vv. 153 and 210 above, the normal form of which will appear in v. 268 below.

unpunished: lit., "without paying his debt" (at *Ag*. 72 the same term occurs, but in an – apparently – different sense, "unhonoured.")

259 his arms twined round ... the statue: where this statue was placed is uncertain; see n. on 235 *Action* and Intro pp. 13–14, above.

260 I have accepted Scaliger's emendation, **debts,** for the word which the MSS offer, "hands."

261–262 blood once fallen cannot be recovered: a clear and forceful echo of statements made by Choruses earlier in the trilogy: "When a man's black blood has once fallen in a deadly pool before him, who could call it back again by singing an incantation?" (*Ag*. 1018–21); "What atonement is there for blood fallen to the ground?" (*Cho*. 48); "Because of blood drunk up by the nurturing earth the avenging gore lies solid and does not flow away" (*Cho*. 66–7, Garvie's trans.). The theme will be reiterated later (vv. 647–8 below; cf. 980). Fraenkel calls it "one of the themes ... which bind the trilogy into a single whole" (his n. on *Ag*. 1018 ff.). (See A. Lebeck, *The Oresteia* 87 ff.)

263 the liquid once spilt to the ground is gone: the phrasing of *Cho*. 400–2 is very similar: "there is a law that bloody drops spilt to the ground demand other blood" (the line continues by mentioning the agency of the Erinys, although the text is slightly uncertain).

264–265 let us suck the red clots from your limbs: the Erinyes seem to take a rather malicious delight in recalling Apollo's earlier charge that they belong "in a blood-sucking lion's cave" (v. 193).

your living flesh: they are distant analogues of the Transylvanian vampires.

Cassandra had envisioned them as a "revel band that has drunk human blood" (*Ag.* 1188–9); Orestes pictures the Erinys "quaffing a third [hence, mystically potent] draught of blood – unmixed" (*Cho.* 578; cf. Soph. *El.* 785–6, *Trach.* 1053 ff.).

266 fodder: continues the grazing metaphor; they seem to accept, for the moment at least, the beast-like role Apollo has cast them in.

267 I shall shrivel you: just as Clytemnestra's Ghost had ordered them to do (v. 138 above; Paley remarks that this was one of the punishments threatened by Apollo's oracle, *Cho.* 296 with Garvie's n.). They can threaten to **take** him **down** to Hades, because even there he will not escape their assaults (v. 175 above).

269 ff. It has often been remarked how broadly the Erinyes here conceive their punitive, that is, protective, functions: **god or guest or dear parents;** they are in effect setting themselves up as guarantors of the "Unwritten Laws" (cf. *Suppl.* 701–9). It is noteworthy that, quite apart from this wider and more general moral supervision which they claim here and to which they return in vv. 545 ff. below, their mention of **dear parents** in v. 271 shows that they are already thinking of an expanded mission beyond punishment only for matricide (vv. 210–12, 268 just above, 605–608). "Mother" broadens out to "parents" again at vv. 496–8, 513–5 and 545–6, and in the course of Athena's preliminary investigation of the litigants, they even seem to extend their punitive watchfulness to murder in general ("We drive murderers from their homes," v. 421). It is of practical importance as well to the dramatist to expand the Erinyes' range of moral interest to its widest possible extent; it will make their so-called "conversion" at the end seem less drastic.

273 ff. Hesiod (*Works & Days* 252 ff.) paints a strange, moving picture of Zeus' "thirty thousand immortal watchers (*phulakes*)" who supervise men's transgressions; in the next lines (256 ff.) he tells how Zeus' daughter, Dikē, also sits by her father and tells him of men's "evil intent." Onto this older view of Zeus' oversight of human wickedness Aesch. has grafted a separate (perhaps Pythagorean) strand of belief in a god of the Underworld, Hades or, as he is sometimes called, "Nether Zeus" (cf. *Cho.* 382 with Garvie's n. on 382–5), who keeps an account of human rights and wrongs, and punishes or rewards men after death accordingly. Yet a third element enters into the way the Chorus express themselves, the official examination of a magistrate's record after his term of office (the *euthunai*).

275 his recording mind: cf. *P.V.* 788–9: Prometheus tells Io he will give an account of her wanderings which she is to "record in the remembering tablets of your mind," and *Cho.* 450: Electra urges the chorus to "write [my sufferings] in your minds." At Aesch. fr. 281a. 21 Radt, Dikē describes one of her functions as "writing [men's] transgressions in Zeus' tablets." Cf. also Soph. *Ph.* 1325 and fr. 597 Radt, with D. Sansone, *Aeschylean Metaphors* 59 ff.; F. Solmsen, "The Tablets of Zeus," *Classical Quarterly* 58 (1944) 27–30; G.F. Nieddu, "La metafora della memoria come scrittura e l'immagine dell'animo come *deltos*," *Quaderni di Storia* 19 (1984) 213–9. (As theology this was ridiculed by Eur. in *Melanippe the Wise*, fr. 506 Nauck.)

276 ff. Orestes ignores the violent threats of the Erinyes and makes another appeal to Athena's statue. By now he (and perhaps also the audience) may be beginning to wonder not when but whether the goddess will actually appear. Aeschylus will delay bringing her on through another entire choral ode, thus raising the tension as high as it can justifiably go (this is akin to his device of bringing on characters like Niobe or Achilles, but then letting them remain silent for long periods while the action goes on about them; cf. Taplin "Aeschylean Silences and Silences in Aeschylus," *Harvard Studies in Classical Philology* 76 [1972] 57–97). Orestes' first address (vv. 235–43) was comparatively brief. Here, he returns to the two main points he had made earlier, his lack of ritual miasma (237–9 = 277–87) and the fact that he acted under orders of Apollo (235, 241 = 278–9), but he expands on the first by going into some detail about specific purifications he has undergone (283) and adducing as a proof of his ritual purity his apparently uninjurious converse with men (284–5). He makes an additional offer which he hopes will tilt the balance in his favour and induce the goddess to accept his suppliancy: the practical benefits of an alliance between the people of Argos and Athens (289–91). Noteworthy throughout this speech are the themes and clichés of prayer: the dire straits in which the petitioner finds himself, local references to other places within the divinity's sphere of activity, possible advantages to be gained by the god from accession to the request (see on this point Taplin, *Stagecraft* 388).

276–278 Orestes means, in effect, that he has been "schooled in suffering," has had a variety of experiences, including an assortment of purificatory procedures, and so knows when he should speak and when not (this last sounds like a proverbial expression: *Cho.* 582, *Sept.* 619, fr. 208 Radt). Sensible remarks in defense of the transmitted text are offered by Taplin, *Stagecraft* 383 n. 1.

279 **a wise teacher**: besides being a compliment to his protector the phrase neatly rounds off the image in "taught" in v. 276.

instructed me to speak: the ref. may be general, or in particular to Apollo's use of the phrase "words that cast a spell" in vv. 81–2 above, although the greater part of these will not be spoken until the courtroom scene (and then by Athena).

280 **the blood is drowsy**: Aesch. used this relatively uncommon word to have Clytemnestra remind Orestes of the way he had "drowsily sucked milk at her breast" (*Cho.* 897–8).

withers: the active voice of this vb. at v. 139 above; it perhaps was a medical term (Hipp. *Epid.* 7. 84 of the disappearance of a tumour).

281 **miasma of matricide**: a similar phrase, with "patricide" for "matricide," occurs at *Cho.* 1028, where it is applied to Clytemnestra.

282–283 Orestes says, in effect, "I went to Delphi and was purified there by Apollo," but when exactly in the action of the play as Aesch. conceived it did the purification take place? It is foretold by the Chorus at *Cho.* 1059–60, "Loxias will touch you and free you from these sufferings," and later Apollo will acknowledge that he was Orestes' purifier (v. 578; cf. 474 where Athena refers to him as "purified"). Yet the Pythia's description at vv. 40 ff. shows that the purification has not yet occurred (cf. her adjuration to her master at vv. 62–3). No very satisfactory solution has been offered to this minor mystery. Since there seems to be no opportunity in the dramatic time of the play for this to take place between Orestes' departure at the end of the opening scene and his arrival at Athens, we must assume a slip on the dramatist's part. (Apollo's purification is in any case just one among the several alluded to by Orestes at vv. 238–9 and 451–2, and none of this will make any impression on the Erinyes. As an Aeschylean chorus say in a different context, "When men of the same blood slay one another, there is no growing old [cf. *Eum.* v. 286] of this pollution", *Sept.* 681–2.)

282 **while it was still fresh**: another possible meaning of the Greek word is "although it was quite unprecedented," and in an article important for its presentation of the evidence for ritual purification at Delphi, R.R. Dyer argues strenuously for this latter sense; he would translate "although it had no precedent, the stain was driven away at a hearth ..." (*Journal of Hellenic Studies* 89 [1969] 38 n. 2). The context, however, seems to me to favour the other interpretation, with the implication, "I intercepted it [the miasma] while it was still fresh, so it didn't have a chance to 'set'." The particle **for** in v. 282 explains the grounds for Orestes' assertion in the preceding line that **the miasma ... has been washed away**, and that certainly is the implication of

the closely parallel passage *Cho.* 1055 (see Garvie's n. there), where Orestes has just said he can see clearly his mother's "angry hounds," and the Chorus-leader replies, "for the blood is still fresh upon your hands."

283 driven out with purifications: compare, for the wording, *Cho.* 967-8, where the Chorus sing of a "defilement driven out entirely by purifications that drive out disasters." **driven out** is a technical term for the expulsion of a curse or pollution (Soph. *O.T.* 98); cf. also Thuc. 1.126.2 on the Alcmeonid curse. Purification by blood of pigs was a standard remedy: Ixion (?) was thus purified by Zeus (Aesch. fr. 327 Radt), and this kind of procedure was brought into relation with Delphi by the painter of an Apulian krater now in the Louvre (K 710: see Intro. p. 30). There is, however, strikingly little external evidence to substantiate a connection between Delphi and purification. P. Amandry suggested that Aesch. was (not altogether innocently) confusing pig-purification at Eleusis, his home-deme, for which there is confirmatory evidence, with a different Delphic ritual by flowing water and laurel (*Revue archéologique* 6th ser., 11 [1938] 19-27). For the ritual of purification in general, see Parker, *Miasma* (n. on v. 168 above) Appendix 6, pp. 370 ff.

284-285 Similarly, Antiphon's client Euxitheos argued that he was innocent of the charge of murdering Herodes: "for one thing, any who took me aboard their ship as a passenger had a fine voyage, and, for another, any sacrificial rites which I attended most assuredly turned out for the best" (*Orat.* 5. 83).

286 time, as it joins ...: the line has been suspected, but with Stanley's change of accent giving **purifies** for the MSS' "destroys," it makes acceptable sense and has a proverbial ring (proverbs concerning both "time" and "old age" occur frequently, e.g. Soph. *Ant.* 1353, *O.C.* 7-8; *P.V.* 981). See Taplin, *Stagecraft* 383 n. 2.

287 So, too, now ...: Orestes takes up the points made at vv. 276 ff.: he is calling on Athena because he has been instructed to do so "by a wise teacher" who has also ensured that his speech is pure.

288 to come to me and "that she come" (v. 297) are expressions characteristically used in prayers to call on divinities for assistance (Taplin, *Stagecraft* 388).

289 as my defender: words formed on this stem can, from Homer on (*Il.* IV.408, XVIII.502), have a semi-technical meaning, "defend before a tribunal, act as advocate" (cf. Fraenkel on *Ag.* 47; compare vv. 486 and 598 below, *Suppl.* 726, with Friis Johansen's and Whittle's n.).

without compulsion of arms, that is to say, not after conquest, or under military duress (with perhaps an oblique ref. to Sparta's "allies").

291 as trusty allies: Orestes offers a *quid pro quo* in return for asylum; this is the first of three refs. in the play to the alliance between Athens and Argos concluded c. 460 B.C. (see vv. 670 ff., 762 ff., and Intro. pp. 19-20 for the possible political overtones).

for all time: see n. on v. 52 above.

292 ff. whether in Libyan regions ...: "the list of places where the god may be found is traditional in Greek prayers," Dodds on Eur. *Bacch.* 556-9 and citing our passage; cf. *Il.* XVI. 514-5, Bacchyl. 16. 5-7, Alcaeus fr. 34 Voigt). This was a tactful compliment to the divinity's wide range of influence and a way of ensuring that the prayer reached its destination; thus Glaucus, in the *Il.* passage just cited, after calling upon Apollo to hear him "whether he may be in Lycia or Troy," adds, "you have power to hear from anywhere a man in distress" (Blass on our passage remarked, "thus the more numerous and distant the places, the greater her power").

How topical is the allusion to Libya in v. 292? Cf. Thuc. 1. 104. 1 and Intro. p. 20.

293 stream of Triton: the lake and river in Libya near which (in one version of the story) Athena was born. The scholiast here notes Athena's epithet "Triton-born" (*Il.* IV.515, VIII.39; *Od.* 3.378). Herodotus (4. 180) mentions an odd variant current among natives in the region: Athena was really the daughter of Poseidon and the water-nymph Tritonis, but got annoyed with her father and passed herself off as Zeus' daughter.

294 The words taken literally mean "she plants her leg erect or covered" (Lloyd-Jones), but what are we to make of that? The standard explanation sees a ref. to archaic statues either standing or sitting (cf. Paus. 1.24.7 and Strabo 13.1.41, C 601, cited by Paley). Some interpret it to mean "walking" and compare *Od.* 17. 158, where Odysseus is described as "seated or moving."

295-296 overseeing: a cognate term occurs in a list of honorific titles given to Athena by Solon: "great-spirited, overseer, daughter of a mighty father" (fr. 4.3 West). In certain contexts it occurs in connection with Athens' interference in her allies' affairs.

Phlegraean plain: the region referred to is almost certainly Pallene in the N. Aegean, the westernmost finger of the Chalcidice peninsula (Hdt. 4. 123. 1), which was the site of the battle of Gods and Giants, in which Athena played an important part (Pind. *Nem.* 1. 67-8; Ar. *Birds* 823-5, Diod. Sic. 4. 15).

297 a god can hear even from afar: the phrase is parenthetic, Orestes giving a perhaps rather naïve justification for his address to an absent Athena. The expression "from afar" links Athena and Apollo (v. 65 above) who are never, so to speak, out of range of their suppliant's needs. Athena's first words will be a confirmation that she has indeed heard "from afar" (v. 397 below). Dodds notes the parallel between our passage and Eur. *Bacch.* 392-4 "the Celestial Ones, though they inhabit the aether far away, see the affairs of men."

298 these creatures here: alternatively, this might be a vague neut. (as at vv. 81, 154, 199 and 224 above), but I prefer Douglas Young's interpretation of it as fem. (A gesture by the actor playing Orestes to the threatening Erinyes would have decided the matter.)

299 ff. The Choral Ode that follows is again prefaced by a short speech by the Chorus-leader, as at vv. 244-53. It is a brisk rebuke to Orestes' hopes: he should expect no help from his divine patrons; his adversaries intend to proceed to wreak their worst upon him. Orestes is not taunted into replying, however (v. 303).

299 strength: Athena shares this word with Apollo (v. 61 above, with n.) and Orestes himself had appealed to that strength (v. 87). The Erinyes are undaunted, and obviously feel themselves to be a match for their divine adversaries.

301 to perdition: the word is sudden, harsh, almost vulgar (the Erinyes will later use the word of themselves, in a conditional way, as the votes are being counted; see v. 747 below). The phrasing at the end of this verse carries a threat to make Orestes shudder, and is substantially repeated at v. 423 below. Translators disagree about exactly how it should be rendered, but Rose's comment comes close to what I take to be the correct view: "so unused to joy as to forget with what part of the mind, what faculty, one rejoices." I think the phrase implies, "in no corner, however remote, of your feelings (see n. on v. 158 above) will you have the capacity for joy." They fully expect to bring his *phrenes* totally under their control (vv. 332, 345 below). A similar phrase occurs at Soph. *O.C.* 1216, where Jebb cites the present passage.

302 bloodless because, of course, they will have sucked him dry (vv. 264 ff. above); so the scholiast, "we shall suck up your blood." He will be a mere ghost of his former self. **Fodder** picks up the pastoral metaphor of v. 197 above.

shade: *skia* was the technical term for a dead 'soul' (*Od.* 10. 495 etc.). As the next verse indicates, this line was followed by a pause (Wilamowitz remarks that the

Chorus-leader was perhaps expecting Orestes, if not to try to escape, at least to cry out in fear; that he does not do so attests his confidence in the divine protection for which he has just been praying.)

303 spit at my words (Douglas Young): see n. on "abominated" in v. 191 above. Although the phrase might be given a different meaning, "scorn to speak," the former sense is likelier: "your silence constitutes a scornful rejection of my threats." So Mazon, "tu rejettes en crachant mes paroles ..."

304 "Like a beast set apart specially to be reared for sacrificial purposes" (Rose). It was customary to rear certain animals and let them roam free in temple-precincts until the time of sacrifice (Plato, *Critias* 110 D for the rearing of bulls in this way to Poseidon). The grisly contrast comes in the next line: Orestes is not to be sacrificed like an ordinary victim, and certainly not at an altar (*bōmos*), which was reserved for offerings to the Olympians (cf. n. on v. 108 above), but – apparently – devoured alive.

306 The Erinyes will cast a spell on Orestes and thereby clinch the consecration of the victim to themselves mentioned in v. 304. In an interesting article, C.A. Faraone argues that some of the motifs in this song (e.g., Orestes' silence at v. 303), might have been paralleled in actual contemporary "curse tablets," deposited before a trial to secure magical superiority over one's adversary ("Aeschylus' *hymnos desmios* (*Eum.* 306) and Attic judicial curse tablets," *Journal of Hellenic Studies* 105 [1985] 150–154).

307–321 These lines form an anapaestic prelude to the First Choral Ode, a feature found only in Aesch. of the tragedians (also at *Pers.* 532–47, 623– 32, *Suppl.* 625–9 and *Ag.* 355–66); "the function of these systems is purely introductory" (Friis Johansen & Whittle on *Suppl.* 625 ff. I see no reason for assuming, as is sometimes done, that they were delivered not by the whole chorus but by the leader alone; for the contrary view, MacDowell on Aristoph. *Wasps* 725–8). It is uncertain whether they were 'chanted' or merely recited; the absence of 'Doric alpha' is generally taken as showing that they were not sung.

This is a genuine *prooimion,* or prelude; its function is to introduce in a straightforward, easily comprehensible and almost prosaic way the main themes of the Binding Song which follows (see n. on vv. 321 ff.). The chorus had previously entered in an unconventional manner, mimicking their role as bloodhounds. Here they exhibit a new and somewhat studied formality. Paley remarks on the significance of this change; their previous "fitful irregularity of huntresses" having been to no avail, they now "propose a new method", more threatening and (potentially, at least) more effective. Dr. Ireland has put it to me that the anapaests might suggest their "coming into formation around their victim with almost military precision."

307 Every chorus in Greek tragedy sang and danced. Here a conventional element of the Chorus' role is skilfully incorporated into the action. Cassandra had anticipated this literal constitution of the Erinyes into a Chorus by her reference to them as a "chorus singing in unison but not euphoniously" (*Ag.* 1186–7).

let us also: that is, presumably, in addition to singing. The phrase in Greek is rather cryptic: "let us link the dance" (Weir Smyth, after Verrall); "nouons la chaîne dansante" (Mazon).

308–309 our frightening Muse (= music): a fairly common oxymoron, whereby the normally joyful connotations of music, dance or instruments like the lyre or aulos are applied in doleful contexts or with pejorative adjs. The image recurs frequently in the *Oresteia: Ag.* 709 ff., 990–1 "the lyreless Erinys-dirge", 1143, 1176, 1186–7 (cited in preceding note), 1473; *Cho.* 467; vv. 331–2 below; cf. *Sept.* 868 "the ill-sounding Erinys-hymn." See J.A. Haldane, "Musical Themes and Imagery in Aeschylus," *Journal of Hellenic Studies* 85 (1965) 33–41. (The root *stug-* connotes 'fright' as well as 'hate'; see West's nn. on *Theog.* 211 and 739.)

310–311 (My trans. is adapted from Lloyd-Jones.) They portray themselves as discharging an official function which, they claim, entitles them to prosecute horrendous criminals like Orestes without interference from the 'higher' gods. The meaning of *lachos* here is 'appointed office'; the phrase should not be interpreted as "fates which men have allotted to them" ("the lots which prevail among mankind", Paley; the schol. is ambiguous), but rather is to be taken, as Verrall rightly emphasizes, in relation to the 'honours' and 'privileges' already mentioned (vv. 209, 227 above). These 'offices' form a dominant theme of this song (vv. 334, 347, 385) and, along with the 'honours' claimed as their due by the chorus, will figure in the resolution of the conflict (vv. 930–1, where the wording is similar to the present passage, but the Erinyes' working among men is beneficent).

discharges: this word is sometimes wrongly interpreted as "apportions."

company: the term had already been applied to the Erinyes by Cassandra (*Ag.* 1117, cf. 1119). If this prelude is delivered by the chorus-leader alone (see n. on vv. 307–21) the word here translated "our" might be rendered "my"; see Friis Johansen and Whittle on *Suppl.* 106–7.

312 The phrase as it stands in the MSS is manifestly corrupt, although the sense is not in doubt. Whatever the exact text, the term "straight judgement" came to have a technical meaning in legal contexts, a "direct trial" on the merits of the case, without exceptions or technical pleas (LSJ *s.v. euthudikia*). (See v. 433 and n. below.)

313 The Erinyes implicitly deny Orestes' claim to have been purified (v. 283 above). The text is faulty and various changes have been proposed; I translate my own suggestion.

316 The phrasing is reminiscent of v. 269 above.

318 **true witnesses** are ones who in judicial proceedings observe their oaths, etc.

319–20 **we have full authority to collect the fine:** the word translated "full authority" also implies "completely, efficaciously." The Greek word *praktores* designated Athenian officials who were responsible for collecting fines, debts and lease-payments due to the city. At 623 below Orestes is described as "exacting the penalty of his father's murder."

321–396 Structure There is a fairly serious structural uncertainty in this choral ode. The MSS repeat the short stanza vv. 328–33 after Stanza 1', as vv. 341–6. Many edd. therefore repeat vv. 354–9 after 366 and 372–6 after 380, but there is no justification for this in the MSS and Page simply leaves the tradition as it is. It is not an easy choice. W.C. Scott argues that whereas vv. 354–9 might be able to be repeated (the explanatory "for ..." of 354 could equally well explain 365–6, which simply echo the thought of 350 ff.), "372–6 ... is disruptive if repeated" ("Nonstrophic elements in the *Oresteia*," *Transactions of the American Philological Association* 112 [1982] 179–96 at 190). Since the MS repeats *Suppl.* 117–22 as 128–33 and *Suppl.* 141–3 as 151–3, edd. generally insert *Suppl.* 162–7 again after 175. On the other hand, in spite of the fact that the MSS repeat *Ag.* 1489–96 as 1513–20, modern edd. generally do *not* insert a repetition of *Ag.* 1538–50 after 1566 ("the words of Clytemnestra 1576 ff. are a direct reply to 1563–6," Fraenkel). See, on this whole complex question, A.F. Garvie, *Aeschylus' 'Supplices': Play and Trilogy* (Cambridge: Cambridge Univ. Press, 1969) 43–4, and Garvie's commentary on *Cho.*, pp. 255–6 and 304.

I propose as an alternative the excision of vv. 341–6. These lines, too, are "disruptive," since the phrase "these offices" in v. 347 must refer to the content of Stanza 1', which ends at 340. In any case, to achieve perfect symmetry we should also have to suppose that a Fourth Mesode has fallen out of the MSS between Stanzas 4 and

4' (i.e. after v. 388).

Content A too superficial reading of this Ode might leave the impression that it lacked coherence, and was intended to make an impression mainly through the incantatory rhythms, refrains, and a general mood of terror and threat. No doubt these irrational (better 'subconscious') elements were important means which the poet used to good effect; but there is also a tightly-knit and quite logical presentation of ideas and dominant themes, points which the poet wished his chorus to leave in the minds of the audience. To bring these out clearly, I give, somewhat schematically, a prose rendering of the Erinyes' message.

They conceive their pursuit of Orestes to be part of a larger cosmic scheme in which they have their assigned functions (311, 334, 347, 385 [line refs. are to the translation, not the Greek text]). Looked at from a slightly different point of view, these are their "honours," the privileges due to them (324, 394 and cf. n. on vv. 208–9 above). (The imagery is frequently borrowed from the language of civic offices and responsibilities: "full authority to collect his blood" 319–20, "immunity" 362, "station" 395, perhaps "test," 364.) These duties were assigned to them by Moira (334, 392), officially ("guaranteed" 348, "guarantee" 362, "guaranteed by Moira" 392) at their birth (347; cf. 321) to be fixed and unshakeable ("firmly implanted" 335). The discharge of these duties must be a manifest example to wrongdoers ("determined to display" 308, "show him" 319).

The range of the Erinyes' activity is universal (322, 387–8) and they are confident of accomplishing their purpose (319–20, 382, 393). They are sudden in attack (377), diligent in pursuit ("versatile" 381, "mindful of wrongs" 382–3), inexorable (338–40; cf. 175–6, 383–4). The effect of their punishment is physically painful (333, 358–9, 369; cf. 302), but in spite of their victims' ignorance or self-deception (368–9, 377), these latter are sinful and polluted (316, 378), so that the Erinyes' justice is deserved, "straight" (312, "true witnesses" 318; cf. 272).

With the solemn discharge of their duties the Olympians may not interfere (349–51, 362–4, 386). Just as the range of their activities is totally different – and the "higher" gods should be glad of being absolved of any responsibility therein, 360–1 – so their feasts and ceremonies are separate (351 ff., 365/6 [cf. 108–9, 191]). Black attire (352–3, 370) is suitable for ones whose domain is dark, subterranean (386, 395–6), and this in turn is matched by the darkness afflicting their victims' sinful minds (377–8). Appropriately, then, these sinners will be brought to the Erinyes' own infernal realm (338–40, 395–6), reduced to their pursuers' status as bloodless wraiths (302, 358–9 [?]). Specifically, Orestes is consecrated to them (306, 326–7) and will be sacrificed (328), but not in an ordinary sacrifice (305). So, too, the dance they are at present engaged in (307) is no ordinary dance (371; the Mesode following Stanza 3, vv. 372–6, is a travesty of a dance). Their music is unmusical (309, 332–3). Their hymnic song does not praise but binds (306, 329, 331–2) and sets to frenzy, maddens (329–30; cf. 377 "his brain is destroyed"). Finally, in the last stanza, there are verbal foreshadowings of developments to come: with "fear" in v. 390 compare 517 ff.; "ordinance" in 391 anticipates 484, and 572.

321 They refer to the fact that they are daughters of Night again at vv. 416, 745, 791–2 (= 821–2) and 844 (= 876) below, and are thus addressed by the Escorts at v. 1034. Their father's name was variously given as Skotos, 'Darkness' (Soph. *O.C.* 40, 106; see n. on vv. 71–2 above), Acheron (Servius on *Aen.* 7. 327), or Kronos (Epimenides fr. 19). Hesiod has them born from Gaia and the severed genitals of Ouranos (*Theog.* 185; cf. Apollod. 1. 1. 4; Schol. Aeschines *in Timarch.* 188), whereas Night numbers among her fatherless children the Moirai and Keres (*Theog.* 217, with

West's n. *ad loc.* for various overlapping genealogies and functions of Moirai, Kēres and Erinyes).

322 They personify themselves as a requital for sin and they repeat their association with *Poina* again in the Second Choral Ode (v. 543 below); see Garvie's n. on *Cho.* 946–7 for additional refs. Dead and living, lit. "blind and seeing," as at vv. 387–88 below. Designation of the dead as "blind" is a natural form of expression (see, e.g., Alcestis' death-bed remark, "night is coming over my eyes," *Alc.* 269).

324 In charging that Apollo dishonours them they refer to their earlier exchange with him at vv. 227–29 above. According to Friis Johansen & Whittle on *Suppl.* 251, a rather rare word for son in v. 323 (*inis*) "imparts a lofty tone."

326 cowering hare: compare v. 252 above, and, for the hunt image, n. on v. 130. The word is that used to describe the portent at Aulis, a pregnant hare devoured by two eagles (*Ag.* 136).

328 Over the victim: Aesch. uses a participle in the perfect tense, which suggests that, in their opinion, Orestes, who is consecrated to them (v. 304), is already as good as dead.

329 to bring delirium: perhaps an echo of *Ag.* 223, where the same word is used by the Chorus to try to explain how Agamemnon could have brought himself to sacrifice his daughter. It was also a medical term.

332–33 For the oxymoron, see n. on v. 308–9 above, where the closely analogous phrase at *Ag.* 990–1 is quoted. The Erinyes' description of their song as a withering (the schol. explains the unusual word used here as "that which dries up"; a cognate form occurs in Archilochus) fits in well with Clytemnestra's description of their noxious breath (vv. 138–9 above) and repeats their own earlier threat to Orestes (v. 267).

334 office echoes "offices" in vv. 310–11 above.

Moira: as daughters of Night, the Erinyes are half-sisters of Moira (Fate) or the Moirai (see n. on v. 321 above), and they will specifically refer to this relationship at vv. 961–2 below. Besides, it is to their advantage to claim that their vengeful activity has the sanction of a settled, fated order of events which, as the *Iliad* makes clear, even Zeus could not easily controvert.

relentlessly: translates a word whose meaning is not quite certain. In some contexts the image is of a weapon that strikes or pierces "right through" (so *Cho.* 380–1, where an apparent synonym, *diamperes,* occurs). Schol. M here paraphrases "(Moira) who avenges thoroughly." It is possible that this word, like so much in this song, is borrowed from the vocabulary of medicine; Hipp. *Peri arthrōn embolēs* 45 (IV. 190 Littré) uses the term to describe tendons running along the whole length of the spine.

335 It is possible that the verb here translated spun out may contain an allusion to the name of one of the Moirai, "Klotho" or "Spinner"; in the *Od.*, Alcinous predicts that when Odysseus gets home "he will experience whatever *Aisa* [= Moira] and the dread Spinners spun for him at his birth" (*Od.* 7. 197–98).

336–7 I mark the text as corrupt. In my opinion, it is unlikely that Aesch. had his Chorus sing about murderers as if their criminal acts simply "happened to them" (see Rosenmeyer, *The Art of Aeschylus*, 306); the most popularly accepted restoration has them "falling in with" their crimes. Secondly, *autourgia* should mean "working oneself, farming one's own land," although LSJ and commentators give it a special meaning here, "murder of kin", presumably by analogy with such terms as *authentēs,* "perpetrated by a kinsman" (used at v. 212 above) and *autocheir,* "murderer," on the one hand, and *panourgia,* "knavery," on the other. Finally, the term *mataioi* seems too weak in the context. The root *mat-* normally denotes "foolish" or "sexually wanton," although admittedly it seems to carry a stronger condemnation at *Cho.* 82 and fr. 281 a. 19 (the Dikē fragment).

338 attend, with a sinister connotation as at *P.V.* 678.

339 The change to singular until he goes ... is surprising. Since the text of the preceding lines is in doubt, we cannot even be sure that the construction does change from pl. to sing., which would be awkward but not unparalleled (see vv. 313–14).

Even in death ...: for the sentiment, compare v. 175 above.

340 not unduly, a sardonic (and idiomatic) way of saying "not at all" (cf. *Ag.* 992–3).

341–46 = 328–33 I have excised these lines and omit them from the translation; see n. on vv. 321–96 above.

347 these offices: refers back to the content of Stanza 1', as if vv. 341–346 had not intervened.

guaranteed: Aesch. uses a word which adds solemnity and weight. It recurs in Stanza 2' at vv. 361–2 (where, however, the text is in doubt), probably with the same suggestion of something pre-ordained and therefore incontrovertible. Cf. vv. 949 and 968 below and, for the simple form, 759–60.

349 keep their hands away: there is a colloquial abruptness about the wording here, reflecting, perhaps, the anger which the Erinyes feel at the infringement of their rights by Apollo. Rosenmeyer comments, "The Furies revel in their separation from the rest of the gods, in spite of the fact that they have their office from the gods" (*The Art of Aeschylus*, 230).

351 partake of our feast: picks up the image of v. 305 above.

352/3 The Erinyes have no share ... in white-robed festivals such as the gods frequent because, among other things, their robes are (appropriately) black (v. 370 below with v. 52).

353a Because of what appears to be an extra clause in the corresponding place in Stanza 2' (v. 367), edd. generally assume that a metrically equivalent line has dropped out here, although the text makes sense as it stands.

354 For ...: either giving a reason for a statement in the assumed lacuna just preceding or explaining in a more general way the basis for the separation between the functions of the 'upper' gods and those of the Erinyes.

354–355 overthrow of homes: Aesch. uses the image elsewhere of the squandering of wealth (*Pers.* 163) or the destruction of a city (*Sept.* 1076).

355 War-god: by a fairly common extension of meaning this term has come to designate any "destructive spirit" (e.g. *Ag.* 1511, *P.V.* 860–1; Pind. *Pyth.* 11.36 [of Orestes' retribution on his father's murderers]; Soph. *Aj.* 254, where Stanford glosses it "a violent death" (by stoning), *O.T.* 190–1, where the "de-militarization" of the image is made explicit). As Garvie remarks in his n. on *Cho.* 461, "Ares regularly appears in this context of crimes in the house of Atreus." The description of the beast which, **tamed and kept in the house,** then reverts to its natural savagery, recalls the striking fable of the lion-cub of *Ag.* 717 ff.

356 slays: a Homeric turn-of-phrase (in this sense), rather unusual for Aesch.

358–359 There is a serious doubt about what image Aesch. intended in these lines. The MSS transmit a word which normally means "make dark, dim, feeble" and the reference to blood seems to show that the Erinyes are threatening to suck their victim dry and make him a mere "shade" of his former self (alternatively, some have seen a reference to the "newly-spilt blood" involved in his criminal deed; cf. vv. 204, 280 ff.), but the force of the preposition in the Greek is obscure (and has been much-emended) and the adj. *neou* ("young" or "recent") inappropriate. Perhaps Aesch. wrote *philou*, "his own blood." Matters get even more obscure in the following lines.

360 ff. The text yields sense of a kind: "We are ones who are eager to remove someone [the "ominous" indef. pron., as (perhaps) at v. 137, taken by the scholiast here as alluding to Clytemnestra] from this concern, and (eager that) the gods grant immunity to my prayers and not come to even a preliminary confrontation." The root *speud–* connotes eagerness or haste; *merimna* is the word Clytemnestra's ghost had used at v. 132 to describe the "concerned involvement" of a hound in the chase. Both *ateleia* and *ankrisis* are technical terms; the former denotes a grant of immunity from taxes or some onerous service (the Erinyes thus appear to be insisting that they be "exempt" from the god's interference in their pursuit of Orestes), while the latter designates either the "preliminary investigation" conducted by a magistrate before he referred a case to a specific court (most commentators interpret it this way and see a ref. to the role Athena later plays in Orestes' trial) or – a somewhat rare but in my opinion preferable meaning here – the examination of magistrates to establish their qualifications for holding office (cf. pseudo-Demosth. 57. 66 and 70). But sense and even syntax are obscure and much-disputed.

This chorus, like others, indiscriminately uses both sing. and pl. pronouns of itself; cf., for example, vv. 347 and 352, 354 and 358. (I have translated my own conjecture *theous t'* in v. 362 for the MSS' *theon d'*.)

365/6 our tribe: the Greek has simply "this tribe," which the scholiast interprets as "tribe of murderers." This is unlikely to be correct, for the whole tenor of the passage is a restatement of the "separation, hands-off" theme, and the chorus here close with yet another, particularly graphic, reiteration of it.

his company: the word Aesch. uses means literally "conversation place," then "council chamber." It picks up the imagery of public or social institutions encountered earlier in this Choral Ode. For "his" Aesch. uses a somewhat rare form of the possessive pron. (also at *Sept.* 640–1, where similarly the sound-pattern seems to influence the choice of words: *litōn tōn hōn*).

367 blood-stained ...: the adjs. give the grounds for their relegation from Zeus' "court."

368 ff. After the obscurities and (probably) lacunae of the second set of stanzas, clarity (for the most part) once again prevails, at least as far as the Erinyes' meaning, although here and there a doubt may persist about their exact words. They contrast the sinful man's grand schemes with the suddenness and violence of the overthrow wrought by their own assaults: "How are the mighty fallen..." The sinner is left at the end shrouded in gloom. The language in particular is noteworthy, for in the Stanza and Mesode there is a pungent play upon their own position as a singing and dancing Chorus.

368–369 In calling human pretensions **solemn** the Erinyes indulge in word play, for at v. 383 they will apply the epithet to themselves (it was a cult-title in contemporary Athens). We have heard the adj. **dishonoured** frequently enough earlier in this choral ode and it will recur at v. 385 below. Here it is as if the sinner were encroaching on their territory, and so they have an additional, personal grudge against him.

pretensions: the word denotes insubstantial thoughts, imaginings, as at *Ag.* 420–21, of Menelaus' dream images of Helen, or Orestes' visions of the Erinyes (*Cho.* 1051–53).

melt ... waste: compare v. 267 above, where the Erinyes say to Orestes, "I shall shrivel you, take you down alive." Note the pointed contrast between "touch the sky" and "beneath the earth."

waste (also at *Sept.* 920) is a medical term (Hipp. *Peri arthrōn embolēs* 53 [IV p. 234 Littré]; *Mochlikon* 19 [IV p. 360 Littré]).

370 in our black robes: contrast "white-robed" in v. 352.

371 angry dancing-kicks: the apparently inappropriate adj. extends the oxymoron of "frightening Muse" in v. 308, since dancing is usually reserved for festive occasions.

angry: the adj. has a range of meanings in Aesch.; perhaps closest to our usage are *Ag.* 134 (Artemis is angry at the eagles' feast on the pregnant hare) and *Suppl.* 201, the Argive people are irascible. (On the other hand, I see no way of ruling out the possibility of a passive meaning, "hated.")

372 For ...: the connective particles ensure a close tie between the Mesode and the preceding Stanza.

372–373 taking a long leap ... come down hard: commentators have long recognized a grim parody of "normal" dancing; the leap is inordinately high and its effect is deadly. The phrase is reminiscent of *Pers.* 515–16, "O Spirit of Suffering, with what a heavy leap – too heavy ! – you jumped upon the entire Persian race." Compare Creon's remark at the end of Soph. *Ant.*: "an unendurable fate leapt at my head" (1345–6); similarly the Chorus describe the *daimon* as "jumping farther than the longest (jump)" at Oedipus (*O.T.* 1300–1).

375–376 The MSS lack a single long syllable; an alternative supplement (*gar* = "for") will give a slightly different meaning, "the limbs of fast runners are easily tripped up" (the "passive" meaning of the adj. *sphaleros* is somewhat more common).

375 nimble hardly does justice to the unique compound which Aesch. uses, "running at full stretch." The phrasing, if not the identical sense, may have been in Soph.'s mind when he had Ajax pray for help to the "august, stretch-footed (*tanupodas*) Erinyes" (*Aj.* 837, where Jebb's note collects the various "-foot" compounds applied to the Erinyes).

376 unbearable ruin: by a fairly common Aeschylean idiom, the "pendant" acc. summarizes and rounds off the action described in the preceding part of the sentence (see Fraenkel on *Ag.* 1645; Barrett on *Hipp.* 755 f.).

377 Although other interpretations are possible (the scholiast, for example, seems to understand it as, "he is unaware of the evil circumstances he is in"), I take the line to mean, "he is ignorant of the Erinyes' agency in his downfall." Cf. v. 933 below.

379–80 I have taken over Paley's trans. (with, however, some uneasiness about the text of v. 380). **a kind of murky mist:** compare, for the same idea and similar phrasing, *Pers.* 667–8, "a kind of Stygian death-mist flutters;" *Cho.* 51–2, "sunless darkness, hated by men, covers the house" (Garvie's trans.).

381 fulfilment awaits: "the notion of an unending perspective of retributive justice is there [at *Eum.* 381] compressed into a phrase of lapidary brevity" (Fraenkel on *Ag.* 1563, he also compares *Ag.* 154 and *Suppl.* 385 f. for *mimnei* placed emphatically at the beginning of the sentence).

382 They are **"accomplishing, efficacious,"** an epithet which looks back to v. 320 and ahead to v. 393. The Erinys or Erinyes are **"mindful, remembering"** also at *P.V.* 516 and Soph. *Aj.* 1390 (*Cho.* 652, "deep-pondering Erinys," is similar and Pindar uses a synonym of the Moirai at *Nem.* 7.1). They thus assimilate themselves to Hades' unforgetting surveillance of men's sins (vv. 273–5 above).

383 august: this may allude to their official title at Athens (Paus. 1. 28. 6, with S. *Aj.* 837, quoted in n. on v. 375 above); cf. vv. 1006 and 1041 below. Their claims are valid, as opposed to the sinner's empty pretensions (v. 368).

383–384 hard ... to appease: similar multiple compound adjs. are found at *P.V.* 34 (of Zeus' "implacable mind"), *Suppl.* 106 and 386.

385 dishonoured recapitulates vv. 310, 334, 347 above.

386 separated from the gods: cf. vv. 349 ff. above.

sunless slime: cf. "sunless gloom" in v. 396 below.

387 rough-and-rocky: Aesch. uses a compound which, though unique, is perfectly intelligible and which has good Homeric antecedents (*Il.* XII. 168, *Od.* 17. 204).

sighted and sightless echoes v. 323 above.

389 respect: Aesch. favours this epic word; cf. v. 1002 below, Friis Johansen & Whittle on *Suppl.* 652 and 884 (where they say that it "regularly denotes religious awe").

390 my role: the Gk. (*tad'* in v. 389) is more vague; either general, "my warnings," or with specific ref. to "offices" in v. 385.

391 ordinance: a word with the prestige of antiquity behind it. It is regularly associated with Athena's creation of the Areopagus (vv. 484, 571 [572 in the trans.], 615, 681).

392 guaranteed by Moira does not do justice to the splendid Aeschylean compound, which takes full advantage of the solemn *krain*-stem (see on v. 348) and once again stresses their relation to Moira (vv. 173, 335 above).

393 fully effective: a final reprise in this ode of the "accomplishment" theme; see n. on v. 382 above. They are making a strong claim: for all the revulsion the gods may feel at the Erinyes personally (so to speak), they not only tolerate their pursuit of criminals like Orestes, they authorize and validate it. Of course, this is a way of forestalling objections from Apollo later.

394 an ancient privilege ... not dishonoured: the Erinyes thus answer Apollo's earlier sneer at v. 209.

395 keep my station: probably a military metaphor; cf. *Pers.* 297–8, where the Queen speaks of "places ... left vacant" by military casualties.

396 sunless gloom: cf. v. 386 "sunless slime."

397 Enter Athena. Neither the method nor the place of her entry can be specified with certainty. It is generally believed that vv. 404 and 405 refer to alternative modes of entry in separate productions (the scholiast on v. 397 at least had no doubts, for he commented 'she comes on a chariot'). See n. on 404/5 below.

What is clear, however, is that Aesch. has heightened tension almost unbearably by delaying her entry so long. The Erinyes have taken full opportunity of the time to sing an elaborate, frightening "binding" song and Orestes must by now be beginning to wonder whether the goddess will, indeed, come to his assistance in person. Apollo had, after all, merely promised Orestes that he would obtain jurors (v. 81), not personal intervention by the goddess herself. From the moment she appears, of course, Athena takes full control of the present situation and of the subsequent course of events. There is never any doubt who is in charge and whose is the guiding hand in the appeasement of the Erinyes. Apollo's role shrinks to that of a mere co-litigant (*sundikos*; cf. v. 579 below).

398 ff. Why is Athena so specific about coming from the region around Troy? The scholiast here saw a pointed ref. to the dispute between Athens and Mytilene over Sigeum *c.* 600 B.C. (Hdt. 5. 94). His further comment, "it seems then that Aeschylus is inciting the Athenians to get hold of Sigeum *again*," suggests he knew, or was guessing, that there had been a renewal of hostilities. Modern writers have seen an allusion of a different and more immediate kind, some sort of recent trouble in the "Delian Confederacy". Inscriptional evidence published and discussed by B.D. Meritt ("Praise of the Sigeians," *Hesperia* 5 [1936] 360–61) shows that in 451/50 B.C. the Sigeians asked for and obtained Athenian protection against an unnamed local enemy, in all likelihood the Persian satrap; Sigeum was possibly at the same time taken into the Confederacy, for the name appears in the tribute-quota lists of the following year. Although there is no direct evidence for trouble at the date of the play, it seems likely that this was an area in which Athens was taking a special interest and therefore one on which Athena might well have been keeping a "watchful eye" in 458 B.C. (E.R. Dodds, "Morals and Politics in the *Oresteia*," *Procs. of the Cambridge Philological*

Society 186 [1960] 21 with n. 2 [= *The Ancient Concept of Progress* (Oxford: Clarendon Press, 1973) 47 with n. 2]; L.H. Jeffery, *Annual of the British School at Athens* 60 [1965] 45 n. 21). C.W. Macleod (*Journal of Hellenic Studies* 102 [1982] 125 [= *Collected Essays* (Oxford: Clarendon Press, 1983) 21]) tried to explain Athena's interest in the area around Scamander as due solely to the 'fact' that she was taking her people's part of the spoils after the Trojan War (vv. 399 ff.). Even if that were so, we have still to ask why the goddess discourses at such length on the point; a poet chooses, organizes, or gives special emphasis to his mythological "facts" often for more than one purpose.

taking control: she has asserted her rights to the land left vacant by the depredations of the Greeks and the exodus of the Trojan refugees.

401 This double emphasis on the perpetuity of the grant may also indicate Athenian sensitivity to their claims to the Troad.

402 The wording is reminiscent of Agamemnon's description of Cassandra as "the select flower of many possessions" (*Ag.* 954–55; cf. Fraenkel II, p. 433). **sons of Theseus:** the first of three allusions in the play to Theseus, the early king whose historicity Thucydides (2. 15) took for granted, and who was to become a symbol of an enlightened, even a democratic, monarch (Eur. *Suppl.*; Soph. *O.C.*). The involvement of his sons Akamas and Demophon in the "rescue" of their grandmother, Aithra, who had gone to Troy under duress as Helen's nurse, was an important episode in the Epic Cycle, and it may have been given more recent prominence for Aesch.'s audience by its inclusion in the great painting of the Sack of Troy by Polygnotus for the meeting-chamber of the Knidians at Delphi (Paus. 10. 25. 8). Theseus' repulse of the Amazons' invasion of Athens is alluded to in v. 686 below.

403 ff. From the parallel at *Sept.* 371, v. 403 taken by itself would naturally mean, "I walked here in a leisurely way, *i.e.* did not have to hurry." The picture changes, of course, with 404.

404/405 It has been maintained by almost all edd. since Paley that either 404 or 405 can stand in the text, but not both (see above, n. on v. 397). Efforts to interpret the lines metaphorically ("this car" = her aegis; "swift horses" = wind), are more ingenious than convincing. My preference is to retain 405 over 404: Athena's use of her aegis as a sail seems misconceived and her appearance in a horse-drawn chariot would have been iconographically appropriate (thus, vase-paintings and various epithets connecting her with horses; cf. also Eur. *Tro.* 536, which Lee explains by citing "Athena's interest in horses and chariot as a goddess of war;" cf. *Il.* V. 745 = VIII. 389; VI. 837–841. (**Without wings** in v. 404 recalls the Chorus' arrival "flying without wings," v. 250, which seems to me to count neither for nor against the authenticity of 404.)

406 - 407 She notices the Erinyes and expresses (to put it mildly) some surprise which would no doubt have been reinforced by the actor's gesture; 408 shows her recovering composure.

This momentary shock is perhaps reflected in the slightly awkward run of thought and syntax in vv. 407–412 (see e.g. H. Friis Johansen, *Gnomon* 48 [1976] 335). On the other hand, David Bain comments, "the reasoned and unhurried description of her [sc. Athena's] feelings is ... characteristically Aeschylean" (*Actors and Audience* [Oxford: Clarendon Press, 1972] 70).

408 Who ... are you?, Athena asks more in surprise than from an immediate quest for information. Her attention naturally is drawn first to the chorus, who are more numerous and exotic, but as she notices the suppliant at her statue she includes him, too, in her enquiry: "I am speaking to all in common."

410 like no other race ... etc.: for a similar formulation, compare the Pythia's comment at vv. 55–6 above.

414 Right stands aside: she "withdraws her patronage from", the opposite of *prostateō*, 'be a patron of' (cf. *prostatēs* 'patron, protector'). There is a similar image at *Ag.* 1103–04, "Help stands far aloof" (Fraenkel, who, however, does not personify "Help").

415 The Erinyes respond (rather belatedly) to Athena's question about their identity in v. 408. The "preliminary enquiry" or *anakrisis* thus begins (see Appendix I below, "Athenian Judicial Procedure ...").

416 They had called upon their "mother, Night" at v. 322 above (cf. vv. 745, 791–2, 844–5, 1033). Although of somewhat weaker MS authority, the text which makes the adj. modify "Night" rather than "children" is to be preferred as making a poetically stronger statement (so, too, Soph. *Aj.* 672 most MSS); a doubt remains, however, about what exactly the adj. means. It is derived either from *aiei*, in which case it means "eternal", or from the exclamation *aiai*, with the meaning "dolorous, lamentable." At vv. 572 and 672 below it certainly has the former meaning; vv. 479 and 942 are, like the present instance, ambiguous, although "everlasting" seems a more suitable description of Night here, and is a possible meaning at 479 and 942. See in general E. Degani, "*Aianēs*," *Helikon* 2 (1962) 37–56 esp. 43–6.

417 They mean, in effect, "our ordinary name is 'Curses'". The line is of interest on several counts. Rose is right to see here an allusion to the occurrence of alternative names (generally, one human, one divine) in early Epic; see M. L. West's n. on Hes. *Theog.* 831. The implication will then be that 'Erinyes,' the name they had applied to themselves at v. 331, is more elevated. Secondly, they seem to be coming down firmly on the side of the "dead man's curse" theory regarding these Avenging Spirits (see Intro., p. 7). It was a common Homeric notion that a wronged individual, especially a parent, might curse a wrongdoer and thus invoke the Erinyes to wreak vengeance (thus, *Il.* IX. 454 and *Od.* 11. 279–80), but the identification of the two cannot be traced earlier than Aesch. At *Sept.* 70 Eteocles calls upon the "Curse, mighty Erinys" of his father and Orestes invokes the "plenipotent Curses of the dead" (*Cho.* 406; the Erinys had been mentioned at 402). Clytemnestra's reaction to the false report of her son's death is to call upon the "Curse of the house, hard to wrestle with" (*Cho.* 692) and later, when faced with death herself, she urges Orestes to "reverence a parent's Curses" (*Cho.* 912).

418 Athena, as presiding magistrate, has to ascertain the legal status of the parties to a litigation (cf. v. 454 below). In contemporary Athens, proof of membership in a *genos* was one way of attesting citizenship.

419 The Erinyes return to the theme of their rights and prerogatives; see n. on vv. 208–209 above.

421 The Erinyes seem to be claiming a much wider jurisdiction even than they had done at vv. 269–72 above.

423 joy has no currency: the Erinyes' rather odd turn of phrase here reminds us of the graphic expression they had used for the total absence of pleasure at v. 301. Here their words mean literally, "... a place where pleasure is never in use" (a similar meaning of *nomizetai* at v. 32 above).

424 cry ... on (*epirroizeis*): the verb Athena uses tells us something about the tone of voice employed by the Erinyes; it is used by Theophrastus of a croaking raven.

426 Athena is as it were leading the witness, or at least anticipating the defense Orestes will later make. (Compulsion was one of the recognized mitigators of legal and moral responsibility.)

427 what could possibly ... : Aristotle makes the point, à propos a scene in Euripides' *Alcmaeon*, that it was ludicrous for a matricide to plead compulsion (*Eth.*

Nic. 1110 a 28–29, cited by Thomson).

goad echoes v. 158 above. Compare v. 466 below, "anguish to goad the heart," which in effect provides an answer to the chorus-leader's question here.

428 She means, in effect, "we still have to hear the other side." She uses a proverbial expression, as the scholiast here notes: "don't judge a case till you've heard both accounts" (Plut. *Mor.* 1034 E; Ar. *Wasps* 425–6, with MacDowell's n.).

429 he would not accept ... nor is willing to give (an oath): the legal point alluded to here (known as *proklēsis*), involved an agreement between prosecutor and defendant "to rest the issue to be tried on the oath of one or other of the parties" (C.O. Müller, *Dissertations on the Eumenides of Aeschylus* [English trans., 1853] 146); "... the parties had to take an oath (the so-called evidentiary oath) as to the truth of their case, and the court had to decide on that basis" (A.R.W. Harrison, *The Law of Athens: Procedure* [Oxford: Clarendon Press 1971] 151). It is to be distinguished from the oath known as *diōmosia* or *antōmosia*, in which both sides swore "specifically to the truth of the pleas in the documents handed in" (Harrison, 99). For the profusion of references to oaths in the trial scene, see Appendix I "Athenian Judicial Procedure ..."

As the scholiast here comments, it is clear that Orestes is unwilling to let the case be decided in this (to us seemingly perfunctory) way, so the question of "giving and receiving an oath" is raised here, only to be dropped after v. 432.

430 Athena's reprimand is rather harsh: "You are more interested in the semblance than the reality of justice." By a familiar Greek idiom, "to hear *dikaios*" means "to have a reputation for being just."

431 The Erinyes respond, rather sardonically, "you are no beggar, when it comes to wisdom"; the expression may be colloquial (*tōn sophōn* neut.).

432 Athena rebukes the Erinyes for even bringing up "oaths" in this case, as if so important an issue could be decided in such a perfunctory way. Presumably the oaths proffered by the Erinyes, as coming from supernatural beings, would have been overwhelmingly powerful (such at any rate is the implication of the scholiast's remark here).

433 The dialogue moves in a more positive direction. The Erinyes urge Athena to do her duty as a presiding magistrate; they thus in effect withdraw their objections to having the trial proceed (the Greek contains two technical terms of Athenian legal procedure, *exelenche*, and *eutheian dikēn* [= *euthudikian*, not, as some commentators and translators interpret, "straight justice;" see Verrall's n.]).

434 For the ambiguity inherent in the word here translated **issue and completion** (it also carries the suggestion of "authority over"), see n. on v. 243 above.

435 Certainly, for ..., exhibiting the regular syntactical interlocking between lines of stichomythia. The notion of reverence (*sebas*) plays a large part in the Erinyes' thinking (vv. 151, 525, 545, 715). (I read here with Hermann, *axi' ant' epaxiōn*; cf. v. 272 above, *epaxia*.)

436 Having elicited from the Erinyes their agreement (albeit somewhat grudging) that the trial should proceed, Athena now turns to the other party in the impending lawsuit to elicit from him his side of the story.

437–438 your circumstances: *xumphoras*, "the facts of what has befallen you" (Douglas Young), a word that has not quite the "neutral" sense as at v. 1020 below, but something, at least, of its usual connotation, "mis-fortune." Athena can surmise from Orestes' suppliant posture and his grim-looking attendants.

these women's: with, no doubt, a gesture in the Chorus' direction.

441 a solemn suppliant: the echo of v. 368 above may be unintentional. **suppliant**: the verb from this stem occurs at *Cho.* 1035. Zeus' purification of Ixion for the murder of the latter's father-in-law is mentioned again by Apollo in v. 718 below;

the story provided material for Aesch.'s *Perrhaibides* and *Ixion*, of unknown date.

442 make me a comprehensible reply: Athena's tone is that of a magistrate exercising full authority over the proceedings.

443-444 Orestes wishes to correct the impression he assumes he must have given (as would appear from Athena's likening him to Ixion), that he has come merely for purification; in fact, it will prove to be more complicated than that. (The constr. in Gk. is rather odd, "take away ... from your last words.")

445 a polluted suppliant: for the ambiguous *prostropaios*, see n. on v. 41 above.

defilement: the word the Erinyes had used at v. 378 above (and Apollo of them at v. 195).

447 Orestes here (as at vv. 276 ff.) launches into a disquisition upon his ritual purity; this is no likelier than his other protestations to have an effect on the Erinyes' attitude. The form of his expression in v. 447 is closely paralleled by Apollo in v. 662 below (**a mighty proof** is the language of formal argument).

448 The argument resembles that used by Orestes at vv. 284-85 above: since his purification, others have come into contact with him, to no apparent detriment to themselves. Eur. has Orestes tell a different story: "When I arrived in Athens, none of the residents voluntarily took me in, since I seemed to them to be loathed by the gods. Those who did feel pity set a table of hospitality for me separately, though under the same roof. Their silence made me silent, too, so that I might be totally apart from them in eating and drinking, and they each took their pleasant draught of wine from an individual cup" (*Iphigeneia among the Taurians*, vv. 947-53).

449-450 The purificatory ritual is the same as that described in v. 283 above.

452 at other houses: the same phrase as at vv. 238-39 above.

flowing streams: because such water was thought particularly conducive to a successful sacrifice (Aesch. *Pers.* 613, Soph. *O.C.* 469-70).

454 my family background: Orestes proceeds to give Athena the particulars she had asked for in v. 437.

455 an Argive: for the possible significance of this relocation by the poet of Agamemnon's household, see Intro. p. 19.

456 organizer of a force of sailors: the Chorus in the first play had called him, more dignifiedly, "elder leader of the Achaean fleet" (*Ag.* 184-5 trans. Fraenkel); cf. also *Ag.* 1227, *Cho.* 723 with Garvie's n. Apollo will return to the point in v. 637 below.

457 Again, we hear a resonance from the opening play: Agamemnon's first words when he finally appears implicate the gods in Troy's destruction (although it has been thought near-sacrilege that he addresses the gods as "co-responsible ... for the just claims exacted upon Priam's city," *Ag.* 811-13 and cf. 813 ff., "the gods cast decisively their votes for Troy's destruction and the slaughter of men into a bloody urn"). Of course, it is to a defendant's advantage to remind the judge that he has some stake in a verdict of acquittal. (The scholiast here comments, "he's making friends with the goddess".)

a non-city: Aesch. is fond of this kind of "privative" locution (*Pers.* 680 "ships no longer ships," *Ag.* 1142 "a song that is no song"), which was perhaps imitated by Eur. at *Tro.* 1292 f., "the great-city has perished un-cited, and Troy is no longer."

458 No sooner has Orestes reminded Athena of her sponsorship of Agamemnon's Trojan enterprise, than he attempts to sway her to his side by using emotional language to describe the manner of his father's death. It is skilful courtroom procedure and Apollo will employ it again later (vv. 631 ff. below).

459 black-souled mother: this powerful compound is unique in surviving Gk. literature, although the image has antecedents (cf. the formula "his black *phrenes* were filled with might, wrath etc." in *Iliad* and the song attributed to Solon [by Diog. Laert. 1. 61 = fr. 42 Bergk], the hypocrite's "shining countenance" belied by a "tongue of divided speech speaking from a black *phren*"). "Black-robed *phren*" at *Pers*. 115–16 is different.

460 a net of cunning design: the adj. suggests not only "with variegated embroidery," but "duplicitous." ("Embroidered robe" in v. 635 below is more univocal.) Orestes had used this same word for **net** in his address to the fatal cloth at *Cho*. 998 (Clytemnestra used a synonym at *Ag*. 1382, and Cassandra had earlier personified Clytemnestra herself as a "hunting-net", *Ag*. 1115–16).

461 gave open witness: as A.L. Brown points out to me, at *Cho*. 1010–11 Orestes had used similar language in referring to the cloak in which Agememnon was entrapped.

463 I'll not deny it: similarly Prometheus at *P.V*. 266, "willingly, willingly I erred, I'll not deny it."

464 killing in requital: Aesch. employs a single compound adj., *antiktonois*, of a type which he affects; cf. v. 268 *antipoinous* and 982 *antiphonous*.

465 answerable: repeated at 467 below ("careless even for Aesch.," Rose). (Many accept Weil's change to "sharing responsibility.")

466 anguish to-goad-the-heart: the same compound as at v. 136; a similar image at v. 427. Orestes tones down his description of the agonies that Apollo had threatened for disobedience (*Cho*. 271 ff., 1032–33). The scholiast on these lines notes that Athena at v. 426 had anticipated such a plea of "coercion."

467 took some action: with a sinister connotation, as at *Ag*. 1564, "... for the agent to suffer."

470–489 Most edd. agree that Athena's speech, especially towards the end, has suffered some textual disarrangement, perhaps with a lacuna of several lines (generally posited after v. 482). It is also clearly, and perhaps irremediably, corrupt at several crucial points. Taplin thinks that "we may have lost here [in the alleged lacuna] several important lines about the procedure of Athena's new court" (*Stagecraft*, 395 n. 1).

470 ff. Athena's train of thought seems to be: the issue is too complex, the passions aroused too bitter (*oxumenitou* v. 472), for any single individual, whether human or divine, to decide the issue by himself. Moreover, any tribunal, however constituted, will, in making a decision, be faced with negative consequences, and intolerably so: a decision against Orestes means rejection of a suppliant claiming to be "pure and innocuous," while one against his adversaries risks releasing their venomous hostility for ever after. Still, as the matter has fallen to me to adjudicate, I shall take steps to summon the best, fairest court possible; it will then be up to both sides to make their respective cases as persuasively as they can.

It is to be noted how convincingly Aesch. has portrayed Athena's dilemma: both sides have claims which are "not easily dispensed with" (v. 476; compare the King at *Suppl*. 407 ff.). Unlike her half-siblings Artemis in *Ag*. and Apollo in *Cho*. Athena refuses to fall too easily into partisanship or favouritism. She devises a characteristically Athenian solution: let there be a full and unhurried presentation of both sides before a (presumably) impartial jury whose sole function it will be to sort out subtleties of argument and weigh the sometimes almost equally balanced claims.

471 not even for me: Athena's words seem to glance at a version in which Orestes was tried before a divine tribunal (Eur. *Or*. 1650–52; Demosth. 23. 66 and 74).

472 that-arouses-sharp-wrath: the compound only here; for *Menis*, see n. on v. 234 above.

473 I mark the trans. "thoroughly inured to suffering" as doubtful. The inappropriate word offered by the MSS at the end of the line has not been convincingly mended and the sense of the participle preceding is doubtful, perhaps "broken in, tamed" (as at Eur. fr. 821.5 Nauck), a meaning which this vb. can have in the passive.

474 Once again, the emphasis on Orestes' ritual purity is to be noted (compare vv. 237 ff., 282 ff., 450 ff.).

475 As most edd. have seen, this line cannot be retained in the position the MSS assign to it (Page, accepting a suggestion and emendation of E. Lobel, shifts it to follow 482). It seems easiest to delete it, with Prien.

476 an allotted office: *moira* "neutral" as at v. 105 above.

not-easily-dispensed-with: the compound *eupempelon* occurs only here, but the idea correlates to Cassandra's vision at *Ag.* 1189–90, "there awaits in the halls a revel band, difficult to expel (*duspemptos exō*), of kindred Erinyes."

477 if they do not obtain ...: there is a syntactical irregularity in this sentence, not a rare occurrence in Aesch. (incontestable exx. are *Sept.* 681-2, *Suppl.* 446, *Ag.* 1008 ff., *Cho.* 520).

obtain victory: the adj. means, more literally, "bringing in victory." Orestes will use it later in his good wishes and leavetaking to the Athenians (v. 777 below); it occurs as an epithet of Justice at *Cho.* 148. Athena had rebuked the Erinyes for trying to win an unjust victory (v. 432 above).

478 poison: the image will be repeated later by Apollo (vv. 729–30) using similar language, and taken up by the Erinyes themselves (vv. 782 ff. = 812 ff.).

479 everlasting blight: for the uncertainty of meaning of the adj., see n. on v. 416 above.

480–481 After a standard formula of summing-up, Athena proceeds to state that she feels herself in an impasse – for that is what the troublesome expression in v. 481 must mean, however it is to be restored. Contrary to most commentators starting with the scholiast, who paraphrases "it is difficult for me to send them [sc. the Erinyes] away unangrily," I feel strongly that her summation ought logically to include both sides of the case to which she has been giving her attention: *su men...* (v. 473) *hautai d'...* (476). She must mean, then, "it is (unmanageable, difficult) for me whether the two contesting sides (simply) stay or (simply) are dismissed," for, in the former case, the Erinyes' threatened harm (vv. 477 ff.) must be taken account of, in the latter, Orestes' just claims (vv. 473 f.) are ignored.

482 Athena now recovers her train of thought and explains how she intends to resolve her dilemma. The scholiast discerns a lightning-metaphor in the vb. *epeskēpsen*.

483 Athena's solution is not very different from Pelasgus' in *Suppl.* He had said, "I shall make haste to call together the people resident here, that I may make the commonality (*to koinon*) well-disposed" (*Suppl.* 517-18) and the decision to accept the Danaids' suppliancy was taken by a vote of the Argive assembly (v. 607). Athena will *convoke* "the best of her citizens" and *constitute* them a court for all time, to take decisions in cases like this.

It seems best to posit with Hermann a lacuna after this line since the participle (Casaubon's emendation to *hairoumenē* seems to me inevitable) is left without a constr. and v. 484, *pace* many commentators, embodies a relative clause. Taplin accepts the hypothesis of a lacuna on grounds of the way things are handled – in his opinion, mishandled – in the succeeding trial scene; see n. on vv. 470–489 above. These details are taken up in Appendix I, "Athenian Judicial Procedure ..."

485 call witnesses, marshal evidence: it was standard legal procedure that the opposing sides be given an opportunity to gather "testimony and evidence;" that in the event only Orestes produced a witness (v. 576) is irrelevant. (See D.M. MacDowell,

The Law in Classical Athens [Ithaca: Cornell Univ. Press, 1978] pp. 242–47, "Evidence." He remarks that "one important kind of evidence was laws, which were evidence of what conduct was right or wrong" [p. 242].)

486 safeguards under oath: "Witnesses too had to swear [i.e. in addition to the prosecutor and defendant], not just that their evidence was true, but that the defendant committed the homicide, or that he did not commit it" (MacDowell, *The Law in Classical Athens* [Ithaca, N.Y.: Cornell Univ. Press, 1978] p. 119; cf. MacDowell, *Athenian Homicide Law in the Age of the Orators* [Manchester: Manchester Univ. Press, 1963] pp. 98–101).

safeguards: almost a technical term in the legal vocabulary; cf. n. on v. 289 above.

487 the best: Athena uses, somewhat oddly, a neut. pl. form. (Verrall compared *Pers.* 1–2, *tade... pista*).

489 Since we cannot be sure where this line originally stood in the MSS (here in M, after 485 in FGTE), it is difficult to be sure of the meaning.

Exit Athena: so the scholiast on v. 490, although it is not quite certain how this was managed. "Into her temple," Hermann thought; but since she has just said she intends to "collect jurors," it is likelier that she departed by the western parodos, the conventional way in the Athenian theatre of signifying movement to or from the city. The scholiast comments in addition that "Orestes remains in supplication, while the Erinyes keep him under guard," but he ought to depart in response to Athena's behest at v. 485, and his physical removal would make it easier for an audience to envisage a change in locale from Acropolis to Areopagus, which the action of the following scene seems to imply (see Intro. pp. 14–15, "Staging").

Whether we imagine a change of scene to the Areopagus or not, some few physical arrangements for the trial must have been made during the Choral Ode that follows, or in the interval before or after it. There will be need of seats or benches for the jurors, two voting urns and other courtroom paraphenalia. And Athena's statue (vv. 80 and 259) was probably removed.

Second Choral Ode vv. 490–565 Although it is linked to the *First Choral Ode* in metrical scheme (the first two stanzas trochaic, the last two dactylic and iambic, see Appendix III), the sense and structure of this song are, by a welcome contrast, almost always straightforward, uncomplicated. The Erinyes begin with the case in hand, the confessed matricide who is to be tried. If he were to be acquitted, it would set an unfortunate example to other would-be parentslayers; a flood of such gruesome deeds, and their attendant sufferings, would ensue, which the Erinyes will be powerless to avert (*St.* 1, 1', 2). They then turn to a more general application of the principle that underlies their whole manner of proceeding – indeed, it might be called their *raison d'être* – the salutary effects of a restraining fear (vv. 517, 522) for individuals and cities alike (*St.* 2'). In fact, this principle can be widened still further, to the whole of life, including political life: "steer a middle course, settle for a prosperity that does not depend on impiety" (*St.* 3, *St.* 4 init.). In short, respect Justice and observe the "unwritten laws" (*St.* 3'), for to do otherwise leads to certain shipwreck (*St.* 4 second part, 4').

To be noted are the unusually frequent moral themes and even images repeated from *Ag.*: the submerged reef, the maltreated altar etc. The effect of this is to have the Chorus of demons begin to take on the ponderous wisdom of the Elders of Argos, and it also provides a coherent summary of the moral message of the whole trilogy. Note, finally, how insistently the Erinyes ally themselves with Dikē. They contrive to give the impression that they are her staunchest – indeed, in their own judgement, perhaps her only – supporters. As they see it, were it not for them, the whole divinely-sanctioned edifice of morality would come tumbling down (vv. 511, 516, 525, 539, 564).

There is a sensible discussion of this ode in D.J. Conacher, *Aeschylus' 'Oresteia'*, pp. 156–58.

490–491 Now will Athena's new ordinances cause a revolution: the Greek is ambiguous. I take the meaning to be (as Dr. Ireland paraphrases), "If Orestes gets off there will now be a general overthrow of all that previously was held sacrosanct." Others interpret: Athena's new ordinances will be overthrown (i.e. undermined) if they result in a victory for Orestes.

492 malicious plea: lit. "legal plea and injury."

497 Orestes' impunity will be a paradigm; parents everywhere have reason to be afraid.

500 maenad: "Aeschylus is certainly thinking of the evil revelry of the Erinyes in the house" (Garvie, n. on *Cho.* 698–9). For a connection between the Erinyes and the Maniai, Spirits of Madness, cf. Eur. *Or.* 36–8, "his [sc. Orestes'] mother's blood sends him racing with *maniaisi*; for I scruple to name the goddesses, the 'Eumenides' ..."

watchers-of-men: see v. 787 below for a similar bold compound.

501 With the deterrent of the Erinyes' anger removed, men will indulge in indiscriminate slaying; it will be "no holds barred."

502 ff. The sense of this passage is obscure, and the corruption may extend further than v. 504. (The real problem lies in "proclaiming." What is wanted is a vb. like "looking at " or "pointing to.")

a man shall enquire of another: the theme of ineffectual recourse to bystanders will recur in v. 558 below; cf. also *Suppl.* 383–4, "... mortals who appeal to neighbours (*tois pelas*), yet do not obtain lawful justice."

505 abatement or remission are medical terms, as Thomson (following Headlam) noted, although he perhaps overstates the case when he comments, "This passage is written as though from experience of the plague." The **sufferings** are those attendant upon the killings which will ensue once the Erinyes' restraint has been removed.

506–507 The text may have suffered corruption deeper than that noted in the Apparatus. The scholion (itself rather confused and perhaps a blend of originally separate notes) suggests an interpretation along the lines, "the sufferer consoles himself with an (empty) hope against us [i.e. the Erinyes];" but that can hardly be got out of the Greek as it stands.

511 Justice is here fully personified. The victim calls upon her to witness the wrong he is suffering and if possible do something to redress it. (The word translated **call out** in v. 510 occurs in a similar context at *Cho.* 828–9: the Chorus envision Clytemnestra calling "child" as Orestes advances against her.)

512 O thrones ...: it is somewhat presumptuous (if understandable) of the Erinyes to picture themselves "enthroned." Thrones were reserved for the "great gods," Zeus (v. 229 above, *Ag.* 1563, *P.V.* 228, 767) and Apollo (v. 18 above, 616 below); or great kings, like Agamemnon.

513–514 Some father or mother: cf. vv. 497–8 above.

517–521 A memorable expression of a principle which another religious culture formulated as "The fear of the Lord is the beginning of wisdom." The Erinyes had already hinted at this doctrine earlier (vv. 389–90 above) and it will be restated by Athena at vv. 698–99. Compare Soph. *Aj.* 1073–76 (although from the lips of an unworthy spokesman, Menelaus), "Never can the laws have prosperous course in a city where dread [*deos*] hath no place; nor can a camp be ruled discreetly [*sophronos*] any more, if it lack the guarding force of fear and reverence" (Jebb's trans.). Pericles put it more simply in the Funeral Speech: "In our public activities it is especially through fear [*deos*] that we do not break the laws" (Thucydides 2.37.3).

518 seated majestically: suggesting perhaps seated statues of divinities; see n. on v. 294 above. Kings also received their subjects seated on thrones, as Orestes remarks bitterly of his mother and Aegisthus at *Cho.* 975 (cf. *Cho.* 572).

519 overseeing: Orestes had used a cognate word of Athena's military watchfulness at vv. 295–6 above. "Overseer of the Constitution" was one of the early titles of the Areopagus; see n. on v. 706 below.

521 prudence: a hardly adequate trans. for the Greek concept, which has no single English equivalent. It implies an instinctive or habitual avoidance of that excess which made a man morally culpable in the sight of the gods or his fellow men. For the thought, commentators cite *Ag.* 180–1, "prudence comes even to the unwilling."

522 ff. In spite of the textual uncertainty, the meaning is not in doubt. In Athena's recapitulation at vv. 698–99 she says, "I advise ... that the fearful not be cast out of the city entirely; for which one of mortals who feared nothing could be just?," where the second sentence probably gives the general sense of vv. 522–3. I have translated my own suggestion.

522–523 What city ... what man : an interesting early example of an argument from analogy similar to that which Plato develops systematically in *The Republic*; the city is simply the human psyche writ large.

526 ff. Give approval ...: The Erinyes, pursuing a hint they had dropped at the end of the preceding stanza, move more fully into the realm of politics and use a term that, in some contexts, can mean "vote formal approval." Their words have sometimes been taken as bearing a quite specific political meaning, and it is true that in certain contexts in the latter part of the fifth century the phrase *to meson* seems to denote a definable socio-economic group, the "middle" class (e.g., Eur. *Suppl.* 244; Thuc. 6.18.6 with Dover's n.). But here, I believe, we are still in the realm of generalized admonition, similar to Theognis 330, "Be not overly zealous in any matter; in all things the 'middle' is best." It is possible, too, that what was to be broadened later into a formula for general moral behaviour retains here – we are still pre-450 – the hint of a medical connotation: "a moderate regimen" (cf. Eur. fr. 79 N , "for mortals those things beyond the moderate breed diseases;" Alcmeon of Croton DK 24 B 4 where, interestingly, "monarchy" of any single element is said to be "productive of disease", and Aristotle, *Eth. Nic.* 1104 a 15–18, where the term used is *summetra*, as at *Eum.* 531).

530–31 his manner of surveillance differs ...: the expression here and in the following verse is rather obscure. I take Aesch.'s meaning to be, "Even if you consistently maintain a middle course, mastery (*kratos*) may not come immediately, because God works in his own way – and at his own pace – in such matters," with the corollary that it is up to men to make sure that they apply the doctrine of "the mean" appropriately in each case. But other interpretations are possible. (Note that the poet has his chorus, in referring to "God," speak in suspiciously human terms; they have for the time being abandoned their character as Nether Powers pitted against the Olympians.) For the sentiment in general, cf. Solon 13. 17 West, Zeus exercises surveillance (*ephorai*) over the completion, *telos*, of all things; "the will [*noos*] of Zeus who holds the aegis is different at different times" (Hesiod, *Works and Days* 483, tr. Evelyn-White).

533 ff. truly Impiety's offspring: another of those moral genealogies of which archaic Gk. poetry was so fond. Cf. (among many possible parallels) *Ag.* 758 ff., "the Impious Deed begets a large progeny .... Old Hybris usually gives birth to a young Hybris ...." In both passages the point being emphasized is that human prosperity is stable only when it does not lead to excessive, "insatiable" (and so sinful) ambition, or Hybris, that is, when it is kept within reasonable bounds by "soundness of mind." As Flinthoff remarks, "*Olbos* [prosperity] appears three times in close succession [vv. 537, 551 and 563] ... on every occasion, it is used by the Chorus to emphasize that without *Dike* [Justice] there is not prosperity at all for anyone anywhere" ("The Treading of the Cloth," 129). The Erinyes' role as defenders of the doctrine of "nothing to excess" is as old as Homer: after Achilles' horse Xanthus, to whom Hera had given speech, predicts his master's death, the Erinyes "checked his voice" (*Il.* XIX. 418), and there was an uncharacteristically lucid dictum of Heraclitus to the same effect: "Sun will not overstep his measures (*metra*); otherwise the Erinyes, ministers of Justice, will find him out" (fr. 94 = no. 226 in Kirk, Raven & Schofield, *The Presocratic Philosophers* [Cambridge: Cambridge Univ. Press, 1983] p. 201, whose translation I quote). The Erinyes' function as chastisers of human hybris is adumbrated at *Ag.* 462 ff.: "the black Erinyes eventually wear out and darken the life of a man whose success comes unjustly." (There was nothing particularly novel in the doctrine that a man's moral outlook and intent were what really mattered: "Insatiable Greed (*Koros*) begets Hybris, when great Prosperity accompanies men whose attitude is not sound," Solon 6. 3–4 West).

539 Justice's altar: compare *Ag.* 381–84, "Wealth provides no means of defense against Greed (*Koros*), for the man who has kicked Justice's great altar into oblivion."

543 Requital will take charge: at vv. 322–23 above the Erinyes identified themselves as a "Requital for living and dead." The metaphor seems to be that of a military commander "placed over" troops (so *Pers.* 241, 555 and esp. 828, Zeus "stands by" to chasten and correct overboastful thoughts). The short, pointed style of the Gk. is to be noted: it reinforces the Erinyes' purpose, which is clear, direct, unswerving. For the idea compare *Cho.* 935–36, "Justice came in time to Priam's sons, Requital just but oppressive."

544 appointed: as at vv. 127 and 326–7 above, "with full authority" and therefore efficacious. The cold simplicity of tone is reminiscent of *Ag.* 1562–64: "the robber is robbed, the killer pays. The rule 'Doer must die' waits while Zeus waits on his throne."

545 ff. let a man show reverence ...: again, as in the First Choral Ode (vv. 269 ff.), the Erinyes portray themselves as guarantors of the "unwritten laws;" here, only two of the usual three are mentioned specifically, the third, reverence for the gods, being assumed throughout (cf. 529–31 and 542, "with a godless kick").

550 voluntarily, not under compulsion: the Erinyes move beyond the rather narrow injunction of vv. 520–21, into a higher order of morality (for the standard view commentators cite, among many passages, Glaucon's dictum, "no one is voluntarily just, but only under compulsion," Plato, *Rep.* 360 C). Ideally, they seem to be saying, dire threats and scare-tactics – their own tools-in-trade, in fact – would not be necessary to force men to be just, they would be so because they naturally wished to be (or with only the incentive of a stable and abiding prosperity as a reward, v. 551).

552 nor ever totally ruined: the same kind of understatement as at v. 340 above, "not unduly (= not at all) free."

553 ff. The picture of the shipwreck recalls *Ag.* 1005 ff. There, however, the moral responsibility of the sufferer was merely hinted at (cf. *Ag.* 1003, "insatiable" [*akoreston*] , which hearkens back to *Ag.* 756, "woe brought on by insatiability"); here, it is fully spelled out: it is gain won boldly and sinfully (553–54), without justice (554), that is at risk.

554 plunders extensively: resumes the theme of "profit" in v. 540. The language is strongly reminiscent of the description of helter-skelter pillaging in the First Choral

Ode of *Sept.* (esp. *pantophurt' Eum.* 554 and *akritophurtos* ["mixed undistinguishably"] *Sept.* 360).

555–556 forced to lower his sail: that is, the time for voluntary action has passed (alternatively, the placement of the adverb *biaiōs*, "perforce," allows the interpretation "plunders ... with force"). An ancestor – not necessarily a direct one – of this shipwreck-image is Alcaeus fr. 208 Voigt (note vv. 7–8, "all the sail lets the light through now, and there are great rents in it," D. Campbell's trans.).

560 the divinity laughs: Eur. uses a similarly chilling image at *Bacch.* 439 and 1021 to suggest the easy, mocking superiority of Dionysus over his victim, Pentheus.

hot for crime: compare *Sept.* 602–3, where a pious man has become a shipmate of "sailors hot and ready for any crime." (Cf. *Cho.* 629, which the scholiast interpreted correctly as "a hearth not bold to crime.")

561–562 The expression is somewhat tortured and compressed and the picture Aesch. intended is anything but clear. (The phrase that I have translated **surmount the waves' crest** has been taken by some to mean "rounding the promontory." Likewise, **foolishly counting himself safe** has been interpreted "boasting that this would never happen.")

564 Justice's reef: cf. *Ag.* 1005–6 "a man's destiny, travelling a straight course, strikes an unseen reef" (trans. Denniston & Page).

Action

Athena, having selected "the best of her citizens" (v. 487), now leads them onstage. If he did not stay behind through the preceding Ode, Orestes now re-enters with her, as does Apollo (probably; see n. on v. 574 below). The trial – the prototype of all future homicide cases heard before the Areopagus – is about to begin.

566 Herald ...: in historical times inscriptions and official lists attest, among other heralds, a "herald of the Council of the Areopagus." Gilbert suggested that the seat in the theatre of Dionysus marked "herald's" – admittedly, from much later, in the Roman period – belonged to this official (*The Constitutional Antiquities of Sparta and Athens*, Engl. trans. [London and N.Y.: Swann Sonnenschein and Macmillan, 1895] 168 n. 2). (A scholiast here remarks that Aesch. is anachronistically introducing contemporary Athenian practices.)

567 shrill: lit., "piercing" (at *P.V.* 76 of fetters, 181 of fear).

567–568 Etruscan (Tyrrhenian) trumpet: the Etruscans, famous as bronze-workers, allegedly invented the trumpet, or were given it by Athena; or the ref. is to a particular kind of trumpet (there was a shrine of 'Athena of the Trumpet' at Argos).

570 this council-chamber: a similar phrase at v. 704 below.

is being filled the locution may be thought awkward in view of "filled" in v. 568, but see n. on v. 465 above.

571 and these men: the MSS and edd. (in v. 573 of the Gk.) offer a choice of "this man," "of these," "these two" (*i.e.*, as Murray says, "accuser" and "defendant"), "these men." The sense is hardly affected, whichever we choose.

572 my ordinances for all time to come: virtually repeats v. 484 above. **all time:** the adj. *aianē* is unproblematic, unlike 416 and 479 (the temporal sense also in v. 672 below; 941–42 echo 479 and are equally ambiguous).

574 My lord Apollo: the same form of address as the Chorus had used at 198. Gods speak thus courteously to one another (so Poseidon to Athena at Eur. *Tro.* 52; cf. v. 892 below). There is a problem about line attribution. I follow Wieseler and Rose and continue the couplet 574–5 as spoken by Athena.

An additional difficulty is that we cannot be quite sure when Apollo enters. Although the absence of a clear marker signalling the arrival of so important a character is unusual (see Taplin, *Stagecraft* 395 ff.), he would not have gone unrecognized by the audience. Friis Johansen posits a lacuna after 572 in which Apollo's entrance would have been announced; he assigns 573 to Apollo (concluding a speech), 574 to the Chorus-leader and 575 to Athena (*Classica et Mediaevalia* 39 [1988] 5–14).

578 I purified him: cf. vv. 282–83 above, with n.

579 will be his advocate: he repeats in more specific terms his promise in v. 232 above. A *sundikos* or *sunēgoros* was one "who spoke in his own person on behalf of a litigant" (Harrison, *The Law of Athens*, vol. II, *Procedure* [Oxford: Clarendon Press, 1971] p. 158, with refs. at pp. 158–60). At v. 761 below Orestes refers to the Erinyes as his "mother's advocates."

I take responsibility: Apollo thus confirms formally and before the court what he had already admitted privately to Orestes (v. 84).

580 begin the proceedings: he uses a technical term to urge Athena to act as the presiding officer over her newly-established court.

582 It is yours to speak: in Athenian legal proceedings it was customary for the plaintiff to speak first.

586 respond by making a statement: in the absence of a public prosecutor, the plaintiff cross-examined the defendant directly.

589 the first of three falls: it took three clear falls for one side to claim victory in a wrestling match, hence Orestes' sharp retort in the following line. See M. Poliakoff, "The Third Fall in the *Oresteia*," *American Journal of Philology* 101 (1980) 251–59.

593 by whom were you persuaded ... : when at v. 426 above Athena had suggested that Orestes might have been acting under compulsion, the Erinyes refused to accept the possibility that external pressure could "goad one to matricide." Here, they offer him the opportunity to plead extenuating circumstances, or shift the burden of guilt; they do not shirk a fight with Apollo, with whom in any case they have their principal quarrel.

595 expounded: a technical term indicating official interpretation of a sacred law or prescription; it occurs again at v. 609 below (compare "exegete"). (See *Cho.* 118 with Garvie's n., and *Cho.* 552.)

598 means of assistance: the stem is the same as that translated "defender" in v. 289 above; see n. there. The Chorus in the preceding play had prayed to the "blessed spirits of the underworld" (including Agam.) to "graciously send assistance" to assure the children's victory over Clytemnestra (*Cho.* 476–78).

600 was afflicted: in Greek, a noun which is "particularly appropriate to [a] hostile visitation" (Garvie on *Cho.* 283, where the phrase "assaults of the Erinyes" occurs).

a double defilement: this enigmatic statement is clarified by Orestes in v. 602.

601 you'd better instruct: their tone is somewhat ironical, as at v. 431 above.

602 Orestes' explanation is less sophistic than it sounds. He means that by one slaying she destroyed two sacrosanct relationships, that of husband-to-wife and father-to-son.

603 death has absolved her: the underlying logic of their retort is that if she was "guilty" or "defiled" in killing her husband, her sin at least has been expiated by her death, while Orestes' defilement in killing her remains to be dealt with, since he is still alive.

604 Orestes affects to ignore the irony in the Chorus-leader's preceding reply and takes a slightly different tack by picking up the reference to his being "still alive"; he points out the inconsistency in their prosecuting him for Clytemnestra's murder, but not her for Agamemnon's. This is the same point as Apollo had made at v. 211 above, and the Chorus' next reply virtually restates v. 212.

608 in her womb: the language is reminiscent of Orestes' comment that Clytemnestra had "borne for her husband the burden of children in her womb" (*Cho.* 991–92).

609 expound: see n. on v. 595 above.

615 I am a prophet and shall not lie: Apollo echoes the words that Orestes had used of him at *Cho.* 559 in referring to the oracle which enjoined the murder of Clytemnestra: a "prophet not formerly given to lying."

616 ff. Never on any occasion ... seems a surprisingly absolute appeal to the higher authority of Zeus. The close relationship between the two was alluded to earlier by the Erinyes (v. 229), but can Apollo really mean that *all* his prophecies must be cleared with his father before being delivered? Or is he – perhaps feeling a bit threatened and on the defensive – simply overstating the general authorization he feels he has? In any case, the recourse to Zeus will not go unchallenged (vv. 640 ff. below).

621 an oath does not have any greater strength: Does he mean some specific oath or oath-taking in general? Conacher and many other commentators interpret as the former: "presumably the juror's oath" (*Aeschylus' 'Oresteia'*, p. 160 with n. 56). Or is the ref. to "the oath which Orestes refused to take [v. 429]" (so Thomson, following Davies)? Perhaps likelier, the signification is general, as in vv. 217–8 above, where Apollo used similar language to argue that "the marriage-bond ... is greater than any oath."

623 exacting the penalty: see n. on v. 320 above.

625 for it is not ... the same thing: Apollo has no hesitation in asserting that Agamemnon's claims cancelled out Clytemnestra's, but he introduces a new and highly subjective argument: Agamemnon's life was worth more than his wife's because of his status as a king, his achievements as a general (v. 637) and his sex as a male. (Ultimately, it is this last argument that is decisive in Athena's eyes: vv. 737–40.)

628 some Amazon: a by-word for female (and hence, unnatural) aggressiveness. Homer designates them "equals of men." According to myth, their Queen was the daughter of Ares and the women themselves reared only girl-children. Aesch. may have in mind their alliance with Priam and attack on the Greeks at Troy, a story told by one of Homer's continuators, Arktinos of Miletus in his *Aithiopis*. See vv. 685 ff. for a different myth concerning Amazons, who are alluded to also at *P.V.* 723–4 (a "man-hating army of Amazons;" Clytemnestra "hated her man") and *Suppl.* 287 ("man-less Amazons"). These ferocious barbarian women and the threat they posed to "superior" masculine Greek cultural values appear in scenes on Greek vases about 520 B.C. Cf. D. von Bothmer, *Amazons in Greek Art* (Oxford: Clarendon Press, 1957) 143–216; P. Devambez, article "Amazones" in *Lexicon Iconographicum Mythologiae Classicae* I.1 (Zurich: Artemis, 1981) pp. 586–653.

631 If the text is sound (which is very doubtful), Rose citing *Sept.* 545–6 explains the metaphor as that of a merchant adventurer returning from a trading voyage. In the following passage Apollo uses the technique of a good courtroom lawyer, recreating the horrors of the crime for a jury asked to condemn it. At 638 below he candidly admits that his purpose is to try to enflame the jurors' feelings.

633 in the bath: At *Ag.* 1540 the Chorus refer to the "silver-sided bath" in which Agamemnon's body has just been wheeled out and at the end of *Cho.* Orestes calls the robe in which Clytemnestra entangled her husband "covering for a bath" (*Cho.* 999). Most edd. follow Schütz, Dindorf etc. in positing a lacuna of one or more verses after 632. I prefer to mark v. 633 as corrupt. The sense of the whole passage is given by Thomson: "she stood by him or assisted him while he was performing his ablutions, and on the completion of them ... enveloped him in the fatal robe."

634–635 endless folds: Clytemnestra after the murder had herself referred to the "endless net ... as for fish" in which she had trapped her husband (*Ag.* 1382).

fettered: Orestes, too, had mentioned these metaphorical "fetters for his (sc. Agamemnon's) hands and feet" (*Cho.* 982).

637 commander of a fleet: see n. on v. 456 above.

638 such a speech: in this idiom a noun in the feminine is regularly to be supplied from the context.

639 to deal authoritatively: virtually the same phrase as at v. 581.

640 ff: The logic of Apollo's argument was that the sanctity of the bond of fatherhood, the obligation Orestes had to avenge his father's murder, overrode all other familial claims (Clytemnestra's rights as a mother in respect of Iphigeneia, and as a wife in respect of Cassandra). Now the Chorus-leader dips into the storehouse of myth to produce a striking case of an instance when Zeus himself violated the code of filial obligation (this same example is flashily produced by the "Worse Argument" in Ar. *Clouds* 904 ff., where it similarly elicits an angry reaction from the opponent). They will score a similar mythological hit against Apollo later, vv. 723–24 below.

640 has preferential regard for: Athena will use the same word at v. 739 below (according to Clytemnestra the reason she killed her husband was that he "showed no regard" for their daughter Iphigeneia, *Ag.* 1415).

641 Hesiod had told large sections of the story of Zeus' struggle for supremacy on Olympus against his father Kronos and the Titans (*Theog.* 664 ff.). True, the upshot was the imprisonment of Zeus' adversaries in Tartarus, where they could "enjoy neither sun's rays nor breezes of air" (*Il.* VIII. 478–81), but the Erinyes are being a little unfair in not giving any of Zeus' side of the story: but for his mother Rhea and grandmother Earth, Kronos would have swallowed Zeus along with his brothers Poseidon and Hades (*Theog.* 453 ff.). Besides, in one version of the story the Titans and, presumably, Kronos with them were freed (*Prom. Luomenos* fr. VIII Griffith).

aged father: the Chorus, too, can use emotive language.

644 objects of loathing: Apollo, bested in argument, descends to name-calling (so, too, Eteocles, in a similar locution, calls the chorus of panic-stricken women "objects of hatred to moderate men," *Sept.* 186). Using the same noun in the sing., Orestes referred to his mother as an "object of loathing to the gods" (*Cho.* 1028).

645 one can unlock fetters: the fetters of Kronos and the Titans were probably so unlocked; see n. on v. 641 above.

647 once a man has died: The Chorus had made the same point about Clytemnestra's murder at vv. 261 ff. above. In his note on that passage Sidgwick rightly calls this "the keynote of the three plays" (he cites *Ag.* 1019 and *Cho.* 48).

649 did not fashion any spells: quite the contrary, when Apollo's son the physician Asclepius tried to do this, Zeus struck him with his thunderbolt (Eur. *Alc.* 3 ff., 123 ff.; the story is touched on obliquely by the Chorus at *Ag.* 1022–24, in a context which uses language similar to that of the present passage: "Who by chanting spells could call up a man's black blood once spilt?" [*Ag.* 1017 ff.]). Spells are among Asclepius' medicinal techniques mentioned by Pindar (*Pyth.* 3. 51 ff.).

650–651 he can turn upside down ...: the effortlessness of the divine power (contrast the hustle and bustle of the Homeric gods, and not only Hephaestus) is a persistent theme in the 'higher' religious thinkers, as Thomson noted. Thus Xenophanes *DK* 21 B 25, "[God] shakes all things without labour by the thought of his mind" and B 26, "he stays always in the same place without being moved, nor is it fitting for him to go about in different ways at different times." Or as Socrates argued, "it is impossible for a god to want to change himself, but being, as is fitting, each of them as far as is possible best and most beautiful, he remains always simply in his own form" (*Republic* II. 381 C 7 ff., trans. Grube). The ease of God's mode of acting is also emphasized by the Chorus at the beginning of *Suppl.*: "all the work of a god is free from toil. Seated, without moving from his holy throne, He yet in some way works His thought" (vv. 100–103 trans. Friis Johansen). It was not always an exalted effortlessness; in Aesch.'s *Carians or Europa*, the heroine complains that Zeus engineered her theft and eluded the supervision of her father, Agenor, "without toil, remaining there (sc. where he was, in Crete)."

and not even pant: there is a similar phrase at *Sept.* 393, where an Argive warrior is compared to a "horse panting with effort at the bit." We remember the Erinyes' description of the way their victim "gasps out his guts with man-crushing labours" at v. 248 above.

653 after spilling to the ground: in language recalling the Chorus' lines earlier (vv. 261–63), the leader picks up Apollo's reference to the irreversibility of death. How can Orestes expect to take possession of his ancestral home when he has such a defilement on his hands?

655 What public altars ... : murderers as ritually unclean were excluded from the city's sacrifices and other religious celebrations. The detail is worked out in Eur.'s *Or.* (vv. 46–47, 430).

656 purifying water: refers to "the lustral water sprinkled over the hands of the participants, and over the victim and the altar, at the beginning of a sacrifice" (Garvie on *Cho.* 129). Again, the point is explicitly taken up by Eur. Towards the end of *Or.* Menelaus rejects Orestes' boast that he will assume the kingship of Argos; "I suppose you'll touch the water for purification ..." (vv. 1601 ff.). Cf. Oedipus' interdiction against Laius' killer, "... I forbid any to welcome him or cry him greeting or make him a sharer in sacrifice or offering to the Gods, or give him water for his hands to wash" (Soph. *O.T.* 238–40 trans. D. Grene). Prof. MacDowell draws to my attention Demosthenes *Or.* 20 (Against Leptines). 158, where a law ascribed to Dracon is cited by which "the murderer is debarred from the holy water, libations, wine-bowls, and holy places in the agora."

his brotherhood: a ref. to the "phratries," which were associations of restricted membership and intermediate between the smaller households and the larger clans, where sacrifices and rituals of less-than-national scope were performed.

657 how correctly: Paley notes that Apollo is acting in his role as "expounder" (vv. 595, 609 above). Apollo pedantically launches into a lecture on biology. The Erinyes had previously raised the issue of blood- relationship (v. 605, cf. 212) and had a moment earlier referred to a mother's "kindred blood" (v. 653). Now Apollo puts forward the doctrine of "father-as-sole-parent," a theory which would perhaps not have sounded as ludicrous to Aesch.'s audience as it does to us. Aristotle ascribed this "mother-as-receptacle" doctrine to Anaxagoras (*DK* 59 A 107), but a later authority, Censorinus, named Anaxagoras with Alkmaion of Croton (c. 500 B.C.) as theorists who maintained that the mother, like the father, contributed semen to the embryo, the baby's sex being determined by the parent who had contributed more.

Of course the point remains that for all Apollo's haughty and even sophistic lecturing, Orestes did violence to one of the most basic and sacrosanct of human relationships, that between a child and a mother.

Eur. takes over the argument and has Orestes voice it almost verbatim in defending himself to his grandfather Tyndareus (*Or.* 552–56).

662 I shall show you a proof: see n. on v. 447 above.

664 to bear witness: Athena will, in fact, corroborate Apollo's testimony, but only partially, in respect of the unusual circumstances of her own birth (see vv. 736 ff. below). Apollo here commits a logical fallacy in generalizing from a particular, and extraordinary, case.

667 Both in other respects and ... is an idiomatic way of giving emphasis: "... and especially ...," but the expression here is too abbreviated to be satisfactory. One or more lines appear to have dropped out.

670 ff. We have here the second of the three refs. in the play to the alliance between Athens and Argos concluded c. 461 B.C. (also vv. 289 ff. and 755 ff.; see Intro. pp. 19–20).

674–675 I punctuate these verses as a question, and interpret the vb. **command** as deliberative subjunctive.

a just vote in accordance with their judgement: Rose cites Demosthenes 39.40, where the speaker reminds the jury that they had sworn to render a verdict "by their most just judgement," if the matter fell under no particular statute.

676–680 The MSS cannot be right in assigning both couplets, 676–77 and 679–80, to the Chorus, for Athena's words at 678 indicate that she turns to the other of the two litigants. The question is, which side speaks first? I follow Thomson, Page and Winnington-Ingram (*Studies in Aeschylus*, 219–221) in assigning the first couplet to Apollo; "our bolt is shot" seems an obvious metaphor for the archer-god. Athena then diplomatically asks the Erinyes whether there is anything else she can do to satisfy them, and their response at 679–80 is in effect a disclaimer: "No, the voting may proceed." (For the opposite arrangement, see D.J. Conacher, *Aeschylus' 'Oresteia'*, pp. 186–7 n. 60.)

680 show respect ... for the oath: the oath sworn by the jurors (off stage), referred to at v. 483, the problematic 489 and perhaps 621 above (see Demosthenes 39. 40 cited in n. on 674–675 above).

681–710 Some edd. transfer this speech of Athena's to follow v. 573. It is sufficient, however, to cite Conacher's answer to the question he poses, "Why ... does the poet have Athena postpone her proclamation," even though she had already at v. 572 called upon those assembled to "learn my ordinances"? It is, Conacher suggests, "to make it easier for Athena to generalize, now that the court has already been seen in operation as a homicide tribunal, on the more wide-ranging powers and political significance which Athena also envisages for the Areopagus" (*Aeschylus' 'Oresteia'*, p. 162).

681 my ordinance: Athena had previously announced her intention of promulgating "an ordinance for all time" (vv. 484, 571–72), which she now does. This has with justice been termed the "foundation document" of Athens' oldest and most venerable court, the Areopagus. It will not have escaped the audience that, for all that Athena's institution is epoch-making and even revolutionary, it also incorporates some of the "conservative" principles previously enunciated by the Chorus (vv. 691, 698 ff. = 517 ff.; 696–7 = 526 ff.).

682 first lawsuit for shed blood: Aesch. ignores or deliberately suppresses the myth which had the Areopagus instituted to hear the case against Ares (hence the name "Areopagus" = "hill of Ares") for the killing of Poseidon's son Halirrhothios, who had raped Ares' daughter (Eur. *El.* 1258 ff., Pausanias 1. 28. 5). He can thus make the Argive Orestes beneficiary of archetypal Athenian legal justice.

683 Aegeus' people: Aegeus was an early Athenian king, father of Theseus.

685–686 Amazons' position and camp: this was a follow-up to the Greek sortie into Asia (see n. on v. 628 above). These warlike women retaliated by invading Greece. An Athenian speaker in Herodotus (9.27.4) mentions this repulse of the

Amazons as one of the glories of Athens' heroic past. Paley suggested (and Verrall agreed) "that Aeschylus borrowed the idea from the capture of Athens in the Persian invasion."

686 a grudge against Theseus: Athena had already referred to the "sons of Theseus" as somehow involved in the distribution of spoils after the Trojan war (v. 402 above). The Amazons' grudge against him was that, after invading their territory in Asia (perhaps in company with Heracles), he had carried their Queen Antiope back to Greece, a scene sculpted on the pediment of Apollo's temple at Eretria (c. 510 B.C.). Antiope's tomb was shown to travellers just outside the city (Pausanias 1.2.1)

690–691 Reverence ... and an in-born fear: the topic is broached here, to be taken up again at vv. 697 ff.; together these lines are a clear and close echo of the Erinyes' warnings at vv. 517 ff. above (in-born fear could alternatively be translated "kindred fear," i.e., akin to Reverence).

693 make no innovations: Dodds (*Classical Quarterly* n.s. 3 [1953] 19–20) saw here a pointed allusion to a current debate, a proposal to relax the eligibility requirements for the office of archon. Before 457 only the two highest of Solon's property classes could enter their names into the allotment-pool; now the Zeugitai (roughly corresponding to the "hoplite class") were admitted (cf. the Aristotelian *Constitution of Athens* 26.2). Ex-archons automatically became members of the Areopagus. (See Intro., pp. 20–1.)

694–695 mud ... never find a drink: a proverbial expression.

697 neither anarchy nor despotism: Athena (and presumably also the poet) counsels a "middle course", a compromise between extremes. Cf. Soph. *Aj.* 1073–76 (cited in n. on vv. 517–21 above). "The goddess sums up the poet's ideals of wise government, and in doing so takes over and puts in a more civilised form what is true and of permanent value in the Chorus's manifesto" (Rose on vv. 681 ff.). "Many commentators have ... discussed the obvious similarities between Athena's advice here and the Furies' earlier warning. Not all, however, have noted the precise parallel in the transition from homicidal jurisdiction to social and political authority through the concepts of Fear and Respect" (Conacher, *Aeschylus' 'Oresteia'*, p. 187 n. 64).

700 such a reverend body: she uses the abstract term, "reverence," as at v. 690, but the reference seems to be to the court she is instituting (so Sidgwick; "with such a venerated object of your righteous dread," Headlam).

703 neither ... Scythians nor in the Peloponnese: these two peoples are chosen to typify, on the one hand, nominally "barbarian" folk who nevertheless conduct themselves with an innate righteousness – "law-abiding Scythians" was a kind of proverb (Aesch. fr. 198 Radt, from *Prometheus Unbound*) – and on the other a developed Greek state, Sparta, which, according to Thucydides, "had a system of good government from earliest times" (1.18.1). With perhaps some justice Verrall remarks that "the phrase, like those in vv. 292 ff. [and 397 ff.] , sweeps the horizon of Athenian ambitions at this critical moment" (i.e. in 458 B.C.).

704 uncorrupted by thought of profit: some commentators take this as merely equivalent to "not open to bribes," but the phrase may have a somewhat wider meaning. Profit can denote payment of any kind, so the poet may be glancing critically at the introduction of payment for service on popular juries, an innovation which perhaps had just been introduced (see Rhodes' *Commentary on the Ath. Pol.* [Oxford: Clarendon Press, 1981], pp. 338–40.)

705 on behalf of those who sleep: Dr. Ireland suggests that the image is of "a military camp at night: there still need to be vigilant guards on the lookout for hostile incursions." (The scholiast here thought the phrase referred to "the dead," but this seems unlikely.) Thomson remarks on the Areopagus' sittings by night (see Intro. p.

5).

706 **ever-wakeful guard-post**: the phrase evokes such titles as "guardian of the laws," "overseer of the constitution," which were applied to the Areopagus from very early times. (Note that Athena uses a similar expression at v. 948 below.)

707 **This rather lengthy advice**: "the reference to the length of a previous speech ... is not meant as an apology for tedium; it simply facilitates a return to the business on stage", A.M. Michelini, *"MAKRAN GAR EXETEINAS,"* Hermes 102 (1974) 524–539 at 531.

710 **showing respect for the oath**: similar phrases had been used earlier by Athena herself (v. 483) and by the Chorus-leader (v. 680)

711 ff. In spite of the suggestion, frequently made, that a single juror steps up to the urns to cast his vote after each of the couplets that follow, Conacher's warning is a salutary one: "In fact we can form no detailed picture of the stage action during these exchanges other than the fact that the jurors' voting was going on and is completed by the time Athena begins speaking at l. 734" (*Aeschylus' 'Oresteia'*, p. 166). See further Appendix II below.

711–712 The Erinyes interject an additional consideration: the jurors are to take account not only of Athena's gentler exhortations but of their own threatening stance, if the voting goes against them. (They make the threat more explicit at vv. 719–20 below.)

visitation to the country: the same phrase as that used by Athena at v. 406 above and v. 1030 below (cf. also v. 57).

713 **fear**: the very word that Athena had used in her admonition to the jury (v. 700) is here echoed by Apollo. He once again insists on the validation provided by Zeus (v. 618 above).

714 **fruitless**: the theme of fruitfulness will recur in a literal context in the Hymn of Reconciliation (see, e.g., vv. 941 ff. below).

715 **your allotted office**: the phrase is similar to that used by the Erinyes in the First Choral Ode of their own "offices" (vv. 310–11, 334, 385 above).

718 **when Ixion supplicated him**: see on v. 441 above. He argues *a fortiori*: if it is conceded that so great a crime as Ixion's slaying of his father-in-law Eioneus could be absolved through purification, so then must Orestes' crime be expiable.

primal slaying: so Pindar, *Pyth.* 2. 31, who names Ixion as the first human to shed a kinsman's blood.

719–720 As the scholiast remarks, they turn from argument to threats.

721–722 **among the young and elder gods ... without honour**: the very thing that the Erinyes feared (vv. 227, 323 ff. etc.). Apollo seems to be taking a certain glee in provoking them.

723 **Pheres' palace**: the Erinyes produce another mythological example, this time of Apollo's deviousness. In the story immortalized for us by Eur., Pheres' son Admetus was able to substitute the life of his wife, Alcestis, for his own, when Apollo, in return for Admetus' previous hospitality to him, duped the Fates into allowing the substitution. The Erinyes had already earlier hinted at Apollo's outrageous behaviour (v. 172 above).

726 **be in such need**: alternatively, the phrase could mean "made the request."

728 **led astray with wine**: this detail in not found in Eur.'s version, where rather Apollo's "guile" is given emphasis (*Alc.* 12, 33–4). Aesch. has been charged with being "crude," "primitive" in introducing it. In fact, given the ineluctability of the Fates, it is hard to see how else the deal could have been arranged. The Erinyes bring it up here as another charge against Apollo: he would even descend to making old ladies tipsy (and so, incidentally, showed himself no more a respecter of age in the case of the Fates than he has been in theirs).

729 total victory in the suit: the form of words is the same as at v. 243 above (cf. also vv. 433–34), but the meaning is slightly different.

730 vomit out your poison: Athena had previously envisaged just this possibility (vv. 477–79 above). The Erinyes pick up the notion at vv. 782 ff. below.

734 to judge the case last: Athena acts as an archon, the presiding officer, in a contemporary court whose vote, in case of a tie among the jurors, was by humane convention assumed to be cast for acquittal.

735 I shall add this vote: but when does she do so? On one view, right now, after speaking v. 735, thereby creating the equality which she mentions at v. 753 below (and cf. v. 795[796 in the trans.]). On another (and in my opinion likelier) interpretation, she holds up the pebble which, as she implies at v. 741, will not be actually added to the pile for acquittal unless the human votes are tied (as turns out to be the case, v. 753). As Sidgwick describes it (n. on v. 741), "the other judges get up and drop their pebbles in, Athena holds hers in her hand until the counting." (But it is hardly an open-and-shut case; see Appendix II, "Athena's Vote... and the so-called 'Vote of Athena'.")

736 there is no mother who gave birth to me: although Athena's expressed reason for voting for Orestes' acquittal echoes Apollo's earlier argument (vv. 663 ff.), there is one substantial difference: she does not generalize and draw the same kind of universal conclusion as he had done. In other words, there is nothing in her speech that corresponds to vv. 658 ff. in his ("the mother so-called is not the child's real parent," etc.). What Athena is doing here is simply explaining her own preference for the male principle (v. 737) over the female. It is as if she were trying to let the Erinyes down gently instead of giving them a rude jolt. (Of course, that she *would* vote for Orestes there was never any doubt. The audience was prepared for it from vv. 79 ff. The question was always: how would Aesch. manage it?)

738 except in the matter of marriage: Athena was, conspicuously among the Olympian goddesses and after Artemis, a virgin ("regularly regarded as a virgin," H.J. Rose, *Oxford Classical Dictionary* s.v. "Athena").

741 even if ... an equality of votes: that is, equality of votes will be the same as a majority of votes in his favour, since her vote for acquittal (v. 735), held in abeyance until the counting is finished, will then come into effect.

743 to whom this function has been assigned: the same line-ending as at *Ag.* 908.

744 O Phoebus Apollo: we have not heard from Orestes for 130 lines. He had used Apollo's epithet earlier (v. 283; see vv. 7–8 for the reasons for its bestowal), but here it has the effect of a full and formal title.

... the contest be decided: the same phrase as at v. 677 above.

745 Night my mother: they had issued a similar appeal at vv. 321 ff. above (cf. v. 416). Compare vv. 844 and 878 below. The structure of v. 745 closely parallels that of 744, a typical feature of stichomythia (perhaps intended to bring out the cut-and-thrust quality of the dialogue).

746–751 It is not certain how these lines are to be divided. In M, vv. 745–7 continue without any change and are given to the Chorus-leader; Abresch in the 18th century first assigned 746 to Orestes. At 748 M indicates a change of speaker, but gives no designation. The other MSS and some early editors continue the lines as spoken by the Chorus-leader, a solution I have (after much puzzlement) adopted for 748–9; I assign 750–1 to Orestes. (Victorius first assigned 748–51 to Apollo, and is followed in this by most modern edd.; Wieseler gave them to Orestes.) According to Taplin, "Orestes may say them, or the chorus may say 748 and 750 and Orestes 749 and 751" (*Stagecraft* 403 n. 3).

751 when a house has fallen: for the image, cf. v. 516 above and *Cho*. 262–3.

753 On my interpretation it is only after she speaks this line that Athena adds her vote to the pile for acquittal, that is, her vote in his favour breaks the tie. (See n. on v. 735 above.)

756 some Greek will say ...: this is the Homeric technique of commenting on the significance of an event by reporting the remark of an anomymous onlooker.

758 Loxias: see n. on v. 19 above. The three divinities mentioned, besides forming a standard triad in prayer-formulas, are literally those most potent in the rehabilitation of Orestes.

759–760 Third ... Saviour: the full title was "Zeus Teleios (Fulfiller, - see v. 28 above) Sōtēr (Saviour)" (Photios s.v. *tritos kratēr*). "The libations at banquets ... were offered in the following sequence: (1) to Olympian Zeus and the Olympian gods, (2) to the heroes, (3) to Zeus Sōtēr [Saviour]" (Adam on Plato, *Rep*. 583 B 10, where the formula occurs); see the Intro. to Garvie's ed. of *Cho*., p. xxxviii and P. Burian, "Zeus SOTER and Some Triads in Aeschylus' *Oresteia*," *American Journal of Philology* 107 (1986) 332–42.

out of respect for a father's death: exactly as the Erinyes had feared (v. 640 above).

765 A third allusion to the Argive alliance (cf. vv. 289 ff., 670 ff.).

771 regret having made the effort: the phrasing is similar to the Pythia's comment at v. 59 above.

772 if they keep their oaths: I have in fact translated what the text ought to mean.

774 am favourably disposed: vivid present.

776 wrestling-grip: cf. v. 589 above for another wrestling metaphor (also *Ag*. 63–4).

777 Possibly Apollo exits here with his protégé, or he may simply remain onstage to join Athena, the Areopagites etc. in the grand procession at the end. (But in that case it is strange that no one refers to him again.) See Intro. p. 15. (That Apollo remains to the end was suggested by W.C. Scott, *Trans. of the American Philological Association* 108 [1978] 265n.18.)

778–793 In this, the Third, Ode, the normal form of metrically corresponding Stanza and Counter-stanza is abandoned in favour of exact repetition of Stanza 1 at 808 ff. and Stanza 2 (837–47) at 870 ff. This is perhaps intended to show the inexorability of the Erinyes' anger, which represents a more serious challenge to Athena's persuasive powers than the mere rendering of a verdict in Orestes' case. Prof. Scott suggests as well that the verbatim repetition may "represent the emptiness of the arguments of the Erinyes against the conciliatory tone of Athena." "The rage of the defeated Erinyes expresses itself in the agitated metre, mostly dochmiacs mixed with iambics" (Rose); see Appendix III.

778–779 have ridden roughshod over: the same charge, and repeating the "young-old" contrast, as at vv. 150 and 731 above.

780 dishonoured: again their earlier worst fears seem to have been confirmed (v. 227 etc.).

782 my heart's poison: Apollo had foreseen this danger at v. 730 above. There is still a real threat that the Erinyes may resort to such noxious tactics as Apollo had repeatedly imputed to them (vv. 183 ff.; although he himself was not above using violence, *Cho*. 271 ff., 1032, *Eum*. 466–7 above). It will be a test of Athena's good sense and inventiveness to find a way of averting their threatened plague.

783 I have accepted Thomson's transposition of the words in the MSS, which removes hiatus and makes a smoother run of language.

785 blight killing crops, killing children: one may compare the plague sent by Apollo in Soph.'s *Oed. Tyrannos:* "a blight is on her [sc. Thebes] in the fruitful blossoms of the land, in the herds among the pastures, in the barren pangs of women" (*O.T.* 25–27 trans. Jebb).

787 deadly plague-spots: Sidgwick's trans.

790 by the citizens: since Athena had said at 741 that an equal number of (human) votes would constitute acquittal – as in fact turned out to be the case (vv. 752–3) – the Erinyes now hold the Athenians responsible for their humiliation (contrast Orestes' gratitude to "the city's people" at v. 775).

792–793 maiden daughters of Night: a sinister, or at least ominous, ref. to their lineage; compare vv. 321–2, 416 and esp. 745.

793 dishonoured: see v. 780 above. My trans. of this line is adapted from Rose.

795–796 a trial in which the votes were equal: this appears to be the meaning of the compound here, as it certainly is in v. 741 above. Alternatively the phrase may mean "a trial where the voting was fair," *i.e.*, the vote could have gone either way, in Orestes' favour (as it did), or yours.

797 Zeus was the source: Athena thus confirms Apollo's claim at vv. 616 ff. above.

shining clear testimony: use of the term shining here (for which see my n. on v. 104 above where it is translated "bright") is reminiscent of Cassandra's statement that her prophecies will be no longer like a bride hidden under a veil but "shining bright and blowing forth against the sun's rays ..." (*Ag.* 1178 ff.).

800 hurl: as if it were a javelin (*Ag.* 366) or thunderbolt (*Pers.* 715, "pestilence's bolt").

your oppressive wrath: she speaks to their threat at v. 780 above.

801 continue in anger: she echoes their exact word (v. 733).

802 emitting ... drops: she once again echoes their threatening image. The MSS offer "from (or of) divinities," which is obviously incorrect; "from throats", "from lungs" are conjectures.

802–803 savage: Aesch. had used this word in v. 14 above. **lances that devour:** Aesch. is fond of figurative uses of the term "lance;" cf. *Ag.* 483 "a woman's lance" (= martial spirit; the use has caused needless difficulty to commentators) and the converse, "a woman's undaring lance" at *Cho.* 630, where Garvie terms it "a characteristic oxymoron." Cf. also *P.V.* 405 and Pind. *Nem.* 9. 37, where Chromius, to whom the ode is dedicated, is praised for having a "spirit (*thumos*) armed-with-a-lance."

804 With this verse Athena moves into a new mode, one of cajolery and "the soft sell." What have they to gain from abandoning their wrath and destructiveness? A great deal: a transformed, pervasive, fructifying role in her *polis*. (But they are not easily to be won over, showing no sign of real interest until v. 892; and she will hint that her fist, though gloved, remains formidable, vv. 826–28.)

805 in the recesses: lit., "caverns, underground holes." The audience would probably have thought of an actual grotto on the N.E. side of the rocky Areopagus hill, which was designated "Eumenides' cave;" see vv. 1007, 1022 and esp. 1036 below.

806 enthroned at lustrous hearths: these in effect replace the "hearth-fire" at which Clytemnestra said she had offered sacrifices to the Erinyes (v. 108 above, with n.). As Gantz remarks, Athena "offers the Furies the chance to transfer their retribution to a new home, a new hearth where it will function under the guidance of Athenian justice" ("The Fires of the *Oresteia*," 38). The first part of the compound "lustrous-enthroned" was regularly applied to Athens by high-flown poets like Pindar, and Aristophanes could not resist a jibe at this affected language (*Ach.* 639–40).

("Lustrous" or "polished" is a stock epithet of stone benches – once, at *Od*. 16. 408, of thrones – in Homer, and it has been thought to imply actual polishing with oil; cf. *Od*. 3. 406–408.) **enthroned** suggests a new and more elevated status for the Erinyes; see n. on v. 512 above.

807 full honours: see n. on v. 15 above for Aesch.'s use of this unusual, purportedly Sicilian, word.

808–823 = 778–793 "The Chorus, totally unconvinced [of Athena's sincerity], merely repeat their former plaint" (Rose).

824 Note that **not dishonoured** picks up "dishonoured" in v. 823 just as "with heavy groans" in v. 794 echoes "I groan" in v. 788. This shows Aesch.'s care to tie the repeated stanzas intimately into the continuing dialogue (contrast vv. 341–346 which I have accordingly excised).

825 goddesses: all tact, she gives them an honorific title, to which mere "mortals" are juxtaposed.

828 his thunderbolt: compare Athena's similar, unsubtle threat at Eur. *Tro*. 80–81, "Zeus has promised my hand the gift of the blazing thunderbolt to dash and overwhelm with fire the Achaean ships" (trans. R. Lattimore). The threat thus raised ("politely but unmistakably," Rose) is quickly dispelled in the following line.

830 a foolish tongue: by a common understatement "foolish" in such contexts signifies almost "morally culpable."

832 black wave's ... force: Thomson notes a similar image at *Cho*. 183–4 (Electra speaking), "over my heart ... there sweeps a surge of bitterness" (trans. Weir Smyth).

833 co-resident: Athena adds an unexpected inducement, naturalisation in Athens, so to speak; cf. also vv. 869, 890, 916, 1011 and 1018. Rose observes that their indignation is necessary if the element of healthy fear that they represent (vv. 517 ff., 698) is not to be lost but somehow incorporated into the very fabric of the *polis*.

835 on behalf of children and the rite of marriage: they are to be included among the divinities (including the Fates; see Sidgwick's n.) to whom were offered *proteleia*, offerings preliminary to and calculated to ensure the success of a marriage. (See n. on v. 214 above.)

837 ff. What the poet intended them to be complaining of here is not entirely clear: either the offer Athena has just made, which seems to them an insult, or more generally the outcome of the trial; possibly both.

838 all my wisdom and years: they return to a point they had already made several times, that their venerable age seems to have counted for nothing against the effronteries of the "youngster," Apollo. (Athena will address herself to this complaint at v. 848 below.)

842/3 seeps into and fills: lit., "comes in under my sides," a graphic medical metaphor. ("The anger and grief which the Erinyes feel is like the pain of a deep wound, or perhaps the stabbing sensation accompanying some acute illnesses of the thorax," Rose.)

844 mother Night: see n. on v. 791 above.

846–847 There is some doubt about what image Aesch. intended. On the basis of the same phrase in v. 213 above, I take it to be "turned me into a cipher," "rubbed me out."

848 I shall bear with your rages etc.: Athena is the very model of diplomacy.

849 Prof. Sansone has convinced me that Bothe was right to excise this line which, as it stands in the MSS, will not scan, and where the adv. *karta* ("very, exceedingly") is misused with a comparative.

851 If you go to some foreign land: compare the Chorus' enquiry of the city's gods at *Sept.* 304–5, "What more delightsome plot of earth will ye exchange for this ...?" (trans. Weir Smyth).

852 you will grow passionately fond: acc. to Thucydides (2.43.1), Pericles asked his audience in the "Funeral Speech" to "behold the city's power in day-to-day actuality, and become her passionate lovers." Aristophanes could not resist poking fun at such an extravagant image (*Ach.* 143, *Knights* 732, 1340–44).

855 palace of Erechtheus: probably designates the Acropolis (non-metaphorically at *Od.* 7. 80–81, "Athena ... came to broad-wayed Athens and went into the well-built palace of Erechtheus").

859–860 incitements to bloodshed ... maddening: a profusion of metaphor (not always clear), typical of Aesch. The literal meaning of **incitements to bloodshed** in v. 859 is "bloody whetstones," and the phrase is reminiscent of *Ag.* 1535–36, "Justice is being sharpened, for another deed of injury, on other whetstones of Destiny" (Denniston's and Page's text and trans.). With **young men's guts** compare the similarly graphic physiological phrase at vv. 248–49 above. As Paley remarks, "the loss of the young was an especial grievance to a military state." He compares the Chorus' prayer at *Suppl.* 663 ff.: "let youth's flower be unplucked and may Aphrodite's mate, man-destroying Ares, not cut its bloom."

a kind of drunken rage: this is probably just an accident of phrasing, but in Greek (lit., "a fury not of wine," Weir Smyth) it suggests the "teetotal" nature of the Erinyes' cult (see n. on v. 107 above).

861–866 This passage has several serious, perhaps insoluble, difficulties of syntax and interpretation, and at one point (vv. 864–65) we must suspend judgement on what Aesch. intended to be the sense. I suggest transposition of 866 to follow 863. The verse thus caps in an epigrammatic – perhaps even proverbial – way Athena's urging that her citizens avoid civil war.

862 heart = "resolution" also at *Cho.* 832 and elsewhere.

of fighting cocks: the scholiast remarks "the cock is a pugnacious bird, and even though other creatures have respect for their kin, it alone does not spare them." Commentators cite Pind. *Ol.* 12. 14 "like a cock, the stay-at-home fighter."

862–863 a war-spirit inbred: "in-bred spirit of faction" is a civic evil condemned by Solon (3. 19 West). Herodotus (8.3) uses the same phrase: "inbred *stasis* is as much worse than war waged with united minds as war itself is worse than peace." (The Chorus will specifically respond to this wish of Athena's in their prayer for blessings on the city, vv. 976 ff.)

864–865 I have little confidence that my makeshift translation captures even remotely the sense of what Aesch. intended. The phrase at the end of 864 is generally taken as a parenthesis, but the meaning assigned, " ... and war is close at hand with no difficulty," seems exceedingly doubtful. The phrasing of the last part of 865 is Aeschylean enough, and the tone more than slightly pejorative; compare *Sept.* 692, where the Chorus disapprove of Eteocles' "too savage passion" (Weir Smyth's trans.) for his brother's blood, but attempts to construe the first two words have been unsuccessful. (Dr. Ireland suggests that there is corruption which masks a conditional sense, "if they have to go after glory, may it be in foreign war.") In any case, I believe it is mistaken to see in these verses an allusion to Marathon or some impending battle ("one might suspect some military enterprise was about to be undertaken," Paley). The sentiment is perfectly general, and by no means approving of war. (Vv. 864–5 are perhaps to be excised. The transition at 867 is in any case rather abrupt, as A.L. Brown points out.)

867 bestowing good etc.: I have borrowed Weir Smyth's trans.

869 have a share is a paraphrase for the more technical term *metoikia*, "non-citizen resident's status," which occurs at vv. 1011 and 1018; cf. n. on v. 833 above. **beloved by the gods**: a subtle suggestion that the Erinyes should join the company of the Olympians in learning to love Athens (v. 852).

870–880 = 837–847

882 a younger goddess: Athena meets head-on the charge the Erinyes had made against Apollo that he, as upstart, had no respect for their venerable age (vv. 150–51, 227–28, 721–22, 731).

883 city's people: recalls v. 775.

884 went to perdition: an expression which the Erinyes had used earlier of their victims (v. 301) and themselves (v. 747).

banished: a political term, found also at *Ag.* 1282 (where Fraenkel suggests it may have been coined by Aesch.) and *Cho.* 1042. Athena thus subtly reminds them (by contrast) of what she is offering if they relent and abandon their anger: the official *xenia*, hospitality, of herself and her citizens.

885 reverence due to Persuasion: compare her remark at v. 829 above. At *Suppl.* 1040 "beguiling Persuasion" is named as a daughter and companion of Aphrodite (see Friis Johansen and Whittle on *Suppl.* 1039–40). But the goddess had a less attractive side: "crafty Persuasion" at *Cho.* 726 and at *Ag.* 385–86 she is designated a "wretched and unbearable child of Ruin." See in general R.G.A. Buxton, *Persuasion in Greek Tragedy* (Cambridge: Cambridge University Press, 1982) 110 ff.

888 in justice weigh out: the phrasing, as Prof. Sansone notes, is reminiscent of the Chorus' enunciation of the "learning through suffering" principle at *Ag.* 250–1: "Justice weighs out understanding to those who have gone through suffering" (Fraenkel's trans.). Cf. also *Cho.* 61 "Justice's scale".

890 to have landholder's status: this interesting word (which, note, is an emendation – though generally accepted – for the MSS' *amoirou*, "share-less"; it occurs also at *Suppl.* 630) was used at Syracuse to designate men whose estates were of considerable extent. At Athens it denoted a class of "landholders" in the archaic social structure, distinct from "aristocrats" (*eupatridai*) on the one hand and "craftsmen" on the other.

891 honour for all time to come: cf., e.g., vv. 824, 833, 839, 868.

892 The Chorus, through their leader, now begin to speak in dialogue with Athena; "they have left off mere lamentation and resentment, and begin to consider the offer" (Sidgwick).

895 that no household shall flourish: Athena had hinted at much the same thing at vv. 834 ff. above, but the Erinyes were then too angry to listen. The Erinyes will allude to this promise (albeit somewhat vaguely) at vv. 1018–20 below.

899 I could just as well ...: Athena's reply is rather brusque; they need not ask for "pledges ... in perpetuity," for her word is her bond.

900 you will cast a spell on me: Apollo had promised Orestes that at Athens he would find "words that cast a spell" (vv. 81–82 above), and cf. v. 886.

902 What blessing ...?: this is not, of course, a genuine question. The Chorus know from Athena's injunctions earlier (vv. 801 ff., 858 ff.), as well as from the conventions in such cases (see, e.g., the similar prayer at *Suppl.* 630–709), what they are expected to pray for. But the technique of naïve question followed by Athena's detailed response gives the scene a solemnity and fulness. They are now ready to take their lead from the Protectress of their adopted city, even down to small particulars.

903 base victory: the same rather cryptic phrase occurs at *Sept.* 716, where it seems to mean, "a victory won by less than totally honorable means."

908 unwearied by the passage of time: a favourite Greek idiom for "forever." The permanence of the blessings here prayed for matches that of the compact between

Orestes' people and Athens (vv. 763 ff. above).

909 seed of human generation: thus they will have a chance to show how misguided was Apollo's attack on them at vv. 187–88 above.

912 these just men: I believe Paley was right to see a ref. here to "the citizens in general, addressed as present in the theatre."

913–914 I for my part shall not fail ...: why does Athena interpose her own intention? First, as a balance to her earlier admonitions at vv. 858 ff. Also, perhaps, as a boost to the possibly flagging spirits of the contemporary Athenians who had been for several years embroiled in what was to prove a disastrous military undertaking in Egypt (see Intro. p. 20 and n. on vv. 292ff. above).

916–1047 A solemn and at the same time joyful choral finale (contrast the end of *Pers.*), the Chorus' lyrics being matched first by Athena's anapaests – cf. *Ag.* 1448 ff. for a structurally similar but emotionally quite different arrangement – concluding with an eleven-line trimeter monologue by the goddess (1021–31) and a lyric coda by the subsidiary Chorus of Escorts (1032–end).

918 Zeus All-prevailing: one of Zeus' traditional epithets, here endowed with special force in view of the "military contests" just alluded to (hence also the appropriateness of mentioning Ares, along with Athena, in a triad of war-divinities).

919 the gods' watch-post: the language recalls Athena's designation of her new court as a "guard-post" of the city (v. 706 above). A similar phrase occurs at v. 948 below.

920 glorious defender of the altars: high-flown phrases, but the function is of great symbolic importance, since foreign invaders were traditionally conceived of as committing sacrilege against national shrines (Agamemnon at Troy, *Ag.* 339–40, 527 – which I believe to be genuine –; Xerxes in Greece, *Pers.* 809–12). Sidgwick well calls this and the preceding line "an imaginative rendering of the favourite idea of 'the piety' of Athens" and he compares vv. 805 and 869.

924 sun's radiant gleam: picks up Athena's injunction at vv. 906 ff. above. This represents a complete reversal for underworld divinities who formerly inhabited a region of "sunless gloom" (v. 396 above).

927 with good intent: Athena echoes the Chorus' "kindly" in v. 923: the tone has now changed to one of relaxed bonhomie. But she reminds us of the magnitude of the change (and of her own skill in achieving it) when within two lines she uses the term **implacable** (cf. vv. 383–84 above, "hard ... to appease").

930 have been allotted the task: the language seems chosen to recall the Chorus' own harsh statements earlier about their "allotted tasks" of hunting down murderers (vv. 310–11, 334, 385). At the same time the wide scope of the powers she allots them has itself already been adumbrated by the Chorus (vv. 336 ff., 421, 545 ff.).

932 oppressive is a word the Chorus had used of themselves earlier in the play (vv. 711 and 720; cf. 800). The Erinyes' old fearsomeness is not to disappear, but rather to be channeled henceforward to more constructive ends.

933 Rose's paraphrase seems to me correct: "he meets sudden and inexplicable disaster" (a similar turn of phrase at v. 377, and cf. 301).

934 the sins of his ancestors: this apparent reversion to a less enlightened concept of hereditary guilt has suprised some commentators, but it is firmly in the tradition inherited, and for the most part absorbed, by Aesch. (see *Ag.* 374 with Denniston and Page's n. on 374 f., with the refs. to *Sept.* 742 ff. and Solon fr. 13. 31–2 West). Another approach is to interpret this as a doctrine of an hereditary *propensity* to guilt. Spatz puts this well in the case of Agamemnon: "... as an heir to the curse as well as the property of Atreus, he has inherited the potential to beget further impiety" (*Aeschylus* p. 101).

hale him off is a technical legal term, "lead off for trial before a magistrate."

935 whether he is silent: I have translated my own conjecture.

936 shouts loudly: the ref. is to the practice of a victim of assault or aggression shouting for witnesses to his maltreatment, so that they may later support his case in court.

937 pulverizes him with an enemy's rage: a fine, jagged, quite Aeschylean blended image.

938 ff. The Chorus here specifically address Athena's behest to them at vv. 905 ff. (Prof. Sansone points out that at Erythrae the Erinyes were worshipped under the cult-title "Ablabiai," that is, "Averters-of-harm.")

941 borders of the land: the phrase in Greek has seemed vague and unsatisfactory to some commentators, but no convincing emendation has been proposed.

942 everlasting sterility: the phrase echoes v. 479 above. For the ambiguity of the adj. translated here "everlasting", see n. on v. 416 above.

945 ff. may earth's rich progeny ...: scholars are correct, I believe, to find here a ref. to the mineral wealth of Athens' silver mines (cf. *Pers.* 237–38, "What do they possess besides their men? Is there sufficient wealth?" – "Silver springs run through their soil, a treasure from the earth for them."), perhaps also to the "lucky strike" that enabled Themistocles to expand Athens' fleet in 483 B.C. (Herodotus 4.144.1). Thomson, after Davies, notes Pausanias' description (1.28.6) of the statues of Earth, Plouton (Wealth) and Hermes (namesake of the mineralogical 'lucky strike') in the grotto of the Erinyes by the Areopagus. The gods are conceived of as "paying honour" to the city by making possible the discovery of new veins of silver. (Others, with less probability, take it as referring to the citizens' increased ability to make thank-offerings to the gods.)

948 city's watch-post: probably the scholiast is right to see a specific ref. to the Areopagus-court (cf. v. 706 above), although others have given the phrase wider extension ("the citizens who are guardians and defenders of the city," Rose).

949 guaranteeing: Erinyes have earned a place with the Olympians as divinities who can authoritatively promise benefits to men. See n. on v. 347 above.

950 reverend: an ancient title for a female divinity which can be traced back as far as Mycenaean times. For Aesch. it seems to have had underworld connotations; it is applied to the Erinys at *Sept.* 887 and, indirectly, at *Sept.* 976 (Eur. uses a cognate term at *Or.* 318 and probably *Bacch.* 664 [see Dodds' n. on 664–7].) See Garvie's n. on *Cho.* 722.

951 among the immortals ...: thus is the gap, of which the Erinyes had themselves made so much in the First Choral Ode (e.g. vv. 347 ff.), bridged.

953 manifestly and completely: an echo of the language used by the Erinyes at vv. 320 and 382 above.

956–960 The two prayers are correlative: men killed before their time make for unhappy widows.

961 who hold authority: the root signifying "authority" occurs also at vv. 127, 326–7, 544, 581 and 639 above. The association predicated between these unnamed gods (perhaps "Zeus, Hera, and Aphrodite, the deities especially concerned with marriage," Mills) and the Fates, *Moirai* (on whom see n. on v. 335 above), effectively dignifies their role in the life-process, whereas earlier the powers they exerted were largely negative (vv. 389 ff.). It is thus highly significant that Zeus and Moira will be conjoined at vv. 1045–46 below. (Reminiscent of this passage is the powerful juxtaposition of divine names at *Sept.* 975: "O Moira whose gifts are oppressive; Reverend [*Potnia*: cf. *Eum.* 950] Shade of Oedipus; and black Erinys – indeed you are one whose strength is great !")

970 **I love Persuasion's face:** Athena had sung the praises of this goddess-abstraction at v. 885 above (see Buxton, *Persuasion in Greek Tragedy* [cited in n. on v. 885 above], pp. 112–13). Athena's attitude contrasts sharply with that of Apollo.

971 **supervised:** the same word as the Chorus had used of Hades at v. 275 above (compare v. 530, "his surveillance differs").

973 **Zeus, Protector God of assemblies:** the epithet in a sense complements that used of Zeus at v. 918. Zeus sometimes, and Athena almost always, prevails by means other than sheer divine might.

975 **our joint ... striving:** a paradox: neither side has "won," for it is not strife between two opponents but a striving, by two newly-associated powers, for a noble not a base objective. The phrasing also suggests Hesiod's doctrine of the "Two Strifes," one reprehensible who "fosters evil war and battle, being cruel; her no man loves," the other "the elder daughter of dark Night." She "stirs up even the shiftless to toil," and incites craftsmen like potters and poets, and even beggars, to beneficial competition with one another (*Works and Days* 11–26, adapted from Evelyn-White's trans.). As Garvie remarks in his n. on *Cho.* 474–5, the Goddess Strife, whose malign influence has been at work earlier in the trilogy (as at *Ag.* 698, 1461, *Cho.* 474), here "becomes at last a creative force."

976 ff. They take up Athena's injunctions at vv. 858 ff. **the growling of Factional Strife (Stasis) ...":** begins an extended metaphorical depiction of Civil War, or Faction, as a ravening beast, which continues in "snatching up" in 981 (I have taken **hungry for evil** from Verrall). Commentators point out that contemporary Athens may, in fact, have been torn by factional disputes over the recently enacted judicial reforms of Ephialtes and the impending relaxation in property qualifications for holding the archonship (for the latter, see n. on v. 693 above).

979/980 **drink ... black blood:** as Apollo pointed out using similar language, such bloodshed is irreversible (vv. 647–48 above, and *Ag.* 1019 ff.).

981 **snatching up:** Paley explains the word Aesch. uses as meaning "eagerly to lick up, to catch at as an animal seizes its food."

982 **Atē's requital:** *Atē* was the term used by the Greeks to denote a state of culpable blindness, "destructive madness" or, in a more fully personified way, "Spirit of Destruction." In the *Oresteia* she is in some ways a double or shadow-image of the Erinys. At *Ag.* 385–6 she "plots in advance" and is genealogized (a favorite way of giving life to these moral abstractions in early Greek poetry) as mother of Persuasion; together the family pair lead sinners like Paris and Agamemnon to destruction. In the fable of the lion-cub (see n. on v. 355 above) the beast turned savage works destruction "like some god-sent priest of *Atē*" (735–6). After the murder of Agamemnon Clytemnestra swears her unrepentance by a sacrilegious triad, "Dike, Atē and Erinys" (*Ag.* 1432–3). In the next play Orestes calls upon Zeus of the Underworld (see note on vv. 273 ff. above) to send as assistance "late-avenging Atē" (*Cho.* 383): the adj. evokes **requital** in the present passage and a scholiast there glosses "Atē" as "Erinys" (a ref. which, among many others, I owe to Dr. A.F. Garvie).

requital: the Chorus had claimed this function at vv. 322 ff. above; and the word occurs in a similarly-formed compound at 464. Cf. also v. 543 above and *Cho.* 946–7, where Orestes' slaying of his mother is attributed to "wily Requital," which according to Garvie, "is to be thought of as the Erinys."

985 **unanimity of thought:** the opposite of Factional Strife (976).

988 **Do they intend to find ...?:** I have accepted Dodds' interpretation of this passage (*Classical Quarterly* 3 [1953] 21).

990 **frightening visages,** lit. "masks": we are reminded of the impression they made on the Pythia (vv. 52 ff. above).

991 great profit: the phrasing recalls the way the Chorus had sung praises of "fear" in the Second Choral Ode (vv. 517 ff.) With **profit** compare Athena's remark at vv. 1008–9 below about what is "advantageous to the city's profit in gaining victory." The train of thought is: "the element of healthy fear which these goddesses inspire will ensure your respect for the laws in an exemplary way."

992 kindly to these Kindly ones: the ancient Introductory Note (*Hypothesis*) says, "After mollifying the Erinyes [Athena] addressed them as 'Eumenides' (= "Well-wishers")." I believe that that comment, and thus the title of the play, derive from this verse, since the word for "kindly," *Euphronas*, and *Eumenidas* are synonymous. As Paley remarks, "In this epithet [*euphronas*] ... the new title of Eumenides is *implied.*" The epithet is repeated at v. 1030 below and (as emended) 1034.

993 honouring them greatly: the "honour" theme is reaching its conclusion (also at vv. 1029 and 1037 below).

994 just and upright: the compound Aesch. uses is close to that in v. 312 above, which I have translated "dispense straight judgements."

996 destined enjoyment: the word suggests "approved by the gods" (and so not subject to catastrophes facing those who seek to aggrandize themselves without limit, as, e.g., *Ag.* 772–80).

1000 wise with the passage of time is, as Rose remarks, "a curious expression." They appear to be calling on the Athenians to match them in showing the "good sense" which they themselves have recently learnt, for which Athena had complimented them at v. 988. **Wise** probably also refers to the theme of "wisdom through suffering" which was heard so often earlier in the trilogy (vv. 520–21 above, esp. *Ag.* 181, 1425). Thomson suggests that they are to show this wisdom "by their acceptance of the deterrent influence of law."

1001 Pallas Athena's wings: some have seen here an allusion to winged statues of Nike (Victory), who was assimilated to and often even identified with Athena (see Ar. *Birds* 574, Eur. *Ion* 457).

1004 deep dwelling-places: Aesch. uses a word that has "netherworld" connotations (cf., e.g., *Pers.* 624, where the Chorus instruct the Queen to "send libations [sc. to Darius' ghost] to dwelling-places beneath the earth").

1005 these escorts: the text puts it beyond doubt that some individuals escorted the Chorus from the orchestra. It is possible that these were merely the jurors redesignated and drawn into extra service, or a subsidiary chorus may have been introduced at this point. They carried torches (1005, 1029) and led animals to be sacrificed (1006). We remember that the Erinyes had used, with some irony, the term "escorts" of themselves early in the play (v. 206). (Whether we should accept the view of Weir Smyth and others of a stage peopled with vast numbers of extras is another matter: "The procession is formed by Athena (at its head), the Chorus, the Areopagites, torch-bearers, the women who guard the Palladium [Athena's statue], and various others. In the rear came the Athenian public" (Loeb trans. p. 367 n. 1).

1006 august victims for sacrifice: the term **august** reflects the Erinyes' own title (vv. 383 above and 1040–41 below).

1010 in charge of the city: cf. v. 775 above.

1011 Kranaos' sons: Kranaos was an early king of Athens, a rather shadowy figure; the Athenians are frequently styled as "descended from, related to, Kranaos." Similarly, she addressed them as "Aegeus' people" at v. 683 above.

for these new residents: they are now fully-fledged "metics," aliens resident in Athens with defined legal rights and responsibilities (the status had been hinted at by

Athena's words at v. 869 above, "take a resident's share," and cf. v. 1018 and n. on v. 1028 below).

1013 for the good done to them: this is Paley's suggested trans., but the meaning is not quite clear; other versions include "of the good powers" (Sidgwick), "good intentions of doing good" (Paley, alternatively). The phrasing of Ar. *Frogs* 1530 is remarkably similar.

1018 my residency: see n. on v. 1011 above.

1024 with female attendants: probably although not necessarily distinct from and in addition to the "escorts" mentioned in v. 1006.

1025 my statue: the olive-wood statue already alluded to in vv. 80, 242, 259, 409, 439 (440 in the trans.) and 446. It is to have a place of honour in the procession.

the eye of the whole land: with some reluctance and a lingering doubt I construe this rather odd turn of phrase as nomin. and in apposition to "a celebrated troop" etc. in vv. 1026–27 (and thus adapt Weir Smyth's trans.); but other interpretations are possible. (Lloyd-Jones translates, "you shall come to the very eye of Theseus' land, O honourable band of children ...").

1026 a celebrated troop: a promise had been made by Athena at v. 856 above which is here discharged (in part at least: there, "men and companies of women" are to pay the Erinyes honour, here, apparently, only women).

1027 ff. I follow those commentators who posit a lacuna after 1027 not because we require a literal naming-ceremony by Athena, but simply because otherwise the syntax of the passage is incomprehensible (see A.L. Brown, *Classical Quarterly* 34 [1984] 272–5).

1028 The widely-held theory, that at this verse mute attendants brought out scarlet cloaks and helped the Erinyes re-robe (or, rather, simply put these over their black clothing; see vv. 352 and 370 above, *Cho.* 1049), is, I believe, correct, although it cannot be proven in the strict sense. Red is an appropriate colour for them to wear, because (a) "blood-red alone would be enough to make the colour suitable to the Furies" (Thomson, citing *Il.* XVIII. 538, where the "destructive Kēr," Spirit of death, is said to wear about her shoulders a "raiment red with the blood of men"); and (b) Athenian metics wore crimson cloaks when participating in solemn processions, the most important being the Panathenaia (see Thomson's long n. on 1027–31 for full refs.). See W. Headlam, "The Last Scene of the *Eumenides*," Goheen, "Three Studies in the *Oresteia*," 115 ff.; W. Whallon, *Problem and Spectacle* 100 ff. Whallon remarks on the "three-fold meaning in the color: as foreigners dwelling in Athens they wear livery on festive occasions, as neighbors of the goddess in their grotto near her temple they have the right to a badge of divinity or royalty, and as former inhabitants in the house of Tantalus they wear a reminder to us of the blood they once drank in long draughts" (*Problem and Spectacle* pp. 104–105). So, too, Conacher: "the trilogy ends with the recurrence of a striking visual symbol: the blood-stained robe of the slain Agamemnon (displayed at the climactic moments of both preceding tragedies) is now triumphantly replaced by crimson insignia proclaiming the new civic status of the Erinyes" (*Aeschylus' 'Oresteia'*, p. 174).

1029 blaze of torch-fire: the carrying of torches was a common feature of religious processions, esp. during the Panathenaia (the festival itself was also preceded by a torch-race: Harpocration s.v. *lampas*, cited by Thomson). Thus, at the end of *Frogs* Pluto bids the chorus of initiates "shine your sacred torches for him [Aesch.]," and escort him to the accompaniment of his own songs and melodies" (*Frogs* 1524–27, where Stanford suggests a conscious parallel with the end of *Eum.*). Torches are moreover iconographically appropriate for underworld divinities, and the Erinyes are thus depicted on several of the south Italian vases and almost all of the Etruscan and

Roman sarcophagi where they appear. As Gantz well remarks, "the line of torches ... summarises and re-echoes all the appearances of fire in the trilogy" ("The Fires of the *Oresteia*," 38).

1030 these visitors to my country: Athena echoes, perhaps consciously, her own phrase at v. 406 ("but with a different tone," as Verrall says).

1031 conspicuously inspiring her men with courage: Sidgwick comments on the "rather emphatic and unusual phraseology" of this line. As Thomson remarks, there may be an allusion to the contests called *Euandriai*, held at both the Panathenaia and Theseia; "they select the handsomest boys and command them to be the first among the carriers [? of the sacred implements]" (Athenaeus 13. 565 F, trans. C. B. Gulick, with his n. there).

1032–1047 The metre is dactylic, stately but at the same time rather sprightly. See Appendix III. Who sang these lines? It is only the scholia in M and F (at v. 1032) which designate this choral exodos as sung by a subsidiary chorus of "Escorts," who are in fact referred to at v. 1005; M itself assigns them simply to "Chorus." Page notes Kirchhoff's theory that vv. 1035, 1039, 1043 and 1047 were sung by a Herald. A.L. Brown suggests that this was all a monody sung by Athena. I feel some sympathy with Verrall's remark, "Here the natural supposition is, that everyone on the scene who could sing, did."

1034 (yet not children): cf. n. on v. 457, "a non-city" (I do not think the usual meaning of this word, "without children," is possible here.)

1035 inhabitants of the land: Hermann's generally accepted emendation of the word offered by the MSS, "go." (Alternatively, some edd. repeat "the city's whole population" from v. 1038.)

keep auspicious silence: the usual injunction by those participating in a sacred ritual to the onlookers (see, e.g., Ar. *Ach.* 241). (There seems to be a change of tone in these commands at the end of each stanza, hence, Kirchhoff's suggestion that a Herald sings them; or Verrall may be correct in assigning them to "another voice or voices.")

1036 primeval: "a strange word of obscure origin" (Sidgwick), is used of "Styx's primeval water" by Hesiod (*Theog.* 806), and is also applied to Thebes and, at *Pers.* 975, to Athens.

1040/41 August Goddesses: their proper title: Paus. 1. 28. 6, and cf. vv. 383 and 1006 above.

1042 fiercely blazing: lit., "devoured by fire."

1044 "This line is thoroughly corrupt and it is hopeless to try to restore it with any confidence," Sidgwick.

1045 Zeus All-seeing: the epithet is· generally applied to Argus of-the-many-eyes, whom Hera had imposed as a spy on Zeus' beloved, Io (so Aesch. *Suppl.* 304), but it is appropriately used of Zeus' benevolent surveillance of human affairs (see v. 530–1 above). "Zeus and the *Moirai* work together" (Garvie's n. on *Cho.* 306–8, where he cites the present passage).

1046 came down to join: I accept A. L. Brown's arguments for interpreting the *sun-* in the compound as requiring an additional referent (*i.e.* not Zeus and Moira "came together"); see *Journal of Hellenic Studies* 103 (1983) 28 n. 74 and *Liverpool Classical Monthly* 11.6 (1986) 2, and so Paley: "... entered the contest on behalf of the citizens of Pallas." **Came down** is probably an athletic metaphor, to descend from the spectators' stands to the lists where the competitions took place (cf. *Cho.* 726–27: "Now is the hour for Persuasion with her guile to enter the lists with him [i.e., Orestes]," Weir Smyth's trans.). In Fraenkel's words, "all Homeric thought is far transcended in this notion of a unified and all-prevailing justice which in the wisdom of reconciliation triumphs in the end over the tangled fates and frightful misdeeds of human kind" (*Aeschylus, Agamemnon* vol. III, p. 730).

Leningrad, Hermitage B 1743 (St. 349);   Apulian calyx-krater by the Konniakis Painter, c. 350 B.C.:   Orestes, sleeping Erinyes and the Pythian priestess in what may be a stage-setting for a south Italian production of 'Eumenides'.   See pp. 29–30. (photo 'Journal of Hellenic Studies' 89).

APPARATUS CRITICUS

Ὑπόθεσις vid. A. L. Brown *CQ* 34 (1984) 270-1, *ibid.* 37 (1987) 427 sqq., qui περισχόμενος pro περιεχόμενος(M) proposuit (429 n.19)

11 Παρησοῦ θ' Robortello : Παρ*νησοῦσθ' (ex Παραν-) M

18 θρόνοις Turnebus : χρόνοις codd.

21 damnavi (δ' εὐλόγως Hermann)

23 ἀναστροφαί GTFE : -φά M -φή MΣ24b

27 Πλειστοῦ Turnebus : πλείστους codd. δὲ Blaydes : τε codd.

31 πάρ' Abresch : παρ' codd.

36 στάσιν codd. et Phrynichus in Bekk. An. 23. 12 : βάσιν MSYP, Et. Mag. s.v. δκταίνω

37 οὐ ποδωκείᾳ GFE : οὐ ποδωκίᾳ MPCT

40 θεομυσῆ M : θεομισῆ GTFE

41 ἔχοντα GTFE : -τι M

44-45 sic scripsi : λήνει μεγίστῳ σωφρόνως ἐστεμμένον, ἀργῆτι μαλλῷ· τῇδε γὰρ τρανῶς ἐρῶ codd. (λήνει μεγίστῳ glossema, ut videtur; "τῇδε...ἐρῶ suspectum, nam valde abnormis est voc. τῇδε usus" Page)

46 λόχος GTFE : λέχος M

49 post h. v. lacunam proposuit Wakefield

53 πλατοῖσι Elmsley : πλαστ- codd.

54 λίβα Burges : δία M βίαν GTFE (λίαν D. Young)

59 πόνον Arnaldus: -νων codd.

63 post h. v. nonnulli post Burges inserunt vv. 85 - 7

76 βιβῶντ' Stephanus : βεβῶντ' M βεβόντ' GTFE (περῶντα δ' αἰεί Wecklein)

77 πόντον Turnebus : -του codd.

93 ὁρμωμένων Blaydes : μενον codd.

95-99 sic disposui: 95, 96, 99, 98, 97 (sic separatim Musgrave)

103 ὁρᾶτε post Hermann scripsi et v. interrogative accepi (variatio ὁρᾶτε...σέθεν nil miranda; vid. 143-5, 180-1, 950-3) : ὅρα δὲ codd.

105 μοῖρ' ἀπρόσκοπος Turnebus ex Σ : μοῖρα πρόσκοπος codd. φρενῶν pro βροτῶν Hermann

107 νηφάλια Robortello : νιφάλια codd.

108 νυκτίσεμνα Turnebus : νυκτὶ σεμνά MGTF νύκτι σεμνά E

110 ταῦτα πάντα E : πάντα ταῦτα cett.

112 ἀρκυστάτων Turnebus : ἀρκυσμάτων codd.

113 ἐγκατιλλώψας Turnebus : ἐκκατ- codd.

116 Κλυταιμνήστρα codd.

117-31 personas paragraphis distinguit M

118 ἀνήρ Dindorf (teste Davies) : ἀνὴρ codd.

119 nondum sanatus (φίλων γὰρ εἰσὶν οὐ κενοὶ προσίκτορες Dodds, *CQ* 1953, p. 18)

121-3 om. M, suppl. MS in marg.

123 ὠγμός Robortello : μωγμός codd.

125 τέτακται Wakefield (vid. infr. v. 639) : πέπρακται codd. (πέπρωται Stanley)

130 φάρξον M. L. West (*BICS* 24 [1977] 100) : φράζου codd.

132 ἐκέλειπων Blomfield : ἐκλιπὼν codd. φόνου pro πόνου Page post Dawe (vel κόπος pro πόνος in 133 Halm)

137 σὺ δ' Pierson : οὐδ' codd. τω Wakefield : τῷ codd.

138 κατισχναίνουσα Robortello : κατισχαίνουσα codd.

139 δεύτερος 'adiunctus' vel 'renovatus' displicet (δ' ἀγρίοις F. W. Schmidt)

140 Χορὸς Ἐρινύων praefixit M, ἐξ ὧν μία add. MS

142 ἰδώμεθ' Turnebus : εἰδώμεθ' codd.

143 πόπαξ Aldina : πύπαξ codd.

145 δυσαχὲς M : δυσαχθὲς GTFE Hesychius (δυσακὲς Lindau)

144 πέπονθα Blaydes : παθοῦσα codd.

161 τι Schütz : τὸ codd. κρύος ἔχειν displicet (vid. 154 et 168)

163 πέρα Heimsoeth : πλέον codd.

164 φονολιβῆ Arnaldus : φονολειβῆ codd.

167 γᾶς τ' Wilamowitz : γᾶς codd.

168 δρόμενον (Abresch : αἰρόμενον M) ἄγος ἔχειν suspectum

169 μάντις ὢν Schütz : μάντι σῷ codd.

170 μυχὸν Robortello : μυκὸν M, σὸν οἶκον T ἐχράνατ' Fᵃᶜ : ἐχρανά τ' M, ἔχρανας Turnebus

172 παρὰ νόμον Parisinus gr. 2886 (= Me Turyn) : παρανόμων M (ω in o mutato), παρὰ νόμων GTFE

174 κἀμοὶ γε Casaubon : κἀμοί τε codd.

175 δὲ Heyse : τε codd. φυγὼν Porson : φεύγων codd.

177-8 corrupti 178 πα°σεται M : πάσσεται GTF, πράσσεται E

186 οὗ Turnebus, καρανιστῆρες Stanley : οὐκαρανιστῆρες M

187 ἀποφθορᾷ Musgrave : -φθοραί codd.

188 ἀκρωνίαι Murray : -νία codd.

189 λευσμοὶ Casaubon : -μόν codd.

190 ὑπὸ ῥάχιν Eᵃᶜ : ὑπόρραχιν Eᴾᶜ rell.

195 τοῖσι A. L. Brown : τοῖσδε codd. πλησίοισι suspectum (πανοσίοισι Newman, παντίμοισι L. Kayser)

197 δ' post τοιαύτης delevit Page, recte

200 εἰς Canter : εἰς codd.

203 πρᾶξαι Bigot, Kirchhoff : πέμψαι codd.

204 ὄκτωρ Mˢ : δ' ἔκτωρ M rell.

207 πρόσφοροι Stanley : πρόσφορον codd.

211 τί γάρ Mˢ : τίς γάρ M rell.

213 ἠργάσω Rutherford : ἠρκέσω codd.

217 μόρσιμος T et sscr. GFE : μόρσιμοι MGFE

219 εἰ Canter : ἢ codd.

220 τίνεσθαι Meineke : γενέσθαι codd.

221 Apollinis nomen praefix. MGFE σ' Robortello : γ' M, om T

222 τῷ μὲν Paley : τὰ μὲν codd. οἶδα Mᶠʸᴾ : οὗτοι GTFE

223 τοῖς δ'...πράσσουσιν Paley : τὰ δ'...πράσσουσαν codd. (sed ἐμφανῶς suspectum)

225 λίπω Porson : λείπω codd.

226 πλέω Auratus : πλέον codd.

230 ἄγει...μητρῷον GTFE : ἄγειν...μητρῴων M

231 κἀκκυνηγετῶ Erfurdt (cf. Eur. Ion 1422) : κἀκκυνηγέτης codd.

232 τε ῥύσομαι codd. (τ' ἐρύσομαι Murray, quod syllaba brevis ante ρ initialem abnormis est; vid. adnotationem eius ad Prom. 713)

235 κελεύμασιν Eᵃᶜ T : κελεύσμασιν MGEᴾᶜ

236 ἀλάστορα codd., fort. ἀλήτορα Taplin (vid. A. L. Brown. JHS 103 [1983] 24 n. 61).

240 "fortasse post 235 traiciendus," Murray

242 πάρειμι, "adsum," scripsi (cf. Eur. Ba.5) : πρόσειμι codd.

243 ἀναμενῶ Stanley : ἀναμένω codd.

246 νεβρὸν Victorius : νεκρὸν codd.

247 ἐκματεύομεν Dindorf : ἐκμαστ- codd.

250 ποτήμασιν Dindorf : πωτή- codd.

255 πάντα λεῦσσε μὴ A. L. Brown : λεῦσσε**τον πάντα M

256 βὰς Hermann : βὰς ὁ codd.

δδ' αὐτὸς ἀλκὰν ἔχων Stanley

χρεῶν Scaliger ex Σ (ἀνθ' ὧν χρεωστεῖ) : χερῶν codd.

πέδοι χύμενον Porson : πέδῳ vel πέδωι κεχυμένον codd.

φεροίμαν βοσκὰν Wellauer : inverso ordine codd

ἰσχνάν- Turnebus : ἰχνάν- M, ἰσχάν- rell.

ἀντίποιν' ὡς Schütz : ἀντιποίνους codd. τίνης GTFE : τείνης (ει super η) M   μητροφόνου
Schütz post Casaubon : μητροφόνας codd.

ὄψει codd.   δὲ κεῖ τις Schütz : δ' ἐκεῖ τίς codd.   ἄλλος Heath : -ον codd.

καθαίρει (purgat) Stanley : καθαιρεῖ (delet) codd.

σκιάν Heath : σκιά codd.

ἀμή Dindorf (ἀμά iam Canter) : ἄμα codd.

εὐθυδίκοι (cf. *Ag.* 761) proposui, αἶδ' Verrall : εὐθυδίκαι θ' οἶδ' οἴμεθ' M

ἔχοντας scripsi (cf. Dem. xxiv. 60 οἱ μὴ καθαρὰς τὰς χεῖρας ἔχοντας) : προνέμοντας
(προσνέμ- M) codd.

ἀφ' ἡμῶν μῆνις ἐφέρπει codd., traiecit Porson hiatus vitandi causa

ἀλιτῶν Auratus : ἀλιτρῶν codd. ἀνὴρ Porson · ἀνήρ codd.

πτᾶκα Sophianus : πτάκα codd.

παραφορά Mᵖᶜ : παράφρονα Mᵃᶜ rell.

sqq. varie tentati, sensus non apparet

341-346 ex 328-333 pauca cum variatione iteratos seclusi

συνδαίτωρ Turnebus : -δάτωρ codd.

352 sqq. renumeravi, ordine servato

2/353 ἄκληρος ἄμοιρος Blass : inverso ordine codd.

3a vid. 367

4 γὰρ secl. Sansone

5 τιθασὸς Par. gr. 2886 (Me Turyn) : πιθ- rell. φίλον Turnebus : φίλος codd.

7 ὧδ' ἱέμεναι E. A. J. Ahrens : ὦ διόμεναι codd.

8 ὁμοίως Murray : ὁμοίως codd.

9 αἷμα νέον obscurum (vid. v. 204); fort. scribendum ἀφ' [Schoemann] αἵματος φίλου
("sanguinem victimae ipsius haurimus") μαυροῦμεν αἵματος κενόν proposuit Dawe
(*Collation & Investigation* 187)

0 σπεύδομεν αἶδ' Doederlein : σπευδόμεναι δ' codd.

2 θεούς τ' scripsi : θεῶν δ' codd.

4 εἰς Pauw : ἐς codd. ἔγκρισιν ('inquisitio' vel 'iunctura') GTFE

5/6 Ζεὺς Mᵖᶜ : Ζεῦ Mᵃᶜ rell. δ' Linwood : γὰρ M, om. rell. αἱμοστ- Bothe : αἱματοστ- codd.

8 δ' Bergk : τ' codd.

9 γᾶς Hermann : γᾶν codd.

0 ἁμετέραις Dindorf : ἡμετ- codd.

1 ἐπιφθόνοις Heath : -φόνοις codd.

3 ἀνέκαθεν J. Pearson : ἄγκαθεν codd. βαρυπετῆ Blaydes : -πεσῆ codd.

5 καὶ suppl. Schoemann

8 τοῖον ἐπὶ Heath : τοῖον γὰρ ἐπὶ codd.   τε ποτᾶται Sansone (*Hermes* 112 [1984] 7 - 8) :
πεπόταται codd.

5 ἀτίετα Canter : ἀτίεται M, ἀτίετον GTF

6 λάπᾳ [= βορβόρῳ] Wieseler : λαμπᾳ M, λαμπαί rell.

ost 388 fort. excidit Mesodion 8

9 οὐχ ἅζεται Turnebus : οὐ χάζεταί codd.

3 ἔτι δέ μοι <μένει> Hermann : ἔπι δε μοι codd.

8 γῆν... μένη Stanley : τὴν... μένην codd.

04,405 dittographias esse affirmant viri docti; 405 retinendus mihi videtur

09 ξένῳ· sic interpunxit Murray post Paley

411 θέαισι Wieseler : θεαῖσι codd.

414 ἤδ' F : ἤδ' M, ἤδ' T

416 αἰανῆς GTFE et Tzetz. ad Lycophr. 406 : αἰανῇ M et M^Σ

417 Ἀραί GTFE : Ἀρά M

422 ποῦ τὸ Arnaldus : τοῦτο codd. φυγῆς Scaliger : σφαγῆς codd.

424 ἐπιρροιζεῖς Scaliger : -εῖ M^pc, -εῖν M^ac rell.

430 δίκαιος Dindorf : δικαίους M^ac, δικαίως M^sGTF
435 sic olim divisit Hermann, Blass (vid. v. 272) : ἀξίαν τ' codd.

438 τῶνδ' GFE : τόνδ' M T

440 ἐμῆς GTFE : ἀμῆς M

445-446 ἔχων... ἐφεζόμην Wieseler : ἔχει... ἐφεζομένη codd.

450 καθαιμάξωσι Turnebus: -ξουσι codd. -σι νεοθήλοος Abresch (νεοθήλου iam Turnebus, εὐθήλου Wunder) : -σιν οθηλοῦ M

461 κρύψασ' ἃ Musgrave : κρύψασα codd. (κλέψασ' Sansone, cf. Cho. 854)

465 ἐπαίτιος suspectum (cf. v. 467) : μεταίτιος (Weil), ἐστ' αἴτιος (Blaydes)

468 δ' J. Pearson : τ' codd.

471 βροτός M^s rell. : βροτοῖς M

472 φόνου Robortello : -νους codd.

473 pro ὅμως codd. fort. legendum πόνῳ (πόνοις iam Burges) κατηρτυκώς 'adultus' (Hesychius) haud possibile

475 delevi post Prien et (olim) Dindorf

478 χωρεῖ Wieseler : χῶραι codd.

479 πέδοι Dindorf : πέδω codd.

481 nondum sanatus (πέμπειν ἀμηνίτως τε δυσπήμαντ' ἐμοί coni. Page post Blaydes et Scaliger)

483 ὁρκίους αἰρουμένη Casaubon : ὁρκίων αἰρουμένους codd. post h. v. lacunam statuit Hermann

489 "non suo stat loco" Page (post 485 GTFE) fort. post 487 traiciendus πορόντας Hermann : περῶντας codd.

492 τε supplevit Heath

494-5 εὐχερείᾳ Turnebus : εὐχερίᾳ M

499 οὐδὲ Elmsley : οὔτε codd.

503-4 προφωνῶν non intellegitur

505 ἐπίδοσίν pro ὑπόδοσίν Stinton JHS 96, 1976, p. 123

506 ἄκεα δ' Schwenk (ἀκέα τ' Schütz) : ἄκετ' M, ἄκεστ' GTFE

506-7 τλάμων δέ τις μάταν codd. : δὲ del. Schwenk, τις del. Pauw

511, 512 ὤ...ὤ Pauw : ἰὼ...ἰὼ codd.

519 δεῖ μένειν Dobraei amicus : δειμαίνει codd.

522-523 lectio incertissima (fort. 522 φόβῳ [Schütz], 523 ἀποστρέφων 'se avertens')

525 σέβει sscr. σέβοι M

529 παντί T : ἄπαντι MGFE

530/1 ἀλλ' ἀλλᾳ Wellauer : ἀλλα ἀλλα' M δ' ἐφορεύει GTFE: δι' ἐφορ- M

533 δυσσεβίας T : -βείας MGFE

538 σοι Lachmann : δέ σοι codd.

548 ἐπιστρ. δωμ. Heath metri causa : δωμ. ἐπιστρ. codd.

550 ἐκὼν δ' Wieseler : ἐκ τῶνδ' codd.

552 δ' suppl. Pauw

553 παρβάδαν F (teste Wecklein, cf. Groeneboom, Murray ad loc.) : περβάδαν T περαιβάδαν M (παρβάταν Hermann ex Σ παραβεβηκότα)

554 ἄγοντα O. Müller : τὰ codd. (τὰ πολλ' ἄγοντα Mazon, Thomson) δίκας GTFE : δίκης M

558 ἐν suppl. Abresch

559 δυσπαλεῖ τε Turnebus : δυσπαλεῖται MGTF, δυσπλανεῖται E

560 θερμῷ T : θερμοεργῷ MFE θυμοεργῷ G

562 λαπαδνὸν Musgrave : λέπαδνον codd. et. Σ

565 ἀκλαυτος Dindorf : ἀκλαυστος codd.

566 κατεργαθοῦ Dindorf (κατειργάθου Porson) : κατεργάθου codd.

567 εἰς οὐρανὸν δὲ Wecklein : εἶτ' (ἦ suprascr. M^S) οὖν codd.   πέλει ante Τυρσηνική TF, post versum G

570 πληρουμένου suspectum (vid. 568)

573 τούσδ' Hermann : τόνδ' ME fort. recte (τῷδ' post Bothe Murray), τῶνδ' GTF

574-575 vv. Athenae tribuit Wieseler, choro M (lacunam post 572 vult Friis Johansen et sic vv. distribuit: 573 Apollini, 574 choro, 575 Athenae [*Classica et Mediaevalia* 39, 1988, pp. 5-14])

576 νόμῳ olim Schütz : δόμων codd.

577 ἀνὴρ Porson : ἀνὴρ codd. ἐφέστιος M^sscr. : -ίως M, -ίων GTFE

578 τῷδ' Robertson : τοῦδ' codd.   v. damnavit A. L. Brown (*JHS* 102, 1982, p. 32 n. 39)

580 τοῦ φόνου Turnebus : τοῦδε φόνου codd.

581 τ' suppl. Hermann

600 μιασμάτοιν Elmsley : -των M

post 602 lacunam vult Sansone

603 τί γάρ; Hermann : τοιγάρ M   φόνῳ Schütz : -νου M

608 φίλτατον M^S : -του M

612 δίκαιον Auratus : δικαίως codd.

615 ὧν δ' Canter : δ' ὧν M

618 κελεύσαι Hermann : -σει M

619 μάθε Blaydes : μαθεῖν M

620 βουλῇ Σ620 : βουλή M et Σ619

623 τὸν M^S : τοῦ M

631-634 lectio incerta; poeta voluit ut vid. "quamvis Clytaemnestra maritum suum a bello Troico bene finito revertentem benigne recepisset, illum de balneo egredientem (interfecit)"

634 περ ἐσκήνωσεν M (sed unum verbum intellexit Σ634a)

638 ταύτην M (vid. Fraenkel, *Aesch. Agam.* II. 415-6 adn. 4) : τὴν δ' αὖ Weil, Page

650 ἄνω τε GTFE cod. Monacensis 546 (= Mf Turyn) : ἄνω M

651 οὐδὲν ἀσθμαίνων GTFE : οὐδ' ἐν ἀσθμαίνω M

653 πέδοι Dindorf : πέδω vel πέδῳ codd.

656 προσδέξεται GTFE : προσδέξαιτε M

658 κεκλημένη GTFE : κεκλημένου M

663 γείναιτ' Wieseler ex Σ : γένοιτ' codd.

665 οὐκ Schütz : οὐδ' codd.

666 θεά Weil : θεός codd.

667 lacunam post hoc v. statuit Dawe

676-677 Apollini tribuit Winnington-Ingram, choro codd.

683 Αἰγέως GTF : Αἰγέωι M

684 δικαστῶν Canter : δ' ἑκάστων M, fort. δικάζον (cum βουλευτήριον) Sansone

692 τό τ' Grotius : τόδ' codd. ὁμῶς Turnebus : ὅμως codd.

693 'πικαινούντων Stephanus : 'πικαινόντων codd.

696 μήτε Guelferbytanus Gudianus Graecus 88 (Mc Turyn) : μηδὲ rell.

710 , αἰδουμένους Canter : αἰδουμένοις M, αἱρουμένοις T (vid. 483)

713 κἄγωγε Robortello : κἀγώ τε codd.

716 νέμων Hermann : μένων codd.

727 διανομὰς schol. Eur. *Alc.* 12 : δαίμονας codd.

733 ἀμφίβουλος F : ἀμφίβολος MGTE

746, 747 nulla nota personae in M : 746 Oresti tribuit Abresch, recte ναῦ pro νῦν habet M

747 ἔχειν Paley : νέμειν codd. (μένειν Wakefield)

748-751 attributio h. vv. res incertissima; 748 paragraphum habet M, sine nota personae (Apollini dedit Victorius) 748-49 choro continuavi cum TF , 750-51 ubi sensus claudicat Oresti tribuo (Wieseler iam 748 sqq.)

751 πεσόντα vel σφαλέντα Blaydes : βαλοῦσα M (ὄγκον pro οἶκον M. L. West)

752 δδ' GTFE : δ γ' M

755 γαίας Dindorf : καὶ γῆς codd.

768 παρβ- MPC GT : παραβ- Mac , προβ- FE

769 nondum sanatus

771 πόνου Butler : πόνος codd.

772 ὀρθουμένοις T (-νων MGFE)

774 αὑτοί σφιν Verralli amicus : αὑτοῖσιν codd.

778-92 (quos om. GTFE) = 808-23 designatio (1) significat lectionem strophae, (2) antistrophae

780 ἁ Dindorf : ἡ codd.

782 ἀντιπενθῆ M (1) : παθῆ codd. (2)

783 χθονὶ σταλαγμὸν Thomson : verba inversa in codd. (1) et (2)

785 λειχὴν Bothe : λιχ- codd. ὃ Δίκα < Δίκα > Lachmann : ἰὼ Δίκα codd. (1) et (2)

786 ἐπισύμ- M (1) : ἐπεσσύμ- codd. (2)

787 βαλεῖ Turnebus : ειν codd. (1) et (2)

788 στενάζω M (2) T : στενάξω M (1)

789 γελῶμαι Tyrwhitt : γένωμαι codd. (1) et (2) δύσοιστ' ἐν Murray : δύσοιστα codd. (1) et (2)

791 μεγάλατοι Porson (cf. Pers. 1016) : μεγάλα τοι codd.

794-807 om. GTFE

794 πίθεσθε Turnebus : πειθ- M

798 θ' ὁ MPC : δ' ὁ Mac ὁ χρήσας Turnebus : ὁ θήσας MPC (ὀρθήσας Mac)

800 μήτε Wieseler : τε M

801 σκήψητε Elmsley : ησθε M

802 δαιμόνων vix sanum (λαιμόνων Wellauer, πλευμόνων Wakefield),

808-23 vid. 778-93 nn.

825 κτίσητε Linwood : στήσητε codd.

827 δώματος Casaubon : των codd.

828 ἐν ᾧ MGFE : ἐν οἷς T

829 εὐπιθὴς Hermann : εὐπειθ- codd.

830 ἔπη χθονί Burges : ἐπὶ χθόνα codd.

835 τέλους MsT : τέλος M

837-47 : (1) = 837-47 (2) = 870-80

838 τε γᾶν M (2) : γᾶν rell. (2), omnes (1)

839 μύσος φεῦ Hermann : φεῦ μύσος codd. (1) et (2)

840 θ' suppl. Hartung metri gr.

842 ὑπόδεται M (1)

843 πλευρὰς ὀδύνα M (1) et (2) post ὀδύνα voc. θυμὸν habent omnes (1) et (2), quod delendum videtur tamquam glossema

845 με γὰρ metri gr. Page : γάρ με codd.

846 δαναιᾶν Dindorf : δαμαίαν Ms (1), δαμαί°ων M (1), δαμίαν M (2), δαμέαν GTFE (1) et (2)

847 δόλοι Msscr (1) et (2)

849 secll. Bothe, Sansone (metrum claudicat [γε μὴν σὺ T], κάρτα cum comparativo non adhibetur)

857 ὅσ' ἂν H. L. Ahrens : ὅσην codd.
860 δοίνοις Robortello : ᾿νους codd.
861 μήτ' Dindorf : μηδ' codd.
862 ἱδρύσῃς Ἄρη Stephanus : ἱδρύσηι κάρη deinde mutatum in κάρα M
866 post 863 transposui 864-5 fort. delendi sunt (οὐ μόλις παρὼν ἐν ᾧ non intellegitur)
865 ἐστι Mᵃᶜ : ἔσται Mᴾᶜcett.
870-60 vid. 837-47 adnn.
882 ἐμοῦ fort. glossema pro θεοῦ (Sansone)
890 τῆσδε γαμόρῳ Dobree : τῆδέ γ' ἀμοίρου MGTˢˢᶜʳFE, ἥδέ γ' ἀμοίρῳ T
895 εὐθενεῖν Scaliger : εὐσθενεῖν codd.
907 βοτῶν Stanley : βροτ᾿ codd..
908 εὐθενοῦντα Mᴾᶜ : εὐσθενοῦντα Tˢˢᶜʳ E, εὐστενοῦντα GFTᵃᶜ
923 βίου delevi metri gr. (vid. 945 ubi viri docti᾿- suppll.) βίου (om. τύχας) E, βίους τύχας Fᵃᶜ, βίους (om. τύχας) GFᴾᶜT
924/5 ἐξαμβρῦσαι Pauw : ᾿αμβρόσαι M
932 ὃ γε μὴν Linwood : ὃ δὲ μὴ codd. βαρεῶν H. L. Ahrens : -έων codd.
934 ἀπλακήματά Pauw : ἀμπλακ᾿ M (ἁμαρτήματα om. νιν GTFE)
935 σιγῶντ' proposui (σιγῶν <δ᾿> Musgrave) : σιγῶν M
940 φλογμοὺς ὀμματοστερεῖς Wilamowitz : φλοιγμὸς ὀμματοστερὴς M
942 εὐθενοῦντα Πᾶν Meineke : εὐθενοῦντ' (εὐθην᾿ T) ἄγαν codd.
947 πόροι A. L. Brown : τίοι codd.
949 ἐπικραίνει MᵃᶜGFT : ᾿κρανεῖ Mᴾᶜ
952 φανεραί Thomson : φανερῶς codd. (φανέρ' ὡς Meineke)
954 δακρύων T (suspectum : fort. κρυερὸν D. Young) : κρύων MGFE
958 δ' Blaydes : τ' codd.
960 κύρι' Mᴾᶜ (υ in rasura)
961 τ' ὦ Hermann : τῶν codd.
964 μετάκοινοι Turnebus : μέγα κοινοι M, μεγάκοινοι GTFE
967 παντᾷ Sansone (πάντᾳ iam Canter) : πάντα MGFE, πάντων T
970 ὄμματα M (ὄμματι GTF, ὄμμα τὸ M. L. West)
985 κοινοφιλεῖ Hermann : κοινοφελεῖ M, κοινωφελεῖ MˢGTF
988 ἆρα T : ἆρα M, ἀρὰ Mˢ
989 εὑρίσκειν Pauw : ᾿κει codd.
995 πάντως G : πάντες MTF
996 χαίρετε iteravit Turnebus
997 ἀστικὸς codd. (᾿Αττικὸς Erotianus s.v. ἴκταρ)
998 ἡμένας Bothe : ἥμενοι codd.
999 παρθένου Robortello : ᾿νους MF, ᾿νοις GT
1005 προπομπῶν Bentley : ᾿πὸν codd.
1007 ἀτηρὸν Bentley : ᾿ριον codd.
1008 χώρας ἀπέχειν Burges : χώρας κατέχειν codd. (χωρὶς κατέχειν Linwood)
1010 ὑμεῖς T : ἡμεῖς MGF
1011 μετοίκοις Turnebus : ᾿κοι codd.
1014 ἐπανδιπλοίζω Hermann (ἐπεὶ διπλοίζω Wieseler) : ἐπιδιπλοίζω MGF
1021 τε Hermann : δὲ codd.
1027 seclusit A. L. Brown; post h. v. lacunam proposuit Hermann
1028 ἐνδυτοὺς Headlam : ᾿τοῖς codd.
1029 πάρος pro πυρός Headlam (cf. Ag. 1057)
1032 Προπομποί praefixit Mˢ, choro tribuit M βᾶτε Wellauer : βᾶτ' ἐν codd.
1033/4 εὔφρονι Burney : εὐθύφρονι MGT

1035 χωρῖται Hermann : χωρεῖτε codd. (πανδαμεί iteravit Schwenk ex v. 1038)
1037 τιμαῖς Hermann : καί τιμαῖς codd. περίσεπται Schoemann : σέπτα codd. τύχαι τε M ((τ. in marg.)
1038 πανδαμεί Robortello : πανδαμί M, πανδημεί GTF
1040/1 < Θεαί > suppl. Hartung
1042/3 ὁδόν Boissonade : ὁδόν δ' codd.

APPENDICES

I. Athenian Judicial Procedure as reflected in the Trial Scene

References

Boegehold, A. "Toward a Study of Athenian Voting Procedure," *Hesperia* 32 (1963) 366 - 374

Bonner, R. J. and Smith, Gertrude *The Administration of Justice from Homer to Aristotle* (Chicago: University of Chicago Press, 1930; repr. N.Y., 1968)

Carawan, Edwin M. "*Erôtêsis*: Interrogation in the Courts of Fourth Century Athens," *Greek, Roman and Byzantine Studies* 24 (1983) 209-226

Gagarin, M. *Early Greek Law* (Berkeley & Los Angeles: University of California Press, 1986) esp. pp. 41 ff.

Harrison, A. R. W. *The Law of Athens, Procedure* (Oxford: Clarendon Press, 1971)

MacDowell, D. M. *Athenian Homicide Law in the Age of the Orators* (Manchester: Manchester University Press, 1963) [= MacDowell 1963]

―――――― *The Law in Classical Athens* (Ithaca, N.Y.: Cornell University Press, 1978) esp. pp. 240-254, "Preliminary Proceedings," "Evidence," "The Trial" [= MacDowell 1978]

Müller, C. O. *Dissertations on the Eumenides of Aeschylus* 2nd. Engl. ed. (London: Parker, and Cambridge: Deighton, 1853) pp. 144 ff. "On the Judicial Proceedings in Aeschylus"

Sealey, R. "The Athenian Courts for Homicide," *Classical Philology* 78 (1983) 279-96

Wolff, H. J. "The Origin of Litigation among the Greeks," *Traditio* 4 (1946) 31-87

Wyse, W. "The Athenian Judicial System in the Fourth Century," in L. Whibley, ed., *A Companion to Greek Studies* (Cambridge: Cambridge University Press, 1905) pp. 383-402

It is important to try to determine the degree of veracity to which the trial scene in the play reflects actual Athenian courtroom procedure. Is it a literally accurate picture of what would have happened in a contemporary court of law, or was the dramatist concerned more to give a general impression of what went on in a lawcourt (and thus familiar to many in the audience), but allowing himself the freedom to highlight some features but to ignore or suppress others?

I shall deal first with a problem that has been touched on from time to time in discussions of this topic. It is not prima facie certain that in contemporary Athens Orestes' trial would "really" have been held before the Areopagus. At the *prodikasia*, "preliminary (or "practice") trial," the appropriate magistrate, the *basileus* (sometimes designated, not altogether accurately, "King archon") heard the pleas from prosecutor and defendant and determined which court was competent to hear the case. In principle, at least, since Orestes and Apollo argue at various times that the killing was justified, Orestes' trial might have been held at the court known as "Delphinion," which held its sittings near the temple of Artemis and Apollo Delphinios in south-east Athens in the vicinity of the Olympieion (see Demosthenes 23. 74; Bonner & Smith II. 170 with n. 3, MacDowell 1963 p. 70 ff.). It has also been argued (rather less plausibly) that the original audience would have understood Orestes' trial to be taking place not at the Areopagus but at the court called "Palladion," which heard cases of "unintentional" (*akousios*, "unwilling") homicide, since Orestes insists that he had no choice but to obey Apollo's command to kill his mother, especially as it was backed up by threats of really horrendous punishments for disobedience; cf. *Libation Bearers* 269 ff., *Eum.* 466 - 7 (W. Ridgeway, "The True Scene of the Second Act of the *Eumenides* of Aeschylus," *Classical Review* 21 [1907] 163 - 8). But arguments of this kind fly in the face of obvious theatrical "fact": Athena is summoning a court which she says will exist for all time to come, a court which is to sit at and so derive its title from "Ares' Rock" (vv. 685, 690). Whatever the legal niceties and hypothetical pleas available to a latter day Orestes, in this primordial, pre-legal period of Athens' mythic history Orestes is to be tried at and by the Areopagus. (Conversely, if Aeschylus had intended some other site for the trial, or before another court, it seems to me that that would have had to be clearly indicated in the text.)

The scene, then, is the Areopagus court. In historical times, the council heard homicide cases only on the last three days of the month, the so called "apophrades", "unlucky days" (cf. the Roman "dies nefasti"; R. Sealey, *The Athenian Republic* [University Park, Pa.: Pennsylvania State University Press, 1987] 71, citing Pollux 8. 117, *Et. Mag.* and *Et. Gud. s.v.* "apophrades"). There is some evidence as well that the Areopagus' actual judicial sittings were held at night (see Intro. p. 5). As with the argument noted above for other historical courts perhaps being more appropriate for Orestes' case, here as well we should avoid pressing for too historicist a reading; this is the Areopagus' first case, and all the later precisions and technicalities can hardly be imagined as being already in effect.

Let us return to the course of the onstage judicial proceedings. Athena's function is that of presiding magistrate; in an actual trial, as was noted above, this would have been the (archon) basileus. Many discussions (including my own; see n. on v. 415) refer to her preliminary scrutiny of the litigants as an *anakrisis*. But the term, as MacDowell points out (MacDowell 1978 pp. 118 and 242 and per litt.; cf. MacDowell 1963 p. 34), is not appropriate for the preliminary investigation by a magistrate in a homicide case, where the evidence points to "three *prodikasiai*, or 'pre-trials,' in three separate months, in preparation for the trial itself, which was held in the fourth month" (MacDowell 1963 p. 34).

At various stages in the proceedings reference is made to an "oath" or "oaths", and there were indeed several oaths to be taken in connection with an actual lawsuit. Ordinary juries were empanelled and sworn in only once each year, and the judges' oath ran as follows: "I will vote according to the laws and according to the decrees of the Athenian people and the Council of the 500, and where there are no laws, according to my honest judgement, without favour or animosity; I will hear impartially both the prosecutor and the defendant" (Wyse p. 388; cf. Harrison p. 48, MacDowell 1978 p. 44). MacDowell notes (per litt.) that there is no evidence for a similar annual oath sworn by members of the Areopagus: "I should certainly expect that they did swear one [he continues], but it could have been either more frequent (at the start of every trial) or less frequent (taken by each man when he first became a member)." Some such formal undertaking to seek the truth seems to be implied by vv. 483 (see my note on the line; probably there is a lacuna following it), 680 and 710, which allude in a general way to the "reverence" or "respect" which the jurors are to have for their oaths. It seems likely that the audience, many of whom may themselves have served on juries, would have felt it appropriate that a newly constituted jury be adjured to "respect its oath."

At vv. 429 ff. Athena and the Chorus-leader exchange remarks concerning an oath which evidently (from the context) Orestes had declined to take. This must be the so-called "evidentiary oath" or "summons to an oath," a primitive judicial procedure whereby both sides swore to the truth of their contentions (the plaintiff to the defendant's guilt, and the latter to his own innocence), and the jurors then decided the issue solely on the basis of which oath appeared to them to be the stronger. Harrison (p. 99) describes the system as follows: "One or both parties would swear to the truth of their contentions; if one did not swear, the issue was decided in favour of the other; if both swore, it was clear that one was perjured, but it was left to the gods to adjust any wrong which resulted if his cause prevailed" (cf. also Bonner and Smith II. 148, 158 ff.). Another term for this procedure was "challenge to take an oath." "A litigant would propose that he and his opponent should each take a solemn oath in a temple that his own statement, on some point which was in dispute, was true. If the opponent did not agree to do this, the challenger could have the terms of his challenge read out at the trial as evidence that his opponent did not really believe in his own case" (MacDowell 1978 p. 247).

Besides this evidentiary oath which the Erinyes claim Orestes refused (perhaps only tacitly or by implication) to take, there was a series of oaths common to homicide trials in general and one specific to cases heard by the Areopagus, none of which appears to be alluded to in the play. MacDowell (1963 pp. 90 ff.) cites and discusses a passage in Demosthenes (Orat. 23 *Against Aristocrates* sections 67 - 8) where we read that in homicide trials held before the Areopagus "...the man who accuses someone of such a deed (namely, homicide) will swear an oath invoking destruction on himself and his family and his house, and no ordinary oath either, but one which no one swears on any other subject, standing over the cut pieces of a boar, a ram, and a bull...." In homicide cases in general, as MacDowell remarks elsewhere (1978 p. 119), "the prosecutor swore that the defendant had committed the homicide, the defendant... that he had not; at the end the winner swore again that he had told the truth and that the jurors' decision was the right one. Witnesses too had to swear, not just that their evidence was true, but that the defendant committed the homicide, or that he did not commit it." R. Parker suggests that "the numerous and distinctive oaths sworn at homicide trials seem to have been intended to transfer responsibility for a false decision from the jurors to the perjured participants" (*Miasma. Pollution and Purification in Early Greek Religion* [Oxford: Clarendon Press,1983] 126). None of this variety of oaths is actually depicted in the play.

In the play's opening scene Apollo had told Orestes to "go to Pallas Athena's city... and there we shall get us judges" (vv. 79 - 81). When after the First Choral Ode she appears "from Scamander" and asks of Orestes and the strange creatures before her "Who in the world are you?" (v. 408), she exercises a magistrate's control over the soon-to-unfold judicial proceedings. In an actual lawsuit the prosecutor would present to the magistrate, generally in writing, a bill of indictment (*enklêma* or *lêxis*; cf. Harrison p. 88); we seem to have the equivalent of this formal written charge in the Chorus-leader's assertion at v. 425 that Orestes is being pursued because "he saw fit to be his mother's murderer." Although the magistrate technically had the authority to quash a case at this preliminary stage on grounds of "errors in form or law," this was generally not done; a magistrate usually simply "introduced" (the Greek verb is *eisagein*, a word used by Apollo at v. 580 and Athena herself at 582) the case to the appropriate jury and let the dicasts decide whether any technicalities might be involved, or whether the case would proceed in the normal fashion. The Erinyes seem to be urging Athena to let the case proceed in this regular way when their leader bids her "reach a decision by a regular trial" (v. 433); the language has a technical flavour, a *euthudikia* being a normal trial which the defendant had agreed to undergo "without demurrers and evasions" (Wyse p. 398; see my notes on vv. 433 and 312). It was up to the magistrate to put up a public notice of the impending trial on a notice-board (*leukôma*) and to appoint a day for the actual proceedings (Harrrison p. 91). In ordinary courts it was also the magistrate's responsibility to "see that [articles of proof and other evidence] were in the proper shape, for nothing was admissible at the trial that was not in writing and had not been disclosed at the *anakrisis*" (Wyse p. 398). Thus Athena takes particular care to instruct both sides to "call witnesses, marshal evidence [the word Aeschylus uses is *tekmêria* which, as Wyse remarks, would have included the speeches presented at the trial], safeguards under oath of the justice of the case" (vv. 485-6).

Athena reappears after the Second Choral Ode and says, "Herald, make your proclamation and keep the people back...," and she orders that the trumpet be sounded (vv. 566 ff.). In the actual trial, the plaintiff spoke first: Athena seems to acknowledge this normal procedure by saying to the Chorus-leader, "It is yours to speak...for the plaintiff, by telling the story from the beginning, can give accurate instruction in the matter" (vv. 582 -4). From this point on, however, one very important element of actual courtroom procedure is lacking: "Each side made two speeches (in the order: prosecutor, defendant, prosecutor, defendant). At the end of his first speech the defendant was permitted to leave the court and go into exile if he wished" (MacDowell 1978 p. 119 [cf. Harrison 161]; so Bonner and Smith I. p.128: "Aeschylus does not reproduce the regular four set speeches of an Athenian homicide trial"). What we are shown instead is a free rendition of the kind of give-and-take questioning that occurred during a trial: "a speaker could interrogate his adversary, and the judges could interrupt and question the speaker" (Wyse p. 399); "a litigant always had the right to question his opponent in court" (Bonner and Smith II p. 122). This phenomenon of cross-examination has been studied by E. M. Carawan, who remarks (p. 211), "The law requiring answers in cross-examination applied at the *anakrisis* as well as at the trial: at the *anakrisis* questions were directed by the archon to each of the *antidikoi*, and by each of the *antidikoi* to his adversary; the archon had the responsibility to define the question at issue and determine the legality of the charges, and the archon had the authority to demand that both parties 'answer according to the law'..."

At v. 579 Apollo says, "I myself will be [Orestes'] advocate" and at v. 761 Orestes uses the same word, *sundikous*, in referring to the Erinyes ("my mother's advocates"). As the trial progresses, it is clear that Apollo is in fact acting as Orestes' *sundikos* or *sunêgoros*, "originally...a man who was ready for reasons of family or friendly relations to speak in court on a litigant's behalf" (Harrison p. 158). In fact there is some blurring or overlapping of roles, for at v. 594 Orestes asserts that Apollo "will be my witness" and at v.

609 he tells him to "testify, expound for me." According to Bonner and Smith (II p. 124), "the advocate himself might be a witness."

In the next Appendix I shall return to the difficult matter of the number of jurors and Athena's own vote. Here I note simply that the text leaves no doubt about when the actual voting begins: it is when Athena says to the jurors, "you must arise, take a pebble and decide the case, showing respect for the oath" (vv. 708 - 710). Among the stage equipment brought in during the Choral Ode vv. 490 ff. will be two urns, "the brazen urn of mercy and the wooden one of death" (Müller p. 150). Müller's distinction in the material used for the urns may be anachronistic for the fifth century, but it appears certain that at the date of *Eum.* each voter had a single ballot or "pebble" which was to be deposited in one of the two urns, one signifying acquittal and the other condemnation. (This same procedure is alluded to in the comic writer Phrynichus' *Muses* [fr. 32 Kock] and Aristophanes' *Wasps* 987, with MacDowell's n.) In fact we may have a foreshadowing of all this at *Agam.* 815 ff., where Agamemnon remarks that the gods have cast their votes for Troy's condemnation into "the urn of blood - and unambiguously ... while into the opposite urn [for acquittal] only the hand's hope approached; it was not filled." It is clear that at vv. 748 ff. (whoever speaks them; see my n. there), the two urns are turned over and the votes are counted; in the later part of the fourth century four jurors were assigned the task of enumeration. Athena then proclaims the verdict at v. 752: "This man has been acquitted...." (For the procedure see Paley's n. on *Eum.* 742 [his 712], Fraenkel's n. on *Agam.* 816 f., Boegehold pp. 366 - 7 and Harrison p. 165.)

O. Taplin in his book *The Stagecraft of Aeschylus* (pp. 395-401) claims to find serious deficiences in the central scene of the play. Certain details seem to him so much at variance with normal Athenian courtroom procedure that he believes consideration should be given to remedying the defects through excision, drastic emendation or wholesale re-arrangement. He enters a minor objection to vv. 485-6, already considered, where Athena tells both sides to "call witnesses" and "marshal evidence." "This [Taplin writes] is strangely explicit since there is only to be one witness and he cannot be 'called' in the usual sense, and only one *tekmêrion* will be cited -- Athena herself (see 662 ff.)" (p. 395). But as I indicated above, it would not be unusual for a presiding magistrate in an Athenian judicial proceeding to request both sides to "summon witnesses" and "marshal evidence;" how could Athena know at this stage that her command would not be met in full? It is true that Apollo at v. 662 uses the term *tekmêrion* of Athena's motherless birth, but he also refers to her as *martus* at v. 664 and she is in fact neither of these in a technical sense (as noted above, the term *tekmêrion* was used in legal parlance to include the speeches adduced as proof by both sides). Taplin is further troubled by the fact that "Apollo is never called or summoned;

instead he is abruptly addressed in 574f. ["my lord Apollo, exercise control over your own sphere of authority..."] and that is the first we know of his presence" (p. 395; like Taplin, I accept Wieseler's re-assignment of vv. 574 - 5 to Athena). Taplin "suspect[s] large-scale textual tampering" in the trial-scene (p. 396), and he adduces as one reason for his suspicions what he calls the "abrupt" and "disruptive" way that the playwright handles the entry of Apollo: "Apollo is a god, and his arrival is something to be noticed" (p. 396). But what if Apollo is a god whose importance is waning, whose presence becomes increasingly more an embarrassment than an aid to Athena who must exercise all her ingenuity to bridge the gap between the Erinyes and herself (and her suppliant)? If she can only achieve this by trying to undo some of the hurt and humiliation that Apollo's coarse and sometimes savage attacks on them have caused, then it is perhaps part of the dramatist's purpose to as it were "ease him in" to the proceedings without formal announcement -- and just as inconspicuously ease him out. I agree with Taplin, however, that the matter of Apollo's entrance is awkwardly handled; see my n. on v. 574. As for his exit -- which, as Taplin says [p. 403], "is hardly less problematical" than his entrance -- in my n. on v. 777 I consider the possibility that Apollo simply stays onstage and takes his place, in silence and without being referred to by the other characters, at Athena's side as part of the grand processional exodos.

Taplin then proceeds to give his main objections to the way the trial is handled. He notes "three suspicious omissions which... are clearly pointed to by the text itself; procedures which are alluded to as though they had been given more attention than they receive in our text" (p. 398). These he lists as: (1) "the calling and registration of witnesses;" (2) the jurors' oath which "is never sworn on-stage nor is there any direct allusion to a swearing ceremony off-stage" and (3) "by far the most conspicuous omission is that of any opening speech to establish the court in the first place." Of these the first two have already been touched on. It seems to me mistaken literalism to expect Aeschylus to have followed actual contemporary courtroom procedure *to the last iota*. But Taplin's third objection has some weight. At v. 484 Athena had announced her intention of "instituting an ordinance for all time;" she refers to her "ordinances" again at vv. 571 - 2 and Apollo uses similar language in addressing the court at vv. 614 - 5, but we are not actually given the formal speech inaugurating the court until 681 - 710. Taplin finds this placement so offensive that he says he has "considerable respect" for Kirchhoff's removal of the lines from their position in the MSS and their placement after v. 573 (see my n. on vv. 681 - 710). Of course it is possible that this was the dramatist's original intention but that by some now irrecoverable process of textual (and perhaps theatrical, in a re-production) garbling, the lines have found their way to their present place in the MSS.

Straight transposition, however, as Taplin himself remarks, will not be enough, for the last four lines of Athena's foundation speech, 707 ff. ("This rather lengthy advice I have given to my citizens for the future, but now...take a pebble and decide the case"), anchor it firmly to where it is now in our texts. My own preference is to leave well enough alone, for to place the inaugural speech where we would prosaically expect it to be found might constitute a violation of the poet's instincts that a certain degree of audience-suspense is appropriate. Thus he may have intended that the goddess make an early announcement of her plan for a permanent judiciary, but not actually institute it until the climactic moment just before the voting. The technique will be similar to her "advance" statement about how she intends to vote (v. 735) but not actually doing so until later, probably after v. 753. It will add considerably to the sense of solemn responsibility with which the jurors cast their ballots if they do so immediately after having been told that their court is to be made permanent and will assume its glorious function as "a bastion to bring safety to the land and city such as no one on earth possesses", a "deliberative council to be uncorrupted by thought of profit, worthy of respect, quick to wrath, on behalf of those who sleep an ever-wakeful guard-post of the land" (vv. 701 - 2, 704 - 6). I note also Conacher's defense of what he calls the "postponement" of Athena's proclamation; it is as a result "easier for Athena to generalize, now that the court has already been seen in operation as a homicide tribunal, on the more wide-ranging powers and political significance which Athena also envisages for the Areopagus" (*Aeschylus' 'Oresteia,'* p. 162).

Taplin's solution, then, to what he feels to be large-scale corruption and disarrangement in the trial scene is to posit a lacuna "somewhere between 571 and 575" of "perhaps 40 lines [which] will have contained Athena's inaugural speech, much of it preserved in 681 - 706, and it will have included the arrival of Apollo. It may also have contained the oath of the jurors, the summoning of witnesses, and perhaps a formal announcement by the Herald (if he went before Apollo arrived, this could be managed with three actors)" (pp. 400 - 401; the theory of a lacuna in the text is accepted and elaborated upon by Friis Johansen in *Classica et Mediaevalia* 39 [1988] 1-14). Taplin admits that he "finds it hard to believe whole-heartedly in this hypothesis," and it seems to me easier to explain the discrepancies between the scene as we have it and actual procedure in the way that I have done, by pointing out that instead of laboriously trying to achieve exact literalness in all details Aeschylus has been content rather to create a flavour of authenticity; the audience senses that it is in a real courtroom because so many (even if not all) of the expected elements are present.

II. Athena's Vote at vv. 735 and 752-3 and the
so-called 'Vote of Athena'

References

C. O. Müller [see under App. I] pp. 149-50, 215-19

M. Gagarin, "The Vote of Athena," *American Journal of Philology* 96 (1975) 121-7

D. A. Hester, "The Casting Vote," ibid. 102 (1981) 268-74.

D. J. Conacher, *Aeschylus' 'Oresteia,'* 164-6

The issue is whether Athena's vote, which at v. 735 she says she will cast in Orestes' favour, is tie-making (with an uneven number of human jurors voting) or tie-breaking (an even number of human votes). Unfortunately the text of the play itself is unclear and has been interpreted both ways. The strongest argument is also somewhat circular: in actual Athenian legal practice a tie was deemed to go in favour of the accused, the president's vote in such a case being notionally cast for acquittal; late sources such as Philostratus (*Lives of the Sophists* 2.3 [p. 185 in the Loeb ed.]) and Julian (*Orat. 3, Eis Eusebian* sect. 114d [ed. J. Bidez 1932, vol. I, p. 87]), refer to this practice as the "vote of Athena." So MacDowell 1963, 110: "...the principle that a tie in the voting meant acquittal seems to have applied in homicide courts as in others." The text of Antiphon, Oration 5 *Murder of Herodes* sect. 51 makes this quite clear: "When matters are equal this goes to the advantage of the defendant rather than the prosecutor, if in fact an equal number of votes aids the defendant rather than the prosecutor;" cf. also Aristotle, *Problems* 29. 13. At Euripides *Electra* 1268 - 9 the equal votes cast in Orestes' case are specifically said to be the reason for the *nomos* that "the defendant's case always wins when the votes are equal" (in practice many juries were constituted of an uneven number of jurors -- we hear of courts of 201, 401 and 1,001 -- presumably in order to avoid a tie, although it is possible that some voters would have remained undecided). Certainly Cicero understood the myth as having Athena break a tied human vote in Orestes' favour (*pro Milone* 3). Pollux (8.90) reports that the archon basileus (whose function Athena symbolically assumes in the play) "introduces actions for homicide to the Areopagus and, after removing his crown, votes with the jurors," but since the actual number of Areopagite jurymen varied from case to case as well as from year to year, this is not decisive; we might, however, be able to infer that the archon, as president, invariably voted for acquittal.

Help with our problem has sometimes been sought in the way Euripides handles the theme in his treatment of Orestes' story. Unfortunately, Euripides' text is only slightly less ambiguous than

Aeschylus'. In *Iphigeneia among the Taurians* Orestes tells his sister that at his trial in Athens Athena "saved him by discriminating (966 *diêrithmêse*, although the text is not quite certain) or judging (1471) equal votes", which could mean "constituted the votes equal by adding hers to those for acquittal", although this is admittedly not the natural sense of the words; it seems easier to conclude that Athena's vote actually broke the tie. The question of equality of votes does not arise at *Orestes* 1648 ff., although the scholiast on line 1650 (Dindorf's ed, 1867, vol. II, p. 341) offers the interpretation that "when the votes were equal Athena, taking pity on Orestes on her own initiative (*par' heautês*), cast one vote, which made him win."

Gagarin and others have tried to make deductions from the voting scene at *Eum.* 711 ff. He remarks that there are 10 sets of paired verses (711 - 730), the sequence being capped by a triplet, vv. 731 - 3, which he takes as indicating that 11 votes were cast by the stage-jurors (Gagarin p.122). Of course, as Hester and others have pointed out, once the sequence of pairs is broken, we really have no way of knowing what stage-action accompanied the triplet: vv. 731-3 might have covered the casting of their ballots by one, two or more jurors (or, for that matter, by Athena). Hester assays an argument which seems (to me at least) to carry some weigh. If Athena's vote had constituted an equality, the human Athenian jurors would in casting their ballots have voted for Orestes' condemnation (if only by a margin of one); "we should expect Orestes to be indignant with the Athenians and extremely grateful to Athena" (Hester p. 270), whereas the Erinyes ought conversely to be "furious" with her but effusively thankful to the Athenians for having done what they humanly could to bring about condemnation of their adversary. But we hear nothing of this in the sequel. On the contrary ,it might be argued that it was precisely the equality of votes among the human jurors that allowed Athena eventually to sway the Erinyes in the direction of benevolence. Gagarin maintains that the goddess' assertion at vv. 795 - 6, "It was not a defeat for you, but a true outcome of a trial in which the votes were equal," might mean "a trial in which the votes (including my own) were equal". The Erinyes, however, could reasonably have been annoyed at Athena for trying to mollify them with what is essentially a sophistic quibble: equality of all the votes counted (including Athena's) constitutes acquittal only because Athena has set up this complicated and artificial system. To me it seems more natural to take the lines as implying: "you must not take it as a defeat, because in fact the voters were unable to render a decisive verdict (so you could not reasonably be angered at them); it was simply the traditional magistrate's vote for leniency that set Orestes free". Thus, in effect, Conacher: "[Athena's] credibility as a pacifier of the Furies would surely have been jeopardized in advance if she had first of all cancelled, by her vote, an actual vote by the human jury *condemning* Orestes and then declared in addition that this single vote converted an actual condemnation into an acquittal" (p.165, his italics).

I find it diccult to imagine the coming to light of new evidence to decide the issue, for even an ancient commentator's note on Aeschylus' text would be no more than that, one person's interpretation. It is rather awkward to have to admit that on this relatively important point an argument that can be said to have clinched the matter has not yet been produced.

Somewhat tentatively, then, I accept Paley's account of how the actual "vote of Athena" was handled in the play (n. on his v. 704 [=734]). "Pallas does not at this point drop her ballot into one or other of the urns.... Only, should the votes prove equal, she announces her intention of adding hers in favour of the culprit; that is, of declaring him acquitted. And this she does *verbally* at v. [752], and *without giving any actual vote* either before or after the counting of the ballots". (The first emphasis is Paley's, the second mine.)

III. The Choral Metres

References

GREEK METRE

Maas, P. *Greek Metre* Engl. trans. by H. Lloyd-Jones (Oxford: Clarendon Press, 1962)

Raven, D. S. *Greek Metre. An Introduction* 2nd ed. (London: Faber & Faber, 1968)

West, M. L. *Greek Metre* (Oxford: Clarendon Press, 1982)

(briefer treatments)

Denniston, J. D. "Metre, Greek" in N. G. L. Hammond and H. H. Scullard, edd., *The Oxford Classical Dictionary* 2nd ed. (Oxford: Clarendon Press, 1970) 679 - 684

Drury, Martin "Metrical Appendix" in P. Easterling and B. M. W. Knox, edd., *Cambridge History of Classical Literature, I. Greek Literature* (Cambridge: Cambridge University Press, 1985) 893 - 899

ANALYSES

Dindorf, G. *Metra Aeschyli Sophoclis Euripidis et Aristophanis Descripta* (Oxford: University Press, 1842) 52 - 61

Scott, Wm. C. *Musical Design in Aeschylean Theatre,* 112 - 133

Dale, A. M. ed. by E. W. Handley *Metrical Analyses of Tragic Choruses. Fasc. 3, Dochmiac-Iambic-Dactylic-Ionic* (University of London: Institute of Classical Studies [Bulletin Suppl. 31.3] 1983) pp. 24-7 for *Eum.* 143-177, 254-275, 778-880; pp. 196-205 for *Eum.* 321-396, 490-565, 916-1020, p. 269 for *Eum.* 1032-1047

OTHER

Dale, A. M. *The Lyric Metres of Greek Drama* 2nd ed. (Cambridge: Cambridge University Press, 1968)

Conomis, N. C. "The Dochmiacs of Greek Drama", *Hermes* 92 (1964) 23-50

Scott, Wm. C. "The Splitting of Choral Lyric in Aeschylus' *Oresteia*", *American Journal of Philology* 105 (1984) 150-164 (pp. 158 ff. for *Eum.* 140 ff., pp. 162 ff. for *Eum.* 244-275)

Chiasson, Charles C. "Lecythia and the Justice of Zeus"

NOTATION

(NOTE: Line numbers are of <u>the Greek text</u>, not the Translation.)

— = a long syllable

˘ = a short syllable

anap = anapaest, ˘ ˘ — or equivalent (generally, this involves "resolution"
        of — into ˘ ˘ or substitution of — for ˘ ˘)

aristophanean = — ˘ ˘ — ˘ —

ba = baccheus, ˘ — — (sometimes treated as "syncopated" [see below] ia:
        ˘ — · —)

catalectic = "ritardando", a metron is shortened, generally by omission of ˘
        in the last foot, thus slowing down the rhythm

chor = choriamb, — ˘ ˘ — ("choriambic dimeter" = chor + ia, or the
        reverse)

cret = cretic, — ˘ — sometimes considered a syncopated ia or tro)

dimeter = 2 metra

dact = dactyl, — ˘ ˘

doch = dochmiac The basic pattern is ˘ — — ˘ —, but a wide variety of
        substitutions is found; thus, any — may be replaced by ˘ ˘, or
        sometimes by single ˘, and — is occasionally found in second-
        last position.

hemiepes = — ˘ ˘ — ͞˘ — ("blunt"), or — ˘ ˘ — ˘ ˘ — —
        ("pendant")

ia = iambic metron (2 iambi treated as a unit, or the equivalent; generally, —
        resolved to ˘ ˘, or — substituted for ˘ ˘)

iambus = ˘ —

ia trim = 3 ia, the normal verse of the spoken dialogue

ithyphallic = — ˘ — ˘ — ˘͞

lekythion = — ˘ — ˘ — ˘ — (See the article by Chiasson , above.)

metron = the shortest natural metrical unit (for the iambus and trochee, 2
        feet)

pherecratean = ˘͞ ˘˘͞ — ˘ ˘ — — (in practice in *Eum.*, — ˘ or ˘ ˘
        ˘ before the chor; vv. 330, 355, 374, 376)

praxillean = 3 dact + — ˘ — —

resolved, or resolution = see under "anapaest", above

spondee = — —

syncopated = shortened, generally by the omission of ˘ within the metron

tro = trochaic metron (2 trochees treated as a unit), — ˘ — ˘͞

trochee = — ˘

ENTRY SONG (PARODOS) 143 - 178

str./ ant. α   143-148 = 149-161

143 2 doch
144 ia trim (perhaps spoken)
145 2 doch
146 doch
147 ia trim
148 ia + 2 cret ("syncopated ia trim", Dale)

str./ ant. β   155-161 = 162-168

155 ia trim
156 doch + ia
157 doch ("free response" with 164, Dale)
158, 159 7 ˘ ending with — (according to Dale, these two vv. together
          constitute a resolved "long" doch, i.e. with one extra ˘)
160 ia + 3 cret ("syncopated ia tetrameter")
161 2 ia (all — resolved except the last syllable)

str./ ant. γ   169-173 = 174-178

169 ia trim
170 doch
171 aristophanean
172 2 doch
173 ia + doch

SECOND ENTRY SONG (EPIPARODOS) 254 - 275 "astrophic",
i.e. there is no metrically corresponding
counter-stanza or "antistrophe"

254 doch
255 doch
256/7 2 doch
258 ?(text corrupt) + ia
259 2 doch
260 2 doch
261 ia trim
262 ia + cret ("syncopated ia dim")
263 2 doch
264 ia trim
265 2 doch
266 doch (cf. v. 961) + 2 cret
267 ia trim
268 2 cret + doch

269 ia trim
270 doch + cret (resolved)
271 doch
272 ia trim
273 ia trim
274 doch
275 2 doch

307 - 320 **anapaestic prelude to the FIRST CHORAL ODE (v. 308, 311, 315, 317, and 320 are catalectic)**

FIRST CHORAL ODE (STASIMON) 321 - 396

str./ ant. α 321-327 = 334-340
321 lekythion + spondee
322 dact + lekythion
323 spondee + 2 cret
324 2 cret + —
325 2 cret
326 2 cret
327 lekythion

mesode α 328-333
328 2 cret resolved
329 2 cret resolved
330 pherecratean
330 lekythion
331 leekythion
332 lekythion
333 lekythion
(I omit 341-346, which repeat 328-333.)

str./ ant. β 347-353a = 360-367
347 3 dact
348 2 dact
349 3 dact
350 2 dact
351 3 dact
352/3 5 dact
353a (missing) = 367 lekythion

mesode β 354-359
354 lekythion

355 pherecratean
356 2 cret resolved
357 2 cret resolved
358 2 cret resolved
359 may be corrupt (— + choriambic dimeter)

str./ ant. γ   368-371 = 377-380
368 5 dact
369 5 dact
370 4 dact
371 spondee + lekythion

mesode γ   372-376
372 2 cret resolved
373 2 cret resolved
374 pherecratean
375 lekythion with first — resolved
376 pherecratean

str./ ant. δ   381-388 = 389-396
381 ia + cret ("syncopated ia dim")
382 ia + cret ("syncopated ia dim")
383 ia + spondee ("contracted ia dim")
384 2 ia
385 2 ia + iambus
386 3 ia
387 4 dact
(Vv. 385-387 are problematic. V. 385 has suffered some textual corruption; if
    ἄτιμ' is kept, μένει or the metrical equivalent in 395 must be added. δυσ-
    in 387 is anomalous [marked † by Dale], yet apparently required by καιπερ
    in 395.)
388 lekythion
(Mesode δ perhaps has been omitted from the MSS after v. 388.)

SECOND CHORAL ODE (STASIMON) 490 - 565

"Meter, as well as sense
throughout, serves to link the First and
Second Stasimon", (Lloyd-Jones, trans. p.
41).

490 lekythion
491 2 cret
492 lekythion

493 2 cret
494 2 cret + ia
495 lekythion
496 2 tro (with resolution)
497 lekythion (initial — resolved)
498 lekythion

str./ ant. β   508-516 = 517-525   ("The metrical purity of this system is
                    striking", Chiasson p. 16)
508 lekythion
509 lekythion
510 lekythion
511 cret
512 lekythion
513 lekythion
514 lekythion (with resolution)
515 lekythion
516 lekythion

str./ ant. γ   526-537 = 538-549
526 lekythion
527 lekythion
528 cret
529-531 a run of 7 dact
532 lekythion
533-534 5 dact, ending catalectic (i.e., the last foot is —)
535 2 dact
536 ia + cret ("syncopated ia dim")
537 aristophanean

str./ ant. δ   550-557 = 558-565
550 ia + lekythion
551 ithyphallic
552 ia + ithyphallic
553 ia + lekythion
554 3 ia
555 ba + cret + ba ("syncopated ia trim catalectic")
556 choriambic dimeter
557 aristophanean

THIRD CHORAL ODE (STASIMON)
778-793 repeated as 808-823;
837-846 repeated as 870-880

str./ ant. α
778 2 ia + doch
779 3 ia
780 3 ia
781 doch
782 2 lekythia
783 iambus + ba
784 doch
785 3 ia
786 doch
787 3 ia
788 2 ba
789 2 ba
790 doch (cf. Conomis, p. 23)
791 doch
792 doch
793 aristophanean

str./ ant. β
837 doch
838 2 doch
839 doch + —
840 2 doch
841 2 spondees
842 — ˘ ˜ ˘ — ("hypodochmius")
843 2 anap
844 doch
845 doch
846 doch
847 2 doch

CHORAL EXODOS 916 - end

str./ ant. α   916-926 = 938-947
916 cret + lekythion
917 lekythion
918 spondee + lekythion
919 lekythion
920 ithyphallic + lekythion
921 lekythion

922 lekythion
923 5 iambi
924/5 3 spondees (= "hemiepes pendant", Dale 203)
926 lekythion

927-937, 948-955 anapaests, 937 and 955 catalectic

str./ ant. β   956-967 = 976-987
956 2 cret
957 lekythion
958 lekythion
959/60 5 dact
961 doch
962 hemiepes blunt
963 hemiepes blunt
964 hemiepes pendant
965 hemiepes pendant
966 lekythion
967 spondee + lekythion

968-975, 988-995 anapaests, 975 and 995 catalectic

str./ ant. γ   996-1002 = 1014-1020
996   praxillean
997   lekythion
998   lekythion
999   lekythion
1000   lekythion
1001   lekythion
1002   lekythion

1003-1013 anapaests, 1009 and 1013 catalectic

CODA (Chorus of Escorts) 1032 - end
str./ ant. α   1032-1035 = 1036-1038
1032 4 dact
1033/4 5 dact
1035 4 dact, catalectic

str./ ant. β   1039-1042/3 = 1044-1046/7
1039 4 dact
1040/1 4 dact
1042/3 7 dact

GENERAL BIBLIOGRAPHY

This bibliography covers works that deal in a general way with Aeschylean drama or in particular *Eumenides*. Not all works cited in the Introduction or Commentary are listed here. Conversely, some of the following titles, although not referred to specifically in the notes, are included here because they might be found useful by students of Aeschylus.

There are separate subject bibliographies for sections of the Introduction and the Appendices.

TEXTS, EDITIONS, COMMENTARIES

Barnett, Lionel D. *The Eumenides of Aeschylus* (London: Blackie & Son, 1901)

Groeneboom, P. *Aeschylus' Eumenides* (Groningen: Wolters, 1952)

Mazon, P. *Eschyle, Tome II* (Paris: Les belles lettres, 1955)

Mills, T. R. *Aeschylus: Eumenides* (London: University Tutorial Press, n.d. [1901])

Murray, Gilbert *Aeschyli septem quae supersunt tragoediae* 2nd ed. (Oxford: Clarendon Press, 1955)

Page, Denys *Aeschyli septem quae supersunt tragoedias edidit* (Oxford: Clarendon Press, 1972)

Rose. H. J. *A Commentary on the Surviving Plays of Aeschylus* ([Verhandelingen der koninklijke Nederlandse Akademie van Wetenschappen, afd. Letterkunde n.r., LXIV.2] Amsterdam, 1958) pp. 229 - 294

Sidgwick, A. *Aeschylus, Eumenides.* (Oxford: Clarendon Press, 1902)

Thomson, Geroge *The Oresteia of Aeschylus* (Amsterdam: Hakkert, 1966)

SCHOLIA

Smith, Ole L. *Scholia in Aeschylum Pars I* (Leipzig: Teubner, 1976)

TESTIMONIA, FRAGMENTS

Radt, Stefan *Tragicorum graecorum Fragmenta v. 5 Aeschylus* (Göttingen: Vandenhoeck & Ruprecht, 1985)

LEXICA, CONCORDANCES

Linwood, W. *A Lexicon to Aeschylus* (London: Taylor & Walton, 1843)
Italie, G. *Index Aeschyleus* 2nd ed. by S. Radt (Leiden: Brill, 1964)
Edinger, H. G. *Index Analyticus Graecitatis Aeschyleae* (Hildesheim: Olms, 1981)
Holmboe, H. *Concordance to Aeschylus' Eumenides* (Aarhus, Denmark: Akademisk Boghandel, 1973)

TRANSLATIONS

Fagles, Robert *Aeschylus, 'The Oresteia'* introductory essay, notes, and glossary by Robert Fagles and W. B. Standford (New York and London: Penguin Books, 1977)
Headlam, W. ed. by C. E. S. Headlam *The Plays of Aeschylus* (London: George Bell, 1909)
Lattimore, Richmond *Aeschylus, Oresteia* (Chicago: University of Chicago Press, 1953)
Lloyd-Jones, H. *The Eumenides by Aeschylus* (Englewood Cliffs, N. J.: Prentice-Hall, 1970; reprint London, 1982)

Murray, Gilbert *The Eumenides (The Furies)* (London: George Allen & Unwin, 1925)
Smyth, Herbert Weir *Aeschylus II* (rev. ed. by H. Lloyd-Jones [Loeb Classical Library] London: Heinemann, and Cambridge, Mass.: Harvard Univ. Press, 1957)
Vellacott, P. *Aeschylus. The Oresteian Trilogy* (Harmondsworth: Penguin Books, 1956)
Young, Douglas *Aeschylus: The Oresteia* (Norman: University of Oklahoma Press, 1974)

GENERAL

Brown, A. L. "Some Problems in the *Eumenides* of Aeschylus," *Journal of Hellenic Studies* 102(1982) 26 - 32
-------------- "The Erinyes in the *Oresteia*: Real Life, the Supernatural, and the Stage," ibid. 103 (1983) 13 - 34
Clay, Diskin "Aeschylus' Trigeron Mythos," *Hermes* 97 (1969) 1 - 9
Conacher, D.J. *Aeschylus' 'Oresteia,' a Literary Commentary* (Toronto: University of Toronto Press, 1987)
-------------- "Interaction between Chorus and Characters in the *Oresteia*," *American Journal of Philology* 95 (1974) 323 - 343

Chiasson, Charles C. "Lecythia and the Justice of Zeus in Aeschylus' *Oresteia,*" *Phoenix* 42 (1988) 1 - 21

Davies, M. I. "Thoughts on the *Oresteia* before Aeschylus," *Bulletin de correspondance hellenique* 93 (1969) 214 - 260

Deforge, Bernard *Eschyle, poète cosmique* (Paris: Les belles lettres, 1986)

Dodds, E. R. "Notes on the *Oresteia,*" *Classical Quarterly* n.s. 3 (1953) 11 - 21

Duchemin, Jacqueline "La triade eschyléenne des *Euménides* et la purification d'Oreste," *Le mythe, son langage et son message* (Lorrain-la-Neuve, 1983) 245 - 74 (I have not seen this.)

Dyer, Robert Rutherford "The Evidence for Apolline Purification Rituals at Delphi and Athens," *Journal of Hellenic Studies* 89 (1969) 38 - 56

Dyer, Thomas "On the Chorus of the *Eumenides,*" *The Classical Museum* 1 (1844) 281 - 298

Edwards, Mark "Agamemnon's Decision: Freedom and Folly in Aeschylus," *California Studies in Classical Antiquity* 10 (1977) 17 - 38

Ewans, Michael "Agamemnon at Aulis: a Study in the *Oresteia,*" *Ramus* 4 (1975) 17 - 32

Flintoff, E. "The Treading of the Cloth," *Quaderni Urbinati di Cultura Classica* n.s. 25 (1987) 119 - 130

Fontenrose, Joseph "Gods and Men in the 'Oresteia,' " *Transactions of the American Philological Association* 102 (1971) 71 - 109

Fowler, B. H. "Aeschylus' Imagery," *Classica et Mediaevalia* 28 (1967) 1 - 74 (676 - 74 for *Eum.*)

Gagarin, Michael *Aeschylean Drama* (Berkeley: University of California Press, 1976)

Gantz, T. "The Fires of the *Oresteia,*" *Journal of Hellenic Studies* 97 (1977) 28 - 38

---------- "Inherited Guilt in Aeschylus," *Classical Journal* 78 (1982/3)1 - 23

----------- "The Chorus of Aeschylus' *Agamemnon,*" *Harvard Studies in Classical Philology* 87 (1983) 65 - 86

Goldhill, Simon *Language, Sexuality, Narrative: the 'Oresteia'* (Cambridge: Cambridge University Press, 1984)

Grube, G. M. A. "Zeus in Aeschylus," *American Journal of Philology* 91 (1970) 43 - 51

Goheen, R. F. "Aspects of Dramatic Symbolism: Three Studies in the *Oresteia,*" *American Journal of Philology* 76 (1955) 113 - 37

Hammond, N. G. L. "The Conditions of Dramatic Production to the Death of Aeschylus," *Greek, Roman and Byzantine Studies* 13 (1972) 387 - 450

------------ "More on Conditions of Production to the Death of Aeschylus," ibid. 29 (1988) 5 - 33

------------ and Moon, Warren "Illustrations of Early Tragedy at Athens," *American Journal of Archaeology* 82 (1978) 371 - 83

Harris, Grace   "Furies, Witches and Mothers," in Jack Goody, ed., *The Character of Kinship* (Cambridge: Cambridge Univ. Press, 1973) pp. 145 - 159

Harrison, Jane E.   "Delphika (A) The Erinyes, (B) The Omphalos," *Journal of Hellenic Studies* 19 (1899) 205 - 251

Headlam, Walter   "The Last Scene of the *Eumenides*," *Journal of Hellenic Studies* 26 (1906) 268 - 77

Herington, John *Aeschylus* (New Haven: Yale University Press, 1986)

Higgins, W. E.   "Double-dealing Ares in the *Oresteia*," *Classical Philology* 73 (1978) 24 - 35

Hogan, James C.   *A Commentary on the Complete Greek Tragedies, Aeschylus* (Chicago & London: University of Chicago Press, 1984)

Ireland, S. *Aeschylus* ([*Greece & Rome* New Surveys in the Classics No. 18] Oxford: Clarendon Press, 1986)

Kuhns, Richard   *The House, the City and the Judge. The Growth of Moral Awareness in the 'Oresteia'* (Indianapolis: Bobbs-Merrill, 1962)

Lebeck, Anne *The Oresteia: a Study in Language and Structure* (Cambridge, Mass.: Harvard University Press, 1971)

Lévy, Ed. "Le théâtre et le rêve: le rêve dans le théâtre d'Eschyle," *Théâtre et spectacles dans l'antiquité: actes du colloque de Strasbourg. 5 - 7 novembre 1981* (Leiden: Brill, 1983) 141 - 68

Lloyd-Jones, H. *The Justice of Zeus* (Berkeley: University of California Press, 1971)

-------------   "Artemis and Iphigeneia," *Journal of Hellenic Studies* 103 (1983) 87 - 102

Maloney, Gilles   "Contributions hippocratiques à l'étude de l'*Orestie* d'Eschyle," *Formes de pensée dans la collection hippocratique. Actes du ive colloque international hippocratique (Lausanne, 21 - 26 sept. 1981)* (Geneva: Droz, 1981) 71 - 84

Méautis, Georges "Notes sur les *Euménides* d'Eschyle," *Revue des études anciennes* 65 (1963) 33 - 52

Moreau, Alain Maurice   *Eschyle: la violence et le chaos* (Paris: Les belles lettres, 1985)

Moritz, Helen E.   "Refrain in Aeschylus: Literary Adaptation of Traditional Form," *Classical Philology* 74 (1979) 187 - 213

Murray, Gilbert *Aeschylus the Creator of Tragedy* (Oxford: Clarendon Press, 1940; repr. 1978)

Owen, E. T. *The Harmony of Aeschylus* (Toronto: Clarke, Irwin, 1952)

Peradotto, J. J. "Some Patterns of Nature Imagery in the *Oresteia*," *American Journal of Philology* 85 (1964) 379 - 93

Podlecki, Anthony J. *The Political Background of Aeschylean Tragedy* (Ann Arbor: Univ. of Michigan Press, 1965)

------------ "The Aeschylean Chorus as Dramatic Persona," *Studi in onore di Q. Cataudella* (Catania: Univ. di Catania Fac. di Lettere e Filosofia, 1972) I. 187 - 204

Prag, A. J. N. W. *The Oresteia: Iconographic and Narrative Tradition* (Warminster and Chicago: Aris & Phillips and Bolchazy-Carducci, 1985)

Rabinowitz, Nancy S. "From Force to Persuasion: Aeschylus' *Oresteia* as Cosmogonic Myth," *Ramus* 10 (1981) 159 - 91

Roberts, Deborah H. *Apollo and his Oracle in the 'Oresteia'* [Hypomnemata Heft 78] (Göttingen: Vandenhoeck and Rupprecht, 1984)

Roisman, Hanna "Clytemnaestra's Ominous Words, Aeschylus, *Agamemnon* 345 - 347," *Zeitschrift fur Papyrologie und Epigraphik* 66 (1986) 279 - 284

de Romilly, Jacqueline *La crainte et l'angoisse dans le théâtre d'Eschyle* (Paris: Les belles lettres, 1958)

------------ *Time in Greek Tragedy* (Ithaca, N.Y.: Cornell University Press, 1967)

------------ "La haîne dans l'*Orestie*," *Dioniso* 48 (1977) 33 - 53

Rosenmeyer, T. G. *The Art of Aeschylus* (Berkeley: University of California Press, 1982)

Said, Suzanne "Concorde et civilisation dans les *Euménides* (*Euménides* 858 - 866 et 978 - 987)," *Théâtre et spectacles dans l'antiquité: actes du colloque de Strasbourg. 5 - 7 novembre 1981* (Leiden: Brill, 1983) 97 - 121

Sansone, David *Aeschylean Metaphors for Intellectual Activity* ([*Hermes* Einzelschriften 35] Wiesbaden: Franz Steiner, 1975)

------------ "Notes on the Oresteia," *Hermes* 112 (1984) 1 - 10

------------ "The Survival of the Bronze-age Demon," *Illinois Classical Studies* 13 (1988) 1 - 17

Sarian, Haiganuch "Erinys," *Lexicon Iconographicum Mythologiae Classicae* [=LIMC] III.1 (Zurich: Artemis, 1986) pp. 825 - 843, with illustrations in vol. III.2, pp. 595 - 600

Scott, William C. *Musical Design in Aeschylean Theater* (Hanover, New Hampshire: Univ. Press of New England, 1984)

------------ "Comedy in the *Oresteia*?," in Karelisa V. Hartigan ed., *Legacy of Thespis: Drama Past and Present vol. IV* (Lanham, Maryland: University Press of America, 1984) 67 - 73

Sider, David "Stagecraft in the *Oresteia*," *American Journal of Philology* 99 (1978) 12 - 27

Smith, Peter M. *On the Hymn to Zeus in Aeschylus' 'Agamemnon'* (Chico, Calif.: Scholars' Press, 1980)

Smyth, Herbert Weir *Aeschylean Tragedy* (Berkeley: University of California Press, 1924; repr. 1969)

Solmsen, Friedrich *Hesiod and Aeschylus* (Ithaca: Cornell University Press, 1949)

Sommerstein, Alan "Notes on the *Oresteia*," *Bulletin of the Institute of Classical Studies, Univ. of London* 27 (1980) 63 - 75

Spatz, Lois *Aeschylus* (Boston: Twayne, 1982)

Taplin, Oliver *The Stagecraft of Aeschylus. The Dramatic Use of Exits and Entrances in Greek Tragedy* (Oxford: Clarendon Press, 1977)

Tarkow, T. A. "Thematic Implications of Costuming in the *Oresteia*," *Maia* n.s. 32 (1980) 153 - 65

Thalmann, W. G. "Speech and Silence in the *Oresteia* 1: *Agamemnon* 1025-1029)," "Speech and Silence in the *Oresteia* 2," *Phoenix* 39 (1985) 99 - 118 and 221 - 237

------------ "Aeschylus' Physiology of the Emotions," *American Journal of Philology* 107 (1986) 489 - 511

Vellacott, Philip *The Logic of Tragedy. Morals and Integrity in Aeschylus' 'Oresteia'* (Durham, North Carolina: Duke University Press, 1984)

Vermeule, E. T. "The Boston Oresteia Krater," *American Journal of Archaeology* 70 (1966) 1 - 22

Visser, Margaret *The Erinyes: their Character and Function in Classical Greek Literature and Thought* (Ph.D. dissertation Univ. of Toronto, 1980)

West, M. L. "The Parodos of the *Agamemnon*," *Classical Quarterly* n.s. 29 (1979) 1 - 6

Whallon, William *Problem and Spectacle: Studies in the 'Oresteia'* (Heidelberg: Winter, 1980)

Winnington-Ingram, R. P. *Studies in Aeschylus* (Cambridge: Cambridge University Press, 1983)

-------------- "Aeschylus," in P. E. Easterling and B. M. W.Knox, edd., *Cambridge History of Classical Literature I. Greek Literature* (Cambridge: Cambridge University Press, 1985) ch. 10.3 pp. 281 - 295

Wüst, Ernst "Erinys," *Paulys Realencyclopaedie der classischen Altertumswissenschaft* Suppl. VIII (Stuttgart: Druckenmüller, 1956) cols. 82 - 166

Zeitlin, Froma "The Motif of the Corrupted Sacrifice in Aeschylus' *Oresteia*," *Transactions of the American Philological Association* 96 (1965) 463 - 508